CENTAUR

THE MYTH OF IMMUNITY

Australian Hospital Ship

CENTAUR

THE MYTH OF IMMUNITY

Christopher Milligan   John Foley

NAIRANA PUBLICATIONS

Frontispiece: *The* Centaur *memorial window in Concord Repatriation Hospital, NSW. This magnificent stain glass window was unveiled on 13th May 1990 by His Excellency the late Rear Admiral Sir David Martin, KCMG, OA, Governor of NSW.*
(Navy Photographic Unit)

2/3 AUSTRALIAN HOSPITAL SHIP

CENTAUR

47

FRIDAY 14TH MAY·1943· 0400·A.M.

·A·H·S·   CENTAUR·

·TO·THE·MEMORY·OF·THOSE·WHO·PERISHED·

1939   1945

Dedication

This book is dedicated to the memory of 268 innocent
non-combatant victims of a callous act of war.

"But you save me, taking me away to my black ship,
and cut the arrow out of my thigh,
and wash the dark blood from it with warm water,
and sprinkle gentle medicines on it,
good ones, which they say you have learned from Achilles,
whom Cheiron taught, most civilised of the centaurs."

Iliad 11. 827–831

Previous books by Christopher Milligan:
  CANADA'S NEAREST NEIGHBOUR: The United States (co-author)
  INSIDE, OUTSIDE, ALL AROUND THE TOWN

Previous books by John Foley:
  REEF PILOTS — The History of the Queensland Coast &
    Torres Strait Pilot Service
  TIMELESS ISLE — An Illustrated History of Thursday Island
  CORAL GATEWAY — The Hydrographers Passage Story
  THE QUETTA — Queensland's Worst Disaster

First published in Australia in 1993 by Nairana Publications,
6A Doncaster Street, Hendra, Queensland.

Printed by Watson Ferguson & Company, 35 Hamilton Road, Moorooka,
Queensland.
Designed and Typeset by Sun Photoset, 7 Mallon Street, Bowen Hills,
Queensland.

Cover design: Watercolour by Stephen S.Bloomer; title design and layout
by Mary Milligan.

Captain John C.H. Foley   **Dr Christopher S. Milligan**

Dr Christopher S.Milligan is a former Director of Teacher Education, and currently a member of the Curriculum and Instruction Department at McGill University in Montreal, Canada. His interest in the *Centaur* stems from the loss of an uncle in the tragedy. He began researching the topic in 1979 and in 1981 released a 100-page monograph on the subject. He lives in Pointe Claire, a suburb of Montreal, with his wife, Mary, and sons Andrew, Thomas and Mark.

Captain John C.H.Foley has been writing books on Queensland maritime history since 1982. A mariner by profession, he obtained his first command in 1966. In 1975 he was accepted into the ranks of the Queensland Coast and Torres Strait Pilot Service.

He is a member of the Australian Society of Authors and the Company of Master Mariners of Australia. He is also a founder member (and now life member) of the Torres Strait Historical Society. In 1990 the Royal Historical Society of Queensland awarded him a Fellowship in recognition of his contribution to Queensland maritime history.

With his wife, Denice, and son, David, he lives in Brisbane.

Contents

Abbreviations

AAMC	Australian Army Medical Corps
AAMWS	Australian Army Medical Womens Service
AANS	Australian Army Nursing Service
AASC	Australian Army Service Corps
ACNB	Australian Commonwealth Naval Board
ADGMS	Assistant Director-General of Medical Services
ADMS	Assistant Director Medical Services
AHS	Australian Hospital Ship
AIF	Australian Imperial Force
AMF	Australian Military Forces
ARCS	Australian Red Cross Society
CMFN	Centaur Memorial Fund for Nurses
CINCPAC	Commander-in-Chief, Pacific
CLO	Central Liaison Office (Imperial Japanese Government)
CNO	Chief of Naval Operations
CO	Commanding Officer
Col	Colonel
DADMS	Deputy Assistant Director Medical Services
DAQGS	Deputy Adjutant and Quartermaster-General Shipping
DDMS	Deputy Director Medical Services
DGAMS	Director-General Australian Medical Services
DST	Director of Sea Transport
ETA	Estimated time of arrival
FA	Field Ambulance
FA(AP)	Field Ambulance Attached Personnel
GHQ	General Headquarters
IJSDM	Imperial Japanese Second Demobilization Ministry
L-Cpl	Lance Corporal
Lt-Cmdr	Lieutenant Commander
Lt-Col	Lieutenant Colonel
MO	Medical Officer
MNWSL	Merchant Navy War Service League
MWT	Ministry of War Transport
NCO	Non-commissioned Officer
NOIC	Naval Officer In Command
OOW	Officer of the Watch
OR	Other rank
POW	Prisoners of War
Pte	Private
RAANS	Royal Australian Army Nursing Service
RAAMC	Royal Australian Army Medical Corps

RAN	Royal Australian Navy
RNVR	Royal Naval Volunteer Reserve
RSM	Regimental Sergeant Major
SATU	Sea Ambulance Transport Unit
SCAP	Supreme Command Allied Pacific
Sgt	Sergeant
SR	Special Research
SRN	Individual translations, Japanese naval messages
SRNS	Summaries, Japanese naval radio intelligence
SWPA	South West Pacific Area
VAD	Voluntary Aid Detachment
WCI	War Crimes Inquiry
WO	Warrant Officer

Foreword
By: Professor Geoffrey Blainey

The sinking of the *Centaur*, by a Japanese submarine, will be discussed in Australia long after nearly all other events of the Second World War have slipped from public knowledge. It will be remembered because so many Australian sailors and nurses and servicemen went quietly to their death, because nearly all who survived were brave and uncomplaining, and because the event happened so close to the city of Brisbane whose citizens for the following 36 hours went quietly about their work, knowing nothing of the disaster. Above all, the *Centaur* will probably continue, from time to time, to influence Australians' attitudes to Japan.

Centaur was a small but luxurious passenger ship built in the 1920s for the Blue Funnel Line of England. Converted into a wartime vessel at the Victorian dockyard of Williamstown she was on her fourth voyage as a hospital ship, steaming from Sydney to Cairns and ultimately Port Moresby, when she was torpedoed and set alight by a Japanese submarine. She sank within minutes. Most of the 332 women and men aboard were either killed in the fire or sucked down when the ship sank about 24 miles east of Stradbroke Island.

It was night, and the ship was so brilliantly lit that she must have seemed like a floating Luna Park. An enemy seeing the vivid red crosses, all illuminated, must have instantly recognised that the ship was immune — under international law — from armed attack. The commander of the Japanese submarine gave her no immunity. Who he was, and why he so acted, are amongst the numerous puzzles pursued in this book and ultimately unravelled.

Australians might well ask why the Hawke-Keating government, in an act of sycophancy, legislated that Australian citizens should be prosecuted for war crimes, committed allegedly in far-off lands at a time when they were not even Australian citizens, but that Japanese officers should be forgiven for war crimes committed against Australians on Australian seas.

Nearly everyone who reads the book will conclude with praise for the two authors, Chris Milligan and John Foley: praise for their persistent research, for their skill in making technical and seafaring matters easy to follow, their fairness in discussing emotional issues, and their ability to tell a story which disloyal leaders would apparently prefer loyal citizens to forget.

Geoffrey Blainey
November 1992.

Preface

There was a light, almost apologetic, knock on the wardroom door. Inside the darkened room the Japanese submarine commander rolled over in his narrow bunk and opened one eye. He saw the heavy curtain being pulled slowly aside.

In the doorway stood the duty petty officer, silhouetted against the passageway's muted red light. He held back the curtain with his left hand and saluted with his right.

'*Captain,*' he called out, softly.

'*Hai!*' breathed the commander in response, closing his eyes again and sighing audibly.

'*San ji desu. Bridge made, onegai shimasu.*' ('It's three o'clock. Come to the bridge, please.')

'I'll be there in one minute.'

'*Hai!*' The curtain fell back into place.

The commander rolled onto his back and stared blankly at the dark deckhead. He was wide awake. He had left the bridge about an hour earlier, after spending the previous six hours scanning the horizon in a fruitless search for Allied shipping. Everything had been quiet — boringly quiet — and this had tempted him to take a short rest. Yet sleep had been denied him. He had tossed and turned, fully dressed on the narrow bunk, worrying all the time about the vulnerability of his surfaced submarine.

Despite the lack of sleep he felt better now, knowing he would soon be on the bridge again. He would be in charge, and able to satisfy himself beyond doubt that all was well. Certainly the sounds around him presaged no hint of danger. The heart of his submarine beat with its usual regular pulse: the familiar hum of the diesel-electric engines; the rush of air down the conning tower; the characteristic intermittent growl of the steering gear. Even the scratching of the ubiquitous rats doing over the nearby galley seemed somehow reassuring.

With a sigh he eased himself out of the bunk. He reached instinctively for his binoculars and his red goggles. He stepped out of the darkened room and walked quietly along the passageway towards the boat's shrine. He was careful to make no noise. He knew that two thirds of the crew — all except those on watch — would be sleeping. Many lacked the luxury of a bunk and simply stretched out wherever they could find a comfortable spot; wedged in convenient corners, on sacks of rice — sometimes even on top of torpedoes.

He kept his visit to the shrine brief, and moved into the central control position. He nodded perfunctorily to the duty crew as they instinctively came to attention at his presence. Then he climbed the first ladder to the conning tower and the second up to the bridge.

Three men were there; a lookout on each side and the OOW in the centre.

'Good morning, Captain,' welcomed the OOW. 'All clear. Still heading west, two knots.'

Without comment the commander raised his binoculars — already set to his personal interocular distance — and scanned the horizon. He trusted the young officer but needed to check for himself. Apart from the low black ridge of land ahead, it was indeed all clear. Peaceful too, the silence broken only by the sea lapping against the conning tower and the occasional whoosh of a breaking wave surging over the trimmed-down hull casing. The ocean lay like a silvery-grey blanket, speckled with daubs of black shadows from scattered clouds. He looked up at the sky. The moon had set — which pleased him — leaving a starlit ceiling pockmarked by puffs of scudding cumulus clouds. He settled into his favourite spot on the starboard side of the bridge, resigned to being there at least until dawn.

He began to mull over the tour of duty. Not much to show for the five weeks since they had left Truk. Only one merchant ship sunk; and he still had nine torpedoes on board. Very soon it would be time to head back to base. Hopefully before then something else would turn up. He began to think of home. But not for long.

The sharp call from the port lookout cut short his reflections. 'Object bearing red one-two-zero!'

Instantly the commander and OOW twisted round to face the port quarter, instinctively raising their binoculars as they did so. The lookout had found a ship.

The OOW acknowledged the report. He looked at his captain, waiting for a response.

'I'll take over,' breathed the commander. He leaned over the voicepipe to the control room. 'Starboard fifteen,' he called down.

'Starboard fifteen!' came the muffled acknowledgment from below.

The submarine soon responded, turning clockwise. 'Midships,' ordered the commander, then, 'steady on three-three-zero.'

His manoeuvre put the target almost right astern, presenting the submarine's narrowest silhouette to any lookouts on the unsuspecting ship's bridge. The commander was glad of the land ahead; it would make his submarine that much more difficult to spot.

He sent a series of sharp, briefly-spaced orders down the voicepipe: 'Diving stations . . .

'Break the charge . . .

'Stop both engines . . .

'Group up, slow ahead together . . .'

And all the time his mind whirled with angles and ranges as he estimated the target's course and speed.

The orders continued: 'Bring all tubes to the ready . . .

'Sonar on; report rev count . . .'

He began calling out the target's compass bearings to the navigator, already hunched expectantly over the plot in the control room.

Soon, from below, came the first opinion of the target. 'Probably a merchant ship . . . diesel powered . . . heading north at about 11 knots.'

The commander acknowledged the report. His eyes never left the target. 'It's not zig-zagging,' he informed the navigator.

At the commander's side the OOW, keeping an intense all-round lookout, reported, 'No escorts in sight.'

The commander was ready. 'Starboard fifteen,' he ordered, then, 'steady on zero-seven-zero.'

The two-way flow of information through the voicepipe continued.

'One hundred degrees track angle,' said the commander to the torpedo officer, who worked with the navigator at the plot.

'Director angle fifteen degrees,' said the torpedo officer.

'Use number one and two tubes,' said the commander.

'Target speed one-three knots,' said the navigator.

'New director angle thirteen degrees,' said the torpedo officer.

The commander clamped his binoculars to the night sight. He set the new director angle. 'Stand by number one tube.'

He could see more and more of his unsuspecting victim. Now he was ready; his calculations done, his plan made. He called out perfuntory orders to the helmsman, adjusting the submarine's course to fine-tune his attack position. He waited.

At last the target's bluff bow came into view on the right side of the lens. Slowly, inexorably, it moved towards the vertical graticule in the centre — and then touched it.

'Fire!' shouted the commander. The weapons officer pressed the red firing button. The submarine shuddered.

In the commander's night sight the graticule traced a path along the target's side.

'Stand by number two tube.'

The target's focsle crossed the line, then its foredeck, a mast, and then another hatch. Its navigating bridge came into the commander's line of sight.

'Fire!'

From below came two shouted reports.

'Numbers one and two tubes fired . . . bow caps shut!' yelled a voice from the forward torpedo space.

'Two torpedoes running correctly,' called the sonar operator.

'Clear the bridge!' shouted the commander. 'Press the diving klaxon!'

The submarine burst into a frenzy of activity.

Already, even before the klaxon ceased its raucous clamour, well-greased valves were spinning in obedience to lightning-fast hands. Sea water thundered into the ballast tanks. In seconds the waves closed over the hull casing and began splashing against the conning tower. The four men on the bridge slid deftly down the ladder. Last to leave was the commander. He swung the upper hatch closed behind him and secured the clips. He called down to the First Lieutenant: 'Take her down to two-fifty feet and shut off for depth charging!'

The commander shinned down the ladder to the control room. The First Lieutenant was already carrying out his instructions. In an aside to him the commander said, 'I don't expect a counter attack . . . we couldn't see any escorts . . . but you never know.'

He moved on to the chart table to discuss the attack with the navigator and torpedo officer.

Head bowed, the torpedo officer looked intently at his stopwatch. 'Estimate one thousand yards,' he told the commander.

Control-room crewmembers watched their commander step back from the chart table. They saw him tug a small towelling cloth from his pocket. He wiped his forehead, cheeks and hands, staring blankly into space as he did so. His facial expression gave nothing away, but they had a good idea what was going through his mind. A thousand thoughts: questions and hopefully accurate answers. What was the target? A merchant ship as it looked to be and as they had calculated — or a warship? His orders were to 'disrupt Allied communications', which meant intercept and destroy primarily merchant ships, but a warship was always more of a challenge and if sunk brought just that extra measure of satisfaction, even if it did attract a greater element of danger. Was this in fact a legitimate target? Were there any lethal escorts nearby? Had he done his calculations correctly? Had he and his team at the plot accurately predicted the target's range, its course, its speed? These they had to know or estimate in advance, if they were to be successful. Experience, educated guesswork, judgement — and luck — were needed in good portion, and the final results were the measure by which the success or otherwise of submarine commanders was finally judged.

The control room crew heard the torpedo officer's revised range estimation of a thousand yards. They knew their torpedoes should cover that distance in about 45 seconds. To a man their eyes fixed on the large circular clock; to its slowly advancing second hand. In less than a minute they would know, one way or another.

Chapter One

THE GOOD LIFE

16th November 1923 to 3rd September 1939

The early 1920s were good years for shipowners. The tragedy
of the Great War — the 'war to end all wars' — had already begun
to dim in peoples' memories. Although wracked economies
around the world still struggled to develop, a prosperous future
beckoned. Burgeoning world trade presaged happy and wealthy
times ahead, and the more progressive shipowners of the day
took full advantage. Among them was Alfred Holt's Ocean Steam
Ship Company of Liverpool, since 1865 owners and operators
of the world-renowned Blue Funnel Line. Ocean Steam embarked
on an adventurous agenda of fleet expansion, thrusting into new
trades and simultaneously replacing old ships with new tonnage.

If ship owners were happy with the times, ship builders were
euphoric. All the leading yards had full order books. One of these,
the Greenock-based Scott's Shipbuilding and Engineering Co.,
had built several previous Blue Funnel ships and stood ready,
able and very willing to meet new demands[1]. In two years, 1923
and 1924, Scott's built six ships for Ocean Steam totalling 44,000
gross tonnes. They were of five different types and design. Two,
the fast passenger steamers *Patroclus* and *Hector*, were twin-
screw, 11,000 tonne sister ships, built for the China trade. The
Adrastus was smaller but at 15 knots almost as fast, and the
Asphalion smaller again with a speed of 14 knots. Even smaller
and slower was the twin-screwed *Dolius*, propelled by an
experimental engine fired by both oil and steam. This hybrid
system, known as a 'Still' engine, could only be described as
technically complicated and operationally cranky, but it worked
and at least it displayed the Holt family's interest in the design
and propulsion of its ships. The progressive Holts also had their
eye on another developing marine engine; this time one with

1

a better future. The internal combustion, or diesel, engine was still then in its early stages of development, but Holts were keen to give one a try. The company chose the model developed by Danish engine builders Burmeister and Wain. To play host to it the company selected the last of this sextuplet of newbuildings — the *Centaur*.

This new vessel was the second in the company's history to bear the name *Centaur*. The first, a single-screw steam reciprocating steamer of 1,900 tons, came from the Belfast yard of Workman Clark in 1895. *Centaur(1)* spent her entire operational life in the company's service in Far East waters. In 1899 Holts sold the ship to Norddeutscher Lloyd. They renamed it *Korat*.

Blue Funnel needed *Centaur(2)* to replace the *Charon* (built in 1903) on the Singapore/Fremantle service[2]. For the previous 20 years the *Charon* and her sister *Gorgon* (1908) had been on the run full-time, save for a four year break by the *Gorgon* between 1916 and 1920. They operated what in modern times would be called a feeder service. In Singapore they linked with the main-line Blue Funnel Liverpool-to-China steamers, transhipping passengers and freight to and from Fremantle and other West Australian ports.

Ocean Steam had learned enough from two decades of experience with the *Charon* and *Gorgon* to know exactly what it wanted in the *Centaur*. A suitable ship could take advantage of good loadings of general cargo and livestock, plus passenger bookings. Holts' designers at Birkenhead were given the task of creating a passenger/cargo vessel of about 3,200 tonnes gross; a ship versatile enough to carry live cattle or sheep as well as general cargo, and with accommodation for about 100 passengers in first and second class configuration. It had to be of light draft and to have reinforced hull plating. This was because the ports of Broome and Derby in particular, where profitable shipments of live cattle and sheep were on offer, were noted for their shallow estuaries and large tidal ranges. At low tide ships were — and still are — left high and dry on the mud.

Scott's began work on this new ship on 16th November 1923. They handed over the completed vessel to Ocean Steam in September the following year. It was given Official Number 147275, and signal letters GMQP[3].

The *Centaur* cost Alfred Holt £146,750. She had the dubious distinction of being the smallest ship in the contemporary Blue Funnel fleet but the first motor ship built for Alfred Holt service in Southeast-Asia. At first, Holts intended naming the new vessel *Charon*, after the ship it was to replace. Why they did not is unclear. Perhaps they wanted to hang on to the old *Charon* a while longer, possibly in another trade. As it turned out the *Charon* stayed on the Singapore/Fremantle trade until 1924, when Ocean Steam sold her[4].

Holts chose instead the name *Centaur*. This conformed with the Blue Funnel tradition of drawing on the names of men (or part-men, part-beasts or part-Gods) from early Greek heroic legend, mostly Homer's *Iliad*. Legend has it that the union between Ixion and a cloud made by Zeus resulted in a half-man, half-horse beast called a Centaur. It mated with the mares on Pelion, and multiplied. The centaurs were lecherous drunkards who terrorised mortals. They were described as having a double nature, and in essence that, albeit unintentionally, eventually summed up this ship's life.

In appearance, the *Centaur* conformed with strict, conservative, Blue Funnel tradition — the world-renowned 'Holts Class' — characterised by the inevitable eye-catching tall, perfectly vertical, sky-blue funnel[a]. Having said that, she also typified the ocean-going passenger/cargo ship of the day. A shipping enthusiast casting a critical eye over her long, multi-decked accommodation block amidships and the short, cluttered cargo-working areas forward and aft, would have immediately identified her as a ship destined for a breakbulk liner trade; not for ocean tramping[5].

In style, she could be classified as neither a 'flush-decker' nor a 'three island type', but something in between. She had a flush deck forward, with no raised focsle, but aft she had a two-level raised poop supporting a docking bridge and a hospital. Amidships sat the triple-decked accommodation block, capped with its Holt-blue funnel sprouting ramrod straight almost eleven metres up from its boat deck mounting. Her bow was raked, but

---

a. The origin of the blue funnel stems from the first ship brought by Alfred Holt, a power-driven three masted sailing ship named *Dumbarton Youth*. When he took possession, Holt found a quantity of blue paint and a number of bibles on board. He used the blue paint on the ship's funnel, liked the appearance, and repeated it on every ship thereafter. What he did with the bibles was not recorded.

conservatively so, and her stern countered over a plate rudder. She had a functional-rather-than-decorative profile, lacking any flamboyance. Apart from the cut of the bow, there were no stylish, raking lines. Her colour scheme was equally orthodox: black hull, white superstructure, blue funnel with a black top. This was the traditional cut of the contemporary Blue Funnel liner (and it would remain so well into the post-WW2 years)[6].

In keeping with Holt tradition the *Centaur*'s scantlings (i.e. the building code: thickness and quality of building materials, sizes of beams and frames, etc.) were above and beyond that stipulated by Lloyds, the preferred classification society of virtually all British companies and of many others around the world. She was 96 metres long, 14.7 metres wide and 6.6 metres deep. She grossed 3,222 tonnes (or tons, as it was in those days; the difference is minimal)[7].

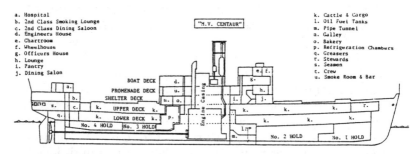

Working from the keel up: immediately inside the extra-thick bottom a web of transverse steel frames, each about 600mm deep and spaced 600mm apart, straddled the width of the ship. Except in the engine room these frames had been plated over, creating double bottom tanks for sea ballast or for storing oil bunkers or fresh water. Then came the four holds: two forward of the engine room, two aft of it; all used for general cargo. No.1 hold, fitted with insulated spaces for stowing fruit or chilled meat cargoes, was in fact two in one, having a separating deck at mid-height.

Above these main holds the *Centaur* had three full-length decks: lower, upper, and shelter. The ship's company would have referred to the two cargo spaces sandwiched between them as the 'lower tween[b] deck' and 'upper tween deck' respectively.

---

b. Strictly *'tween* deck, from 'be-tween' decks.

As with the main holds their purpose was cargo stowage, adaptable to either breakbulk goods (cartons, boxes, sacks, etc.) or livestock, depending on the booking list. When required to carry cattle, of which the *Centaur* could take up to 450 head, the crew erected portable stalls. To enable livestock to physically walk aboard, rather than be unceremoniously slung on board one at a time by the ship's derricks, the *Centaur* had hinged doors, or side ports, in the hull. To improve ventilation the *Centaur*'s architects had designed her two tween decks as open as possible.

The shelter deck, the uppermost full length deck, covered the upper tween deck cargo spaces. The term 'shelter deck' is a misnomer; in truth there is less shelter from the elements on this deck than on any other. In truth it means 'the deck that shelters the upper tween deck cargo spaces'. The name originates amongst the legal machinations of minimising net tonnage measurement. In practical terms this was the true upper deck, but we'll stick with the official nomenclature.

Lloyd's Register listed the *Centaur* as having '2 decks and a shade deck[8]. By shade deck Lloyds referred to the shelter deck, no doubt called a shade deck because of its forest of steel uprights and awning spars, over which canvas awnings could be drawn in tropical seas. These awnings helped cool the decks; something particularly important with livestock below or, as sometimes happened in the East, when carrying native deck passengers.

Right forward on this teak-sheathed shelter deck was the electric windlass, the motive power for the *Centaur*'s two bow anchors. Abaft the windlass a broad V-shaped steel cutwater or breakwater straddled the deck, its purpose to quickly deflect any breaking seas. This knee-high barrier also gave the cooks and stewards, whose only access to their accommodation below was via a nearby central stairwell, a chance of getting in and out without being drenched or washed overboard. Then came the foredeck hatches: No.1, 4.6 metres by 4.8 metres, and No. 2, 7.3 metres by 4.6 metres, separated by a masthouse and foremast. The foremast supported two pairs of pitch-pine derricks of five-tonne SWL (Safe Working Load) — one pair over each hatch — plus a single steel, heavy-lift 15-tonne SWL derrick plumbed over No.2 hatch. The power for this cargo gear came from electric winches, themselves contemporarily innovative. At sea the five-tonne derricks were stowed horizontally, resting in support

5

clamps, while the heavy lift derrick stood vertically, lashed securely to the mast.

At mid-length, immediately over the engine room, sat the accommodation block, three decks of cabins and public rooms draped around the engine casing like a stack of deck quoits. All the exterior decks here, like the shelter deck, were sheathed with teak. From the middle of this structure sprang the proud blue funnel, and forward of this stood the bridge structure.

On the afterdeck, between the central accommodation block and the raised poop, the picture was much the same as on the fore: two hatches, Nos. 3 and 4, separated and served by the mainmast and two pairs of five-tonne derricks (but no heavy lift derrick).

The *Centaur* had a maximum passenger capacity of 72: 50 first class, 22 second class.

First class passengers lived in 14 cabins on the promenade deck and eight cabins on the shelter deck, all quaintly — but at that time seriously — referred to as 'staterooms'. The 'bloods' could take their choice of eight three-berth, 12 two-berth and 2 single-berth staterooms. The need for fresh air circulation in tropical seas had been given special attention; all rooms sported that most modern of ventilation devices — an electric fan. Three-berth cabins had bunks, wardrobes, desks and washbasins (probably not with running water). Two-berth rooms had no desks, for some reason, but at least had beds, rather than up-and-down bunks, and a small settee. At about seven square metres in area these rooms were tiny, but in all likelihood they matched the contemporary average and were anyway more than compensated for by three very spacious public rooms.

Gentlemen wishing to enjoy their cigars and port did so in the padded and masculine elegance of the smokeroom, a room some ten metres by four metres in size, sited near the after end of the promenade deck. Right aft on this deck, adjacent to the smokeroom, an open-air social area — the Verandah Cafe — overlooked the after deck and stern.

Mixed social gatherings on the other hand took place in the lounge, similar in size to the smokeroom, but located at a prime spot across the forward end of the promenade deck. Settees and sets of tables and chairs, and a piano for musical entertainment, comprised the decor in this graceful room, so tastefully panelled in light oak. Passengers entered this lounge via a vestibule; a spacious void with a two-deck-high skylight ceiling. From this vestibule central stairs led down to the dining saloon immediately beneath the lounge, on the forward part of the shelter deck. This dining room, which seated 50, stretched the full width of the ship.

Sanitary facilities for first class passengers comprised three baths, seven showers and nine WCs. All the running water was cold, the *Centaur* at that stage having no running hot water system. Attentive stewards brought hot water to the passengers' cabins and bathrooms, as required.

Second class passengers, understandably, weren't quite so well attended. The ship's designers had tucked their accommodation down aft on the upper deck, successfully maintaining that discreet but effective segregation between classes that the mode of the day demanded. It could only be described as cramped and spartan. One cabin accommodated ten passengers, another eight, the other four. The second class dining room and smokeroom were small and no doubt of commensurate modest decor to the second class cabins. Sanitary facilities amounted to just one bath, two showers and three WCs. Adding to the discomfort in this area would have been the clangorous noise of the steering gear immediately above. At sea these passengers lived with unrelenting but intermittent groaning and growling, thumping and crashing, as every turn of the steering wheel on the bridge clanked its mechanical instruction to the steering-flat motors to turn the rudder.

Accommodation for the crew, 39 European officers and 29 Asiatic ratings, presented an even greater range of contrasts.

At the top end of the scale were the officers' cabins on the boat deck. The captain and his three mates lived immediately beneath the bridge, in the officers' house. Farther aft on this deck, and separated by a cross-alley, came the funnel casing, the wireless room and then the engineers' house, home to the chief and his four other engineers. Except for the captain's quarters, these boat deck cabins were small (about three metres square) though comfortable and well-appointed. Each had a bunk with drawers beneath, a washbasin, office desk and chair, full-length settee (or daybed, as it was known), and a small wardrobe. Like the passenger cabins, they lacked any private bathroom facilites.

The captain, as his esteemed rank would suggest appropriate, enjoyed more comfortable quarters, savouring the comfort of a spacious dayroom and an adjoining bedroom with double bed. His privileges did not extend to private bathroom facilities, all the same, and he had no choice but to share the sole bathroom with the other boat deck occupants. Fortunately it adjoined his cabin, and he at least had the luxury of an internal connecting door. For everyone else the access to this bathroom was from the deck.

The remaining officers — chief steward, electrician and ship's doctor — lived down on the shelter deck, in quarters of presumably similar quality to those on the boat deck.

Less commodious were the rating's quarters, all sited below the shelter deck. Chinese cooks and stewards lived right forward on the upper deck, immediately beneath the windlass. The noise when the crew worked the anchors must have been incredible! Suffering a different kind of noise, but one equally as unpleasant, were the engine room ratings, the greasers (also Chinese), who lived right aft on the lower deck, immediately over the threshing propeller. Sleep would have been difficult enough here at the best of times, but impossible in rough weather when the *Centaur*'s stern lifted out of the water and sent the suddenly unburdened propeller racing madly.

The Malay deck seamen were only marginally better off than the greasers. Their quarters were slightly farther forward, away from the worst of the propeller noise, but they too lacked any vestige of luxury. They lived in one large, sparsely-furnished messroom-cum-dormitory; eating, sleeping and recreating in the one room. In the centre of the mess were two long tables with bench seats. Around its perimeter were a dozen pairs of up-and-down bunks, bolted directly to the steel plating. Wardrobes were non-existent; the men kept their possessions in tiny lockers.

Ratings' meals were prepared in two separate galleys right aft on the upper deck.

Rating sanitary facilities were sparse all round; only one toilet and wash place for each of the three departments.

These conditions were draconian by today's standards but apparently acceptable to the Malay and Chinese seamen destined to crew the ship for many years. Not surprisingly, they failed to come up to scratch later, when Australian seamen took over. Extensive modifications were needed before this accommodation could be considered habitable.

Crew recreational facilities, mandatory on modern ships, were non-existent on the *Centaur*. The officers enjoyed some creature comforts; they ate in the dining saloon with the passengers and no doubt also socialised with them in the lounge and smokeroom[9].

For the mechanically minded, in the *Centaur*'s engine room was a 4-stroke, 6-cylinder, blast-injected diesel engine built by Burmeister and Wain of Copenhagen, Denmark. History would vindicate Holt's choice; this engine turned out to be the most reliable of all the early diesels[10].

At 110 rpm, the *Centaur*'s engine developed 1400 brake horse power. Transmitted via the 30-metre shaft to the propeller at the stern, this thrust gave the ship a modest but satisfactory 12.5 knots service speed. The four-bladed propeller had a pitch of 3.3 metres and a developed area of 2.8 square metres. Auxiliaries included a starting air receiver with a capacity of 66.75 cubic metres and working pressure of 330 psi, and a main-engine-driven compressor. Also fitted was an auxiliary boiler with a pressure of 100 psi, for domestic hot water.

The fuel needed to feed all this machinery was oil, diesel oil. The *Centaur* had a maximum bunker capacity of 419 tonnes in five tanks, all in the same area; immediately forward of the engine room. This concentration of bunker fuel may well have spelled the *Centaur*'s eventual death knell, as we shall see.

Moving from the power house to the command centre, the *Centaur*'s bridge, like most bridges of the day, was open, with narrow wings jutting out to the ship's side. Providing the only protective shield from the elements was a tiny square wheelhouse and adjoining chartroom. The wheelhouse was there purely to shelter the man at the wheel, the quartermaster; not out of concern for him personally but merely to make sure that whatever the weather he could see the marks on the steering compass card. Neither was it there as a shelter for the Officer-of-the-Watch (OOW). The company expected him to spend his four-hour watch out on the wings. Woe betide any young turk of an officer who got caught by the captain swanning it inside the wheelhouse!

Compared to the range of navigational equipment with which modern merchant ships are equipped, the *Centaur* came sparsely provided. What she had was very basic: sextants, a chronometer, a steering compass in the wheelhouse and a standard compass on the monkey island above the wheelhouse. Devices common to every ship today — gyro compasses, automatic steering equipment, satellite navigators, radar sets and echo sounders — were unheard of at that time.

At sea quartermasters manned the *Centaur*'s steering wheel 24 hours a day. They shared this duty in one-hour 'tricks' at the wheel, their guide no more than a swaying, yawing circular compass card that in basic design had changed little over the previous century. The card was graduated in 90° quadrants, from North (0°) to East (90°) to South (0°) to West (90°) and back to North. Compasses graduated to 360° did not appear until WW2.

When deep sea, the *Centaur*'s officers navigated by means of sextant observations of the sun, moon, stars and planets. When coasting, the OOW took regular bearings of shore objects, using the standard compass on the monkey island above the wheelhouse. He had to squint through an azimuth mirror, line up the objects with the graduated compass markings, and note the readings. In good sea conditions and in clear weather this was simple, but when the ship rolled or pitched, or in rain or otherwise poor visibility, the officers often stood hunched over the binnacle for several minutes. Afterwards, in the chartroom, the OOW would lay out his bearings on the chart to fix the ship's position, and thus deduce the new course to steer. Then it was back to the monkey island where, by a series of timely taps on the brass voicepipe next to the binnacle, he aligned the quartermaster to the new heading.

When in poorly-charted coastal waters, depth soundings were vital. They were taken by a seaman with a lead-line, reaching out from either of two hinged teak gratings — the 'chains' — at the forward end of each side of the boat deck. This 'leadsman's' line was graduated with strips of leather and different coloured flag bunting; the lead itself baited — or 'armed' — with tallow to sample and help identify the nature of the bottom.

Communication around the ship was also primitive, if effective. Engine orders from the bridge to the engine room were transmitted via brass telegraphs. Oral communication with the engine room and with the captain's quarters was by means of voicepipes. A brass whistle at each end drew attention to the caller. Most long-distance communications from the bridge were by means of the crude but very effective open megaphone, its range limited only by the resonance of the caller's voice. If the captain should be berating someone for a misdemeanour, the message usually got through loud and clear.

Lifesaving appliances consisted of the usual scattering of lifebuoys around the ship, plus enough lifejackets for everyone on board. The *Centaur* had eight boats: six 8-metre lifeboats, a 7.3-metre lifeboat, and a 5.5-metre dinghy. She also carried a doctor, and had a separate 4-berth hospital aft, on top of the steering gear house. To control the ship if communication from the bridge were lost, from whatever cause, an emergency compass, steering wheel and engine room telegraph had been installed on the docking bridge aft, above the hospital.

Radio transmitters on ships were becoming less of a novelty in the 1920s. It is likely the *Centaur* had two medium frequency (MF) 'spark transmitters'. In daylight their effective range was possibly no more than 400 miles, but at night, depending on the conditions, contact could be made with other stations thousands of miles away.

Her fitting-out complete, our spanking new cargo-liner eased away from her Greenock berth and turned her bows towards the Firth of Clyde. Next stop Liverpool, ancestral home of the Blue Funnel fleet. Now completely in Ocean Steam's hands, she would be readied here both for her outbound voyage and for her future career in the eastern Indian Ocean.

Ocean Steam had appointed as the *Centaur*'s first commander a man well familiar with the intended trade. Captain Rose had for many years captained the ship the *Centaur* would replace, the *Charon*. He travelled from Fremantle to England to take over the new ship, together with the *Charon*'s chief officer and chief and second engineers[11]. The *Centaur*'s first 3rd engineer was a Scot from Gourock named Ernest Smith. He turned out to be her last chief engineer.

Like a young eagle leaving its nest, M.V. *Centaur* left England in October 1924, never to return. She took passengers and cargo to Singapore, then reloaded for Fremantle. Her first southbound cargo included a large consignment of sheep; over 2,000 head. She arrived at Fremantle's Gage Roads at 0900 on 19th December, picked up her pilot, and was all secure to 'G' Shed at 1025. What sort of fanfare she received is unknown; *The West Australian* afforded her a lengthy paragraph in its Shipping News section but had nothing to say about any special reception. The newsitem nevertheless ran comments by some passengers who spoke highly of the ship's cool comfort in the tropics and its excellent seakeeping qualities.

On 23rd December the wharfies completed discharging. Soon after, the first northbound cargo started coming over the rails. Yuletide festivities intervened, and it was not until 4th January

1925 that the *Centaur* set off without much ado or fanfare into the trade that would occupy her for the greater part of her career. This first voyage more or less set the pattern for dozens to come, with calls at Geraldton, Carnarvon, Onslow Roads, Point Sampson, Port Hedland, Broome and Derby, and then on to Batavia and Singapore.

And such was her early life, voyage after voyage, year in and year out. A regular pattern broken only when, in response to cargo inducement, she called at other ports; places with exotic-sounding names like Semarang and Banjowangi in the Dutch East Indies, and other West Australian ports. Her cargoes would include rock salt, tea, timber, cattle, drums of molasses, lubricating oil and grease, casks of cement, bags of tin ore, bales of fodder, hides and wool, crates of Java and Carnarvon bananas and, on the odd occasion, a dog or a race horse[12]. Passengers went both ways, treating the ship like a regular (for the most part) bus service between intermediate stops. In 1925 the local agents, West Australian Steam Navigation Company, set the fare for a first class passenger travelling to or from Singapore at £45. Often the ship would be swamped by schoolchildren — up to 250 of them — travelling between Fremantle schools and their northern cattle-station or Singapore homes. On those trips no other passengers were carried and even the public rooms were converted to temporary accommodation.

She was a comfortable ship. Passengers could relax and sip tea on the Verandah Cafe, read a book in the lounge, or just sun themselves on the open deck. And all the while the *Centaur* steamed sedately along, giving her guests a front row view of the passing parade: rugged coastlines, mostly calm seas, and tropical islands. For the crew, seeing these mystical sights trip after trip, the run's exotic appeal inevitably wore off, but each voyage nevertheless had enough of its own highlights to offset any boredom.

In 1928 the *Gorgon* left the run. Her captain, J. Ward-Hughes, transferred to the *Centaur*, replacing Captain Rose. Five years later, in 1933, the company appointed Ward-Hughes to the brand new *Gorgon*, virtually a sister to the *Centaur* although larger. His place on the *Centaur* was taken by a Captain Ireland. Ireland commanded the *Centaur* until 1936, and then handed over to Captain George Alexander Murray[13].

Murray, from Buckie in northern Scotland, had been a loyal servant to Blue Funnel Line for 19 years. His first Holt ship was the *Telemachus* which he joined in 1917, two years after passing his Masters' Certificate[14]. Before taking over the *Centaur*, Murray had commanded three other ships. He came with a reputation as a first class seaman and navigator.

Murray was a stocky man, very much the typecast old seadog. He walked with his legs wide apart, as if bracing himself against the heaving deck of a windjammer. Like many Scots in positions of authority, he tended to keep his own counsel. He was a shy, dour man, of reserved manner with his officers. He had a distinct, wheezy sort of laugh. His officers heard it only when their captain was in the company of passengers, yet they all regarded him as a fine master and a thorough gentlemen. On occasion he could let his hair down; as he did at the wedding of Fourth Engineer Maurice Cairnie in 1941, when he danced the Scottish reels. He also enjoyed participating in passenger activities; dances, horse racing and the like.

Murray soon settled in to his new command and the *Centaur*, as she had done for so long before he came, continued her regular and repetitious trade — just one of the 'Black Boats', as the Holt trio were locally known.

Mostly, apart from an occasional cyclone, a sick passenger, a minor mechanical problem, or the myriad of little incidents that crop up on most days at sea, the *Centaur* enjoyed a happily mundane existence; no doubt just as Murray preferred it. So the interruption to his routine on 13th November 1938, on voyage 91 North, when something out of the ordinary happened, probably irritated him.

That morning the *Centaur*'s wireless operator picked up a distress signal. It came from a 385-tonne Japanese whalechaser, *Kyo Maru II*, bound from Japan to the Antarctic. She had broken down with boiler problems. At the mercy of the currents, the *Kyo Maru II* was drifting rapidly towards the treacherous Houtman Abrolhos Archipelago. Captain Murray quickly turned the *Centaur* towards the given position, which fortunately was not too far away. Reaching the scene in time, he hove to and sent a line across to the crippled vessel. In the calm conditions it was not difficult to pull the *Kyo Maru II* away from the Abrolhos. The *Centaur* then towed her across Geelvink Channel to safety at Geraldton. Ernie Smith, now chief engineer, married, (to a lady he met during a voyage on the *Centaur*) and living permanently in Fremantle, later recalled that it had been a relatively easy and short tow[15].

After rendering this maritime courtesy the *Centaur* resumed her voyage to Singapore. This diversion must have delighted the passengers; a high seas drama to write home about.

Perhaps Murray should have expected something unusual on that trip. It was already a unique voyage. For the first time in more than ten years the *Centaur* would break out from her regular schedule. After discharging at Singapore, Murray's orders were to take the *Centaur* to Hong Kong for a major overhaul.

The *Centaur* spent Christmas that year in Taikoo's No. 2 Dock. She emerged on New Year's Day 1939 with a turbo-blower supercharger in the engine room and a new, slightly larger and coarser-pitched propeller at her stern. The old propeller came aboard as a spare, stowed at the bottom of No. 4 hold.

Freshly painted and refurbished, the *Centaur* went back to her business[16].

For most of 1939 her trade continued as it had before. The events happening in Europe, while terrible and difficult to comprehend, seemed so very far away. Surely nothing would bring an end to this idyllic existence?

Then, on 3rd September that year, came the ominous message that Britain had declared war against Germany.

Chapter Two

A MERCHANT SHIP AT WAR
3rd September 1939 to 11th January 1943

Like all British ships, wherever they were the moment war was declared, the *Centaur* came under the immediate authority of the British Government. Thereafter, although still owned by their shipping companies, every vessel flying the Red Ensign became an integral part of a British Merchant Navy mobilised for war. Some, for example those engaged on established liner trades, were allowed to continue their usual employment, at least for the time being. This applied to the *Centaur* and her two trade sisters[1].

For the remainder of 1939, and during the so-called 'phoney war' of 1940 and on into 1941, the War seemed far distant from Western Australia or the East Indies. For the *Centaur*, *Gorgon* and the new *Charon* (built 1936), life went on much as it had before[2]. Their schedules stayed much the same, varied only by an increase in shipments of flour to Singapore and Java (so much so that more ships came onto the run). Even the customary periodic dockings in Singapore went on as in pre-war years[3]. During 1940 the *Centaur* drydocked three times for her regular 'haircut and shave'.

As quiet as life may have seemed then in that part of the world, however, everyone on board well knew that in other oceans a bitter struggle already raged. The war at sea had begun early and in earnest, long before any ground battles. In fact the first British casualties of WW2 were seamen and passengers of the liner *Athenia*, torpedoed by the U-30 within a few hours of war being declared[4]. Before long, German U-boats ranged with arrogant invincibility in the North Atlantic; a veritable orgy of attacks on unarmed merchant ships. Each month upwards of 50 ships — valuable steel hulls full of vital war materials — plunged to the bottom, many taking their entire crews with them. Complementing the U-boats were surface raiders, converted merchantmen bristling with hidden weaponry. Like the U-boats, they enjoyed spectacular successes. It did not take long for the carnage to spread to the South Pacific. New Zealand got a nasty shock in June 1940 when the liner *Niagara* exploded and sank almost within sight of Auckland, a victim of mines laid by the German raider *Orion*. The *Orion* had slunk across the Pacific undetected. The sombre message could not be ignored in Australia. It generated no little concern in Canberra. Would the Tasman Sea and Indian Ocean be next? Yes indeed. Only four months later came reports of a Norwegian ship lost to a German raider in the Indian Ocean. On 7th November the British freighter *Cambridge* struck a mine near Wilson Promontory. She sank and one man, carpenter J.Kinnear, died — the first casualty of WW2 in Australian territory. Next day the US ship *City of Rayville* followed suit, also losing one man. Suddenly the war at sea did not seem far away at all. Among seafarers, unease grew. Seamen were not stupid. They had well-merited misgivings about the vulnerability of unescorted ships to any unwelcome attention by the *Kriegsmarine*. They knew they had but one effective defence — the sheer vastness of the seas[5].

Captain Murray soon learned that the war brought with it many changes. No longer was he the sole boss of his ship, answerable only to his owners in Liverpool. He had become a servant of the Admiralty, subordinate to any person authorised to act in its name. Naval Control Service Officers in any port he visited could at a moment's notice change or amend his sailing instructions — always of course leaving in place that immunising rider 'the master is at all times responsible for the safe navigation of the vessel'. Often he was 'routed', instructed to proceed as directed along specified routes. Occasionally his ship had to join a convoy, although these were rare on Australia's west coast. No longer could he use his radio transmitter as required. 'Radio silence' had become the fundamental and inviolable rule. Government control brought with it bureaucratic paperwork — forms to be filled in, reports to be written, procedures to be followed — giving Murray more clerical drudgery to add to the already onerous paper chase for which Blue Funnel was renowned.

The *Centaur* too, changed. Protection became the catchcry. First, she had to be made less conspicuous. Gradually, in stages,

M.V. Centaur *as a passenger-cargo ship on the West Australian trade.*

(N.Smith)

Captain George Alexander Murray . . . went down with his ship.

(Mrs Murray)

Above and left: the Centaur *at Broome, high and dry at low tide.*

(N.Smith)

seamen armed with long-handled paint brushes and drums of battleship grey paint transformed the former smartly-liveried cargo liner into a drab freighter. Steadily but inexorably, the *Centaur*'s black hull, white upperworks and sky-blue funnel succumbed to the grey tide. To give some protection to those on the bridge, sandbags were packed around her tiny wooden-walled wheelhouse and chartroom. To counter magnetic mines the *Centaur* was degaussed; that is, internally circled by wire cables laid around her tween decks. A switch on the bridge activated this anti-magnetic system, which was always on at sea when in shallow, mineable waters. Another anti-mine device, the paravane, gave protection from moored mines. Looking like miniature aircraft, the paravanes swept out either side of the ship on the end of wires attached to a steel boom slung over the *Centaur*'s starboard bow. When the paravane fouled a mine, a cutter on the paravane wire severed its mooring and let it bob to the surface, where it was destroyed by gunfire.

Firepower was another thing that war brought to the *Centaur*. Two Lee Enfield .303 rifles appeared on board, to take care of floating mines. For more active defence (though many experts doubted their effectiveness in a serious contest) a Vickers .303 machine gun appeared on each bridge wing. But the main piece of ordnance was a 4" Mark IX, breech-loading, low elevation naval gun. The navy installed it on the *Centaur*'s poop in Fremantle in December 1940[6]. Two naval gunners joined the ship, their task being to maintain these guns and if necessary put them to serious use. Some of the ship's crew had to help man the 4" gun, which called for a crew of seven.

Despite the comforting presence of the two gunners, no-one on board really believed they could offer much more than token opposition to the predatorial advances of German merchant raiders or U-boats[7].

Fortunately for the *Centaur*, the quiet life continued for the first two years of the War. Then, one day in late November 1941, she came face to face with the enemy for the first time.

It happened on Voyage 119 South. Captain Murray was on shore leave, his place taken for one round voyage by Captain W.F.Dark. M.V. *Centaur* was about to play a pivotal and important role in the aftermath of the War's most tragic, nationally embarrassing, and certainly most contentious naval engagement in close Australian waters.

17

The scene for this drama was set about 150 miles west of Carnarvon on the morning of 23rd November, when the Sydney-bound British liner *Aquitania* came across a rubber raft with men on board. The captain stopped and picked up 26 Germans. He gleaned enough from the mostly tight-lipped survivors to suspect the presence of a German raider, so chose not to break radio silence by reporting the incident. The next day, and not far away, the British tanker *Trocas* came across 25 Germans on another raft. Her captain sent a brief coded message. That same afternoon a lifeboat with German seamen on board beached at Red Bluff, about 50 miles north of Carnarvon. Another arrived in much the same place the next morning.

The men picked up by the *Trocas* admitted they were from a merchant raider. They told of a battle with a cruiser, in the aftermath of which their ship sank[8].

This information, when received by the Naval Board, prompted an aerial search, not only for the remaining German survivors but also for the mentioned cruiser. The navy knew it must have been HMAS *Sydney*. Strangely, and disturbingly, the *Sydney* had made no contact for several days. She was already four days overdue at Fremantle.

All available search aircraft took to the skies. Waves of Hudsons, Wirraways, Ansons and Catalinas scoured the ocean west of Carnarvon. Their search grids extended south to Geraldton and north to Onslow. The navy ordered all ships known to be nearby to pass through the area and to keep watch.

One of these was M.V. *Centaur*, on her way to Carnarvon to pick up a consignment of wool.

Early on the morning of the 26th, searching aircraft found two lifeboats containing survivors. They were about 30 miles apart. The two nearest ships were the *Centaur* and an Australian freighter, *Koolinda*. The aircraft contacted and diverted both of them. The *Centaur*'s given target was a lifeboat thought to hold about 50 men, in position 24°39'S, 112°02'E[9].

As the *Centaur* steamed towards this position, Captain Dark began to make his plans. Having lost two previous ships to German U-boats, and mindful of the *Centaur*'s limited ordnance, Dark had some misgivings about taking German seamen on board the *Centaur*, even if they turned out to be suffering from exposure. As they were most likely members of the German Navy they would miss no opportunity of seizing his ship; not too difficult a task with the aid of a few concealed weapons. As well as a valuable ship and cargo, he had 44 passengers and a mixed-race crew of 48 in his care, and they, despite all the traditional obligations to aid distressed seamen, had to be his first priority. Moreover, although he did have two gunners, he lacked both the trained personnel and the necessary armoury to mount an effective guard over 50 prisoners. Just in case, he called for volunteers among the passengers to help as sentries. Several men came forward. Some had served in WW1 and knew how to handle a rifle. What Captain Dark lacked was the rifles to give them.

M.V. *Centaur* reached her given search area in the late afternoon. With the sunset Captain Dark elected to stay in the area, despite the poor chances of sighting a lifeboat in the dark. As it turned out he didn't have to wait until dawn. As darkness pushed the last of the dwindling twilight into the west, a lookout spotted two red star-shell rockets arching through the sky. Dark immediately turned his the ship about and with the aid of a searchlight soon picked out the source of the signals. He found a lifeboat packed to overcapacity[10].

As the gap between ship and boat narrowed, seamen threw ropes from the *Centaur*'s stern. The boat's occupants grasped them and made fast. They called up to the ship asking for drinking water and bread. Captain Dark gave orders for the stewards to send down some bread, butter, jam, and some tea.

The crew rigged a ladder over the stern. Dark gave orders to allow just one man to come aboard.

A young officer clambered up the ladder. Chief Engineer Smith noted that he appeared a 'typical Merchant Navy officer'[11].

The *Centaur*'s 3rd Mate, Gordon Rippon, witnessed the confrontation between the officer and Captain Dark[12]. He recalled that the man introduced himself in fluent English. 'I am the Sturman[a] of a Norwegian merchant ship sunk by an Allied warship.'

'You're a bloody liar!' Captain Dark interjected angrily. 'You're an officer of a German raider!'

Unmasked, the young man's arrogance withered. 'I am the First Lieutenant of the German ship *Kormoran*,' he confessed. 'We have been in an engagement with a British cruiser. We were lucky; our torpedoes hit and hers missed.'

---

a. First Mate.

The man's name was Kurt Foerster, executive officer of the *Kormoran*. And his story rocked the *Centaur*'s officers to their bootstraps.

Seven days earlier, Foerster said, their ship had fought a battle with a cruiser. Both ships had been damaged and after breaking off the engagement eventually drifted out of each other's sight. The *Kormoran* had later sunk, and the crew took to the boats. During the next few days they had seen two aircraft and then the *Centaur*, when they sent up the star shells.

In the lifeboat, Foerster said, were 61 men, all German except one Chinese[13]. Among the Germans was the captain of the raider. His name was Commander Theodor Detmers[14].

Captain Dark listened to the story. He still would not allow the Germans to board the *Centaur*. In her excellent analysis of the *Sydney/Kormoran/Centaur* story[b], author Barbara Winter explains why.

> Captain Walter Francis Dark was relieving *Centaur*'s regular captain, George Murray, who was on holidays. *Titan* had been torpedoed under him in the South Atlantic in September 1940; he had been awarded Lloyd's War Medal for his work in saving his crew. Then *Ixion* on 7 May 1941; he recalled the carnage of convoy OB318, the thud of torpedoes in the bowels of his ship and the pillars of fire from blazing ships as they dropped out of the convoy. He recalled his bombed-out home in Liverpool.
>
> Then Foerster appeared before him.
>
> The Reich's eagle over the right pocket of the naval uniform had been too conspicuous on the bridge of a supposed merchantman; it could be seen through glasses from another ship at a fair distance. Before and during the engagement, Foerster had been wearing a jacket without the eagle, and between fighting fires and launching lifeboats, he had had things to do more urgent than going to his cabin to change jackets. until his cabin was no longer accessible.
>
> Until this point, Dark had been willing to take the men on board, but he had not known there were so many of them. He knew they were naval personnel in the lifeboat, and here was this fellow out of uniform. What were they trying to put over him?"[15]

Dark told Foerster the *Centaur* would tow them, at five knots, to Carnarvon. Foerster went back to the lifeboat. The Germans were less than impressed about having to spend another night in the boat.

Things went reasonably well during the night. Early the next morning, however, a sea swamped the lifeboat, drenching

---

b. *HMAS SYDNEY. Fact, Fantasy and Fraud.*

R. Gordon Rippon, the Centaur*'s 2nd Mate. Rippon survived the sinking.*
(R.G.Rippon)

Ernest D. Smith, the Centaur*'s first 3rd Engineer and last Chief Engineer. Smith survived the sinking.*
(N.Smith)

German Raider Kormoran. *In a battle in the Indian Ocean in 1941 the* Kormoran *and HMAS* Sydney *sank each other. 61 survivors from the* Kormoran, *including the captain, were picked up by the* Centaur. *All 645 men in the* Sydney *perished.*

(W.Muller

Theodor Detmers, captain of the raider Kormoran . . . *credited with capturing or sinking eleven merchant ships plus the cruiser* Sydney.

Survivors from the Kormoran. *Captain Detmers, in white jacket, is seated in the stern. One of several photographs taken by R.G.Rippon.*

Kormoran *survivors transferring from their waterlogged boat to one of the* Centaur *'s lifeboats.*

(R.G.Rippon)

The German survivors in two Centaur *lifeboats. At rear is the* Kormoran *'s boat.*

(R.G.Rippon)

Trappings of war on a merchant ship: a seaman paints a paravane, used for sweeping mines, on the Centaur's *foredeck. Unlike guns, paravanes were allowed on hospital ships.*

(F.Chidgey)

A common sight on a merchant ship: a cook (name unknown) works on deck to escape the heat of the galley.

(F.Chidgey)

everyone on board. Detmers told his boatswain to cut the painter. Almost immediately the boat began to sink. Fortunately the airtight compartments took hold, but not before all the men were up to their chests in water. Detmers wrote later: "It was an odd situation altogether, standing there on a submerged platform . . . every time a wave slopped up we lost our footing because the swim vests lifted us up with it"[16]. (Ironically, the then third officer of the *Centaur*, Gordon Rippon, would go through a similar experience about 18 months later.)

It did not take long for the *Centaur*'s lookouts to spot what had happened. Again, Barbara Winter:

> Captain Dark suspected that the boat had been swamped deliberately as part of a plot to get aboard his ship. He would have none of it. *Centaur* returned to the lifeboat and lowered the two port lifeboats, P2 and P4. Detmers again asked why Dark would not take them aboard. Dark replied that he did not want to wake up in the morning and find the German flag at his masthead.
>
> 'Be careful', said Detmers, as the men transferred cautiously to the new boats. 'I don't want to lose even one more man.'
>
> 'If they manage to sink those two, they can swim to Carnarvon,' Dark told his officers[17].

As the Germans quit the *Kormoran*'s damaged lifeboat it bobbed to the surface. *Centaur* seamen hoisted it onto the foredeck[18c].

In the early afternoon this motley towing combination entered Geographe Channel and by 1500 the *Centaur* had berthed at Carnarvon. The crew rigged and lowered the gangway on the outboard side, and brought the two boats alongside. Even then Captain Dark insisted the Germans stay in the boats. The local Volunteer Defence Corps came aboard to keep an eye on them. Detmers later described them (somewhat inaccurately) as 'a group of civilians on deck armed with all sorts of odd firearms: shot guns, rook guns, hunting rifles — guns anyway, and, presumably, capable of peppering us'[19]. Finally the *Kormoran* survivors were taken aboard. Captain Dark had no misgivings this time; the transfer was made under the watchful eye of armed soldiers.

The first man out of the lifeboats bounded up the gangway two steps at a time. At the top he halted, gave the Nazi salute, and shouted 'Heil Hitler!' He very smartly brought his out-

---

c. Later, this lifeboat was exhibited in several West Australian towns to help raise money for charity.

stretched arm down when he felt the tip of a guard's bayonet prodding his stomach.

The soldiers searched each man in turn as they came up the gangway. Dr Pickles, the *Centaur*'s doctor, quickly checked them over. Soldiers then marched them down into No. 1 hold. A meal of piping hot goulash awaited them, plus some cigarettes and, for a lucky few, cots. Most made themselves comfortable on bales of wool.

Early next morning a Lt-Cmdr James Rycroft, RAN, went aboard the *Centaur*[20]. He called out Detmers and Foerster and took them ashore. The remaining Germans were devastated to see their two senior officers taken away. German propaganda had convinced them that the Allies shot all POWs; they felt sure this was the beginning of the massacre.

Rycroft began his interrogation of Detmers and Foerster. He asked them if they knew anything of HMAS *Sydney*. The Australian cruiser, he told them, was overdue. For the first time — and with immense satisfaction — Detmers realised he had struck the Royal Australian Navy a savage and highly embarrassing blow; his merchant raider had probably destroyed a modern, well-armed and heavily-armoured cruiser. He knew intuitively that his David and Goliath victory would earn him the hero-worship of his nation, and no doubt the effusive praise of Adolf Hitler[21].

It is worth briefly recounting what happened[22].

The *Kormoran* was formerly the 8,736 gross tonne Hamburg-Amerika Line *Steiermark*, built in 1938[23]. At the outbreak of war the Kreigsmarine took her over and converted her into a merchant raider (designated *Schiff 41*). By November 1941 Detmers had been happily plundering Allied shipping in the Indian Ocean for six months. He already had eleven merchant ships chalked up on his honour board: ten sunk, one captured. At that time HMAS *Sydney* was returning to Fremantle after escorting a troop ship to Malaya. The two ships first merged into visible distance on the afternoon of the 19th November, about 150 miles southwest of Carnarvon.

Detmers had the *Kormoran* disguised as the Dutch *Straat Malakka*. His armoury, which included 5.9inch, 37mm and 20mm guns, six torpedo tubes, two Arado 196 seaplanes and a mine laying launch, was cunningly concealed[24].

The *Sydney* closed on the raider, her signalmen flashing NNJ — 'MAKE YOUR SIGNAL LETTERS'.

Kormoran signallers read it as NNP or possibly NNF: either way it didn't make sense. Detmers couldn't reply; he had no idea what the signal meant. The cruiser demanded identification. At Detmers' instructions the signalmen put on a good act of delaying bungling. They finally raised the signal flags for the *Straat Malakka*, PKQI. Meanwhile the *Sydney* had closed to within 2,000 metres, steaming abeam of and parallel to the *Kormoran*.

Eventually Detmers knew he could stall no longer. With typical daring he took the initiative. At his signal the German battle flag fluttered free. In an instant the shutters concealing his weapons swung away, and within six seconds the first salvo was on its way.

Although caught totally by surprise, the *Sydney* quickly retaliated.

Both ships took massive damage. Lethal 5.9″ shells from the *Kormoran* blasted the *Sydney's* bridge and forward control room. A torpedo exploded into her hull near the forward turret. The *Kormoran* fired some 450 shells. In return the *Sydney's* 6-inch guns found their mark on the *Kormoran's* funnel and engine room. The raider soon burned fiercely out of control. After more than half an hour of intense mutual bombardment the action ceased and the two mortally wounded ships drifted apart. Detmers' priority was his own ship, but he did watch the cruiser continue to move away, burning fiercely. After about 2100 he could see it no longer. Around that time, reluctantly accepting the *Kormoran's* inevitable doom, he gave the order to scuttle. He figured, wrongly as things turned out, that his adversary had sent off a radio signal, in which event retribution was already on its way. The *Kormoran's* crew took to the boats[25].

So ended what is arguably the Royal Australian Navy's most humiliating experience[26]. All that remained was for the Australian Government, after holding onto the dreaded news for as long as it dared, to announce to a stunned Australian public that a merchant raider had sunk one of the nation's most modern cruisers — and that all 645 men on board had perished.

Detmers was right about the reaction in Germany. Hitler rewarded him with the Knight's Cross of the Iron Cross. Berlin boomed out that the engagement had been 'an encounter without precedent in the annals of naval warfare.' The German Press made much of the irony that an Australian cruiser named *Sydney* should be sunk by a mere raider within a few hundred miles of the spot where an earlier *Sydney* outgunned the German light cruiser *Emden* in WW1[27]. It brought its own sweet revenge.

Another irony of this incident was that the *Centaur* should play a role, however peripheral, in the greatest WW2 loss of RAN personnel to a German vessel — because her own tragic end some 18 months later caused the highest loss of Australian lives on any Allied merchant ship sunk by the Japanese in the Pacific.

The *Centaur*'s final role in this saga was to transport the bulk of the *Kormoran* prisoners, 160 of them, to Fremantle. The army confined the ratings to No.2 hold, while the officers enjoyed more airy accommodation in the after tween deck. This time they travelled under the watchful eye of 40 regular army guards. The Germans took some amusement from the discomfort of their captors, however, as the soldiers suffered miserably from seasickness for the next four days. Mighty were their thanks when they landed onto solid ground at Shed 'B' in Fremantle[28].

Detmers and Foerster were taken overland instead, under armed guard.

In Fremantle Captain Dark happily handed the *Centaur* back to Captain Murray. No doubt he figured he had put up with more than his fair share of drama. Voyage 119N got underway shortly before noon on 4th December, when the *Centaur* steamed out of Fremantle bound Singapore, this time by way of Geraldton, Onslow, and Batavia[29].

By now, late 1941, the world had come to realise that Germany was not the only superpower with world dominance on its agenda. The evil fruits of Japan's signature on the 'Tripartite Pact' with German and Italy, forged in September the previous year, were becoming all too apparent. Japan's grumblings and intensifying belligerency became daily more alarming. The Imperial Japanese Army's rape of China and its roller-coaster sweep southwards into Indo-China posed a grave threat to the stability of the Northwest Pacific region.

This must have been increasingly on Captain Murray's mind as he pointed the *Centaur*'s bows once more towards the East Indies, towards the very area the Japanese coveted. He kept a keen ear on the daily radio broadcasts. Three days after leaving Fremantle he shared the world-wide shock at the news that Japan had launched savage air attacks on Pearl Harbour, Manila and Hong Kong. Japan was now at war with the mighty USA, and with Britain.

Another world war had broken out.

Murray probably expected fresh orders cancelling the trip to Singapore, particularly with the added tidings the next day that Japanese forces had landed in northern Malaya and begun their sweep south. The *Centaur* called at Canarvon and at Onslow, and then, receiving no instruction to the contrary, set off for Singapore. Soon after leaving Onslow, however, the navy ordered the ship to return. Among the passengers were 58 school children and four adults whom the authorities thought might be safer returning to Perth. They transferred to a southbound ship. Murray continued his voyage to Singapore[30].

After an incident-free run, the *Centaur* arrived at Singapore on Christmas Eve. She completed her cargo work, again without incident, and departed on New Year's Day 1942. She never returned to Singapore.

The second day of the New Year brought more disturbing news. Rabaul on the island of New Britain had fallen to the advancing Japanese forces.

By mid-February Singapore had been overrun[d].

The *Centaur*'s schedule changed. From then on she went no further north than Broome. Even so, the Chinese crewmembers asked to be discharged, and were. Australian stewards and greasers took their places. The deck crew remained Malay. This brought the ratio of European to Asiatic crewmembers to 41:29[31].

In April 1942 the *Centaur*, *Gorgon* and *Charon* were withdrawn from the Western Australian trade altogether and sent to Melbourne.

On the coastal voyage eastwards the *Centaur*'s turbo-charger (the one recently fitted in Hong Kong) began to play up. So serious were the problems that after four days in Melbourne the authorities made arrangements to dock the ship in Sydney for repairs. The *Centaur* limped around the coast to Port Jackson and docked at Woolwich. Unfortunately, the repairs were beyond the dockyard's restricted capability. The only option was to isolate the turbocharger; to run the ship without it, pending instructions from Blue Funnel in Liverpool. During all this waste of time the withdrawal of the three ships from Western Australia

d. The *Gorgon* did a final trip to Singapore in late January. At the time, personnel were being evacuated and the ship left in a hurry with 358 evacuees on board. Little of her cargo had been discharged. The *Gorgon* came under attack from Japanese bombers in Singapore Strait but emerged unscathed.

began to create a serious vacuum. Someone applied the right pressure, and all three went back west. The *Centaur* returned to Fremantle on 5th June[32].

From the 9th June until early October 1942 the *Centaur* made three trips along the west coast. Then, in Fremantle on 6th October, news came that the Australian Shipping Control Board had officially taken over the ship[33]. Captain Murray received new orders: go back to Melbourne first, and then Queensland. The *Centaur* spent three weeks in the Victorian capital before heading north to the sunny climes of Queensland. Off Caloundra (outside Brisbane) on 14th November, she joined a Townsville-bound convoy. It took the 'Red Route', up inside the Barrier Reef. At Townsville the *Centaur* waited two weeks while convoy TN11 formed, then sailed with it to Port Moresby. She had a cargo of war supplies. On her return she loaded sugar at Cairns, Lucinda and Townsville for Sydney[34].

Meanwhile, to Australia's north, the disconcerting and seemingly unstoppable spread of Japanese forces into the South Pacific continued. Rabaul on New Britain became the nerve centre of the Japanese advance. It had already served as an effective launching pad for advances into New Guinea. Japanese soldiers soon took Lae and Salamaua on the eastern shore of lower New Guinea, and the islands of Buka and Bougainville in the Solomons. Port Moresby trembled before the breathtaking advance. A strategic jewel for the Japanese should they ever hope to mount an invasion of Australia, Moresby sat just a tantalising 175 miles south of Lae — across the formidable Owen Stanley Range. Pragmatically baulking at an overland assault, the wily Japanese opted for a seaborne invasion, swinging around the southeast point of New Guinea. It is history that in what became known as the Battle of the Coral Sea, the Allied navies blunted this thrust. The Japanese now had but one choice; if they wanted Port Moresby they had to take it with ground forces. First they continued their thrust along New Guinea's northeast coast, towards Milne Bay. General MacArthur sent a small detachment of Australian troops to Buna to slow the advance. Outnumbered ten to one, the diggers could do little but spasmodically resist and retreat. Meanwhile Major General Tomitaro Horrii, in preparation for the attack on Moresby, moved in his task force of more than 11,000 men. The scene was set for a prolonged and bloody battle.

New Guinea's rugged terrain, however, turned out to be a neutral force. At once it assisted and plagued both the Japanese and Australian forces, playing favourite to neither. The 3,000-metre peaks of the jungle-draped Owen Stanleys lay hidden often for days beneath a misty cloak of low hanging clouds. In this forbidding territory a daily diet of muddy swamps, energy-sapping humidity, insects, and debilitating malaria took their toll on these men engaged in arguably the most bitter fighting of the War. In Australian lore the name Kokoda Track was destined to become synonymous with all the worst possible horrors of modern warfare.

By September — and by good fortune — Australian diggers blunted the enemy advance on Port Moresby. For the first time since the outbreak of war the Australians, admittedly aided in some degree by Japanese logistical problems, were on their way to victory. Triumph came at a high price, however. The Japanese resisted with ferocity and fanaticism. By the time Gona and Buna were taken, the Allies had lost about 3,000 men, with many more disabled by disease. The Japanese had lost 12,000 men, and with them any residual hopes of an invasion of Australia. But the fighting was by no means over[35].

It was because of these continuing hostilities in New Guinea that in late 1942 the Department of the Army (Melbourne) wrote to the Department of the Navy asking for another hospital ship. The army's requirements were straightforward; a ship with a 200-patient ward, an emergency-type operating theatre, pack and linen storerooms, a dental surgery, orderly room and dispensary. The army intended running the ship mostly between Townsville and New Guinea, so ideally the chosen vessel would be of light draft. The planners had in mind a medical staff comprising seven officers (doctors), five warrant officers, 38 other ranks and 12 nursing sisters. Urgency was the key, and as the ship's intended voyages would last no more than about four days, there should be no need for expensive and elaborate modifications[36].

Australia already had three other hospital ships at that time. They were the Adelaide Steamship Company's *Manunda* (designated 2/1 AHS), Huddart Parker's *Wanganella* (2/2 AHS), and the Dutch KPM Line's *Oranje*. *Manunda* and *Wanganella* were requisitioned Australian-owned vessels; the *Oranje* a generous loan from the Netherlands Government. All three were converted passenger ships[37].

The command of Australian hospital ships, while clear cut, nevertheless depended on the cooperation of a tri-partite mix of disciplines: army (medical), merchant marine, and naval (operations). Each ship was treated as a complete medical unit, administered in the same way as an army general hospital; the only difference being its mobility. Invariably, the senior army medical officer on board (whatever his actual rank) became Officer Commanding Troops, usually known by his more popular title of 'O.C. Troops' or the even more compact 'O.C.'. In command of the ship, from the point of view of its navigation, safety, day-to-day maintenance and crew discipline, was the captain, a merchant navy officer. Usually the entire crew were merchant marine. Where the ship went, its schedule or any special routeing orders, became the responsibility of the RAN, no doubt in consultation with other military sources[38].

For the RAN this traditional chain of command was not the most ideal arrangement. Many senior naval medical officers held the view that hospital ships should be operated, manned and run wholly by naval personnel. Even some army medical officers agreed that hospital ships should be controlled by just one service. In fact, the military did consider sole naval control for the *Wanganella*, but changed its mind after extensive debate and a final recommendation against it by the Committee of Medical Services.

In practice, and despite the potential for administrative chaos, the system chosen for Australian hospital ships worked well. As things turned out, the personalities of the O.C. Troops and the captains on all Australian wartime hospital ships were remarkably compatible, their mutual relationships highly professional. Anything else would have presaged disaster, and one can only be thankful for an element of good luck in the selection of personnel.

Except on the *Oranje*, where Dutch medical personnel worked alongside Australian, hospital ship medical staff comprised members of the Australian Army Medical Corps and the Australian Army Nursing Service. The AAMC provided the men; usually a half dozen or so doctors, several orderlies, dental technicians and other specialists. From the AANS came a band of sisters, usually about 12, one of whom was appointed Matron. The army supplied a chaplain and the International Red Cross its own representative.

Life at sea on board a wartime hospital ship was busy and sometimes frenetic[39].

On the outbound voyage the catchword was preparation: readying the wards, checking medicines and dressings; in general getting the house in order. Drills were interminable: lifeboat drills, emergency embarkation drills, respirator drills, and so on. Similarly lectures: senior officers lecturing sisters, sisters lecturing orderlies; again and again until every staff member knew exactly what the officers expected of him or her in a variety of emergency circumstances. Organised recreation was important also, as a means of moulding a cohesive, harmonious and efficient unit. Most recreation took the form of sporting activities, musical or thespian performances; sometimes even a dance.

The Red Cross representative played an important supportive role. As an adjunct to his official function, he was invariably a great organiser. Through his Red Cross contacts he obtained movies, books, and transport for shore excursions. From his Red Cross Store came such diverse items as clothing, cordials, even materials for craftwork. The chaplain was another with a supportive role, bringing that essential spiritual succour to all in need. When it came to boosting casualties' spirits and restoring and maintaining morale, both the Red Cross man and the chaplain were magnificent. They could be seen regularly doing the rounds of the wards. They chatted to the patients, bringing a kind word here, a receptive ear there, and like Santa Claus they distributed drinks, cigarettes and sweetmeats such as Minties.

Homeward bound, naturally, the entire work routine revolved around the needs of the patients. Incredible as it may seem, the routine on board a hospital ship differed little to that of a shore hospital. Surgery, physiotherapy, dentistry, and medicine dispensing went on as in any hospital. General nursing was likewise similar, although the environment did create its own hazards — like tending to patients in double-decker cots when the ship rolled and pitched in a seaway.

During the early years of the War the three hospital ships under Australian control spent most of their time running to the Middle East, bringing home Australian casualties from the North Africa campaign. This changed when Japan joined the fray. In mid-January 1942, when Australian and Japanese forces clashed in Malaya, the authorities dispatched AHS *Manunda*, then in Sydney, to Singapore. She never reached the Lion City. Instead, and due to the breathtaking advance of Japanese forces down the Malayan Peninsula, the *Manunda* was diverted to Darwin. There, in friendly and supposedly protected territory, she could await the outcome of the battle, ready at a moment's notice to continue on to Singapore[e].

What followed was a dramatic incident that served as an instructive warning of the fragility of assumed safe conduct for hospital ships; the dangers of relying too much on a display of red crosses, however large or prominent.

The Japanese had already targeted Darwin. They saw this Top End outpost as a potential thorn in their side, knowing that from airfields in and around Darwin, Allied aircraft were well placed to harass their forces advancing through the Dutch East Indies. Plans for an attack on the city and surrounding airfields to snuff out Allied interference were already in place.

The blow fell shortly before 1000 on 19th February. Waves of bombers from a carrier force some 220 miles northwest of Darwin zoomed in over the harbour. Their assault came as a total surprise to the defenders. Surprised also were the Japanese, who could not believe their luck to find the harbour so full of merchant ships.

In Darwin harbour on that day were 45 vessels. Some were Australian and US cargo ships licking their wounds after a convoy to Timor came under attack and had to be aborted. Others, coastal cargo ships, lay at the wharves discharging their precious cargoes. A smattering of U.S. warships and small RAN vessels stood by — as did AHS *Manunda*.

This scene of nautical tranquillity was shattered by a whining, screaming roar of more than 150 aircraft. Almost immediately a wail of sirens and the replying chatter of anti-aircraft fire from the shore batteries added to and amplified the cacophony. Then came a litany of thunderous explosions as bombs found their targets. The Japanese pilots chose their victims at will, dropping sticks of bombs and incendiaries. Within a few horrifying minutes dozens of ships were ablaze, as was the wharf and part of the town. Smoke and flames filled the sky. Panic struck and confusion abounded.

The *Manunda*'s crew launched motor boats to pick up casualties from burning ships all around her. At first, the

e. That no Australian hospital ships were sent to Singapore at this critical time was a matter of some contention.

Manunda lay unmolested. Her Red Cross markings were clearly visible and, it seemed, the enemy was respecting them. But with all the confusion and thick smoke, and the close proximity of other ships, it is no wonder she suffered damage. A bomb exploded on impact in the sea nearby, and flying shrapnel killed four men. Then one Japanese bomber pilot, for whatever reason, decided this large white ship in his bombsight had to go. He dropped into a low attacking dive (so low that crewmembers on the *Manunda* could see his goggled head) and at the prime moment released a bomb. His aim was spot on. His missile struck in the music room, abaft the bridge, and exploded. It blasted a great hole down as far as D deck. Fortunately, even though the bomb destroyed the radio room and part of the bridge, the medical working spaces were intact, although filled with smoke, and the staff were able to go on tending the wounded.

At 1040 the raid ended. As the drone of departing aircraft faded the defenders caught their breath, still reeling from the savagery of the attack. Not long afterwards, a second bombardment seemed imminent. The dreaded drone — that harbinger of death — returned. Japanese aircraft soon filled the sky once more. But this time they had a different target. They were land-based bombers from Ambon and the Celebes bent on destroying the nearby RAAF bases (which they largely achieved).

On the *Manunda* the casualties mounted; injured *Manunda* personnel and wounded from other ships. Most were severe burn cases. Later more came, this time from ashore. Bombs had severely damaged the shore hospitals, which could no longer cope with the unabated arrival of casualties.

The *Manunda* left Darwin for Fremantle the day after the raid, badly damaged but seaworthy. In her wards were more than 260 wounded. The raid had taken a dozen lives on the *Manunda*: three ship's medical staff (including one sister), and nine merchant crew. Controversy still surrounds the total number of deaths and injuries in Darwin on that fateful day, but it is certainly close to, and possibly higher than, 250.

Much was made after the raid of the deliberate Japanese bombing of a clearly marked hospital ship, despite an expression of regret from the Japanese Government. Lt-Col J.Donaldson, however, the *Manunda*'s O.C. Troops, reported that in his view one airman only was to blame. Apart from the near miss, the ship suffered a direct attack only from this one man, and only once. Had the Japanese deliberately set out to sink the *Manunda*, he maintained, they could have done so very easily[40].

Almost as if AHS *Manunda* courted trouble, she found herself in a similar predicament a few months later. After patchy repairs in Fremantle she made one round trip from Brisbane to Port Moresby and back, then went to Milne Bay in New Guinea to evacuate sick and injured troops. Arriving in the evening of 6th September, she anchored well up in the head of the bay, close to Gili Gili jetty. Her orders were to transfer the wounded the next day. That night two Japanese warships (the cruiser *Tenryu* and destroyer *Arashi*) entered the bay. The *Manunda* swung quietly to her anchor close offshore, brilliantly illuminated. She could not have been mistaken for anything other than what she was. A merchant ship, the *Anshun*, lay alongside, discharging vital military supplies. Both ships were sitting ducks for the Japanese naval gunners. Pensive watchers on the *Manunda* saw the flash of the warships' guns and winced, remembering Darwin. They breathed sighs of relief when the shells passed overhead, relief that turned to immediate anxiety for those who were about to suffer them. Accurate Japanese gunnery found its target. The *Anshun* heeled over and capsized. The Japanese warships left soon after. They did not molest the *Manunda* in any way.

Before closing the account of this incident, mention should be made of someone on the *Anshun* who later played a role in the *Centaur* saga. Captain Richard Mumford 'Jock' Salt, a senior-ranked Torres Strait Pilot, had piloted the ship from Townsville. While she discharged her cargo in Milne Bay, Captain Salt stood by on board to take her back south. When the bombardment came, Jock, like everyone else on the *Anshun*, hightailed it up the wharf to safety. He saw the ship heel over and sink, and then came the moment that he later recalled was the worst of the night — the realisation than he had left his wallet on board![41]

Getting back to the army's request for another hospital ship, it is unfortunate but true that the selection of a suitable vessel can be a tricky process. It takes a panel of experts from the navy, the army, military medical units and the merchant service to flesh out the requirements. There are several fundamental needs.

Size is the first priority. The ship must be large enough to carry a worthwhile number of casualties, yet light-drafted enough to work shallow estuaries or beaches[42]. To bring home the casualties as quickly as possible it must have a respectable speed. It should have an adequate fresh water storage; enough to supply about 150 litres per head per day. And of course it must be suitable for conversion; have adequate and suitable spaces for the installation of hospital wards, and the means of adequately ventilating them. Not surprisingly, passenger ships with spacious accommodation decks were logical candidates.

Two ships appeared to meet these requirements: the (Western Australian) State Shipping Company's *Koolinda* and the *Centaur*. Both had passenger accommodation and open cattle decks that lent themselves to ready conversion into spacious wards[43]. On 14th December 1942, however, while the *Centaur* lay at Lucinda loading sugar, the army agreed with the Director of Naval Engineering that she was the more suitable of the two. They made arrangements to send the *Centaur* to Melbourne for conversion as soon as possible[44].

The *Centaur* arrived in Sydney with her sugar cargo on the afternoon of 22nd December. Her crew celebrated both Christmas and New Year there, and she sailed on 4th January. Those closing days of 1942 brought her commercial life to an end. New Year 1943 was to herald a new and exciting, but brief, career.

The *Centaur* berthed in Melbourne at 1530 on 6th January 1943[45].

Exactly how news of the ship's new career reached those on board is unknown. No doubt at least Captain Murray had for some time either known or suspected that his ship was under consideration for something special. When the official announcement did come it received differing responses. In a recent letter to the authors the then 2nd Mate, Gordon Rippon, said, 'As regards the English officers, we could hardly believe our luck ... No more panic stations, no more blackouts.' They would also have appreciated going on to the more generous Australian rates of pay. The Malay crew, however, thought differently. They asked to be discharged[46].

At first glance the *Centaur*'s selection as a hospital ship would seem to breach some of the fundamental requirements. At around 3,000 tonnes, for example, she was much smaller than the existing vessels. As well, her service speed of just 12 knots seemed inadequate. But this time the army wanted a ship small enough to work the shallow lagoons and estuaries of New Guinea. Its intended voyages, Townsville to New Guinea, were short, so speed did not figure high in the argument. The *Centaur* therefore qualified on those counts. The army needed hospital wards with room for about 200 patients, and she seemed to have that capability. Moreover, as mentioned earlier, urgency was paramount and the army most of all needed a ship that could be easily, and thereby swiftly, converted — and it was probably this more than anything that finally tipped the scales.

Formal acquisition (by charter, not ownership) was soon settled. On 4th January 1943 Sir Thomas Gordon, the British Ministry of Transport (MOT) representative in Australia, wrote to the Department of Defence in Melbourne with the news that the MOT would put the *Centaur* at the disposal of the Commonwealth Naval Board — so long as the Allied Consultative Shipping Council agreed. As there was little chance the request would be turned down, Sir Thomas suggested the Board contact Messrs Dalgety and Company, the principal Blue Funnel agents in Australia, to arrange a transfer date for the ship and make arrangements for the necessary pre-charter inventory[47].

Part of the process of handing over a ship for charter is an inspection to determine its 'bare-boat' value. Lloyd's Register of Shipping sent one of its surveyors, B.P.Fielden. Nothing escaped his probing eye. His observations focused on the general, such as the condition of the hull and steel plating, to the particular, like the cracked washbasins in the captain's and fourth engineer's bathrooms. They ranged from precise measurements and detailed calculations, such as those used to determine the .023″ wear on the main crank shaft at the No. 4 bearing, to simple statements like the one that concluded his investigation — that the electric gramophone was in unserviceable condition. His later thirteen-page report appraised the market value of the *Centaur*'s hull, machinery and equipment at 125,000 pounds Sterling at the outbreak of the War[48].

On 11th January 1943 the *Centaur* completed discharging her Melbourne cargo. On that same day she received her first 'Certificate of Readiness for HM Service'[49]. From that moment on, all Alfred Holt's remaining control over the M.V. *Centaur* — as little as remained by then — passed from its hands. Ocean Steam didn't know it but they had lost her forever.

* * * * *

December 1942 was a month of pivotal significance to this story. In that month the *Centaur*'s days as a merchant workhorse drew to a close, and she readied herself for a military career. At the same time, about five thousand miles away in Japan, the military career of another vessel, one with which AHS *Centaur* would one day make a fateful rendezvous, was likewise about to begin. Throughout that last month of 1942, in the Kawasaki Dockyard at Kobe, shipyard workers put frantic finishing touches to a new submarine in readiness for commissioning.

The *I-177* was the second of ten Kaidai D7 type (or KD7 class) submarines appropriated as part of the 1939 Fourth Replenishment Law. Construction contracts went to a mixture of Japanese shipyards. The IJN originally numbered the boats *I-76* to *I-85*, but in May 1942 for some reason, and before it commissioned any of them, changed this to *I-176*, *I-177*, etc. Kure Dockyard laid down the keel of the first, *I-76*, in June 1940. An improvement on the previous KD6 series, the KD7 class boats could submerge to a depth of 80 metres[50].

The *I-177*'s dimensions were 105.5 metres by 8.2 metres, with a draft of 4.6 metres. When submerged she displaced 2,600 tonnes. In the engine room, two diesel-electric motors of 1,800 shaft horsepower gave her a top surface speed of 23.1 knots and a maximum submerged speed of eight knots. Her range, while cruising on the surface at 16 knots, was 8,000 miles. When submerged and travelling at five knots this range cut back considerably, to just 50 miles. At the forefront of the *I-177*'s array of strike power were six 21-inch torpedo tubes, for which she carried a stock of 12 torpedoes. On deck she had one 4.7-inch gun, a 40mm calibre gun and two 25mm guns. She had a complement of 88 men[51].

Kawasaki Dockyard took a full year to transform the empty cylindrical steel shell launched on 20th December 1941 into a fully equipped fighting machine, ready for duty. On 26th December 1942 the *I-177* was officially completed. At the commissioning ceremony two days later her first commander accepted her on behalf of the Imperial Japanese Navy. That commander's name was Lt-Cmdr Hajime Nakagawa[52]. To that stage of his life, Nakagawa's naval record can best be described as mixed. As a submarine commander he was credited with having sunk three ships — unfortunately one of them was Japanese.

Nakagawa was born on 25th January 1902, the son of a teacher. From his family he inherited the Buddhist faith. He entered the

Naval Academy in 1919, earned his commission as a 2nd Sub-
Lieutenant in 1923, and entered the Naval Submarine School in
1926. Two years later, promoted to First Lieutenant, he took
command of his first submarine. For many years he gave
exemplary service, but in 1939 an accident in Bungo Strait blotted
his copybook. Nakagawa had command of the *I-60*, on sea trials
in company with a sister boat, the *I-63*. Both boats were on the
surface, taking up station to begin the trials, when Nakagawa's
submarine rammed the other vessel amidships. Apparently the
I-63 lay stopped in the water, in the *I-60*'s station position, and
Nakagawa did not recognise her in time. The *I-63* sank and 81
of her crew perished. Nakagawa was roundly reprimanded in
the subsequent inquiry. The IJN took away his command and
reduced him to shore duties. He spent some time on the staff
of a submarine squadron. In 1941 he went back to sea, again
a submarine captain, and served in the Pacific and Indian Oceans.
His *I-4* sank two ships. His career began to look more respectable. When he took command of the *I-177*, Nakagawa was 40
years old. Despite the taint on his record, he was by then
unquestionably a highly experienced career submarine commander. By all accounts he was a personable, sociable character,
very popular with his colleagues[53].

The navy assigned the *I-177* to the Kure submarine squadron[54].
Nakagawa made arrangements to get under way as quickly as
possible. No time for fanfare; things were not going well for the
Japanese in the Southwest Pacific, and they needed the *I-177*
desperately.

Chapter Three

FROM PASSENGER LINER TO HOSPITAL SHIP

11th January to 12th March 1943

After the selection of a ship for conversion into a fully-mobile medical unit, the responsibility for physically transforming it fell to the Department of the Navy. Invariably the job had to be done in a hurry; the army always wanted the ship to be ready for sea yesterday and to be in place at the front line tomorrow.

Conversion entailed two concurrent processes: physical re-fitting; and official notification of the ship's non-combatant status to all appropriate countries, friend and foe alike.

On the ship itself, what happened next was nothing short of the nautical equivalent of a lobotomy. Unceremoniously ripped out were most of the ship's comfortable furnishings and the ornate decor of peacetime sea travel. In their place went spartan, functional, clinical, easy-to-clean fittings. Public rooms and tween decks were converted into wards, to meet the need for airy spaces with ample room for rows of single and double-tiered iron cots. Somewhere the architects had to find space for operating theatres, X-ray theatres, plaster rooms, special wards, therapy areas and orderly rooms. The ship's existing lighting, having too much glare, would be replaced with softer, more indirect lighting.

The embarkation system was given a lot of attention. The crew had to transfer stretcher-borne casualties from the dockside (and often from boats alongside) up onto the ship and then down into the wards, all by the most efficient means possible. An orderly flow of traffic around the ship was essential. Alleyways and stairways had to be wide and clear; sometimes the installation of special cot-lifts improved access.

Emergency disembarkation was another headache. Should the ship suffer damage, either by running aground, striking a mine or — heaven forbid — by deliberate hostile attack, the staff members had no choice but to evacuate perhaps hundreds of bed-ridden casualties. The existing lifeboats invariably lacked that sort of capacity, and in any case getting wounded men into normal ships' lifeboats can be extraordinarily difficult, particularly if the ship is listing badly. For this reason hospital ships were equipped with dozens of easily-manageable rafts and Carley floats.

The *Centaur* went to Williamstown, at the mouth of Melbourne's Yarra River, for conversion. Before her arrival the contractor (United Ship Services) had the necessary specifications and engineering drawings already prepared. The planned alterations, which ranged from simply giving existing spaces new names to major alterations to the ship's interior, included:

— converting the upper and lower decks to hospital wards and staff accommodation;
— converting several existing storerooms to medical storerooms and adding new ones; and,
— converting the smokeroom on the promenade deck to an operating theatre.

These were straightforward; technically very simple[1]. United Ship Services wasted no time getting stuck into the work, under the supervision of Lt-Cmdr(E) F.L.George, RAN[2]. No sooner did they get started, however, than something happened to change the whole program. The Department of the Army reassessed the progress of the war in New Guinea — and immediately also reassessed its requirements for the *Centaur*.

The army now wanted ward capacity increased to 280 cot cases (up by 80) and the installation of a special ventilation system for tropical use. It also wanted the *Centaur* to be equipped for voyages up to about 18 days in length, considerably more than the original three to four[3].

This caused a major rethink. The navy discussed it with United Ship Services, and then asked the army for an additional £10,000 to cover the extra work[4].

With all that sorted out, the conversion continued. The navy thought there would be no more heavy demands, but it was wrong. One day some army officers inspected the ship, and an official request for several more improvements soon followed[5]. They included a central hot water system, the enlargement of the operating theatre, the relocation of the dental surgery and workshop, an extensive galley refit, an increase in storeroom space and domestic refrigeration capacity, lagging of the hospital deck over the engine room (only the bulkheads were to be lagged), provision of two observation cabins for mental patients, and an extra duty room and pantry on the lower deck[6].

Even more demands came later in the conversion, this time from the maritime unions. Officials representing the seamen, firemen, stewards and cooks visited the ship almost every day. They rarely left without giving Lt-Cmdr George a new list of 'requests'. Some were important items; a range of extensive improvements to the crew's accommodation. The Seamens' Union of Australia insisted on single berth cabins for the boatswain, carpenter, storekeepers and engine-room donkeymen, four-berth cabins for the seamen, greasers and boys, and hot and cold running water to showers and wash basins throughout the crew's quarters. Greasers rejected the accommodation in the old Malay quarters above the rudder. Stewards demanded cork insulation and new linoleum on the deck in their accommodation, plus an additional shower room on the upper deck. Other minor demands included new iron beds and spring mattresses, bed lights, cabin fans, radiators, full-length wardrobes, electric urns, new galley ventilation, wash troughs, extra sinks, and three additional domestic refrigerators. The accommodation had to be repainted, most of the deck linoleum replaced, and additional small furnishings fitted[7].

That the navy was stunned by these demands is evident from a minute paper written later by the Director of Naval Engineering. The navy had no choice but to totally rework the plans for the crew accommodation. Plumbing modifications alone were a monstrous headache. Certainly the navy knew it had to upgrade the crew's accommodation to meet the standards demanded by Australian seamen, but it was not prepared for the lesson in Australian maritime unionism that it got. In fairness, both sides were at fault. The navy would have done well to confer with the unions before drawing up the conversion plans. By failing to consult early and fully, the navy left itself vulnerable to these later, most irritating demands. Moreover, any impartial observer would agree that most of the unions' requests were for no more than basic necessities. The unions for their part could have made their requests early, but as anyone associated with the Australian maritime scene will attest, that is not how the game is played[8].

Inevitably, all these late demands delayed the work. But when it was all over, the *Centaur* emerged as a fully-fledged, modern hospital ship fitted for tropical duty and capable of accommodating 252 cot cases (not quite the 280 asked for by the army) on voyages up to 18 days in length.

In the process the *Centaur* had changed considerably.

Without going into too much detail, and if for no other reason than that the geography of the ship is important later in this story, we should take a quick look at what had been done to her.

Beginning down in the lower spaces, the cargo holds — for years used to stow all manner of general cargo — now contained permanent ironstone ballast. This counterbalanced the weight of new fittings higher up in the ship. Unfortunately it became another annoying cost-escalation item. An inclining experiment showed that the original tonnage estimates were inadequate — but to add more would increase the ship's draft, which the army particularly wanted to restrict to six metres. A delicate balancing act between stability and draft ensued. Eventually, 900 tonnes

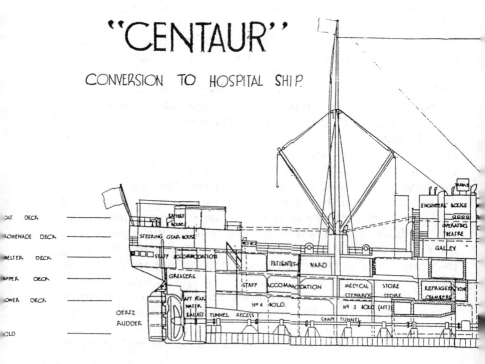

"CENTAUR"

CONVERSION TO HOSPITAL SHIP

went in. Riggers floored over the ironstone with wooden decking, making use of the otherwise dead spaces above it and giving room for about 100 tonnes of material; stores, equipment, whatever.

Most of the lower tween deck had become staff accommodation: orderlies forward, medical stewards and deck crew aft. Just aft of the orderlies' accommodation was a small ward for convalescence patients (Ward F), over No. 2 hold. Adjacent to Ward F were a duty room and pantry and two observation rooms, or 'restraining rooms', for mental patients. A cluster of existing lockers between Ward F and the casing around the engine space were now dedicated to Red Cross and linen storage. On the other side of the casing the old refrigeration chambers had been retained, although extensively overhauled and refurbished, with a new large storage area alongside. Here was a home for the medical, quartermasters' and stewards' stores.

The upper tween deck became the principal hospital area. Apart from small pockets of accommodation right forward and

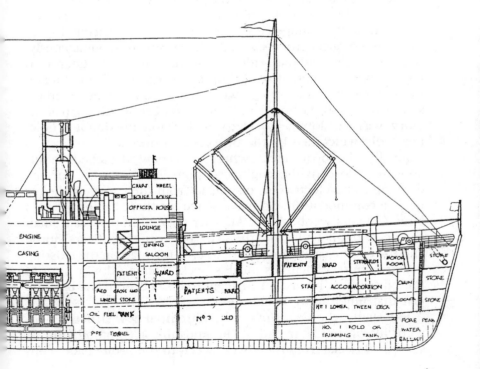

right aft, the new wards stretched almost the full length of the deck. Rows of double-decker cots were strung out along both sides of the tween deck hatchways. The hatchways themselves were left bare, to keep them clear for embarkation. In the cross-over areas between the hatches, underneath the mast houses, were duty messes, mess rooms for orderlies and patients, and pantries.

In the midships accommodation on the shelter deck no dramatic changes had taken place. The ship's medical staff took over the former passenger cabins. The galley, extensively renovated, stayed where it was. On the starboard side the former crew's library and purser's cabin had become a vegetable preparation room and cooks' mess respectively. The dining saloon across the forward end was still there.

Down aft on this deck the old second class smokeroom, and former hospital above it, had become staff accommodation. The gun, like the sandbagging around the wheelhouse and all the other trappings of war on board, was gone, removed.

The only major alteration on the promenade deck was the conversion of the stately smokeroom and Verandah Cafe area into a modern, fully-equipped operating theatre with adjacent dispensary. Two surgical processes could be carried out simultaneously. Nearby, on the starboard side, two former first class staterooms had become the dental workshop and surgery. All the remaining staterooms on this deck were occupied by senior medical staff, officers to starboard and nurses to port. Retained in all its glory was the lounge forward, a decision no doubt whole-heartedly welcomed by the officers and nurses.

Finally the boat deck, where two new detached cabins appeared close to the engineers' house. These were for the carpenter and electrician, displaced from their former shelter deck accommodation. To make space for these cabins the two after lifeboats went ashore. Another new addition was a small shower and toilet built into the space between the officers' house and the engine casing, no doubt to ease the load on the existing meagre sanitary facilities on this deck. This no doubt pleased the captain; the bathroom adjacent to his bedroom had become just that much more exclusive.

Externally, the *Centaur*'s only substantial new structure was a cot lift on the after end of the midships accommodation. It served all decks from the lower tween to the promenade, connecting the wards with the operating theatre. It obviated the need to manhandle stretchers up and down stairs. The installation of wide companionways connecting all decks improved the general movement around the ship. Also, depending on the height of wharves and the tides at various ports, the transfer of cot cases on or off the ship could be made through the ship's old side-port cattle doors.

Internally, to offset the oppressive heat and humidity of the tropics, the designers had installed a ventilation system and increased the fresh water capacity from 450 to 750 tonnes.

Life saving equipment had also been upgraded. Hundreds of additional lifejackets came on board, plus several liferafts and Carley floats stowed in convenient spots[9].

Towards the end of the conversion process a consignment of hospital stores arrived, requisitioned from the Royal Edward Victualling Yard in Sydney. The list included:

> 900 blankets.
> 700 coverlets.
> 340 mattresses, hair.
> 700 mattresses, hair, covers.
> 400 pillows, hair.
> 600 pillows, feather.
> 2,000 pillows, covers.
> 3,000 sheets.
> 15 sets each of mattresses, fracture, cot and covers.

All these the Department of the Navy supplied, officially processed on Form T274, quaintly entitled 'Master's Account of Bedding, and all Horse Gear, etc'. At the same time the navy shamefacedly admitted that service latrine paper was unsuitable for hospital purposes. It noted that the army would supply this product itself[10].

So much for the *Centaur*'s structural alterations. What about her appearance? Her silhouette had changed little. Only an expert would have picked out the cot lift. Yet on the water she somehow looked totally different, thanks to a vibrant new colour scheme and her hospital ship markings. No trace remained of the sombre, all-over battleship grey. Painters had replaced it with a kaleidoscope of vivid white, green, red, black and dark yellow. The hull and upperworks were pure white. A green band 1.2 metres wide stretched from stem to stern on both sides, interspersed in three places by red crosses two metres high and wide. On each bow, above the green band, was a black square with the *Centaur*'s hospital ship identification number — 47 — stencilled in white. The once-blue, once-grey funnel was now dark yellow with a 1.2 metre red cross high up on each side. Another red cross, this time six metres, glared up from the deck of the monkey island above the wheelhouse, plus another, 7.3 metres, from the deck of the docking bridge aft. One more stood vertically down from the docking bridge, facing aft. The lifeboats were painted white, with a green band to identify them as belonging to a hospital ship[11].

To complete her identity, the *Centaur* flew the Red Cross flag on the foremast and the Blue Ensign at the stern.

At night, internal red neon lights lit up the crosses on the funnel and the one facing aft from the docking bridge. Floodlighting illuminated the red crosses on the ship's side; a row of green lights the green band. When AHS *Centaur* later put to sea, the deck officers complained that the starboard forward floodlights interfered with their night vision, so were left off. Regardless of this minor infringement, it mattered not from which angle or under what conditions (bad visibility excepted) an observer viewed the *Centaur* — from sea level or in the sky, day or night — her red crosses were blatantly visible. She could not fail to be recognised as anything other than a non-combatant hospital ship — or so one would have thought.

As the *Centaur*'s conversion neared its end, the army announced the intended make-up of her medical staff: 10 officers, 12 nurses, 5 non-commissioned officers and 40 attendants. On 10th March the navy learned that the commanding officer would be Major C.P.Manson, AAMC, from Gippsland in Victoria, and that he would embark at Melbourne. Also nominated to join in Melbourne were the quartermaster, Lt A.E.Johnson, two NCOs and two ORs (Other Ranks). The rest of the staff would join later, at Sydney and Brisbane[12].

Clement Polson Manson ('Clem' to his friends) had been with the AAMC since September 1937. A graduate of Scotch College and Melbourne University and a resident of the Melbourne suburb of Hawthorn, he had served with the 10th Field Ambulance (Militia) and the AIF. He was appointed to AHS *Manunda* in July 1940. A year later he transferred to AHS *Wanganella* when she commissioned. He learned of his appointment as O.C.Troops *Centaur* on 9th March 1943. Manson came to the *Centaur* with a reputation as a man with a love of the sea. He was a large man with a jolly, handsome, moustached face; every bit the epitome of a career army officer. He took very seriously his responsibility for coordinating relations with the ship's crew and achieved this with such ease, and in such a jovial manner, that he soon endeared himself to all on board. He had the type of dynamic personality that enabled him to join in any social activities with subordinates without losing their respect.

The appointed quartermaster was Lt A.E.Johnson, another Victorian. As it turned out, two other officers, not initially mentioned, joined at the same time. They were Captain Gethyn L.Thomas and Chaplain/Captain Ernest G.Laverick, both Victorians. Chaplain Laverick, 48, had been attached to the 39th Battalion in WW1 and between the wars held the post of rector at the small Victorian town of Kyabram. When the second world conflict took hold, the army put him in charge of Australian POW and internment camps. He earned the reputation for determination in that role when, against official wishes, he gave communion to some Christians among the Japanese POWs. He even gave one a Christian burial. When he learned about his appointment as Church of England padre to the *Centaur*, Laverick reportedly tossed his hat in the air with elation.

The two NCOs were Staff Sergeant George Carter of Victoria and Cpl Tom Hobden from Tasmania. Hobden, who had also previously served in AHS *Wanganella*, had the task of caring for a male nursing section. The two ORs were Pte Fred Chidgey, a dental assistant, and his good friend Pte Tom Hegarty, both recently from the *Oranje*[a].

As for the merchant crew, all the remaining Malay seamen, many of whom had served on the *Centaur* for years, signed off[b]. Their places in the crew's accommodation, now luxurious compared with its former state, were taken by Australian seamen drawn from the Melbourne Shipping Office 'pick-up'[13]. Captain Murray opened the Articles, a contract between master and crew, on 6th March. They were British Articles (the *Centaur* was still a British-registered ship) but the seamen enjoyed the benefits of Australian industrial awards. They were also Foreign-Going Articles, permitting the master to take the ship anywhere in the world within 65°N and 60°S latitudes.

---

a. Private Chidgey had turned in a Warrant Officer commission to give himself a better chance of being assigned to active duty.

b. Many remained in Australia. Some married Australian women and settled.

The British officers, all Blue Funnel Line personnel, remained with the ship. Why is not clear; it may have been because of a shortage of Australian officers, the insistence of Blue Funnel Line, or possibly as a condition of the charter party[14]. Captain Murray still held command. He was virtually an Australian citizen by this time anyway, as he and his wife had some time earlier taken up residence in Nedlands, WA. Murray's chief officer was Henry 'Harry' Lamble, a 31 year-old Devonian. Although a shy, retiring type, Lamble was enjoying a romantic interlude in Melbourne with a section officer in the WAAF. Second officer R.Gordon Rippon, a medium-build, smart, jovial-looking 29-year-old from Yorkshire, had been with the *Centaur* since early 1941. Holts had told Rippon he could expect a promotion to chief officer of the *Centaur* sometime in 1943. Third mate Ernest 'Monty' Banks came from Western Australia, although he had been born in South Africa. Tall and thick set, with fair curly hair, the soft-spoken Banks was already a veteran of three earlier disasters, having since the beginning of the war been torpedoed in the North Atlantic, off St.Nazaire (France), and near Gibraltar.

That stalwart *Centaurian* chief engineer, Ernie Smith, missed the conversion phase of his favourite ship. Blue Funnel sent him in a hurry to relieve the chief engineer on the *Charon*, who had taken ill. His place was taken by Alf Jackson, a 54-year-old Tynesider. Smith would soon return to the post.

Not surprisingly, the turnabout in the *Centaur*'s career brought with it new procedures — and the inevitable increase in clerical work. A set of guidelines arrived: *Regulations and Instructions for H.M. Transport Services*. Henceforth everything had to be done by the book, *this* book. Between its covers were strict guidelines for dealing with a whole range of diverse matters, including the use of naval facilities, victualling requirements and procedures, and accounting methods for liquor sales, the dry canteen and bar[15].

Two other documents, *Red Cross Rules for Hospital Ships* and *Standing Orders for Australian Hospital Ships and Transports*, received equal attention.

Dockyard overhauls are always busy times for ships' crews; conversions even more so, as the ship is beginning a new career. Old working practices count for nought; new ideas are accommodated, new procedures established. Despite this, the crew did find time to get ashore at Williamstown. Some, including Captain

Murray, visited the St.Nicholas Seamen's Church and signed the 'Notable Events' page in the Holy Bible. Harry Lamble also signed, as did Sparks-cum-Purser Eric Summers, Chief Steward Jim Capper, Linenkeeper Sid Sandwell, and the stewards Jessy Stutter, Stan Strack, Jim Watterston, Alex Cochrane and John Buck.

The metamorphosis of M.V. *Centaur* came to fruition on Saturday 12th March 1943. Unfortunately, the process had cost a lot more than expected. When all the bills came in, overruns had stretched the cost to a whopping £54,763.0.11 (Australian pounds) — an increase of some 175% on the original estimate![16]

While the dockies hammered away at Williamstown, the Australian Commonwealth Naval Board (ACNB) pushed ahead with the *Centaur's* registration as a hospital ship. It had taken the first step on 11th January 1943, the day Captain Murray signed the Certificate of Readiness for HM Service. The following message, in cipher, went to the Admiralty in London (to be precise, to the C-in-C Eastern Fleet):

> M.V. 'Centaur' requisitioned by RAN as a hospital ship 9th January[17].

Ten days later the Director of Sea Transport (DST), London, replied that he had assigned the *Centaur* identification number 47, this being the next number on the British Series of Military Hospital Ships list. The DST instructed the ACNB to notify enemy powers through diplomatic channels[18].

On 25th January, at 0820, the Department of External Affairs in Canberra sent a cable to the Secretary of State for Dominion Affairs, London, informing him that the *Centaur* would be commissioned on March 1, 1943. (This estimate wasn't *too* far out.) It also requested the Secretary to pass on the following particulars to the enemy powers:

> Gross tonnage 2469. No. of masts 2, No. of funnels 1, distance from bow to foremast 72 feet, foremast to funnel 80 feet, funnel to mainmast 82 feet, mainmast to stern 81 feet. Outstanding features: two large cowl ventilators fore-end No. 1 Hatch, comparatively large cross trees and funnel[19].

A later telegram asked London to include identification number 47 when making the notification[20].

Dutifully, on 31st January the Foreign Office sent a coded telegram of instructions to its representatives in Berne and Washington. They were to ask the Swiss to inform the Japanese, German, Italian, Hungarian, Bulgarian, Romanian and Siamese

Governments, and ask the Americans to likewise inform the Finnish, that Australia proposed employing 'S.S. Centaur' (sic) as a hospital ship[21].

The efficient Swiss acted promptly. Over two days, 4th and 5th February, they passed on the information to the five nominated governments, then told London that this had been done. The Japanese government received its notification on the 5th.

The first official recognition of the AHS *Centaur* came from the Hungarians, on 18th March[22]. The Italians were next, although they asked for more details of the hospital ship markings, in particular the size, location and illumination of the red crosses[23]. The answer went to the Swiss again who passed it on to the Italians and to all other Axis powers[24].

This diplomatic version of 'Twenty Questions' took so much time that the additional details about the red crosses did not reach the Japanese until 13th May[25].

Taking a brief leap into the future, there was an interesting postscript to this notification phase. As late as 1st July 1943 the Italians notified the *Legazione di Svizzera* in Rome that they recognised 'nave ospedale austreliana Centaur'[26]. Nine days later, Berlin informed *die Schweizerische Gesandtschaft* that it too recognised 'des australischen Lazarettschiff Centaur'[27]. However, as the *Centaur* had already been sunk by then, the Foreign Office saw no point in copying the two messages to its various service departments.

The *Centaur*'s last two days in Melbourne were frantic. To United Ship Services and Lt-Cmdr George, the rapidly nearing sailing time frustrated their efforts to attend to the scores of items still on the worksheets. Workers scurried around the ship in a frantic bid to meet the impending deadline. The gangway groaned beneath the tramping feet of embarking personnel; medical staff and freshly signed-on seamen heaving bulging kit-bags and strapped suitcases. But despite all the last minute panic, the confusion, the disorientation of a batch of new men joining a ship that had been metaphorically turned inside out, by the afternoon of 12th March 1943 the *Centaur* was pronounced ready for sea; destination Sydney. Throughout that afternoon the gangway would have echoed again, this time to the reverberating clamour of workers' boots as all the small *accoutrements* of dockyard work were manhandled ashore:

power cables, paint pots and brushes, tools, staging gear, welding equipment, and so on. In the captain's cabin, Captain Murray, his agents and representatives of United Ship Services and the navy, shuffled sheets of paper across the desk for the signatures that would put the final seal on the conversion of M.V. *Centaur* into *AHS 47*[28].

*   *   *   *   *

While the *Centaur* lay in Williamstown under conversion, the Japanese submarine *I-21* attacked six Allied merchant ships off the NSW coast. On 18th January a torpedo sent the Australian freighter *Kalingo* to her doom with the loss of two lives. Later the same day, three seamen perished on the US tanker *Mobilube* after another successful torpedo strike. Fortunately the *Mobilube* stayed afloat and was towed to Sydney. Three weeks later the enemy struck again. This time the Australian cargo ship *Iron Knight*, full of iron ore and not far from the picturesque coastal town of Eden, took a torpedo and disappeared beneath the waves in only two minutes, taking 36 crewmembers with her. The *I-21* also attacked the *Peter H Burnett*, *Giang Ann*, and *Starr King*[29].

Meanwhile, there was naval action aplenty in New Guinea waters — only it was extremely bloody and the Japanese were getting the worst of it. On 26th January, not far from Wewak on New Guinea's northern coast, the US submarine *Wahoo* sank a Japanese troop transport carrying an estimated 9,500 soldiers. On the premise that the survivors might swim ashore and thus remain a threat to the Allies, the *Wahoo*'s commander gave orders to eliminate them by gunfire. Thousands — the exact number will never be known — perished by gunfire during the next hour. As she pursued her grim task, the *Wahoo* moved slowly through a sea red with blood, her bow slicing into a carpet of floating bodies[30].

To the surprise of many US submarine commanders, this action was enthusiastically endorsed by the US submarine high command. It appeared to amount to tacit approval to behave in this manner. Few commanders followed the example[31].

More slaughter was on the way, however. In early March came the strikingly successful 'Battle of the Bismark Sea'. US bombers sank about 22 Japanese ships, most of them troop transports. That battle was clean, if onesided. Then, for the next several days, A-20s and Beaufighters criss-crossed the scene of the battle, mercilessly strafing the survivors in an orgy that ceased only when no living thing could be found at which to fire. PT boats joined in the turkey-shoot. Once again, observers could only guess at the death toll; no-one contested the estimate of 3,000[32].

Chapter Four

AHS 47

12th March to 8th May 1943

Two events on Saturday 12th March 1943 marked a milestone in the *Centaur*'s career.

The first was her commissioning as an Australian hospital ship. What official ceremony sanctified the great event — if any — is not known. The historic moment seems to have passed virtually ignored; whatever took place went unrecorded. With the change in status came a new title. Gone was the prosaic *MV* in front of her name, replaced by the more prestigious *AHS*. Officially, as the third Australian hospital ship in the second world conflict, she had become *2/3 AHS Centaur*, although *AHS 47* was also correct. Occasionally, but wrongly, officials used the more grandiose *HMAHS* (His Majesty's Australian Hospital Ship).

Later that same day her second great moment arrived. Like a swan that has shed its ugly duckling plumage, the gleaming white ship festooned with green stripes and red crosses slipped its moorings and moved out from the colourless dockyard into public view. Sadly, as with the commissioning, no fanfare heralded this new beginning; no spontaneous effusive farewell from a gathered crowd, as was her due. Instead, almost unnoticed, she turned her bows seaward, heading for Townsville via Sydney and Brisbane. Slowly the browned-out lights of Melbourne fell astern.

Midnight had come and gone before AHS *Centaur* sliced through the tidal maelstrom of the infamous Rip at the exit to Port Phillip Bay. Outside, the waiting pilot steamer *Victoria* wallowed in a choppy sea, an ominous portent of worse weather to come. Captain Ernest Stein, the pilot, asked for 'Slow Ahead'. The *Centaur* lost headway. Stein deftly manoeuvred her to windward of the *Victoria,* making a lee for the five-metre, open dinghy that would be rowed across to pick him up[a]. Captain Stein made his farewells to Captain Murray, then took his leave. OOW Gordon Rippon escorted him to the pilot ladder. He swung over the bulwark rail and shinned down the ladder into the waiting boat. He was in for a bumpy, wet ride across to the *Victoria*, but he was used to it[1].

Captain Murray watched the dinghy pull clear. He obligingly waited until the tiny boat had safely disappeared around the *Victoria*'s stern before ringing down once more for 'Full Ahead'. He called to the quartermaster to come to port.

Naval Control had ordered Captain Murray to proceed to Sydney via the Blue Route, at a speed of 12 knots. This track took the ship well offshore to start with; to a point 100 nautical miles to seaward of Wilson's Promontory, the southernmost tip of the tongue of Victoria. From there it swung around to the northeast, parallel to the shoreline up to Cape Howe, then backed to north-northeast for the run up the NSW coast.

True to form, Bass Strait turned on a five star display of bad weather. In no time the *Centaur* pitched and yawed, and rolled heavily. While seasickness caused no problems (even among the few medical staff, most of whom had acquired their sealegs on other hospital ships), the after-effects of a rushed dockyard job certainly did. Very soon the rough weather exposed many dockyard oversights and shortcuts. Sea water poured in through leaking portholes, flooding the wards and turning the recently-laid linoleum flooring into a soggy mess. With every roll came the sounds of sliding and crashing, as dislodged equipment, flying crockery and loose furniture charged unrestrained from side to side[2].

Medical staffers Hobden, Chidgey and Hegarty spent most of the voyage working with the crewmembers, securing equipment against the constant jarring and rolling. Very little had been properly stowed in Melbourne. They spent hours mopping up water and plugging leaking portholes[3].

Not surprisingly, this legacy of poor workmanship impressed neither O.C.Troops Manson nor the fastidious Captain Murray. They were furious. They compiled a lengthy list of defects. The chief engineer threw in a few of his own, just for good measure.

---

a. Outboard motors were fitted to the transfer dinghies later that year.

Lt-Col Clement P. Manson, Centaur's O.C. Troops (lost). Last seen helping his nurses leap off the sinking ship.
("Lest We Forget")

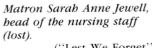

Matron Sarah Anne Jewell, head of the nursing staff (lost).
("Lest We Forget")

Sister Ellen Savage, the only woman survivor.
("Lest We Forget")

Two views of the Centaur after her conversion to a hospital ship.
(Australian Army Archives — courtesy G.McGrath)

Netherlands Hospital Ship Oranje. *At least 27 of the* Centaur's *medical staff had previously served on the* Oranje.
(F. Chidgey)

The Centaur's *Red Cross representative, W.F. Darwin Clarke (lost).*
(Mrs R.McC. Brown)

Captain Bernie Hindmarsh, adjutant (lost).
(Mrs Hindmarsh)

Close pals Pte Fred Chidgey and Pte Tom
Hegarty (both saved).

(F.Chidgey)

Right:
Cpl Tom Hobden
(saved).
(T. Hobden)

Left:
Pte Vince McCosker
(saved).
(V. McCosker)

Group posing in a raft similar to the one that survived the sinking. Pte
Cliff Jones is at right with the Maynard twins next to him. Pte Jim Coulsen
is at left. The other two are unknown.

(F.Chidgey)

L to r — Ptes Jim Coulsen (saved), Ray Hutchinson (lost). 'Tich' Isherwood (saved), Bill Burrett (lost).
(F.Chidgey)

Below: l to r — Ptes Burrett, Isherwood, Jim Coulsen (saved), N.McLean (lost), Len Warren (missed the ship on last voyage), Percy Kelly (saved).
(F.Chidgey)

Above: Pte L.George Ockwell (lost).
(F.Chidgey)

Right: l to r — S/Sgt George Carter (pathologist, saved), Capt Gethyn Thomas, (dentist, lost), WOII Allan K.Thomas (quartermaster, lost).
(F.Chidgey)

Ten of the Centaur's twelve Nursing Sisters. Top: l to r — Merle Moston, Edna Shaw, Margaret Adams, Ellen Rutherford, Alice O'Donnell. Bottom: Jennie Walker, Evelyn King, Doris Joyce Wyllie, Helen Haultain, Mary McFarlane. All were lost.

("Lest We Forget")

WO L.L.Williams,
Quartermaster Sergeant
(lost).

(F.Chidgey)

Pte Percy Clegg (lost).

(M.Wales)

Pte Cliff Jones (saved).
(Mrs Wood

Left: Ptes Allan and John
Maynard, twin brothers
(both lost).

(Mrs F.Gardner)

The US submarine Greenling *gives personnel on the* Centaur *a fright in the* Whitsunday Passage.

(F.Chidgey)

The *Centaur* arrived off Sydney on the Monday afternoon. Captain Murray conned his ship through the mine-swept outer channel to South Head and embarked a Sydney pilot. Like their Melbourne counterparts, Sydney pilots at that time used a cruising pilot steamer (the renowned clipper-bowed *Captain Cook*) and open dinghies. Gathering speed, the *Centaur* passed in through the Heads and turned to port into the East Channel. She slowed as she neared Green Point. Strung across the harbour from there to Georges Head was the boom defence net. Obligingly, the attendant Boom Defence Vessel tugged aside the 120-metre floating gate to grant the *Centaur* safe conduct inside. She passed gingerly through the narrow gap, and steamed on. She hauled to starboard around Bradleys Head. It was regular wartime practice to test the ship's degaussing gear at this point. An officer flicked a switch on the bridge and specially-trained WRANs on Bradleys Head checked the ship's magnetism. It should read negative. If it didn't, naval staff came down to the ship and checked the equipment for faults.

The *Centaur*'s bow then pointed straight towards Sydney's world-renowned symbol — the Harbour Bridge. Slowing, AHS *Centaur* dipped beneath its grey Meccano-like structure. She then turned to port around Dawes Point, crept past Walsh Bay, and inched into her Darling Harbour berth.

Unlike most shipping movements in Sydney at that time, the *Centaur*'s arrival probably turned a few heads. In those mid-war years a ship as colourfully decked out as the *Centaur* was a rare sight indeed. Her eye-catching livery — splashes of red, green and yellow on a white background — offered a welcome contrast to the insipid grey hulls and superstructures of the ships that visited Sydney in those dark days. Sydneysiders were more accustomed to sombre-looking freighters and drab, menacing warships; men-of-war of all types. As grey shadows they came and went, their missions and their destinations cloaked in secrecy. They barely drew a second glance from onlookers along the foreshores.

The next morning the local engineer officer in charge of naval construction came aboard for an inspection. Manson and Murray had a great deal to say to him. Even the local Sea Transport Officer expressed his surprise that his counterpart in Melbourne had allowed the ship to leave in that condition. The engineer drew up a priority worklist. Murray asked him to include some

53

sort of flooring over the upper and lower hatch covers; he feared
the possibility of fire caused by cigarette butts falling through
the gaps to the deck below. The engineer concurred. Then he
had something else to add to his worklist; a minor technical fault
but one with the potential for damage and inconvenience. The
problem had shown itself that day, when the ship took on fresh
water. To reach the fresh water filling pipes on board, the crew
had to run the hoses through the wards. Unfortunately water
spurted from leaky joints in poorly made hose fittings and once
again flooded the wards — much to Manson's disgust[4].

It took the navvies almost an entire week to make the necessary
repairs.

During this week Major Manson continued his task of preparing the hospital. There was a moment of jubilation and con-
gratulation on 18th March when news arrived of his promotion
to Lieutenant Colonel, but the formal celebration had to wait[5].
He was a busy man. He supervised the completion of the painting
in the wards; one of the many tasks left unfinished when the
ship left Melbourne. He organised the loading and storage of the
balance of medical stores. He supervised the preparation of the
accommodation for his embarking staff.

The day before the *Centaur*'s planned sailing date, the next
group of medical personnel embarked. It comprised three
officers, 12 nurses, three NCOs and ten ORs.

Of the three officers, Majors Geoffrey Cooley and L.L. Holland,
both graduates of the University of Sydney, had already served
in the Middle East. Cooley, a surgeon, had also been to New
Guinea, from where he had twice been invalided home. Captain
Bernie Hindmarsh, at 44 the oldest doctor on board, came to
the *Centaur* from the *Oranje*, where he had earned the praise
of that ship's O.C. Troops, Lt-Col J.P.Major, as 'one of my most
valued medical officers'. The product of a highly respected NSW
pioneering family, Captain Hindmarsh had been in the army for
three years. Before joining, he ran a medical practice for 18 years
at Macksville, where he lived with his wife and three children[6].
Manson appointed Hindmarsh his adjutant.

The dozen nurses that embarked in Sydney comprised a matron
and eleven sisters, all members of the Australian Army Nursing
Service. Like the AAMC, the AANS has a proud history. Created
in 1902 as an auxiliary service, its members well and truly earned
their stripes during WW1, when they accompanied Australian

troops in the AIF. Wherever the troops went, these girls went. More than 2,000 sisters served overseas in that conflict; 21 lost their lives and 388 received decorations. Between the Wars the service went into reserve, although it maintained a register of qualified nurses who, when hostilities broke out again in 1939, instantly rallied to the call. By happy coincidence with the flow of this story, in the same month that these twelve sisters joined the *Centaur* all AANS members were granted commissioned rank. They had not held commissions hitherto, although traditionally had always been accorded the respect due to officers. As of March 1943 they became a corps of officers with military ranks ranging from lieutenant (for sisters) to colonel (Matron-in-Chief). The Matron-in-Chief became automatically attached to the staff of the Director General of Medical Services (DGMS). Not all AANS members welcomed the new status. Many questioned its benefit, wondering if it might inhibit lower-ranked military patients and jeopardise the traditional warm and open nurse/patient relationship. Despite their 'elevation', AANS staff neither saluted, preferring the age-old bow and smile, nor, other than formally, did they use their military titles[7].

At the head of the *Centaur*'s AANS contingent was Matron Sarah Anne Jewell. Originally from Western Australia, where she trained at Perth General Hospital, Miss Jewell gained her extensive nursing experience mostly in Victoria. In December 1940 she accepted the post of Sister-in-Charge of the Sea Ambulance Transport Unit. This led to an appointment as Matron on the *Oranje*. While there, she transformed a disparate, multi-national group of nurses into a well-knit, efficient unit. She earned the reputation of an excellent disciplinarian, yet someone uncompromising in her concern for the welfare of her staff. She was shortish in stature, reserved in nature, and somewhat Victorian in attitude; stern in appearance yet a most pleasant conversationalist. In many ways Matron Jewell differed markedly from Lt-Col Manson — she tending to be strict, he much more relaxed — although Manson noted in a later report that she was always cooperative and efficient. Perhaps, reading between the lines, they each recognised their respective differences in their approach to the job, and learned to live with them, making sure that they in no way inhibited the efficient running of the hospital. Miss Jewell found the *Centaur* immensely different to the much larger *Oranje*. It took her some time to adjust. As on the *Oranje*, she exercised firm but benevolent discipline over her nursing sisters and the other medical staff; perhaps more so than had she not felt the need to counterbalance her commanding officer's more relaxed approach. Even so, she too joined in all the social activities with undisguised pleasure[8].

Seven of the joining sisters, like Matron Jewell, had recently served on the *Oranje*. Sisters Margaret Adams, Ellen Rutherford and Wendy Walker were Victorians; Helen Haultain, Evelyn King and Ellen Savage came from NSW. Mary McFarlane hailed from South Australia. Before leaving Melbourne to travel up to the *Centaur* in Sydney, Matron Jewell and Sisters Adams, Rutherford and Walker were farewelled by Lt-Col Major, their former boss on the *Oranje*. Major later wrote that they showed off with pride their new colour patches. They were beside themselves with joy at having been chosen for the *Centaur*. 'Nan' Rutherford, Major remembered, was a happy girl with remarkable talents in the operating theatre; a girl who could always find a laugh and a smile no matter what stress she might be under. Margaret Adams, he said, was 'charming, keen and capable . . . liked by everybody'. 'Jennie' Walker, at 24 the youngest of the group, he remembered as 'always calm and collected and withal so efficient . . . beloved by patients and staff'.

Sisters Haultain, King and Savage were contemporaries and great mates; inseparable. Helen Haultain's brother commanded an Australian warship (he was to play a role in this story, of which more later).

Of Ellen Savage special mention must be made. She fills a very important role in the story of the loss of AHS *Centaur* — the only woman survivor.

Ellen Savage was born in Quirindi, northern NSW, in 1912. She went through her basic nursing training at Newcastle Hospital before 'topping up' her qualifications in midwifery and mothercraft at other centres. In 1941 she joined the AANS. Her first posting was to the *Oranje*. She made several voyages to Egypt and South Africa. Then she transferred to the *Centaur*[9]. Ellen was a curly brunette with a dimpling smile. She held very strong religious beliefs.

Mary McFarlane also warrants a mention. The most senior of the sisters, and Jewell's deputy, she had spent longer on the *Oranje* than any other Australian sister. Lorna Howlett, in her warm account of the *Oranje*, described Mary McFarlane as 'a slender, lovely young woman, her wonderful smile, her gentle manner, the fun that sparkled in her brown eyes and the shining dark hair peeping from beneath her immaculate veil.' Mary McFarlane, said Howlett, 'was a favourite with everyone.' In a letter to a former *Oranje* colleague[b], Mary McFarlane described her affection for 'our cattle ship — oh, how the mighty have fallen!' She found her cabin small but not too small. She lamented the lack of an *en suite* bathroom, but appreciated other little luxuries such as a washbasin with running cold water, an electric fan, a bunklight, and a thermos filled with ice water. She seemed surprised to find beds rather than up-and-down bunks. She reported joyously that a steward[c] actually cleaned her shoes, brought her early morning tea and made her bed. Presumably such attention was lacking on the *Oranje*. The food she described as 'an absolute joy: plenty of salads, fruit, grills, lobster mayonnaise — it really is grand.' At 9 pm, she declared, they have 'supper in the lounge — coffee and sandwiches'. Happily the ship had several proficient pianists and at least one good singer amongst the staff, and sing-songs took place almost every night. Her seniority ensured her a responsible role, that of the single night sister, but three ex-*Oranje* orderlies — Malcolm, Murphy and Cooke — held loneliness at bay[10].

The remaining four AANS sisters to join in Sydney, non-veterans of the *Oranje,* were Merle Moston, Alice O'Donnell, Edna Shaw and Joyce Wyllie. Bundaberg-born Sister Wyllie was the only Queenslander, although she lived in NSW.

Among the NCOs and ORs now on board were 18 former *Oranje* staff: Tom Malcolm, M. Thomas, Fred Chidgey, Jim Coulsen, Tom Hegarty, Ron 'Tich' Isherwood, Cliff Jones, Percy Kelly, George Murphy, S. Burroughs, A. Cooke, C. Le Brun, Bill Burrett, Ray Hutchison, N. McLean, George Ockwell and the twin brothers Alan and John Maynard[d].

On 21st March, in mid-morning, the *Centaur* left Sydney for Brisbane, where she was to embark the remaining quota of medical staff. From there the orders were to proceed to Townsville, to embark Australian casualties from the campaign in New Guinea and evacuate them to Brisbane.

---

b. Reproduced in Lorna Howlett's book.
c. Arthur Waddington.
d. The last nine mentioned were to perish on the *Centaur*.

In contrast to the trip from Melbourne to Sydney, this two-day journey along the designated Blue Route to Brisbane was thankfully calm and uneventful. Manson's staff busied themselves cleaning, scrubbing, unpacking medical supplies and taking inventory. The sisters were keen to get everything ready. They worked with enthusiasm, even attending to the more menial tasks that were usually the lot of the orderlies, most of whom were yet to board. Manson and Jewell jointly prepared the work routines and practices best suited for the conditions on AHS *Centaur*. By the time the ship reached Brisbane things were beginning to fall into place. The musty aromatic legacy of a busy dockyard — paint smells — had at last succumbed to the all-pervading and distinctive whiff of antiseptic.

The *Centaur* berthed at Dalgetys Wharf in the Brisbane suburb of Teneriffe at 1400 on Wednesday 23rd March.

As he had done in Sydney, Captain Murray gave the naval authorities a repair list, albeit one by no means as long. Mostly, it called for joinery work. Manson had discovered that the cupboards in the pantries would hold only 35 sets of crockery, hardly enough for the 100 mouths that were fed from each pantry. The solution was to move some of the cupboards from the orderlies' quarters to the upper deck pantries. This deprived the orderlies, so Manson decided they should eat at the tables in Ward F on the lower deck, after the walking patients, rather than in their own mess[11].

While in Brisbane, officers from Advance Land Headquarters Queensland and Movement Control accompanied the Deputy Director of Medical Services on an inspection of the ship. Manson's arrangements for the hospital impressed them a great deal. Some expressed amazement that such a small vessel could comfortably carry so many beds[12].

On Thursday, the remaining AAMC staff, mostly orderlies, embarked. They had little time to settle in before knuckling down to a rigid training program. Manson and Jewell were acutely mindful of the mere ten days that remained before AHS *Centaur* was scheduled to embark her first patients; ten days in which to mould their group into an effective, cohesive unit. They had prepared an intensive schedule of training and drills for the new arrivals, and it began the very next day. Ward sisters instructed the newcomers on their duties in the wards; officers gave lectures on the embarkation procedures and patient handling methods.

Practical drills finetuned the theory: simulated embarkations, practice sessions carrying stretcher-borne wounded around the wards and companionways. The officers gave medical and surgical lectures to the whole staff; discourses on tropical diseases and debilities, on wound infection and tropical hygiene[13].

Manson now had a full staff; 67 strong. This included one person who, while carrying neither military rank nor membership of the AAMC, nevertheless played an integral role in hospital ship proceedings — the Red Cross representative. AHS *Centaur*'s Red Cross man was Mr W.F.D. Clark of South Australia, formerly of the *Oranje*. Known by his third name, Darwin, he was a direct descendent of Charles Darwin, the famous corsair, adventurer and theorist after whom Australia's Northern Territory named its capital city[14]. A director of W.M.Martin & Coy's Stonyfell vinyards, Darwin Clark had held the rank of honorary Red Cross officer for two years.

On April Fool's Day — not that it had any significance — the *Centaur* sailed from Brisbane. The time had come to put Australia's newest hospital ship to a practical test. By good fortune the circumstances were such that this could be done before she had to enter any active war zones. Manson thus had the luxury of a trial run to test out his ship and his procedures, with back-up support from the navy in Brisbane to correct any technical faults.

As if to help Manson shake down his staff in readiness for whatever the future might hold, the *Centaur* again ran into inclement weather. Those members prone to seasickness suffered, and with two exceptions soon got it out out of their system. Those with more durable stomachs (Manson's key personnel, fortunately) continued the intensive training schedule. The effects of the weather constantly reminded them that they were on a *mobile* hospital, and they knew they would rarely enjoy a stable working platform.

The weather improved as AHS *Centaur* rounded Sandy Cape on the northern tip of Fraser Island and turned into the sheltered waters inside the Great Barrier Reef. Soon, with reefs to starboard and mainland to port — but neither visible at that early stage — the *Centaur* entered what is known as the Inner Route, a well-surveyed shipping channel that traces a safe path all the way to Torres Strait.

In many respects the Inner Route resembles some of the great rivers systems of the world. Broad and open at its southern estuary-like entrance, it gradually constricts as it meanders north-wards until, over the last 500 miles, it thins to a maze of narrow channels. It is not a route that is hazardous, except to those who lack a detailed knowledge of its intricacies and idiosyncrasies. Rather, it gives ships a welcome shelter from the sometimes heavy seas and swells of the Coral Sea. Back in the 1880s a group of experienced master mariners pooled their talents and their knowledge to create what is now heralded by the Guinness Book of Records as the 'longest single-handed pilotage service in the world'. The Queensland Coast and Torres Strait Pilot Service boasts a proud record of more than a century of unbroken service[16].

Gradually, as the *Centaur* pushed farther and farther up into the Inner Route, the rolling abated, and with it the *mal de mer*.

About noon on the day before the *Centaur*'s expected arrival at Townsville, somewhere near the Whitsunday Group of islands, Dental Assistant Pte Fred Chidgey and some of his pals took their lunchtime break on deck, near the stern on the port side. Chidgey had with him his trusted old Kodak Brownie camera. He enjoyed photography. Since joining the *Oranje* he had collected an impressive visual record of both the ship and the personnel with whom he had served. Today he wanted to add to his collection. He snapped various members of the staff in varied poses. Suddenly a cry went up: "Submarine!" Someone had spotted a periscope off the port side, some distance away. A crowd quickly gathered at the rail. They could see the eyepiece of the periscope pointing in their direction, scanning them. It rose slowly, and soon a dark sinister-looking conning tower broke the surface. The observers on the *Centaur* waited with anxious anticipation for some proof of this intruder's friendly intentions. Conventional wisdom had it that enemy submarines would avoid the shallow waters of the Inner Route, for fear of detection from the air, but one never knew for certain . . . Figures appeared on the tiny bridge. One moved aft. Then the "Stars and Stripes" broke free on the flagstaff[17].

Chidgey happily snapped two photographs of this friendly ally.

Three quarters of an hour earlier, the watch had changed in the control room of the USS *Greenling* (SS-213). The *Greenling*, a Gato class submarine, had been submerged for the previous six and a half hours, executing a zig-zag pattern on a base course of 090 °T. It had made no contacts during the morning watch. The new OOW had almost completed his initial periscope sweep of the horizon when he spotted a wisp of smoke almost dead ahead. He ordered "down periscope!" and "condition one submerged!" He noted the time: 1202 hours. Two minutes later an attack approach on this unidentified contact began[18].

The *Greenling*'s encounter with AHS *Centaur* was brief, the passing courtesy made, and then the US submarine moved away to submerge and resume her patrol[19].

AHS *Centaur* reached Townsville in the early hours of the following morning and berthed at breakfast time.

Ready and waiting for their passage to Brisbane were a batch of wounded Australian diggers. They had been flown across from New Guinea. An ambulance train brought them from Charters Towers to Townsville. It ran along tracks on to the wharf itself, right alongside the ship. Manson and his doctors and nurses graded the casualties and allocated them into the various wards. Embarkation began without delay. Fortunately, the height of the wharf enabled the orderlies, acting as bearers, to bring the stretcher cases aboard through a side-port door. They brought them straight into the hospital deck and their assigned wards; they did not need to hoist them aboard by the derricks or manhandle them up or down staircases. The embarkation went rapidly and smoothly and the *Centaur* was easily ready for sea by the nominated 1600 sailing time. She got under way promptly and Captain Murray noted in his log that the harbour pilot disembarked and pulled clear at 1632[20].

The *Centaur*'s visit to Townsville provided an enchanting diversion for the two nurses on duty in the ambulance train, Sisters G.Pollock and K.Breen. During the day their AANS colleagues invited them on board, proudly showing off the ship. The two women cringed with envy. How nice this ship seemed, compared with their grimy train.

The three days it took to return to Brisbane gave Manson and Jewell an opportunity to assess, under practical conditions, the success of their planned work routines. Manson decided that considering the short training period his staff had worked remarkably well. This brief trip to Townsville and back also gave the staff members a hands-on opportunity to sort out their own working arrangements; to develop their routines and isolate the pitfalls and potential problem areas. Manson particularly liked the way the messing routine fell into place. Orderlies fed bed patients from the pantries fore and aft on the hospital deck. Walking cases on full diets had their meals served by the general staff at the dining tables in Ward F (the convalescent ward) on the deck below.

In Brisbane, at Newstead Wharf, the disembarkation went smoothly. This time, because of the height of the wharf, the gunport doors could not be used. The staff hoisted the stretcher cases ashore. Taking the casualties in order of injury (serious cases first), the orderlies transferred each man from his bunk to a stretcher and carried him to the tween deck hatchtop. Through the open hatchway above, a derrick hook came down, bringing six slings to be secured around the stretcher. When ready, the winches hoisted each stretcher up out of the ship and over the side to the waiting ambulances.

Manson later reported that the disembarkation kept pace with the steady stream of ambulances onto the wharf. He estimated the *Centaur* to be capable of handling 100 stretcher cases an hour, either to or from a wharf or from boats alongside. He made the point that stretcher cases lifted on board landed directly into the ward[21].

Manson's satisfaction with the *Centaur* showed in his report. In his eyes the *Centaur* had proven her worth as an effective hospital ship. He also knew that her baptism within the chrysalis of a voyage virtually safe from belligerency was over; now it was time to face the supreme test, the challenge for which Manson had prepared her — a foray into the war zone. To his way of thinking, she was ready.

AHS *Centaur* left Brisbane for Port Moresby the very next day, 8th April. This time her wards were occupied by almost 100 passengers. The list included four US medical officers, 21 female US nurses, one officer and 32 orderlies of the 2/1 Australian Mobile Operating Unit, and eight officers and 33 orderlies of the 2/2 Australian Dental Unit. In the holds were 40 tonnes of equipment and medical supplies[22].

On this voyage, having no doubts about their new ship's immunity, the authorities routed the *Centaur* to Moresby outside the Great Barrier Reef, across the open waters of the Coral Sea. This did not particularly meet with the approval of those on board, particularly the passengers, as a heavy southeasterly sea greeted them when they cleared Brisbane. Huge waves breaking off deep easterly swells battered the *Centaur*'s starboard quarter, sending her rolling, pitching and corkscrewing as she

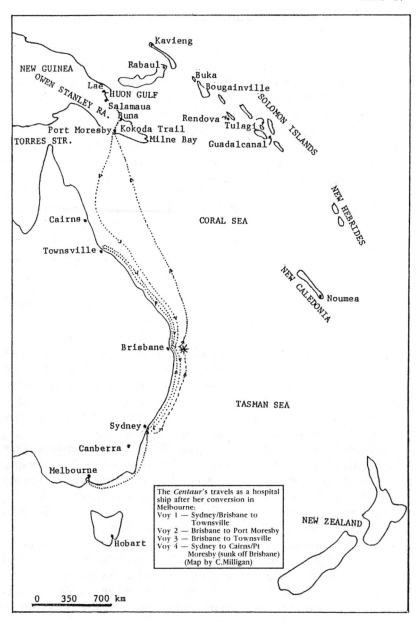

The *Centaur*'s travels as a hospital
ship after her conversion in
Melbourne:
Voy 1 — Sydney/Brisbane to
          Townsville
Voy 2 — Brisbane to Port Moresby
Voy 3 — Brisbane to Townsville
Voy 4 — Sydney to Cairns/Pt
          Moresby (sunk off Brisbane)
(Map by C.Milligan)

laboured her way northwards. The relentless pounding went on for three days without respite. Murray had a schedule to keep and could do nothing but plug ever onwards on the same heading. Although hardened to these conditions himself, he could nevertheless sympathise with the bulk of the passengers — and also some of the medical staff — whom Manson had told him were suffering badly from sea-sickness.

Eventually the seas abated. Seasickness was soon forgotten, and the passengers for the first time began to enjoy life on the ocean wave. Heaven only knew what awaited them in New Guinea, so they might as well make the most of this cruising indolence on board ship. Some took it to extreme lengths. One evening, Chief Officer Lamble trotted down the ladder from the bridge after his watch — and nearly tripped over a couple engaged in some vigorous horizontal refreshment. With typical British aplomb, Lamble deftly stepped over the threshing pair with a polite 'Excuse me'. Apparently they didn't even notice him.

The crossing took five days. At breakfast time on 13th April the *Centaur* entered in through Basilisk Passage, the narrow gap between two reefs that is the doorway to Port Moresby Harbour. She berthed at the main town wharf at 1000. Disconcerting news awaited. Only the previous day the Japanese had bombed the harbour and town, leaving evidence aplenty of their determination and accuracy. No one on the *Centaur* could be blamed for wondering 'will they come back today, and if they do will they respect our hospital ship markings?'

A rapid turnaround was essential. While the passengers were hurriedly disembarked, along with their supplies, the nursing staff began organising the 200 Australian and American wounded waiting on the wharf, readying them for a swift embarkation. Sisters moved among them identifying and tagging each man according to his condition. Half were stretcher cases and the rest 'walking wounded'. Fortunately they were all stabilised, following first aid at casualty clearing stations near the front line, and later treatment at field hospitals. Embarkation got under way as soon as possible, with all the staff helping out. Urgency was the key. Fortunately the wharf height allowed the orderlies to use the side-port doors[23].

While the staff sorted things out on the wharf, Darwin Clark, the Red Cross representative, moved among the wounded to offer a greeting or a word of encouragement; to hand out cigarettes and other small comforts. Off to one side he noticed a group of about ten walking-wounded Japanese POWs, under guard. Australian soldiers stood watch over the very sullen bunch with their rifles at the ready, bayonets fixed. They offered no objection when Clark offered one Japanese a packet of cigarettes. The man took it, then promptly and contemptuously threw it back at him. Instantly, a guard took aim at the prisoner. The Japanese stood his ground defiantly. A few tense seconds passed, then one of the other guards muttered some profanities, picked up the packet and handed it back to Clark. This incident had an interesting postscript. The officer commanding the Australian soldiers put to Manson that it showed the need for armed guards to travel on the ship for the return voyage. Perhaps he saw a golden opportunity for a quick trip home! It was a persuasive argument, forcefully put, but not one that convinced Manson. He had no doubts his staff could handle anything with which it might be confronted. If the need arose they had access to firearms with which to protect the patients. He had the final say. The guards supervised the embarkation of the Japanese POWs and saw them placed in confinement in wards D and F, but then, and with reluctance, they disembarked[24].

After a mere six hours, the *Centaur* put to sea. Fortunately there had been no raid. By good fortune the navy routed the ship back to Brisbane via the sheltered waters of the Great Barrier Reef. During the voyage, the nurses treated the Japanese wounded with the same attention they gave Allied soldiers. Some orderlies felt they gave them more attention than was warranted. Pte Chidgey, for one, found it galling to see these girls' genuine compassionate care for the Japanese so callously rebuffed. Their oriental inscrutability, petulance and absolute resistance to any form of communication shocked the *Centaur*'s staff, many of whom were seeing the enemy for the first time.

Five days after leaving Moresby, on a quiet Sunday morning, the *Centaur* berthed at Hamilton Wharf. As before, the stretcher cases were disembarked by slings through open hatchways[25].

So ended the *Centaur*'s first war-zone voyage as a hospital ship. On the day she returned to Brisbane, Manson compiled a detailed report to DGMS on the first two trips. It has survived; much of the information given in this chapter came from it. Besides a chronological account, Manson also made several

Centaur

pertinent remarks about personnel and some general comments
and recommendations — all of which are worth reproducing
here:

>*Military Personnel* — The officers in this unit are particularly satisfactory. They have given me their whole-hearted support and are settling down to life in this small ship without difficulty. They are all willing workers and moderate in their habits. Capt. Hindmarsh has been appointed Adjutant and is very keen to help with administrative matters.
>
>*The Nursing Staff* are also very satisfactory and their previous experience on a hospital ship has proved invaluable. Matron had a little difficulty first in rearranging her ideas from the "Oranje" to this smaller vessel, but has at all times been co-operative and efficient. The other ranks have with few exceptions been keen and hard-working. I hope to bring the exceptions into line during the next few weeks' training.
>
>*Ship's Merchant Naval Officers* — The relations between these officers and the military staff is excellent. The Master has been more keenly interested in the hospital than any others I have had contact with, and his attitude has had a very good reaction on the whole crew.
>
>*Food and Messing* — The chief Steward, contrary to our expectations, has at all times, provided punctually an adequate supply of well cooked food. His department, and the messing arrangements have been excellent.
>
>*Sanitation* — The latrines and ablution arrangements for the patients and orderlies is adequate and well planned. I have arranged for salt water showers for patients to be available, thus making a considerable saving in fresh water.
>
>*Life-Boat Accommodation* — This is the worst feature of the whole ship. When the ship is full of patients, or passengers, there are 120 military personnel who have no more life saving apparatus than rafts to which they can cling by hand only. This means that the whole of my male staff and about 50 of the patients will have no boat accommodation. The Merchant Navy crew are entitled to a seat in the boats before patients, by virtue of their agreement when signing Articles[e]. The Sea Transport Officer in Sydney has intimated to me that they have some large rafts available in their store in Sydney. I request that arrangements be made to embark as many as possible of these on our first return to Sydney. This will alleviate the position.
>
>*Carriage of Passenger Personnel* — I have pointed out to Adv. LHQ here that we are able to carry as passengers medical personnel, both male and female, by partitioning portion of the ship with curtains and with the same way marking off latrines and ablution places for females. At the most 50 extra officers is all the first class Steward's pantry can deal with. Only in emergency can we carry well females and patients together. Sick prisoners of war can be very conveniently carried in Ward D or Ward F.
>
>*Cargo* — There will be space available for about 100 tons of cargo in the lower holds when the rearrangement of the ballast is completed,

---

e. Manson was not correct here.

66

together with about 60 tons of light cargo in No. 2 tween decks.

In conclusion, I find the ship well planned and equipped. Progress has been satisfactory and I hope to reach a high standard of efficiency in the near future. This unit should be invaluable in areas where large ships cannot go and we look forward to whatever work comes our way[26].

Manson's remarks about the life-saving equipment were accurate. No. 1 and No. 4 lifeboats held 51 persons each; No. 2 and No. 3 52 each, making space for 204 in all. A spare wooden lifeboat with a capacity of 34 brought the total to 238. With a possible full complement of crew, staff and patients of beyond 330, obviously there were not enough lifeboat seats to go round. The requested extra rafts, while not solving the problem altogether, would certainly help[27].

After two hectic trips to Townsville and Port Moresby, at last the pace settled with an eleven day break in Brisbane. Her third voyage, an uneventful trip to Townsville again, began on 29th April and ended with her return to Brisbane on 5th May. The now usual one-day disembarkation process took place and the *Centaur* was once again ready for the next voyage.

She did not have long to wait. Orders came to proceed to Sydney. She left Brisbane after only 28 hours in port.

Captain Murray knew from recent naval reports that by heading out into the western Tasman Sea for the coastal run to Sydney his ship was poking its nose into a veritable nest of very active enemy submarines. Once again, everyone on board had to live with that nagging doubt; would Red Cross markings guarantee the *Centaur*'s safety?

*   *   *   *   *

By the middle of March 1943, the primary Japanese naval objective was to isolate eastern New Guinea and the Solomons from both Australia and the US by interceptive activities in the shipping lanes. Naval forces, particularly submarines, were reinforced. As part of this build-up, on 15th March the IJN transferred the 22nd Submarine Flotilla from Kure to the new naval base at Truk Island in the East Caroline Islands. Submarines *I-177*, *I-178* and *I-180* arrived at Truk in early April. They became members of the 3rd Submarine Squadron under Commander Katsumi Komazawa[28].

On 20th March 1943, Vice-Admiral Hisashi Mito, the Truk-based commander of the 1st Submarine Squadron, sent a dramatic message to all his units, then on patrol off Fiji. It outlined new guidelines for a more rigorous prosecution of submarine warfare. Elements of this message were crucial to the later Japanese conduct at sea, with possible direct pertinence to the *Centaur*. The most critical extract follows:

> MILITARY — ULTRA-SECRET (GUNKI)
> Flagship HEIAN MARU at Truk, 20 March 1943
> 1st SUBMARINE FORCE SECRET // 2-43
> 1st Submarine Force Order
> B.   Attacks on Enemy Shipping.
> 1.   All submarines shall act together in order to concentrate their attacks against enemy convoys and shall totally destroy them.
> 2.   When enemy convoys have been sighted at your skirmishline stations, take into consideration, when attacks are to be carried out, the distance which must be travelled in order to maintain contact with and to attack the enemy naval vessels. Submarines on the skirmish line shall be under the command of the senior submarine commander present.
> 3.   Attacks shall be vigorously repeated until a complete victory is assured.
> 4.   Do not stop with the sinking of enemy ships and cargoes; at the same time that you carry out the *complete destruction of the crews of the enemy's ships* (emphasis added), if possible, seize part of the crew and endeavour to secure information about the enemy[29].

A directive of the Naval General Staff, this infamous order had come to Mito from the Commander-in-Chief of the 6th fleet (which comprised the 1st, 3rd and 8th Submarine Squadrons). While no direct evidence exists that the same message was officially sent to the 3rd Submarine Squadron, either by Mito or its own commander, Komazawa, it *is* known that it went to the 8th Squadron[30]. Furthermore, at least one 3rd Squadron submarine commander, Lt-Cmdr Hajime Nakagawa of the *I-177*, personally saw the order[31].

The strategists assigned the 3rd Submarine Squadron to Australia's eastern seaboard. At 1505 on 10th April, after several days of navigational exercises around Truk, this squadron, comprising submarines *I-11*, *I-177*, *I-178* and *I-180*, left for Australian waters on a patrol expected to last about six weeks. Squadron commander Komazawa travelled in the *I-11*[32].

In this squadron's destination zone an earlier submarine patrol neared the end of its tour of duty.

Searching for something worthwhile to destroy before heading back to Truk, the *I-26* skulked around off Fraser Island, north of Brisbane. Her commander hoped to snare a ship entering or leaving the Inner Route of the Great Barrier Reef. In the late afternoon of 23rd April, the small John Burke Ltd freighter *Tinana*, Rockhampton-bound, rounded Fraser Island's Sandy Cape and turned in towards the coast. Captain Doug McCormack's evening meal was rudely interrupted by yells of 'Submarine! Submarine!' McCormack raced to the bridge. Off to starboard and not far away was a submarine's conning tower. McCormack knew that submarine commanders liked to get their targets silhouetted against the sun. The *Tinana*'s course would soon put her in just that position. McCormack didn't hesitate. He called out 'Hard a'starboard!'. His ship turned towards the submarine and crossed its stern. McCormack set course due east as fast as his little ship could go. After two hours he turned the ship back and continued to Rockhampton, this time via a more circuitous route. Nobody on board slept much that night[33].

The *I-26* soon made amends for this missed opportunity. The next day, in the same area, it put a torpedo into the Australian cargo vessel *Kowarra*. The Howard Smith freighter, fully laden with sugar, quickly sank, taking 21 lives. The crew of the *I-26* went back to Truk well satisfied.

The replacement patrol did not take long to notch up its first success.

Two days after the *Kowarra* sinking, Convoy GP48 steamed slowly northwards near Cape Byron, northern NSW. The group comprised five merchant ships escorted by HMAS *Colac* and HMAS *Ballarat*. One of the freighters, the Union Company's M.V. *Limerick*, had no end of trouble staying in the convoy. An engine fault prevented her steaming at less than ten knots, so she had to keep zig-zagging across the ocean. Her meanderings came to a sudden and dramatic halt when a torpedo struck her amidships on the port side. Five hours later she sank. Two lives were lost. Her attacker was Lt-Cmdr Nakagawa in the *I-177*. The life and death of the *Limerick* in many ways paralleled the *Centaur*'s. She too came into existence in a Glasgow shipyard (one year after the *Centaur*) and like the *Centaur* was one of the earliest motorships. She had the same six-cylinder blast-injected diesel engines. When built she was the highest powered motorship afloat. It is ironic that after careers spanning almost 20 years she and the *Centaur* should meet their ends within 18 days and possibly no more than 100 miles of each other, and at the hands of the same Japanese submarine commander.

The *Limerick* was able to send off an SOS. One of the ships that responded was the Australian freighter *Wollongbar*. Unfortunately, and tragically for the *Wollongbar*, three days later when off the mid-north NSW town of Port Macquarie she herself fell victim to a well-aimed torpedo from the *I-180*. She sank, with a death toll of 32[34].

On 5th May, just as the *Centaur* arrived back in Brisbane after her second hospital ship voyage to Townsville, the Norwegian vessel *Fingal* came to grief off the NSW north coast (again, at the hands of the *I-180*), with a dozen lost lives[35].

Japanese submarines off the east coast of Australia were having a feast.

Chapter Five

SYDNEY SWANSONG

8th to 12th May 1943

At mid-morning on 8th May, a Saturday, after an uneventful trip down the northern NSW coastline, AHS *Centaur* arrived off Port Jackson. Two hours later she lay all secure, port side alongside, at the extreme northern end of No. 1 berth Darling Harbour.

The local naval control officer and the ship's agent came on board. The naval officer would brief Captain Murray on the ship's program. The agent would attend to the ship's mercantile needs. He almost certainly brought Murray a copy of that day's *Sydney Morning Herald*. An item in the paper quoted General MacArthur speaking about shipping losses attributed to Japanese submarines on the Australian east coast. MacArthur had divulged that the enemy sank five Allied ships during the previous six weeks: three Australian, one US and one Norwegian. He did not reveal that four of these ships were lost over a 6-day period, between 24th and 29th April[1].

The *Centaur* lay serenely at her berth for the whole weekend. Sydney residents among the crew and medical staff went home for a few days. The ship was unusually quiet.

On Monday, Sydney put on one of its classically beautiful autumn days; sunny and bright. On the *Centaur*, not much was planned for the day.

About mid-morning, war correspondent Rita Dunstan and war photographer Jack Hickson from the *Sydney Daily Telegraph* climbed the gangway to the deck[2]. Their editor had assigned them to check out the *Centaur* for a possible human-interest story. That the ship was almost deserted surprised them. They were pleased to see a small group of men down aft. As the two journalists made their way along the cluttered deck to the stern,

Dunstan remarked to Hickson that the ship gave her an immediate sense of safety; it seemed a safe haven from the horrors and sadness of war. The seamen aft were enjoying a smoke and a yarn. They were in good spirits, despite having to stay aboard as part of the skeleton crew. They were only too pleased to chat with the attractive young reporter.

Dunstan asked some probing questions but soon came to the conclusion that there was no 'hot' story aboard. She ribbed the seamen. 'You're no good. No news in you lot!'

They all laughed. Dunstan and Hickson said goodbye and made their way back to the gangway.

On the way they met Cpl Joe Moss, a fine looking New Hebridean hospital attendant. Hickson decided his fuzzy hair and dark skin made him a good subject for a photograph. Joe happily posed. Dunstan and Hickson left the ship without a story but not entirely empty handed; they had a good picture. On the wharf they looked back up. Several other crew members lined the rail to wave them a cheery farewell. News of an attractive female on board any ship spreads like lightning. The media pair felt good as they walked away, warmed by the feeling of having made friends. Maybe they would visit the ship again when next it came to Sydney[3].

Another visitor to the ship that day was Chaplain Ernest Laverick's sister-in-law, Mrs T.Ryan. She came aboard to see Captain Laverick, but ended up meeting most of the medical staff and crew[4].

Later that same day, Murray and Manson received their orders from the Commander, South-West Pacific Strike Force. Clear and unambiguous instructions: 'At Sydney ship is to be refuelled and watered and stored to capacity. When ready, to be sailed to Cairns direct, thence Port Moresby'[5]. That the *Centaur* would be returning with wounded servicemen was gainsaid. A later amendment decreed that on the northbound trip the ship would carry a Field Ambulance unit and its equipment. This stemmed from a message sent on 8th May by Major Alister MacKinnon, DA & QMGS at LHQ Melbourne, to his 'Q' Branch counterpart in Sydney. MacKinnon specified the movement of the 2/12 Field Ambulance, which comprised 11 officers, three warrant officers, 14 sergeants and 192 other ranks; 220 in all. One of these officers and 48 of the other ranks would make up the 2/12th's attached ASC unit of ambulance drivers. These ASC personnel would take with them their rifles and ammunition but not their ambulances[6].

The next day, Tuesday 11th May, serious work began to prepare the *Centaur* for sea. Gangs of waterside workers mustered on the wharf in the crisp early-morning air. They filed up the gangway to begin loading the Field Ambulance equipment, stowing it bit by bit in the lower holds, beneath the wards. The crew busied themselves with a myriad of tasks: replenishing oil bunkers and fresh water tanks, loading and stowing fresh provisions, and giving a fresh coat of paint to the red crosses and the green band on the ship's hull. Medical staff prepared the wards, this time as temporary accommodation for a full complement of healthy passengers. All day the scene at No. 1 Darling Harbour hustled busily, a hive of typical waterfront activity: vehicles of various types bringing cargo, stores and fuel to the ship's side; fresh water and bunker hoses running everywhere and always in the way; and through it all a generous helping of good-humoured wharfie profanity bellowed over the clamour of clattering winches.

In the late afternoon, around five o'clock, as the flurry of waterside activity eased, there came a new sound, a clamour totally alien to an Australian cargo wharf. It was the crunching beat of tramping hob-nail boots.

Onto the wharf marched over 200 soldiers in distinctive khaki uniform; the three companies that made up the 2/12 Field Ambulance, plus its attached unit of ASC personnel. At their head strode the 2/12th's commanding officer, Lt-Col Leslie McDonald Outridge.

The origins of the 2/12th dated back to late 1940, in Sydney, when Lt-Col N.D.Barton formed it as an extra field ambulance for the 2nd AIF. It became the 2/12 Field Ambulance. The designation was appropriate; the 1/12 FA had served with the 1st AIF in the Great War. Basic training took place at Cowra, NSW, where the unit went initially in support of the 23rd Australian Infantry Brigade. In March 1941 the 2/12th went with the brigade to the Northern Territory, to a camp at Winnellie, near Darwin. From there small support groups of about 40 men accompanied the *Sparrow* and *Gull* forces sent for the defence of Timor and Ambon. With those forces, they were captured by the Japanese soon afterwards. Other support groups joined the seaborne reinforcement draft to *Sparrow* and *Gull*, but the convoy came under a heavy aerial bombardment which forced it to return to Darwin. The core of the 2/12th held station at Darwin during the savage Japanese air raids in the early months of 1942, witnessing over 60 attacks. A year later the unit redeployed to Reidtown, near Wollongong, NSW. It was from Reidtown that the 2/12th's three companies and its attached personnel travelled by train to Sydney for embarkation on the *Centaur*[7].

On deck, Lt-Col Manson and Second Officer Rippon, with several others of the ship's medical staff and crew, watched with interest as the marching soldiers came to a halt half-way down the wharf[8]. At a shouted command they turned smartly right to face the *Centaur*. Another command, and they stood at ease. They dropped their knapsacks at their feet. Lt-Col Outridge and WO A.K.Thomas (in charge of the attached personnel) immediately began allocating small groups of men to berths — the double-decker patient cots — in the upper and lower tween decks wards. As Thomas called out names the men broke ranks and moved off in single file towards the gangway.

To the observers lining the *Centaur*'s rail, all these soldiers looked to be wearing the same uniform. (The only difference between the FA and the ASC uniforms was the colour of a patch on the puggaree of the hats; brown for ambulance, blue and white for ASC.) Some, however, were seen to have rifles slung over their shoulders and others bore holstered revolvers. On board, a buzz went around that quickly turned to consternation when these armed men lined up to come on board the ship with the others.

Without hesitation, Manson and Rippon went to the top of the gangway and stopped them. Outridge and Thomas moved forward when they heard the commotion. Manson told the two officers he had serious doubts about the legitimacy of soldiers taking firearms on board a hospital ship. Outridge tried to reassure Manson that these weapons — for which his men had no ammunition — were ASC equipment. As these men were ambulance drivers and dispatch riders travelling as a complete medical unit, he maintained, the weapons were permitted on board. He said he had been instructed to take his full war equipment table (about 2000 rounds of ammunition and 52 rifles) but no other weapons[9].

Manson was not so sure. He told Outridge he would get the matter checked and insisted in the meantime that the rifles remain on the wharf.

Outridge acquiesced. WO Thomas returned to his men and explained what was happening. 'Leave your rifles and revolvers against the wall of the wharf,' he told them. He gave each man a blank label on which to write his name, and a length of string with which to tie it to his rifle and bayonet. The men complied, standing their tagged rifles and revolvers neatly side by side against the shed wall. Then they followed the 2/12th personnel onto the ship[10].

To get the matter resolved without delay, Manson went straight to the headquarters of the First Australian Movement Control Group at 1 Bent Street in the city. He spoke to the man in charge, Colonel Hector Clayton, and also to the Sea Transport Officer supervising the *Centaur*'s embarkation. He asked them to confirm that the Convention permitted ASC personnel taking arms onto a hospital ship. Both Clayton and the STO gave Manson a concurring opinion. They produced a document (SM 176 of 5th January 1943), which dealt with this precise matter. One section said:

> For the purpose of maintaining order and for defending the sick and wounded, weapons may be carried on a hospital ship by
> — a) the staff of the hospital ship;
> — b) all personnel on the ship entitled to the protection of the Red Cross Convention, including personnel attached to a medical unit, e.g., attached AASC personnel[11].

To resolve the issue beyond doubt, Clayton telephoned Major MacKinnon in Melbourne. MacKinnon assured him that both Movement Section and the navy had agreed that the embarkation was in order[12].

Apparently, the key to the argument was whether or not the ambulance personnel travelled as a *complete unit*. If they did, then the carriage of their ambulances and their equipment — including their weapons — was legitimate. Top brass had exhaustively debated this issue in late 1942, when becoming aware of the advantages of hospital ships to transport medical units to SWPA war zones. Contemporary army instructions were imprecise about who and what could legally be taken on hospital ships. The Adjutant-General consulted the Army Legal Services and the navy, and then issued a statement (the document SM 176 of 5th January 1943 mentioned earlier). It clarified precisely who could be transported on a hospital ship, and set out the rules governing the carriage of arms and material[13].

Armed with this assurance, Manson returned to the *Centaur*. He told Outridge the weapons could be loaded. The waterside workers put them on board later in the evening.

There the matter should have ended; *should* have.

Unfortunately, the incident on the wharf that Tuesday afternoon had not gone unnoticed. Word of it spread like wildfire. And as so often happens, the facts in themselves were not spicy enough for the rumour-mongers, who embellished the story with lurid half-truths and distortions. By the time the waterside workers turned-to on Wednesday morning, the incident had been blown out of all proportion. If, the tale went, armed troops were embarking on the *Centaur*, then the ship must be loading munitions too![14]

The wharfies, as is their want under such circumstances, had a meeting. This would have surprised no-one; at a time of great upheaval on the Australian waterfront wharfie militancy was renowned. What was surprising was a resolution to cease loading. Very little cargo remained to load and the *Centaur*'s sailing time was set for 9 o'clock. Once all the cargo was on board and stowed, the wharfies could go home and would be paid for the rest of the day. So their interests lay in finishing the job as early as possible. This decision to down tools therefore underscored some strong feelings about the possibility of munitions being on the *Centaur*.

At much the same time, the *Centaur*'s seamen became embroiled in the issue. When Bill McIntosh, the greasers' delegate, heard about the munitions rumour from cooks' delegate Bill Davidson, he called a combined crew meeting; deck and engine-room ratings, cooks and stewards. McIntosh was a communist, like most maritime union delegates, and there can be little doubt that his comrades in the Waterside Workers Federation had briefed him on their actions. The seamen resolved not to take the ship to sea until satisfied it carried no munitions.

About 10 o'clock, McIntosh and the other union delegates — Ron Paige (seamen), Bill Davidson (cooks), and Ronnie Moate (stewards) — went to see Captain Murray[15].

They found the master in his day cabin, chatting with Captain Salt, the Torres Strait Pilot, who had just reported on board.

What happened next appeared later in statements made by both McIntosh and Salt.

'Come in', Murray called out, when McIntosh knocked on his door.

McIntosh took off his cap and led the delegation into the room. 'Excuse us, Cap'n. Can we speak to you for a minute?'

Murray asked, 'Yes, what is it?'

McIntosh got right to the point. 'We have heard that there is ammunition on board this ship.'

'Where did you hear that from?' Murray asked.

'From Bill Davidson, who heard it from one of Colonel Manson's orderlies.' Davidson nodded in agreement, and McIntosh continued, 'We held a meeting and decided to investigate'. He added, 'If there is any ammunition on board we will not take her to sea.'

McIntosh could tell by the expression on Captain Murray's face that the allegation surprised him.

'I'm fully prepared, here and now, to open any hatch of the ship for you to investigate,' said Murray. 'We do have sixty rifles on board that belong to the ambulance drivers who are ASC. But we are not carrying ammunition for them.' In this, of course, Murray was incorrect. He should have known about the ammunition by that time. But he would also have known that its carriage was legal. Possibly he did *not* know, or maybe figured it would be easier to deny its existence on the premise that the crew were complaining not about the ASC ammunition but about a *shipment* of munitions — quite a different matter. We will now never know. Whatever his reasoning, his denial and his willingness to allow the seamen to go ahead with a search convinced the delegates of his sincerity.

McIntosh spoke first. 'As long as there is no ammunition, Captain, I will take your word for it.' The rest of the group murmured their agreement. Murray nodded in approval.

The delegates thanked Murray and left his cabin to report back to their respective members. No doubt McIntosh briefed the wharfies, who examined the cargo they had not yet loaded. The seamen looked over the ship. Neither group found anything to concern them. Satisfied that the cargo was legal and the ship strictly non-combatant, all hands then resumed work to get the ship ready for sea[16]

Centaur

To revert briefly; as the delegates left Captain Murray's cabin they bumped into 1st Mate Harry Lamble. McIntosh asked him if he could use the ship's telephone to ring through to his union's office. One of the seaman had hurt his arm, McIntosh explained, and he wanted to make sure the ship could sail with an unfit man. Lamble agreed and McIntosh made the call. The Seamens' Union officials sensibly decided the injured man would have all the medical attention he needed on board the ship. Seamen were extremely scarce at the time, and the union could see no merit in delaying the *Centaur*. McIntosh accepted the ruling and thought no more about it, but some months later this communication came under scrutiny by intelligence officials keen to find out about a telephone call, made within minutes of the ship's departure, from someone on the *Centaur* to the office of a militant union. By that time, as we shall see, rumours of fifth column activity were rife[17].

At last the wharfies completed loading and stowing the 2/12th's equipment. Satisfied, the Sea Transport Officer gave notice that he was about to leave. Manson and Rippon saw him off at the gangway. AHS *Centaur* was now ready for sea.

The *Centaur* at this time, unbeknown to and certainly unsuspected by anyone, was spending her last few minutes of friendly contact with any person or thing outside her steel hull. She was about to sail off into oblivion. It is perhaps fitting to take a brief look at the makeup of this disparate group of people who so innocently accompanied her to her doom.

As far as is known, and one cannot be implacably definite about it, on board AHS *Centaur* were 332 souls. This sum comprised 75 members of the merchant navy crew (including the Torres Strait Pilot), 64 men and women of the ship's medical staff, 149 men of the 2/12 Field Ambulance, and 44 ASC attached personnel.

At her helm, figuratively but aptly speaking, still loomed the comforting figure of Captain George Murray. Now 53 years of age, Murray had been with the *Centaur* for the previous seven years. He had not visited his home in Nedlands since the ship's last call at Fremantle seven months earlier.

Assisting him with navigation on this voyage was Torres Strait Pilot and fellow Scot, Captain Richard (Jock) Salt. At 67 years of age, this weather-beaten mariner was the oldest person on board. He had been a pilot with the Torres Strait service since

78

1916, and but for the demands of wartime pilotage would have retired years earlier. Pilotage traffic throughout the war was frenetic, not only in Great Barrier Reef waters but also around New Guinea. New Guinea's reef-studded channels and coastal routes lacked navigational beacons and were for the most part uncharted. To the many young American captains of both warships and merchant ships who found themselves in this theatre of war, the intricate and treacherous waters were a nightmare. Money for pilotage was no object, and word of a Torres Strait Pilot in the district brought keen competition for his services. It was not unusual for a pilot to find himself drawn into a pilotage circuit in New Guinea and not return home for six months. In that time he would pilot dozens of ships, varying from Liberty-type freighters to submarines and destroyers.

Despite the workload — or possibly because of it — Captain Salt had been trying very hard to retire. He did not enjoy the best of health. In early 1943 he put his foot down and announced his retirement. The Pilot Service secretaries pleaded with him to stay. They persuaded him to take one more ship. Jock reluctantly took the *Anshun*, a British-flag freighter owned by the China Navigation Company. His adventures on the *Anshun* in Milne Bay were detailed in a previous chapter. Needless to say, when Jock returned to Sydney he made it clear to the secretaries that he had completed his last trip. But once again the secretaries, desperate for men, leaned on him. He withstood their entreaties, reminding them of his *Anshun* trauma. They persisted. 'Look,' they said, 'just one more trip. Here, take the hospital ship *Centaur*. Nothing can happen to you there.' So once more, with great reluctance, Captain Salt obliged[18].

All the deck officers who had been with the *Centaur* during her conversion to a hospital ship — Lamble, Rippon and Banks — were still there. In the engine room the Scot Ernie Smith once more held the reins; he had rejoined the ship in Brisbane. Now 45 years old, the aquiline-faced Smith had been with the *Centaur* on and off for almost two decades. Two newcomers, Bill Cuthill and George Alexander, also Scots, held the posts of second and third engineers. Cuthill, a survivor of three previous sinkings during the Battle of the Atlantic, had been sent by Blue Funnel to a 'safe ship' to help him get over his experiences. While in Sydney, he got news from home that his wife had given birth to twins. Maurice Cairnie and an Englishman, Harry Hall, were fourth and extra-fourth engineers. Sandgroper Cairnie had by that time been with the *Centaur* for three years. The ship's electrician was a Victorian, Keith Sykes. Three radio officers manned the *Centaur*'s wireless room: Eric Summers, Tom Morris and Bob Laird. James Capper from WA, the chief steward, completed the 14-man officer complement.

Among the seamen, firemen, greasers, cooks and stewards, a number of changes had taken place since Captain Murray opened the Articles back in early March, the changes occurring for various reasons as the *Centaur* moved from port to port. The crew were a motley bunch; a mixture of true seamen and whatever other misfits could be persuaded to go to sea in those personnel-scarce times. Most of the, what could be termed 'career' seamen, were fervent unionists and at least a dozen were communists. One of these, Bill McKinnon, the *Centaur*'s 3rd Cook and delegate for the cooks, met a party colleague on a street corner one day. He told his fellow-traveller his previous ship had been sunk under him by a Japanese torpedo, but now he had a much safer job.

One of the *Centaur*'s crew, David Ireland Milligan, warrants special mention, if for no other reason than that a nephew of his, Christopher S.Milligan (who in May 1943 had not even been born), would later devote over 14 years of spare-time investigative skills to a study of the incident that claimed his uncle's life. Able Seaman Milligan, 40 years old in 1943, had moved to Australia from his native Seaforth in England in 1926. He settled in Oakleigh, Victoria, and joined the Australian Merchant Navy. He was an active man, a runner, a one-time member of the St Stephen's Harriers. He had a happy personality; full of good will and boundless generosity[19].

The *Centaur*'s medical staff had also been shuffled a bit with discharges and replacements since the first round-up, but Manson had managed to hang on to his key personnel.

New to the *Centaur* were the men of the 2/12 Field Ambulance and their attached personnel. Their commanding officer, Lt-Col Leslie McD.Outridge, 43, a Queenslander, had trained at Sydney University before establishing a private practice in Gympie, north of Brisbane. A quiet man with a love for orchids and music, he nevertheless volunteered promptly for military service when war broke out. He first served in the 5th Lighthorse Regiment, then with the AIF Medical Corps at Darwin, before taking over the 2/12th[20].

Taking a collective look at the 332 people on AHS *Centaur*, we find 12 women and 320 men, ranging in age from 15 (Ordinary Seaman Bob Westwood) to 67 (Captain Salt). While most were Australian, other nationalities appeared: England and Scotland predominantly but also Sweden (ship's carpenter Brandin), Iceland (AB Long), Finland (AB Kaki), Norway (steward Jonassen) and Canada (AB Le Blanc). There were at least eight sets of brothers aboard: Annis-Brown, Bayley, Bracken, Clark, Fortier, Hayward, Hoggins, Leask and Maynard. In all probability there were more; the names Evans, McGuire, Richardson and Williams appear more than once within their respective departments. Of the known brothers, John and Paul Bracken, Leslie and Neville Clark, the Annis-Browns and the three Leask brothers were all privates with the 2/12 Field Ambulance[a]. John and Alan Bayley and Fred and Alan Fortier were drivers, ASC attached personnel. Having a representative in each camp were the Hayward brothers; one in the 2/12th, the other attached personnel. That they ended up on the same ship is remarkable. Mark and Trevor Hoggins were merchant crew; a baker and cook respectively. Twins John and Allan Maynard were privates on the ship's medical staff.

The tragedy ahead was going to bring sudden, unbelievable grief and loss to dozens of wives, fiances, sweethearts, children, friends and colleagues; too many individual tragedies to detail here, even if they were all known. Some examples are pertinent, nevertheless.

The Maynard brothers came from Queensland. John was married; Allan not. John wrote to his wife Frances shortly before the *Centaur* sailed. He told her about the wildfire rumours doing the rounds that the *Centaur* had munitions in her holds, and with tragic prescience spoke of his concern that both he and his twin brother were on the same ship — in case a Japanese submarine got them.

The story of the Bracken brothers, John and Paul, is as poignant: unbeknown to Paul, his wife was pregnant with their first child.

Fred Fortier, the day the 2/12th left Cowra, managed to send what in the light of the later tragedy was a heart-rending letter

---

a. There was a fourth Leask brother, also amazingly a member of the 2/12th, who did not travel on the *Centaur*.

to his wife Elsie. Forbidden to mention his future movements, he could only assure her he would write as soon as possible. 'Do not worry too much if you do not hear from me for a while,' he begged her. 'I was sure I would be home tonight, but everything has happened so quickly ... I was coming home last night but missed the train ... Bub (*brother Alan*) was lucky and managed to get the train up ... You don't know how I feel about this, Pet, I would give anything to see you and Pam (*their daughter*) just to say goodbye ... I feel rotten'.

The Leask family of Marylands, NSW, suffered a triple-tragedy when not one of their three sons returned from this fatal voyage.

Captain Stephen Foley of the 2/12th had became engaged only a few days earlier. The evening before joining the *Centaur* he and driver George McGrath shared a celebration at the Illawarra Hotel at which they announced their respective engagements: Stephen Foley to a Margaret Cameron; George McGrath to Bombardier Marie Mullins.

There were dozens more pitiable human tragedies about to befall many families.

One pair of brothers fated for a happier outcome were the Hoggins; baker Mark and assistant cook Trevor. They both survived. For Mark, it would be the second time he had been on a ship torpedoed by a Japanese submarine.

Mark Hoggins was by no means the only member of that exclusive club of valour. Mention has already been made of 3rd Mate Monty Banks' three earlier altercations with submarines, and at least five others — 2nd Engineer Bill Cuthill, AB J.Ivan Cecich, 3rd Cook Bill McKinnon, nightwatchman Frank Drust and steward Jack Stutter — had been through that same harrowing experience.

As with most shipping disasters, the *Centaur* story has its share of anecdotes about miraculous last minute escapes. Staff Sergeant Gordon Charles of Warwick in Queensland, one of the ship's medical staff, ironically attributed his survival to his proneness to seasickness. On the *Centaur*'s last round trip to Townsville, Sergeant Charles became horribly seasick. His suffering caused him to leave the ship in Brisbane. His place was taken by Staff Sergeant J. Taylor (who sadly ended up on the list of casualties). George Lamb of the ship's crew was another who missed the ship for medical reasons. On the previous voyage Lamb had an accident involving a fan. He went to hospital in Sydney for treatment, and paid off. A legal matter probably saved the skin of Dr Alan Bryson of Sydney. Subpoenaed to give evidence at a pending court case, Bryson was taken off the ship shortly before departure. Alan Hickson of the 2/12th may well have to thank some incompetent railway official for saving his life. On the list to travel with the *Centaur*, Hickson sought some compassionate leave when his wife became ill. He got it, but on the proviso that he join the ship before sailing. He tried, but a foul-up on the railways got him to the wharf two hours too late. Another to miss the ship at the last minute was medical staffer Pte Len Warren. The army sent him up to Brisbane by train for ongoing transport to wherever the *Centaur* was bound.

Ironically, this phenomenon worked both ways. Cpl Albert Taylor, a dental assistant, was on leave. He was recalled to assist Captain Bedkober give a dental check to each man earmarked for the *Centaur* voyage — and suddenly found himself added to the list! Another man joined the ship even though he should not have been there. Private Clem Lynne, a barber with the 2/12 Field Ambulance, had been left off the nominal roll. Lynne decided he was not going to miss all the fun he figured his mates had ahead of them in New Guinea. He took matters into his own hands and simply went on board; a fateful move, as things turned out.

Pte Neville Clark (2/12th) should have allowed a minor act of insubordination become a major one; it might have saved his life. He took some unofficial time off to visit his pregnant wife Beryl, but obeyed his sense of duty and returned to the ship before sailing.

Ambulance driver George McGrath also nearly missed the ship. He had taken leave to visit his family when the Alert-for-Movement signal arrived at Corrimal. The telegram to recall him went to his father's home, but George had already left there to call on his sister. Another driver and friend, Dick Cavanagh, contacted George's fiancé. She knew where George was and passed on the message[21].

At around 1030 on this partly sunny and mild autumn day, AHS *Centaur* went through the traditional sequence of activities that presage a ship's departure. Seamen threw off the lines securing the gangway, waiting with moderate patience for the harbour pilot to board and the last officials to leave before hauling it aboard. Rat guards straddling the mooring lines at the bow and stern were shaken clear and lifted over the rail. Flags fluttered; up with the pilot flag, down with the Blue Peter. On the bridge a deck officer laid out binoculars and megaphones, turned the steering wheel hard over each way, and clang-clanged his way through an engine room telegraph check. A resonant blast from the ship's whistle high up on the forward edge of the funnel sent an unmistakable audible message across Sydney Harbour that AHS *Centaur* was about to sail.

Before long figures appeared on the bridge. Orders were shouted fore and aft and moments later the heavy mooring lines, one after the other, fell slack. Shore linesmen heaved the great rope eyes off bollards and tossed them into the water. The last umbilical cord had been cut; AHS *Centaur* was on her own. From deep within the hull came a muffled blast of starting air, followed by an accelerating rumble of pistons. A boil of white water appeared at the stern. The *Centaur* began to move, sternwards, backing slowly out into Darling Harbour. Third mate Monty Banks recorded in the movement book that the *Centaur* departed at 1044 hours. The day, 12th May 1943.

For the first time in many a long day (possibly since quitting the Fremantle/Singapore trade) the *Centaur*'s decks teemed with passengers. Unlike the gaily dressed fare-paying individuals of the heady days of old, however, these were all young men needed for a more sombre purpose on the battlefields of New Guinea. In light jungle-green uniforms, having changed from the heavier khaki, they filled every inch of deckspace; every man-Jack determined to miss not one moment of the trip out of the harbour to the open sea[22]. In their eagerness to reach the best vantage points, they shinned up the masts and stays, clinging precariously to whatever support lent itself. For many this was their first sea voyage, and they were making the most of it. With some irony, on the *Centaur*'s last departure from anywhere, it is unlikely that she had ever before had so many people on board.

Majestically, the *Centaur* moved slowly sternwards, curving away from the berth. Once clear, the pilot ordered 'Slow Ahead' and 'Port your helm'. The white lady with its seething mass of green humanity seemed to pivot on her stern as she turned slowly to port and began to move forward. On the now vacant wharf, the military officials — no wives, families, sweethearts or friends could be present — followed her progress until the corner of No. 9 Walsh Bay's cargo shed seemed to rudely interpose itself between them and the ship.

e Allan Pettiford (saved).
(A.Pettiford)

C.O. of 2/12 FA, Lt-Col Leslie McD.Outridge (saved).
(Mrs B.Outridge)

river George McGrath (saved).
(G.McGrath)

Cpl James Thorpe (saved).
(Mrs J.Knight)

Above: Cpl Albert Taylor, dental technician (saved) . . . saw the white wake of the torpedo heading for the Centaur.

(A.Taylor)

Right: Driver Jack Walder . . . survived the sinking but died of severe burns the next day.

(G.McGrath)

Sgt Bill McDougall (lost).
(Mrs A.Clare)

Pte A.Reid (lost).

(A.Pettiford)

Right: Able Seaman David Milligan, uncle of co-author Chris Milligan (lost).
(C.Milligan)

Below right: Third Officer 'Monty' Banks (saved). Banks had been torpedoed three times before the Centaur.
(F.Chidgey)

Below: Ordinary Seaman Robert Westwood, youngest man on board (saved).
(R.Westwood)

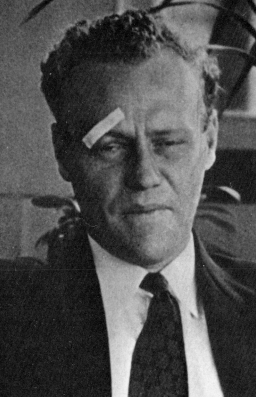

Looking aft along the Centaur's *foredeck. Note the raft slung in the rigging. The enlisted men used this cluttered space as their recreation area.*

(F.Chidgey)

In the hospital ward, showing the rows of iron cots.

(J.Jeppessen)

And then the *Centaur* was gone.

On her packed decks, the men turned their attention to the harbour, especially the great bridge that loomed loftily before them. They gazed upwards, wide-eyed, as the ship slid beneath its imposing arch.

Some excursion ferries took it upon themselves to provide the departing *Centaur* with a spontaneous and unofficial escort through the harbour. They came close, paralleling the ship, and their musicians and passengers began to serenade the troops with *Now is the Hour*, followed by *'Til We Meet Again*. The men waved and whistled at the girls on the boats, and needed no encouragement to join in the singalong[23].

The euphoria of this rowdy departure rubbed off on some of the *Centaur*'s crew and medical staff. Despite the melancholy nature of their mission, this was a lighthearted moment, one to be savoured. They could not help but share in the frivolity, either actively or by amused observation.

On the bridge 2nd Mate Gordon Rippon found the sight of over 200 green uniforms swarming over the ship most memorable. It did bring one sobering thought to his mind however; the concern that some fifth-columnist, not knowing the true status of the *Centaur* and of her mission of mercy, might report to his Japanese masters that she was a troopship — ripe for the picking — rather than a hospital ship taking medical personnel to a theatre of war.

When Fourth Engineer Maurice Cairnie came out of the engine room he, too, was taken by the cacophony of wolf-whistles and yells. The sharp contrast of the swath of green against the white of the ship engraved itself in his memory[24].

After a few verses the 'escort' began to pull away amid a final farewell of waves and shouts. AHS *Centaur* continued, through the boom gate once more and up the East Channel to the Heads. Here one last ceremony of farewell took place. The harbour pilot handed back control of the ship to Captain Murray, and disembarked.

AHS *Centaur* slipped out through the Heads and into a moderate-to-rough Tasman Sea.

* * * * *

On 11th May 1943, eleven merchant ships and four Australian warships formed up outside Moreton Bay's swept channel. Designated Convoy PG50, bound for Sydney, this was the first of the double-size convoys reintroduced because of the increased submarine threat on the east coast. By early afternoon on the 12th, just as AHS *Centaur* was pulling clear of Sydney Harbour, PG50 had reached the vicinity of Coffs Harbour. At 1412 the Japanese submarine *I-180* launched an attack. Captain Kusaka must have been having a bad day. He managed to get torpedoes into two ships, but sank neither. His first target was the AUSN liner *Ormiston*, fully laden with Queensland sugar for Sydney. *I-180*'s missile struck her on the port side, in No. 1 hold. The explosion caused extensive damage to the *Ormiston*'s fore part, but she stayed afloat. With drooping bow, like the nose of a Concorde aircraft, she limped into Coffs Harbour, escorted by HMAS *Ballarat*. The Patrick Company's freighter *Caradale* took Kusaka's second torpedo, but it failed to explode[25].

Chapter Six

NORTHWARDS FROM SYDNEY

1440 12th May to 0410 14th May 1943

With the departure of the Sydney harbour pilot, the navigational control of AHS *Centaur* once more returned to Captain Murray. He in turn was happy to hand it to his Coast Pilot, Captain Jock Salt. Salt immediately began manoeuvring the *Centaur* out through the swept channel, the only part of the Sydney approaches known to be free of mines. Naval minesweepers swept the channel daily to a clear width of two miles. Being wartime, no marker buoys delineated its width or its limits, so the navigator's task — at that time Jock Salt's — was by no means an easy one. Two hours elapsed before the ship reached open waters[1].

During this time, Captain Murray took his young 2nd Mate and navigator, Gordon Rippon, into the chartroom to discuss the route north. Although the NSCO in Sydney had told Murray about his pending voyage several days earlier, he did not pass over the official written sailing orders until the day before departure[2]. They detailed the track known as the 'Green Route'. Starting at the pilot grounds, the first nominated courses took the ship through the swept channel: '151° for 3.8 miles, thence 127° for 16 miles'[3]. From there the *Centaur* was to follow a series of courses connecting several given positions. They were all well offshore: 150 miles east of Newcastle, 110 miles east of Cape Byron, 110 miles east of Cape Moreton, 55 miles northeast of Sandy Cape, and on to the curiously precise '10.2 miles east of Bustard Head'. From Bustard Head (near Gladstone) Murray was given more freedom of movement; told simply to proceed 'inside the Barrier Reef to your destination'[4]. In mineable waters, i.e. shallow areas, the *Centaur* was instructed to stream her paravanes, and when steaming at more than ten knots within

200 miles of the coast she was to zig-zag both by day and by night[5].

These instructions were precise and unambiguously specific. Captain Murray, however, after discussing the matter with Captain Salt, decided to take a different, more inshore, route and a direct one, with no zig-zagging. Murray told Rippon he considered the Green Route would take them too far out to sea, much farther away from the coast than was necessary for a non-combatant. The captain felt that the navy had mistakenly given him a route usually taken by normal merchant ships. This was evident from the specific order to zig-zag. Ships zigged-zagged only to make it difficult for a submarine to take aim. Hospital ships most definitely did not zig-zag; the manoeuvre could arouse suspicion about their *bona fides*. Murray told Rippon where he wanted the courses laid for the run up the NSW and southern Queensland coasts, at least as far as Sandy Cape, from where Captain Salt would dictate the progress. He told Rippon to lay the tracks to seaward of the 100-fathom[a] line, thereby keeping the *Centaur* clear of possible minefields on the continental shelf.

Rippon concurred with Murray's change in plan. To him it was logical. As long as they avoided minefields there seemed no point in adding extra miles to the voyage. He began pencilling in the new courses on the chart. He casually noted, as he went, that they were about 80 miles inshore of the Green Route tracks[6].

Captain Murray's decision to vary his orders was sound, even if the navy was hardly likely to applaud him for disregarding official sailing orders. Unfortunately it unwittingly led the *Centaur* into mortal danger; straight to a rendezvous with an adversary who had less regard for the sanctity of hospital ships than anyone could have imagined. Murray made his decision and he would not, had he survived, have resiled from it. He could not possibly have known or imagined what it might lead to, and he cannot be blamed for it.

Captain Murray, O.C. Troops Manson and Chief Engineer Smith were the only ones on board to know officially that AHS *Centaur*'s destination was Cairns, then Port Moresby. Murray did not even tell his navigator, Gordon Rippon. Individual theories naturally abounded; secrecy about any ship's destination immediately fires up the 'latrine wireless', and speculation

---

a. A fathom is six feet, approximately two metres.

— always based on 'impeccable sources' — runs riot. Milne Bay and Port Moresby were popular, and logical, punts. One wag even tipped America!

Exactly *why* the *Centaur* was going to Cairns is not totally clear. No-one now seems to know for sure. As the *Centaur*'s eventual destination was Port Moresby, one might assume that her arrival in New Guinea had some urgency, and wonder why the authorities had not sent her there direct. Perhaps there was no urgency. Perhaps she would be arriving there earlier than the date the medical officers expected their casualties to be assembled for repatriation. Military authorities would not want a hospital ship hanging around a war-zone before they were ready for it. So the *Centaur* could have been going to Cairns (being the nearest safe port to Moresby) to await the order to move. She might also have been going to Cairns to join a convoy for the run across to Port Moresby. Cairns, Townsville and Gladstone were common assembly points for Coral Sea convoys. But being a hospital ship she should have had no apparent need of a naval escort's security blanket — unless the authorities entertained doubts about her immunity. Another possibility is that at Cairns she was to take on additional staff or some special equipment. This is unlikely, if for no other reason than that there would scarcely have been room. The answer may lie in a *Unit War History* of the 2/12 Field Ambulance, written in Kuching in 1945, which states that the unit was bound for the Atherton Tableland to join 2 Australia Corps[7]. Thus the *Centaur* would call at Cairns first to disembark the 2/12th, and afterwards go on to Moresby. In support of this, ambulance driver George McGrath told the authors he believed the army chose the 2/12th to support the 9th Division landings at Lae (which did not take place until several months later). It is interesting that the NSCO's sailing orders, as originally typed up, instructed Murray to 'Proceed to Townsville . . . ' Even details of the latest depth in Townsville's entrance channel were given. Before the *Centaur*'s departure, for some now obscure reason, the authorities changed this to Cairns. Someone crossed out the typed word 'Townsville' and hand-wrote 'Cairns' above it[8].

Captain Murray had estimated the *Centaur*'s arrival at Cairns as 0700 on 17th May.

As the afternoon wore on and the *Centaur* drew farther out into the Tasman Sea, those on board settled down for the voyage ahead. The merchant crewmembers, as they had done on countless previous sailing days, slipped easily into their normal sea routine; bridge, radio room or engine room watches, or daywork duties. The daywork seamen were already busy cleaning up, squaring away and washing down.

Lt-Col Manson's medical staff got on with their normal hospital practices. For them, apart from the hype of the departure from Sydney, this day was much the same as any other; routine procedures in the wards, lectures and training sessions.

By contrast, the men of the 2/12 Field Ambulance and their attached ASC personnel had no specific duties. Being on board merely as passengers, they could spend their time as they wished. Some, finding the strange motion of a ship at sea not to their liking, went below to their bunks in the wards. (ORs had been allocated two-tiered cots in the main wards, while the luckier NCOs enjoyed slightly more secluded two-bedded alcoves on the same decks.) Most, however, stayed up on deck, enjoying the novelty of being at sea. Some watched — no doubt with mixed emotions — the gradually diminishing grey strip of land on the port quarter. They may have been suffering the wrenched stomachs of lovesickness or homesickness, but mostly were in good spirits. None had any illusory doubts about the ugliness that awaited them in New Guinea, but for the next week at least life should be very pleasant. They might as well enjoy it. They were on a hospital ship; surely that meant they were in no danger?

Their commanding officer did not share their complacency. Lt-Col Outridge had heard rumours before leaving Sydney. Disturbing rumours, about possible Japanese reprisals for claimed attacks on Axis hospital ships by Allied forces. Some of Manson's staff had heard them too. Outridge asked Captain Murray to order additional boat drills, as an added precaution. Murray agreed[9].

Captain Murray had already organised an 'action stations' drill for that afternoon. At 1530 alarm bells summoned the entire ship's company. All hands assembled for instruction by the deck officers. The officers allocated every person on board a lifeboat or raft. Fortunately, during the time in Sydney, the navy had resolved all Manson's earlier complaints about lifeboat capacity. Manson had detailed his punctilious adjutant, Captain Hindmarsh, to supervise the improvements. Now, as well as the *Centaur*'s four 52-man lifeboats on the boat deck and the motor boat and dinghy either side of the steering gear house, an extra 40-man lifeboat sat on deck near No. 4 hatch. The crew had attached it to a bridle slung from a topped derrick; ready for instant use[10]. As well, four four-drum quick-release Carley floats were slung outside the wire rigging, one on each side of both the foremast and mainmast. Four six-drum liferafts sat on deck. About 20 small, flat rafts sat in various places around the decks, unsecured.

The officers issued lifejackets all round. Attached to them were whistles and small, automatically-activated red lights. They told everyone to keep the lifejackets handy always; at night under their bunks.

One man most thankful to be given his lifejacket was L-Cpl Ron 'Spud' Jones. Jones had an almost paranoiac fear of the water (probably because he could not swim!) and furthermore had had a premonition of disaster. While the *Centaur* had steamed up Sydney Harbour and out of the Heads — and almost every member of the 2/12th remained on deck enjoying the view — Jones was below, checking out escape routes from the wards. He surveyed the porthole nearest his bunk to see if he could get through it in an emergency. He couldn't, so ruled it out as a means of escape. This knowledge at least saved him valuable time when the crunch came. He waited eagerly for the afternoon boat drill. When he found out his boat station, he planned the quickest route to it from his bunk. He hung his precious lifejacket immediately above his pillow, ready for instant use.

At 1800 the stewards began serving dinner in the dining room. With so many passengers on board, they were obliged to serve the meal in four sittings.

Usually, evenings were a time for relaxation and social activities, and this first night at sea was no exception. The day's work done, it was time to relax, to socialise, to write a letter home, to read quietly, or to 'make and mend' (attend to one's kit). After the evening meal, groups large and small gathered all over the ship; to talk, to sing, or to play cards. This was usually the time for David Milligan to entertain his mates in the seamen's mess with his piano accordion[11]. His performance did not last long; Milligan had the 12-4 watch and needed to garner a few hours sleep before midnight. In the lounge the merchant and medical officers, including the sisters, would meet. Some gathered around the bar for a casual drink and conversation; others listened to the collection of phonograph records. Padre

Laverick was particularly taken with a Stanley Holloway record about some land girls who went to work on a farm with one strong man and learned all about 'rakes and ploughs, and pigs and sows, and bulls and cows!'[12] This evening the socialising probably became even more lively than normal, thanks to an infusion of 'fresh blood' — the Field Ambulance officers Outridge, Bedkober, Chadwick, Foley, Johnston, Jones, Miles, Sender, Thelander and Wheeler[13].

It was in the lounge that Mr Darwin Clark, the Red Cross representative, wrote letters to his family on Red Cross letterhead paper. In the top left hand corner a warning glared upwards:

> FOR SAFETY. IN YOUR LETTERS DO NOT REFER TO:
> The name of your ship or other ships in the convoy, or its escorts;
> The date of sailing, ports of call, or probable destination;
> The description of troops, their location or any other information which, if intercepted, would be of value to the enemy.

To give his family some idea of his whereabouts, Clark wrote in conundrums, which made his letters meaningless to anyone except them. It gave them the added enjoyment and entertainment — and sometimes the frustration — of trying to decode his delightful cryptic clues[14]. His last letter, dated 26th April, described a shore excursion he and cabin-mate Padre Laverick had taken in Brisbane. 'On Sat(urday) aft(ernoon) Padre and I thought we would go and see some of the seaside resorts a little north of Phuskits Gulf. We took the train to Crushed stone door ... at last we pulled up to Oldwoundville ... so after an ice cream caught the next bus back to Purplepatches.' Clark's family deciphered *Crushed stone door* (Sandgate) and *Oldwoundville* (Scarborough), but not the other clues[b].

Socialising for the ambulance personnel, lacking any formal lounge or bar, was more difficult. To keep them occupied and possibly amused the officers organised a film and a lecture.

The next day, 13th May, was for the crew and medical staff once more one of routine; for the ambulance personnel one of mostly idleness interspersed by frequent, and unexpected, emergency drills. The ship's alarm bells summoning everyone to lifeboat drill went four times that day, each time without advance warning. George McGrath remembered that one of them went the moment they sat down to a hot lunch. By the time they got back to the table the meal was cold.

---

b. *Purplepatches* was probably Redcliffe.

The medical staff — doctors, nurses and orderlies — spent the morning working in the wards; attending to the many details needed to keep this floating hospital in a constant state of preparedness. In the afternoon they practised a range of embarkation scenarios, simulating the movement of stretcher cases around the ship. The orderlies then went to lectures; two hours of discourses on various medical topics.

Sister Ellen Savage worked on Regimental Aid Post duties that day, assisting Dr Thelander. An uninterrupted stream of men turning up for treatment — mostly with minor complaints — kept the pair busy. But whatever they were doing when the alarms went, like everyone else they had to down tools, grab their lifejackets, and head quickly for their lifeboat stations. After being dismissed from the fourth — and as it turned out the last — drill for the day, Sister Savage, who still had a backlog of patients to attend to, raced to the promenade deck cabin that she shared with Sister Merle Moston and more or less tossed her lifejacket into the room, rather than carefully stowing it above the wardrobe as she usually did. It landed next to her bunk. Paradoxically, that singular act of impatience might just have saved her life[15].

Around 1600, as the *Centaur* neared the latitude of the coastal city of Coffs Harbour, Lt-Col Outridge and Lt Johnson (the medical staff quartermaster) took a break and went on deck for a chat. The *Centaur* pitched gently as her bow cut into a shallow swell from the north. The afternoon was fine with clear visibility; a comfortable 24 °C. Outridge stood with his back to the sea, leaning against the port side rail. Johnson faced him, the fresh northwesterly breeze blowing in his face. They began comparing rumours they had each heard about possible Japanese revenge attacks. Suddenly Johnson drew back slightly. He peered out to sea, trying to focus on something in the distance. 'That's a submarine!' he exclaimed, extending his arm and pointing.

Outridge spun around. He saw an object about five miles away. It had what looked like a conning tower. It punched down into the sea, then reappeared. There was spray. He saw what he thought might be a periscope. Whatever this object was, it seemed to be moving south[16].

Second Mate Rippon had also seen it from the bridge[17]. He dismissed it as American. In hindsight, it is interesting to speculate about this. If it were an Allied submarine, surely its

commander or OOW would have signalled to this passing ship
— as had the *Greenling* — if only to allay any fears? A Japanese,
one might think, would hardly deliberately expose itself to an
enemy vessel (although consider the incident off Sandy Cape with
the John Burke ship).

Outridge, unlike Rippon, adopted a more ominous conclusion.
Instinctively he wheeled around and quickly scanned all the
Centaur's markings to make sure they gave a clear visual message
of her status as a hospital ship, a non-combatant. He noted with
satisfaction that they were all very plain and unambiguously
prominent. Again in hindsight, Outridge's concern had some
merit. It if *was* a submarine they had seen, it was most likely
Captain Toshio Kusaka's *I-180*, heading south after his attack
on the *Caradale* and the *Ormiston* the day before.

An hour or so after that sighting, as the sun set and dusk took
hold, Captain Murray and Jock Salt were conferring on the bridge
when a radio officer came up and handed Murray a message. He
read it and passed it to Salt. It warned of a submarine in the area
and gave details of the attack on the *Ormiston*. Salt plotted the
position given. It was NNW of their current position and about
20 miles inshore, near the Solitaries, a cluster of rocky islets not
far from Coffs Harbour. Salt asked Murray if they should change
the course. Murray replied, 'It won't affect us. We are immune
from any attack by submarine.' Nevertheless, he issued pre-
cautionary orders to the lookouts to be particularly vigilant. He
also went around the ship himself to check that all the mandatory
lights were on and shining brightly[18].

Indeed they were. By coincidence, at about that time, the aircrew of an Avro Anson heading back to Coffs Harbour from
convoy escort duties spotted the *Centaur.* The sighting drew
particular comment. A ship so brightly lit was a rarity in wartime[19].

Darkness fell, and the seemingly festooned *Centaur* took on
all the appearances of a floating fun-fair. The overside floodlights
and the row of green lights encircling the ship at deck level
illuminated its white hull, green band and red crosses. Deck
floodlights bathed its white superstructure in light. On the funnel,
cross-shaped red neon striplights took over from the painted
symbols visible during the day. As Outridge later succinctly commented, AHS *Centaur* was 'lit up to glory'[20].

For the merchant and medical officers at least, that second
evening at sea turned out to be one of celebration; a surprise

birthday party for Matron Jewell. Her staff had clubbed together in Sydney to buy a cake. The *Centaur*'s cooks iced it. Also in a celebrating mood was Radio Operator Eric Summers, who had just learned by wireless of the birth of his first child, a son. The party went off magnificently, but coming as it did immediately after the already hectic eating arrangements, it took its toll on the catering staff. Steward Ron Moate later recalled that he worked himself off his feet that night.

The sisters and doctors were not the only ones enjoying themselves. On deck, down aft, some 2/12th and medical staff men gathered to savour the sweetness of evening and the bright, moonlit, star-bedecked sky. Musical instruments appeared, and someone started a sing-song, reviving several popular melodies. Soon a group of hearty lads were bellowing their lungs out, their vocal cords no doubt happily lubricated by the issue of beer. Before long, and inevitably, someone burst forth with a range of alternative bawdy lyrics, either well-known or made up on the spot. They got a rowdy and welcome reception, adding spice to the evening gaiety.

Less frivolous activities were in progress in other parts of the ship. In the lounge some officers began a game of bridge. Medical staff orderly Tom Hobden joined in. L-Cpl Spud Jones and one of the 2/12th surgeons locked horns over a chess-board.

By this time the thought of an early night had germinated in many minds. Staff Orderly Tich Isherwood probably led the charge. Very tired, he went to bed at 2030. He slept soundly. L-Cpl Ken Murray (2/12th) had the same idea and chose an early night. Medical staffer Pte Jack Argent went off at 2130. So did the two Bayley brothers (2/12th), whose bunks were near each other[21].

Cpl Albert Blair (medical staff) went to bed at his normal time of 2200. His quarters were aft, two decks below the main deck and on the port side. His alcove accommodated 22 of the ship's medical staff in double bunks arranged in two rows. He had a top bunk[22].

When the game of bridge in the lounge ended, about 2200, the party broke up. Tom Hobden made his way forward, away from the noise at the stern, for a smoke and a few minutes peace and solitude before turning in. He found a good spot by the port side rail near the bow, opposite the forward companionway. As he stood there one of the ship's officers on his watch inspection passed by. Hobden greeted him. 'Evening, sir. Looks like it'll be another nice quiet night.'

'This ship will be torpedoed tonight,' replied the officer, cryptically.

Hobden was startled. 'How's that, sir?'

The officer smiled. 'Well, it's the thirteenth and there's a full moon,' he teased. 'Are you superstitious, Private?'

'No, not me,' replied Hobden, adding facetiously, 'No need for me to worry. I was born with a caul on my face!'

The officer laughed and went his way. Hobden turned his attention back to the sea and finished his smoke. He flicked the spent butt into the frothing bow wave and decided to call it a night. He made his way down the companionway to the lower deck, to the quarters he shared with 16 other men. He noticed that two of his mates, dental assistant Fred Chidgey and orderly Tom Hegarty, were already asleep. Hobden passed them to get to his bunk on the other side of the room[23].

Spud Jones emerged the chess victor in his game with the doctor. His vanquished foe booked him for a return match the next night. Jones went down to his bunk, wrote a letter to his wife, then read a detective story for a couple of hours before putting out the light.

Down aft the 'concert party' began to wind down. Orderly Vince McCosker (medical staff), an active participant in the sing-song, felt a shiver run through his body as a cool breeze sprang up. He decided to go below. Maybe there'd be a card game to join in or watch; if not he'd just turn in. McCosker passed the steering gear house and went down the companionway through No. 4 hatch, descending two decks to the same 22-man cubicle that Cpl Blair occupied. He went to bed[24].

Captain Salt paid a last visit to the bridge before turning in. He scanned the southwestern horizon with his binoculars for Cape Byron light. He couldn't see it; not even the loom. He stayed for a while chatting to 3rd Mate Monty Banks, then left him to it. Luckily the ship would hold the same course all night, so Jock could enjoy the rare luxury of a full night's sleep. He retired about 2200, and fell asleep about an hour later[25].

Sister Ellen Savage also went to bed at 2200. Although dark outside, the nearby floodlights shone in through the window ˄d lit up the cabin[26].

˄M Jim Johnston came off duty at 2200. He handed over to ˄ief and went straight to the two berth cabin on the poop that he shared with RQMS L.Williams. Within 15 minutes of coming off duty he had hit the sack. He read for about 45 minutes, then put out the light[27].

This was the scene, the common thread of activity as the night drew on and the ship began to settle. On deck only the engine's familiar pop-popping — so distinctive to the *Centaur* — and the whoosh of the sea rushing down the ship's side, could be heard. Below decks, apart from the creaking noises of a ship working gently in a seaway, and the occasional coughs and murmurings of men asleep, all was quiet.

In some parts of every ship at sea, however, sharp eyes and busy hands maintain an uninterrupted, active and alert presence. On the bridge, 3rd Mate Monty Banks kept a watchful eye on the *Centaur*'s progress, making sure she followed the track laid down on the chart. Not far away, in the radio room on the boat deck, 3rd Radio Operator Bob Laird listened intently through big black headphones for incoming messages and warnings. All he could do was listen; wartime conditions strictly enforced radio silence. Operators made transmissions only under special instructions or in the most serious circumstances. Down in the bowels of the ship, in the hot, noisy engine room, 4th Engineer Maurice Cairnie and two greasers, McIntosh and Grainger, had the watch, keeping the big pistons threshing away. Cairnie spent some time during that watch checking the welds on the repaired supercharger, something that had concerned the engineers for the previous few days. Fortunately they were showing no signs of stress or fatigue[28]. During a spare few minutes he managed to fix a watch that Sister Ellen Rutherford had asked him to repair. He was happy to help; Sister Rutherford had a wonderful personality and was always doing things for other people.

At midnight the watch changed. Gordon Rippon appeared on the bridge to take over from Monty Banks. Automatically, as part of the changeover procedure, Rippon checked the log book. He found everything in order. AHS *Centaur* was now in Queensland waters, 27 miles due east of the Gold Coast town of Surfers Paradise.

Third Engineer George Alexander took over from Maurice Cairnie in the engine room. Two fresh greasers, the close pals Mattie Morris and Walter Tierney, relieved McIntosh and Grainger. Cairnie left them all to it. Before quitting the engine room he routinely checked the degaussing gear. He then climbed the steel-runged engine-room ladder to the shelter deck and went aft to check the steering gear; his last duty inspection. The decks, as always, glowed in bright light like a city's main street. This was something totally alien to the merchant crew; merchant ships at sea are invariably blacked out in the dark hours, especially in wartime. Leaving the steering gear house Cairnie ascended the external stairs to his boat deck cabin. He put Sister Rutherford's watch on his table, took a quick wash, and went to bed.

Gordon Rippon meanwhile, had said goodnight to the departing Monty Banks and was taking stock of the ship's progress. He went out to the bridge wing to see what shore lights he had to work with. He noticed how very pleasant the night was. So clear. The stars put on a magnificent display across an almost cloudless sky. Low in the west a still bright half-moon reached down for the horizon. Within two hours it would be gone. The wind had backed since the afternoon, and now blew from the southwest. A low, wind-generated swell surged languidly eastwards. The *Centaur* swayed lethargically from side to side; no more than a degree or so, not enough to disturb the sleepers below.

Rippon's three watch ABs were David Milligan, Ivan Cecich and Alf Ramage. They took their duties — steering, keeping a focsle head lookout at the bow, and 'doing rounds' — in turns, one hour about. When on lookout they kept their eyes peeled and reported anything they saw to the bridge by ringing the focsle head bell; one peal for an object to starboard, two for port, and three for right ahead. On 'rounds' they inspected the ship from bow to stern, visiting all decks and probing every accessible area to make sure there were no fires. They also checked the entire network of deck lighting. Occasionally bulbs here and there would need replacing. For some reason the lights along the top rail of the shelter deck aft, and those between the promenade and boat becks, blew more often than the others.

* * * * *

About 60 miles WNW of the *Centaur* in those early hours, at 23 Radar Fort Lytton, on the south side of the Brisbane River mouth, a young Air Force radar operator named Mabel Hess sat with two others peering into dim radar screens. Their job was to check for aircraft approaching the Brisbane region. About 0130, not long after Mabel began her shift, a blip came up on her screen; a target east of Moreton Island. It puzzled her. Most targets she tracked came in from near the edge of the radar screen; this one appeared instantly where it was.

'I have a contact,' she reported with some hesitancy to her two colleagues. 'But you'd better see this one for yourselves because I don't know where it came from. It just appeared out of nowhere.'

The girls leaned across and peered over her shoulder, intrigued. What could this object be? It was moving far too slowly to be an aircraft. They asked the duty mechanic to check the equipment for a malfunction. He could find nothing wrong. The trio could only conclude that their strange target must be a ship. They converted its range and bearing into equivalent grid coordinates and made a 'surface vessel plot' report to No. 8 Fighter Sector in Brisbane. Fighter Sector replied rather testily that their job was to watch out for air traffic, not surface contacts. By this time, Mabel Hess had begun to doubt that her target was a ship. It had moved only fractionally on her scope. Then abruptly, and as quickly as it had first appeared, it vanished. Gone. Not tracking outwards until out of range as an aircraft or ship contact would, but instantly.

'Only a submarine could do that,' Hess remarked. She was tempted to make another report to Fighter Sector but given the previous petulant response, and as her mysterious contact had now disappeared, she decided against it[29].

* * * * *

Back on the *Centaur* at that time, Staff Sergeant George Carter was very annoyed. The orderly officer had disturbed a most pleasant sleep. Four 2/12th men had broached the bonded stores. They had got stuck into the beer and were legless. The *Centaur* had no jail as such so Carter opened the restraining rooms for mental patients on the after part of Ward F on the lower tween deck. The offenders were summarily bundled inside to sober up[30].

About this time, Pte Percy Kelly, two decks down, had a vivid dream. He dreamt he was with his mother. She turned to him and said, 'You will be alright'. He woke up, worried, because he rarely had dreams, and lay awake for a while before falling asleep again. Then the dream came back. This time his mother called to him again, only louder. The same words: 'You will be alright'. Kelly woke with a start and instinctively swung himself

upright. He looked at his mates around him, all sleeping peacefully. He was tempted to wake them, but knew what sort of
reception he would get[31].

On the bridge, 2nd Mate Rippon's latest fix put the *Centaur*
about 27 miles due east of Porpoise Point on the southern tip
of Stradbroke Island. He updated the position every half an hour
by 'running fix', the method used when navigators have only
one reference point to work on. Before long, hopefully, he would
pick up Point Lookout light and then the loom of Cape Moreton
light on the northern tip of Moreton Island. The two lights would
give him more accurate cross-bearing fixes.

At 0330 Point Lookout light bore due west, distance 23 miles.
Rippon plotted the position on the chart. Working back from
the last beam bearing, he calculated the ship's speed to be almost
11 knots. He took the dividers and from the 0330 fix stepped
off dead reckoning[c] positions for 0400, 0430 and so on, every
half-hour through the four-to-eight watch. He then picked off
the latitude and longitude of these positions and wrote them on
a special chit. This was for the duty radio operator. It gave the
'Sparks' a reasonably current position to transmit in a hurry if
the ship were attacked or struck a mine . Rippon tucked the chit
in his pocket, ready to drop off at the radio room when he
finished his watch.

At 'one bell'[d] the four-to-eight watchkeepers were called.
They had a quarter of an hour to stretch, dress, pay a visit and
maybe catch a quick mug of tea before heading off to their watch
station.

Harry Lamble came up to the bridge a few minutes before
0400. Second Engineer Bill Cuthill made his way below to take
over the engine room from George Alexander. The age-old
routine change-of-watch process was in train once again.

ABs Milligan and Ramage, and greasers Morris and Tierney,
wasted little time handing over the watch to their reliefs. Their
work behind them, they headed quickly for the messroom for
a 'cuppa' before turning in[32].

Also on the move around the ship at that time however, was
someone who need not have been: Pte Albert Taylor, a dental

---

c. Estimated, derived from the logged speed of the ship, likely effects of winds and
   current, etc.
d. Traditionally, 15 minutes before the change of each watch. The time when the next
   watchkeepers are called.

technician with the 2/12th. Shortly before 0400 Taylor awoke to that message nature so often cruelly transmits in the early hours. He conceded the contest, got up, and sleepily ambled aft to the nearest heads. He didn't need to switch on the light; the glow from outside lit up the washroom enough for what he had to do. Afterwards, as so often happens, he found himself wide awake. He decided to take a stroll on deck.

Eight bells sounded at 0400. The ringing woke Pte Tom Hegarty. He rolled over and wondered what time it was. He drifted in and out of sleep. The bells also woke Tich Isherwood, but he soon went back to sleep. At this time the two butchers, Frank Reid and Frank Davidson, got their wakeup call. Nature also woke driver George McGrath. He answered the call, but unlike Taylor went straight back to bed.

Albert Taylor ambled down the starboard side of the deck to the stern. The spinning wheel of the taffrail log caught his eye. Out of interest he peered down at the dials on the circular brass face to see how far the ship had travelled since leaving Sydney. In the dim light he figured it showed about 500 miles. He walked around the stern to the port side to see if he could make out the land. He saw two shore flashing lights, one, quite dim, abreast of the ship, the other, brighter, farther to the north[e]. He leaned against the rail and stared out over the sea. The *Centaur*'s lights shone a fair distance outward onto the surface. They had attracted a school of porpoises[33].

Gordon Rippon left the bridge in Lamble's care. On his way to his cabin on the port side of the boat deck, he made a visual check of the illumination. All was as it should be, except for the two lights over the forward red crosses. They were usually left off because their glare blinded the watchkeepers on the bridge. Passing the radio room, he popped his head in with a greeting and handed Eric Summers the position slips. Then it was time for bed[34].

ABs David Milligan, Alf Ramage and Ivan Cecich, sat in the messroom and chatted over a cup of coffee. In the greaser's mess Mattie Morris and Bob Tierney did the same.

In the engine room big Bill Cuthill made a cursory inspection of the machinery. Then, as was his custom, he settled himself on a seat near the tunnel door with a cup of coffee.

---

e. Point Lookout and Cape Moreton lights. During the war years they were often dimmed under naval orders, and sometimes extinguished altogether.

On deck Albert Taylor could plainly see the porpoises cavorting in the water. He stood watching, captivated by their antics. A flash of white caught Taylor's eye, out beyond the porpoises, perhaps 200 metres away. It moved towards the ship, heading towards the bow. He thought it was a porpoise. Then he saw another one. This one seemed to be heading towards the foredeck area.

Chapter Seven

THREE MINUTES OF HORROR

14th May 1943: 0410 to 0413

Rous Battery, on the eastern shore of Moreton Island, was in mid-May 1943 still under construction. The men of 'O' Australian Heavy Battery (AIF) under Major R. Fullford[a] were laying concrete foundations for a gun and a searchlight due to arrive in June. Fullford had built a temporary campsite and established protective picquets at the battery position, about 20 kilometres south of Cape Moreton lighthouse. Early in the morning of the 14th May, the battery orderly officer, Lt Russell Ward, and his orderly sergeant, Dermot Riley, did the rounds of the picquets. At one of them they stopped briefly for a chat with Sapper Rudi Glass. Suddenly the eyes of all three men were drawn seaward, to a burst of bright light on the horizon. It erupted into a great fiery orange ball over an arc of about ten degrees. The spectacular display lasted but a few seconds before it subsided and soon disappeared entirely.

Lt Ward raced to the campsite about 400 metres away and woke Major Fullford. He told him he had seen a ship on fire at sea and asked what should be done about it. Fullford was sceptical. He knew that Ward was a field artillery officer with no coastal experience. Fullford had been with coastal artillery since 1939 and had heard several ship-on-fire-at-sea reports. 'It's the moon rising,' he told Lt Ward sleepily. 'Go back to bed.'

Ward, who knew that what he had seen was not the moon, persisted. Eventually, Fullford gave in. 'Okay, call CDH and report it.'

Getting through to Combined Defence Headquarters in Brisbane could be a problem. Rous Battery had a tenuous and

---

a. Later Brigadier Fullford, OBE.

unreliable telephone contact. Fullford's signallers had made a single-wire connection to the main line running up the island to the Cape Moreton lighthouse. More often than not it didn't work. This morning, surprisingly, it did. Lt Ward's report read:

> Large all-round orange glare sighted 0400 hours 90 degrees from Rous Battery. Range unknown[1].

* * * * *

Undoubtedly, those three soldiers had seen the death strike on AHS *Centaur*. From that moment, and for the next three horrific minutes of time, the effects of a well-aimed submarine projectile brutally terminated the very existence of a non-combatant merchant ship, an unsuspecting victim with but a singular role of bringing succour and comfort to the casualties of war. At 0410 AHS *Centaur* was a proud, fine and well-found vessel. Most of the 332 people on board slumbered peacefully in presumed safety. By 0413, three minutes later, she had disappeared off the face of the earth; gone, destroyed; a shattered, fiery hulk plunging downwards through an unforgiving sea to a grave a thousand fathoms deep. With her went most of those 332 lives, cruelly snuffed out. Many, mercifully, died instantly, without realising what had happened; many others did not, and many perished in unbelievably cruel and agonising circumstances.

What had happened? How could one torpedo, however well-aimed, cause such devastation? What made the *Centaur* sink in such a short space of time — not longer than the time needed to boil an egg? Now, half a century on, perhaps not even an examination of the wreckage would give a definitive answer. Fortunately, survivors' comments about those three dramatic minutes do allow us to piece together an informed and reasonably accurate description of the *Centaur*'s cruel demise[2].

One thing is beyond dispute. The torpedo struck the ship on the port side, just forward of the bridge, most likely between the 98th and 110th frame.

Unfortunately for the *Centaur* this torpedo, unlike so many supplied to Japanese submarines at that time, did what it was supposed to do — it worked. When it struck the steel hull and drove back the firing pin, its detonator functioned perfectly. The lethal warhead exploded, and blew a hole in the hull possibly eight to ten metres in diameter, from well below the waterline to the top of the green band. Speared in her side, the *Centaur* lurched to port. The blast penetrated the engine room, the upper and lower tween decks (the ward decks), and the main oil bunker tanks. About ten seconds later — all the time it took for the heat of the blast to vaporise the diesel oil — the bunkers exploded. Ironically, had the torpedo struck as little as five metres or so farther forward, in the holds, AHS *Centaur* might possibly have survived or at least stayed afloat long enough to save many lives. With brutal bad luck, this Japanese missile had hit the bunker tanks, and there was no escaping its effects. This second, tremendous blast heaved the ship over to starboard. A sheet of flame burst like a fireball in all directions, sky-rocketing high into the air and into the ship itself. The *Centaur* was doomed.

Exploding oil immediately engulfed the engine room. Bill Cuthill — probably still seated near the tunnel door, cup of coffee in hand — and his watchkeepers were cooked or concussed to death in an instant. They never knew what hit them. The crippled diesel engine rocked off its mountings and began to disintegrate, spitting chunks of crumbling cylinders and pistons around the engine room. The propeller shaft stopped turning almost immediately, probably snapped off at its mounting on the after end of the engine. Her motive power gone, the *Centaur*'s forward motion slowed, although momentum would have carried her onwards until the moment she sank.

The hold forward of the engine room and the two hospital decks above it were engulfed by a shockwave. Immediately afterwards, a searing whoosh of fire roared unimpeded through the open decks like a blast from a flame thrower. A wind tunnel effect sucked the lethal blaze into every nook and cranny, with devastating results. Those men not killed instantly by the concussion wave of the first blast were incinerated moments later. In seconds the wards were an inferno of burning mattresses. If any men on the lower hospital deck were lucky enough to survive both the shockwave and fireball, with tragic irony they suddenly faced death by a totally different means — drowning. For immediately following the second explosion, sea water thundered in unimpeded through the gaping wound in the *Centaur*'s side, straight into the hold and Ward F. The flooding that would soon overcome the ship had begun.

On deck the sky rained burning globules of diesel oil and other debris. Where they landed they mostly found wood, more oil or other inflammable material to ignite. Individual fires sprang up all over the decks.

The after end of the foredeck and forward part of the accommodation block suffered badly from the initial upward blast of flame. No. 2 hatch caught fire. So did the port side of the accommodation and the bridge. Its wooden structure fueled the flames. The blast dislodged the wheelhouse. The bridge collapsed. Soon smoke and fire belched out of the accommodation, the central galley, and the funnel. The explosions had seriously damaged two of the four main lifeboats.

Within a minute of the initial strike the sea had taken a steadfast grip on the *Centaur* as seawater flooded into the forward hold and the lower tween deck. She was already down by the head. Her reserve buoyancy evaporated rapidly, yielding inexorably to the enveloping ocean. As she nosed downwards unsecured ironstone ballast and equipment loosened by the blast obeyed gravity and slid towards the bow. The ship's longitudinal centre of gravity moved forward and intensified the capsizing force. After a minute or so she may have stabilised, the demanding sea held temporarily at bay by the main deck's watertight integrity, but not for long. The sea would not be denied. The *Centaur*'s equilibrium worsened second by second; the capsizing moment gathered force and soon overcame all reserve buoyancy. Her bow dipped deep into the ocean. Her stern lifted high in the air, raising the propeller out of the water. At the end she hung there, just for a little while as if delaying her departure for a final farewell, and then she heeled over to starboard and speared down into the depths.

The human tragedy that accompanied those two to three brief minutes of horror is almost unimaginable. We know enough from contemporary interviews with survivors to take a guess at the unbridled terror and agony meted out to so many who never made it. Those who died instantly were the lucky ones.

The sea not only took the *Centaur*, it took hundreds of examples of human courage, agonising death, despair, perhaps cowardice, and numberless futile battles for survival. The best stories of the *Centaur* will be those that can never be told.

The accounts that we do have, however, give a good insight into what it must have been like during those death throes.

On deck, near the stern on the port side, Cpl Albert Taylor had a grandstand view of the onrushing torpedo. He thought it was an innocuous porpoise. His illusion was shattered in an instant when the advancing stream of white converted itself into a massive explosion, followed seconds later by another. Suddenly oil rained from the sky, coating him. He looked up in time to see the bridge collapse in flames. Wood splinters flew through the air, then droplets of burning oil. The deck lights went out, but the fire amidships illuminated the whole scene in a frightful, eerie light.

A group of ship's medical staff lived right forward on the upper and lower hospital decks. Staff-Sgt George Carter had not long been back to bed after organising the cells for the four light-fingered drunks. The initial blast threw him out of his top bunk to the deck. He stood up, shocked, and was immediately thrown off his feet again by the second explosion. He grabbed his lifebelt and raced up the stairs to the deck.

A few bunks away, Cpl Tom Malcolm amazingly slept through the blast. Someone woke him and he reached up to switch on the bunk light. It didn't work and he wondered why. From his bunk he could see the underside of No. 1 hatch. One corner was ablaze. He leapt out of bed and almost landed on top of Staff-Sgt Dick Medcalf getting out of the bunk below. They exchanged a few words as they reached for their lifejackets. Malcolm tried to wake a man seemingly still asleep in a nearby bunk. He could not. The lights were off but he could see well enough by the light of the flames. He saw mattresses on fire. On his way to the stairway he bumped into L-Cpl Lebrun. It was the last time he saw him.

Pte Tich Isherwood had just drifted off to sleep after a restless night when the torpedo struck. He woke to the explosion. Almost immediately blazing oil dropped on him from the burning hatch above. Startled, he vaulted out of his bunk. He hit the deck so heavily he fractured his arm. With his good hand he grabbed his lifejacket and raced for the companionway.

Privates Fred Chidgey and Tom Hegarty were both woken sharply by the explosion and jumped quickly out of their bunks. Even in that initial darkness they knew where their lifejackets were and how to get to the companionway. They wasted no time heading for the deck, but paused briefly at the entrance to the upper hospital. They could see nothing but a wall of flame. All they could hear were the piercing screams of burning victims. There was nothing they could do to help.

107

Tom Hobden followed closely on the heels of Chidgey and Hegarty. Already, sea water gushed down the companionway and Hobden had to fight his way up through the flood.

Pte Percy Kelly had little time to dwell on his mother's supernatural assurances about his safety. He had to endure the frustrated anguish of failing in a brave attempt to save a colleague's life. Kelly woke to the initial crash to find both flames and water belching down the stairway. He could see other men already out of their bunks, streaming towards the companionways to fight their way up through the deluge. One young man stumbled and slipped over the edge of a hatchway. Kelly leapt out of bed and grabbed hold of him, but lacked the strength to lift him out. Kelly called out to two nearby men to help. They came forward, but had to pass a ladder to get to Kelly and could not resist the temptation to flee up it. Kelly struggled frantically and almost had the man out when burning debris fell down on them both. The unfortunate man slipped through Kelly's fingers[b]. Kelly could do no more. He raced back to his bunk for his lifejacket and dashed for the stairway. Half way up a torrent of water swamped him, knocking him back. He managed to hold on to a step and as soon as the wave passed he ran up to the upper tween deck. The same thing happened on the next ladder but he finally made it to the foredeck[3].

Amidships, both the upper and lower tween decks, where the bulk of the Field Ambulance men had been sleeping in rows of double-decker cots, were in utter devastation. Those who survived the initial blast and barrage of fire ran around in panic, in frantic search of a safe exit. Desperate men clogged stairwells, which were already running with burning oil. Bottlenecks formed. They thickened by the second and were soon totally blocked.

Lt-Col Leslie Outridge was wrenched awake by the explosions. His bunk was on the starboard side amidships in the upper hospital deck. The wall of his cabin and his lifejacket had caught fire, and the whole interior outline of the ward glowed in flames. He raced for the companionway at No. 2 hatch, but a tongue of flame roared down the stairway and drove him back. He would have to find another way out. Around him were men still in their bunks. He shook seven or eight of them, but only two

---

b. Kelly did not name the man, but mentioned his nickname was Mac and he had been married only seven weeks. It was probably Pte N. McLean.

showed any signs of life. Already the deck was awash as sea water flooded up from below. Outridge headed back towards the companionway but the onrush of water quickly filled the compartment and lifted him off his feet. He banged his head on the deck above, and for a while found himself trapped in a tiny pocket of air between two beams. Somehow he managed to work his way across to the stairway and staggered up to the deck.

From the port side only one man survived. Driver George McGrath had not got back to sleep after visiting the heads when the torpedo struck. The blast blew him not only out of his bunk but out of the alcove he shared with eight others. He landed in the passageway. Blood ran from his nose. Something warned him not to go back to his bunk for his lifejacket, but to head aft. He raced through the main ward to the after stairway to the deck. On the way he passed Major Thelander. 'Don't panic, Mac,' said the Major calmly.

Sgt Bill Cornell was blown out of his bunk and landed on the deck next to Pte Charlie Lambert. A hot steampipe above them fractured off its mounting and fell, pinning the pair to the deck. Cornell tried to lift it off, badly burning his hands in the process. The sea thundered in around the two men. Cornell managed to squeeze clear, and began to help Lambert. He couldn't free his friend. Lambert said, 'You go, mate . . . I won't make it.' Then the sea enveloped them and the surging water picked Cornell up and swept him out through the hole in the ship's side into the sea.

Pte Allan Pettiford woke to find himself on his feet, standing next to his lower level bunk. How he had got there mystified him. He woke to a ward in utter confusion but surprisingly little panic. His little pocket of bunks on the upper tween deck had somehow missed the worst of the blast, although when he tried to rouse his friend Jack Lynagh, in the upper bunk, he failed. The shock wave must have killed him. He saw other men nearby, already out of their bunks. The interminable boat drills they had been through since leaving Sydney paid dividends at that moment as each man reached without thinking for his lifejacket. They heard Major Thelander's calm voice nearby. 'Now lads,' he said, almost as if he were mustering a detail, 'don't panic. Just go to your boat stations.' Dressed in only a singlet and underpants — as were most men — Pettiford made for the after companionway, tying on his lifejacket as he went. On the way up he passed a major[c]. He made it to his boat station on the boat deck, where he found men struggling to clear the boats.

That supreme pessimist Pte Ron 'Spud' Jones woke in pitch-blackness and immediately assumed the worst. Instinctively he reached up for his lifejacket. If he was glad of anything at that moment it was that he had had the presence of mind to hang it immediately above his head. He yelled out to his mates: 'We're going down! Get on deck!' Surprisingly, no-one answered him. He assumed they had already gone. From his practised evacuations he also knew exactly which way to run. Hugging his lifejacket he groped his way towards the ladder. Fire chased him as he neared it and set his pyjamas alight. He ran up the ladder in fright to the deck.

Ambulance driver Allan Dickson awoke to find himself standing beside his cot. Oil covered everything around him. The ward had become an inferno; bunks blazed furiously, incinerating many occupants where they lay. He tried to stand. He was facing aft and found it strange. He seemed to be leaning forward. He raced through the conflagration to the nearest stairs.

Pte Rupert Paton woke up wondering why he was suddenly in the companionway, and why water sloshed all over the deck. Panic threatened to grip him, but he overcame it and ran up the stairs to the deck. Pte Vince McCosker, whose bunk was near Paton's, got blown out of bed as well. He followed Paton up the stairs.

Farther aft on that lower deck, on the port side, in the 22-man space occupied by medical staff, Cpl Albert Blair woke to a deafening explosion. It sounded to him like a bomb detonating or a huge gun going off nearby. He lurched out of bed just as the second explosion rocked the ship to starboard, and almost lost his footing. He grabbed what he thought was his lifejacket and ran.

Nearby, Pte Leo Bidmead had a rude awakening indeed. He found himself flying through the air across the room. An unpleasant jolt followed when he hit the starboard bulkhead and crashed to the deck. Dazed, he crawled around in the dark, fumbling for his lifejacket. He never found it. He gave up and made for the stairs. He managed to grasp the stair handrail, then lost it when a blast of flame burst down the companionway. He

---

c. Probably Geoff Cooley.

recognised Pte Cliff Jones alongside him. When the tongue of fire receded, the pair raced up the two flights of stairs to the deck.

In the crew's messroom aft ABs Dave Milligan and Alf Ramage were still enjoying their post-watch cuppa with Ivan Cecich. Milligan had the coffee pot in his hand, topping up the mugs, when the blast came. He dropped the pot. Ramage started, inadvertently splashing coffee over his face and shirt. He swore. The lights went out, leaving them in total darkness. They realised in an instant what had happened. They fumbled for their life-jackets, yelling out to the other seamen as they did so. Some had been thrown out of their bunks by the blast.

One was Ordinary Seaman Bob Westwood, the youngest person on board. He seized his lifejacket and followed his mates on their dash to their lifeboat stations. Halfway up the stairs the ship lurched ominously. Westwood stumbled. As the group scampered up the stairs Milligan did his best to curb any hysteria before it took hold. 'Now don't panic!' Ramage heard him call out, 'Just take things calmly!'

In the greaser's mess Mattie Morris and Bob Tierney had finished their cuppa and were ready for bed when Charlie 'Nobby' Clark came into the room. Morris suggested he join them in a drink. The blast interrupted his answer. All three men raced for the deck.

Two other greasers, Bill McIntosh and Bobby Grainger, were woken by the blast. McIntosh leapt out of bed. He shouted to Grainger. 'Let's go up and see what's happened.' Still in their pyjamas the pair raced up to the deck.

In the shelter deck accommodation amidships, nightwatchman Frank Drust was in the pantry making a cup of tea for the 3rd Engineer when the torpedo struck. The ship rocked to the explosion and Drust watched in horror as the pantry floor began to cave in beneath his feet. He realised in an instant what had happened. 'Oh no!' he thought, 'not again!' He had been torpedoed twice before, as a young lad in the 1914-18 Great War. He rushed out on deck.

Farther aft on that deck, Frank Davidson and Frank Reid, the two butchers, were finding it hard to get out of bed that morning. At 0410 both had managed to sling their legs over the side of their bunks and haul themselves upright. They sat there for a few moments, taking their time to confront the new day. With a sigh, Davidson leaned forward to stand up — and was blown

111

out of his bunk by the blast. Amazingly he landed on his feet. Reid stayed were he was on the edge of his bunk, but in horror saw a great flame shoot past his porthole. Both men raced on deck and went straight to their boat stations. On the way, they met Frank Gannon, the scullion.

Above them, on the promenade deck, confusion reigned. Sister Ellen Savage woke with a start. Her lifejacket lay on the deck near her bunk, where she had hurriedly tossed it the previous afternoon. This saved her valuable time in a predicament where seconds were crucial (and for many on the *Centaur* undoubtedly tilted the scales of fate). She threw it on over her silk pyjamas. She reached for her rosary beads on the bedside table. She later described those moments in observant detail:

> . . . my cabin mate, Merle Moston, and myself were awakened by two terrific explosions and practically thrown out of bed. In that instant the ship was in flames. Sister Moston and I were so shocked we did not even speak, but I registered mentally that it was a torpedo explosion. The next thing Sister King, a very great friend, who was in the next cabin, screamed near my door 'Savage, out on deck!' As we ran together we tied our life-jackets in place. We were so disciplined that we were making for our lifeboat stations when on deck we ran into Colonel Manson, our commanding officer, in full dress even to his cap and 'Mae West' life-jacket[4]
> . . .

In his port side cabin, close to the lounge, Captain Jock Salt woke to a loud crash beneath his room. He jumped out of bed and fumbled for his clock. It had fallen under the table. The hands told him it was 0410. He rushed out of his room, got a shock to see flames belching out of the nearby galley, and set off instinctively for the internal stairs to the bridge. Flames beat him back. He ran back to his room. He pulled the blanket from his bunk and plunged it into a bucket of water near his sink. He slung it around his upper body and dashed out into the blazing alleyway. Sea water was already flooding up from below. He bolted along the alley towards the door at the after end. The onrushing water followed him. He made it to the deck. His face and hands were badly burned.

2nd Mate Gordon Rippon took only five minutes or so to make the mandatory inspection rounds of the deck before entering his boat deck cabin. He thankfully undressed, more than ready for a welcome sleep. Down to his cotton shorts he climbed into his bunk and switched off the light. At that precise moment, as he pulled up the sheet and fell back into the exquisite luxury of cosy bedclothes, he heard and felt the first explosion. As he later wrote to his father:

> Then there was the most almighty crash and I was picking myself up from the floor. I got up and looked out of the door of my room which was near the bridge on the boat deck and saw a sight I will never forget, and which has since been flashing through my mind hundreds of times. The ship was way down by the head. All the forepart was one vast sheet of flames, and it was raining drops of burning oil. At first I thought I was cut off but I grabbed my life jacket and dashed outside[5].

Chief Engineer Ernie Smith was sleeping deeply in his cabin farther aft on the boat deck when what he later described as a 'thud, immediately followed by an explosion' woke him. He jumped out of his bed like a shot. Leaving his cabin he banged on 4th Engineer Maurice Cairnie's door, bellowing at him to get a move on. Cairnie needed no second bidding. He came out of his cabin shrugging on a jacket over his underclothes and carrying his lifejacket and a torch. Smith tried to open the door leading to the deck. It was jammed. It took the two of them heaving with their shoulders to open it. They rushed out on deck.

AHS *Centaur*, mortally wounded, rapidly neared her demise. Fire ravaged her upperworks; a merciless sea claimed her from below. Nothing could save her now. Her burning decks bustled with humanity; oil-covered figures thankful they had escaped the twin nightmares of inferno and flood but aware that perhaps even more traumatic ordeals lay ahead. They sought salvation by whatever means available.

Once again, survivors' recollections give us an insight into the horror of the moment as they paint a picture of a crippled, disintegrating ship in its death throes.

Among the first to reach the deck were the two butchers, Davidson and Reid. They went straight to the port side and looked over. They saw a gaping hole, with flames shooting out of it. Davidson noted that the jagged edges of the hole were pointing outwards, confirming that the last explosion had taken place inside the ship. He saw one of the sisters standing nearby, obviously stunned and confused. He helped her put on her lifejacket and told her to jump. She did. Meanwhile Reid raced back to his cabin to get his lifejacket. On the way he made a gruesome discovery. The body of John Buck, a barman-cum-storekeeper, lay across the companionway. Buck's body had been split down the middle.

113

Up forward, Carter, Malcolm, Chidgey and Hegarty reached the deck virtually together, and within half a minute of the torpedo strike. Sgt Len Hooper was already there. Kelly soon followed. The bow was already under water; the focsle deck awash. They stood knee deep in a rising flood. They looked aft. The entire port side of the accommodation block burned furiously. The fire spread aft as far as they could see. They had no chance of reaching the boat deck. There were some rafts on the foredeck but those near the bridge were already on fire. Chidgey, Carter and Hegarty decided to abandon ship. They dived over the side. Chidgey later said they 'began to swim as fast as Johnny Weismuller had ever swum!' Those left behind heard a voice yelling from the region of the bridge (probably Chief Officer Lamble's). 'Throw that raft over! Man that raft!' They tried to release a lashed raft nearby. They never had time. The *Centaur* listed slightly to starboard and dipped, and the sea overwhelmed them. They were lifted up off their feet and swept away.

Tom Hobden reached the deck soon after the first group. Emerging after his fight against the sea pouring down the stairwell, he found the foredeck awash. He saw his good friend Pte Ray Hutchison nearby. 'Don't worry, Tom,' said Hutchison, comfortingly, 'we're now in God's hands.' Almost as he said it the sea swirled up over the deck and the ship fell away from under them. Hobden later claimed that he did not desert the *Centaur*; the *Centaur* deserted him.

Caught in the swirl of surging water and the suction created by the vessel sinking beneath him, Hobden was bounced in every direction like a cork. He had no lifejacket and thought for sure he would die. He lost sight of Hutchison; he never saw him again. Hobden went under. 'I'm a goner, I'm a goner,' he kept saying to himself. Then he shot to the surface. He gasped for air. The sea pulled him down again, and this time he kept going — deeper and deeper.

By the time Lt-Col Outridge reached the open foredeck, only about ten metres of it remained above the water. He turned to run aft but stepped into a swirling wave that picked him up and washed him along the deck. He became entangled in a jumble of ropes but managed to break free. He floated off, although he had no lifejacket. A loose raft washed up right next to him. He clambered aboard. At that moment, with incredible good fortune as events were to prove, a complete medical kit surfaced alongside him. He grabbed it. Then a swell lifted his raft and pushed it away and clear of the ship.

Allan Pettiford remembers making it to his boat station on the boat deck. Under wartime rules the boats were swung outboard, ready for lowering. There were already too many men working at the falls and gripes so he hopped across into the boat. As he did so the sea swamped the boat deck. The boat broke free. Pettiford was the only occupant — and a very temporary one. He was catapulted out into the sea.

When Spud Jones reached the deck he could not contain his surprise that everything was so quiet. It took him a while to realise that he had been deafened by the two blasts. This explained why he had heard no responses from the men he spoke to earlier. He ripped off what remained of his smouldering pyjamas and slipped on the lifejacket. He took care to leave the back flaps untied, remembering with typical thoroughness being told to do this by the officers at drill instruction. It was so the back pillow of the lifejacket would keep his head out of the water. He tried to release a raft nearby, couldn't, and mentally cursed the efficient seamen who had lashed it to the deck. Then the ship sank, and took him with it.

Pte John Bayley and his brother reached the deck together. They tried to unlash a raft but felt the ship sinking beneath them and decided to jump for it. They jumped over the rail simultaneously. Only one surfaced. The first thoughts of another pair of brothers, the cooks Mark and Trevor Hoggins, whose cabins were at opposite ends of the ship, was for each other. They each raced along the deck calling out the other's name. Miraculously they met up and immediately dived into the sea together.

Albert Taylor, whose nature call had saved him at least from the inferno below, still stood on the after deck. When he watched his 'porpoise' spear into the ship's side, and then heard and felt the explosion, he stood rooted to the spot, mesmerised, staring with disbelief. Then he snapped out of his trance and ran along the port side towards the liferaft slung against the thick wire stays of the mainmast. By the time he got there he had been joined by Boatswain Brandin with Milligan, Ramage and some of the other merchant crew. Frantic hands worked to free the supposedly quick-release senhouse slip that held the raft in place.

115

Milligan took some men to launch the extra lifeboat slung on No. 4 hatch.

Gordon Rippon, dressed in cotton shorts and a lifejacket, was on deck within seconds of the initial explosions. He raced around the officers house to his lifeboat station, the No. 3 boat on the starboard side. He found it smashed and hanging vertically on the after falls. No. 1 boat was also useless. Rippon spun around and raced back to the port side. Amazingly No. 2 and No. 4 boats seemed intact, even though they had taken the full brunt of the blast. No. 2 lifeboat was tangled in its ropework, but Captain Murray and the stewards Ron Moate, Jack Stutter and Charlie Carey were doing their best to free it. Rippon went to No. 4 boat. Here he found the Chief Officer. Lamble had his face cupped in his hands. Rippon thought he had given up hope. 'Come on, Lamble!' he yelled out to encourage him. He didn't realise that Lamble had been on the port bridge wing at the moment of explosion and had suffered the full upward blast of fire. His face and hands were badly burned. Lamble nevertheless stoically ignored his agonies and joined in the efforts to launch the boat.

Rippon soon realised that the *Centaur* was foundering fast. They simply would not be able to launch either of these boats in time. He yelled out, urging everyone to leave them and head for the rafts on the afterdeck. He hurried down the after stairway. The young engineers George Alexander and Harry Hall, and electrician Keith Sykes, followed him.

When Ernie Smith and Maurice Cairnie burst out onto the boat deck they rushed off in different directions. Smith went left, around the engineers house, past the carpenter's cabin and the radio room to the emergency dynamo room just forward of the engine casing. His plan was to switch in some emergency lighting. He never reached his objective. As he passed the WC opposite Rippon's cabin the sea surged across the deck and swept him up and over the side.

Cairnie turned right, past the other engineers' cabins, heading for his No. 4 lifeboat station. He saw his colleagues Alexander and Hall making for their boat stations. At his station he found Lamble and some others trying to clear the gripes and launch the boat. Behind them the bridge decks burned fiercely. Out over the water the reflection of the flames danced across the wavetops. To Cairnie's nostrils came the familiar smell of burning diesel oil. The smoke was already thick and suffocating. To help Lamble and the others untangle the rope falls, he flicked on his torch. The beam of light showed up a wall of white water advancing menacingly up the deck. 'Jump!' he yelled, then followed his own advice and vaulted over the rail into the sea. Captain Murray and his helpers failed in their valiant efforts to free No. 2 lifeboat. They stayed around too long. The rapidly advancing sea surged into them and lifted them up over the deckhouse before sucking them beneath the surface.

When Ellen Savage, Evelyn King and Merle Moston met Lt-Col Manson on deck he seemed quite composed. He climbed up on the side railing and held his hand out to them. 'That's right, girlies,' he said comfortingly, as if directing a sports picnic, 'jump for it, now.'

Ellen Savage, clad only in her thin pyjamas, asked Manson, 'Will I have time to go back for my great-coat?' He said she did not. Evelyn King reminded Savage she couldn't swim. Savage knew. They had often practised life-saving in the swimming pool on the *Oranje*. King used to say jestingly, 'We have to practice. If we're shipwrecked Nell will save me!'[6] Savage would tell her, 'Don't worry, I will crocodile you.' They saw Maurice Cairnie fall past them from the deck above. Manson jumped, and then Savage, followed by King. Ellen Savage's later account described the next few moments:

> I endeavoured to jump as we had been instructed, but the suction was so great I was pulled into the terrific whirlpool with the sinking ship. It would be impossible to describe adequately that ordeal under water as the suction was like a vice, and that is where I sustained my injuries — ribs fractured, fracture of nose and palate by falling debris, ear drums perforated, and multiple bruising. When I was caught in ropes I did not expect to be released. Then all of a sudden I came up to an oily surface with no sign of a ship, and very breathless from this ordeal[7].

Ellen Savage lost sight of her friend Evelyn King and cabin-mate Merle Moston. Later she learned that falling timber killed them both.

By the time Captain Salt emerged onto the promenade deck, still draped in the wet blanket, the torrent of water was at his heels. It caught him and lifted him off his feet. The ship fell away from under him.

The after deck area, around No. 4 hatch, was the scene of the last spasm of activity on AHS *Centaur*. Several of the deck crew were there. Boatswain Gustav Brandin, the 50-year-old Swede, organised them into parties to release the rafts.

Albert Blair made it to the after deck — only to realise that
what he had picked up in the belief that it was his lifejacket
turned out to be nothing more than a pillow! He saw two
colleagues free a raft near him. Then he jumped over the side.

Ship's writer Ron Bull had no end of trouble releasing a raft
on the starboard side of the deck. He had to keep dodging
burning spars and other debris that rained down on him. Nearby
a helpful medical orderly yelled out a warning of another falling
spar. Unfortunately it hit him instead, and killed him.

Allan Dickson found a small raft on the starboard side of the
deck. It seemed jammed and he struggled to release it. It broke
free and with him straddled across it slid down the deck, crashed
into the accommodation and jammed him against the bulkhead.
Then the sea swirled around and lifted the raft away, freeing
him. Afloat, he swam off the starboard side and headed towards
a large white raft he could see nearby. He had almost reached
it when a large spar came down and crashed onto the raft, taking
it under. Dickson had to make do with a floating plank for
support.

When the two 8-to-12 watch greasers, McIntosh and Grainger,
reached the after deck they realised instantly that the ship was
doomed. The stern area physically trembled. McIntosh, in a later
graphic, if occasionally fanciful, interview with author Jean
Devaney[d], described what happened next.

> ... I could see she was going down fast. It was pitch dark, high seas
> were running. Flames were coming out of the funnel. I watched it fall
> off and heard the crunch of the steel of the bridge deck collapsing.
>
> Some of us were panicky; I could tell that by the shouts. I tried to
> quiet a couple of men by telling them to get themselves lifebelts out of
> the locker in the alleyway leading to the foc'sle[e]. It's hard to describe
> how I felt myself. My main point was to keep my senses. I realised that
> meant life or death to me. When I got to the alleyway the lifebelts were
> all gone so I rushed back to the foc'sle to get my own. No noise now;
> except some swearing among the men about the Japs and the swirling
> of the seas over the ship. We kept quiet to hide our position from the Japs.
>
> When I got up on deck again she was just going, slipping from under
> me. She had broken in two. Her ends were beginning to buckle up. I
> saw my pal, Bobby Grainger, of Melbourne, hanging onto the ship's side.
> I shouted to him: 'Get over! She's going!' then took a long dive myself

---

d. Published in 1945 in the book *Bird of Paradise*.

e. 'Foc'sle' is the seamens' name for the crew's quarters, regardless of where they might
actually be located on a ship. The term has largely fallen into disuse in modern times.

from the foc'sle over the side. I hit the ship's rail and smashed the shin-bone of my right leg. But I felt no pain. I was too excited. It put me in hospital for two months, that.

The ship's suction took me down. It kept on pulling me down; tore off my pyjama pants. I'd only had time to tie the top strings of my Mae West jacket and more or less she helped me to come up. The bottom ends floated and resisted the suction. Under water I knew that I had to swim away from the suction and I battled hard, I can tell you, but I was so long down that I swallowed a lot of oil. It was terrible sickly in my mouth.

When I came up on top I was hit on the head with a float from a broken raft and that sent me down again. The suction got me again. I fought hard. I came up again. I couldn't see anything; the night was pitch[8].

Rupert Paton and Vince McCosker arrived on the after deck to see David Milligan and five other men trying to launch the lifeboat on No. 4 hatch, and Rippon, Ramage and Taylor on the port side working to free the big raft on the mast stays. They figured Rippon's chances were better, and they joined his group. Bidmead and Cliff Jones also came and helped. The raft was jammed, fouled by a derrick guy wire. It couldn't be budged. The already steep incline of the deck only hampered the group's frantic efforts. Some smaller rafts stacked right aft broke adrift and slid forward, smashing down into the midst of Milligan's group and knocking them off their feet.

Rippon sensed that the *Centaur*'s final moments were at hand. The big raft was just starting to come free, but he knew it was too late. He shouted out his final order: 'Jump for it!' As he later told his father:

> ... she started to go with a rush so I just hopped over the side and swam away from the ship. The torpedo must have struck number two hatch and blown in the after bulkheads and ignited 350 tons of oil and fuel in the bunkers. The funny thing is that I never felt a bit frightened only dazed, although I never thought for a moment I could get out of it. I just couldn't believe it[9].

Boatswain Brandin had also sensed the end was nigh. 'Every man for himself!' he yelled out. And every man heeded his advice. They gave up on the rafts, went to the railing, and dived into the sea.

Abandoning ship was all that those poor souls still on board AHS *Centaur* had left to do. Some had no option; the sea claimed them as the ship sank under their feet. Others dived into the sea as soon as they realised the hopelessness of their plight. Among the last to leave were the two greasers and close friends Mattie Morris and Bob Tierney. They shook hands in farewell, then shinned up onto the starboard rail and dived overboard.

Chapter Eight

A STRUGGLE FOR SURVIVAL

14th May 1943: 0413 to dawn

Survivors' accounts of the *Centaur*'s final moments varied. While those who saw the death plunge agree that she went down in flames and that her stern was the last part to disappear beneath the waves, they differed in their recollections about what happened immediately beforehand. Some said she knifed straight down and the final nosedive was fast, smooth and silent. Others thought she heeled to starboard in the final seconds and sank with a loud anguished roar.

Some survivors said she broke in two at the last moment. This may well be (we now know that this happened to the *Titanic*), but it does seem unlikely. The *Centaur*'s hull remained largely intact, despite localised damage caused by the torpedo and the exploding fuel. Fire was undoubtedly consuming her, and rapidly, but in three minutes could have done little harm to her steel structure. AHS *Centaur* foundered because the sea overwhelmed her; she lost her watertight integrity and she sank, bow first. She went quickly because the rent in her side allowed the sea to pour in at a staggering rate. Heavy ironstone ballast in her holds accelerated the movement. No doubt the explosion also opened seams in other parts of her hull, but not to the extent that it significantly shortened her life. Given her generous scantlings, the extra strength that Blue Funnel Line demanded for its ships, it is unlikely that even the unsupported weight of her stern suspended high in the air could have caused enough pivotal stress for it to break off. More probably her death throes created an agonising groaning, and this, coupled with the blast of escaping air from the hull, sounded for all the world like a ship breaking apart. As well, the collapse of the bridge, the funnel and the mainmast in the dying seconds may have triggered a visual illusion of the ship splitting in two.

While respecting the recollections of the survivors, at that climactic moment they had but one overriding aim — to get as far away from the doomed ship as possible. Given the trauma of the moment, what they later firmly believed they had seen of the *Centaur*'s dying seconds may have been no more than what they imagined at the time.

Most survivors had something more important on their minds — survival.

Exactly how many people were still alive in the water when the *Centaur* sank will never be known. Gordon Rippon later estimated it to be about 200. Some survived the inferno on board, only to be later cruelly pulled beneath the surface by suction and held down until their lungs burst. Others, non-swimmers, perhaps without lifejackets and not able to find a raft or some supportive debris in time, simply drowned, probably in the first few minutes. All we know for sure is that the number of survivors to this stage of the tragedy was *at least* 68. Each one had already cheated death once; now another dance with destiny beckoned. Three minutes earlier, most of them had been asleep in their bunks; now they were bruised, burned or otherwise injured, scantily dressed if not naked, cold and frightened, confused and disoriented. And they were all doing the same thing; struggling to stay afloat and alive.

The moment the burning hulk dipped beneath the waves a sudden eerie silence descended. The final roar of flames had gone, as had the growl of grating steel, the rumbling of loose internal fittings, the gurgling of escaping air, the sizzling and spitting of cold sea water on red hot metal, and the whoosh of the sea as it closed triumphantly over its victim; all gone with the ship. Quiet prevailed, like the sudden silence at the end of a phonograph record, broken only by the hoarse voices of survivors calling to each other, an occasional scream of agony, an anguished plea for help. Even the sea itself was quiet, the wavelets dampened by a thin film of diesel oil.

Oil covered everything. It coated the debris. It coated the survivors and irritated their eyes. They tried hard not to swallow it. Fortunately the water had cooled it to the point that it was no longer inflammable, otherwise the fire would have spread from the *Centaur* to the sea. Providence, apparently, had averted one hell at least.

In this oily waste the survivors wallowed, waiting to confront what fate had in store. Their plight was woeful, yet they rose to that most basic of nature's instincts — the will to live. After the initial shock receded, their minds began to clear. The fight for survival began.

Jim Watterston, one of the *Centaur*'s storemen, after merely stepping off the after deck into the sea, swam about ten metres from the ship before turning over onto his back. As he said to a newspaper interviewer not long after his rescue:

> The ship was then almost vertical, about 60 feet of the stern showing up out of the water. She seemed to hesitate for a second and then disappeared. I had heard the screams of the nurses and the shouts of the men trapped down below. I swam round till I saw one of the big rafts[1].

Vince McCosker, after diving over the *Centaur*'s side, came to the surface still quite close to the ship, which sank moments later. He struck out as best he could to distance himself from the swirling whirlpool left behind, to no avail. Suction pulled him beneath the surface; suction so strong it ripped off all the buttons on his shorts. When he finally surfaced he had as much trouble keeping his shorts up as he did keeping himself afloat!

As 2nd Mate Rippon swam away from the ship he heard it plunge past him into the depths. He found that in the oily water he could swim reasonably well, despite his cumbersome life jacket. He swam some 30 metres and by good fortune came across one of the large rafts. Already about 30 men clung to its rope grablines. Some had managed to climb aboard. Despite their overcoats of oil, he recognised 3rd Mate Monty Banks and Chief Engineer Ernie Smith. For a while he joined them, holding on to one edge of the raft. When his eyes got used to the dark he and a few others saw an overturned lifeboat not far off, amongst some other debris. He decided to swim over to it. Banks and Smith and one of the stewards, Sid Sandwell, went with him. From the raft the boat did not seem very far away, but it took them a long time to reach it. The swim tired them out. Righting the boat called on their combined efforts. Much to their disappointment they found it badly charred and severely holed. Only by pairing off two men at each end could the boat support them, and even then the sea washed over the gunwales amidships. Smith was exhausted and dearly wanted to sleep, but the physical demands of keeping up this balancing act demanded his constant attention.

Rippon peered at the other debris around them. One large piece proved to be the wheelhouse roof, the monkey island. Somehow it had escaped the inferno that ravaged the bridge.

123

Still attached to it were timber fragments of the horizontal red cross. Rippon left the lifeboat and swam to it. This floating platform, some six by nine metres in size, had also been spotted by the men on the big raft. Some of them, seeing their raft rapidly becoming overcrowded, followed Rippon's example.

The buoyancy of Sister Ellen Savage's lifejacket eventually overcame the ship's suction and she bobbed thankfully to the surface. Still wearing nothing but her silk nightgown, she wallowed in the oily sea and gasped for air. Around her, and under her, all manner of flotsam was shooting to the surface. She saw ropes and spars floating nearby; moving ropes and spars, being drawn down by the ship to which they were still attached. She knew if she became entangled in one she would be taken down too. Terrified, she wallowed around in her lifejacket, not knowing what to do next. All the while she clutched her rosary beads. They were to become a source of comfort to her in the long hours to follow. The first person she came across was her old *Oranje* shipmate Pte Tom Malcolm, who had been swept off the foredeck. Malcolm gasped and gulped for air. When he recovered they exchanged a few words and vowed to stay together. They soon found a piece of timber debris. It had once been the roof of the hospital aft. It was awash but large enough to support them both. With great difficulty they hoisted themselves onto it. Ellen Savage lay in agony from her injuries, but she mentioned not a word of complaint to Malcolm. Now that she had time to think, she wondered what had happened to her eleven colleagues. She worried that the girls might have stopped to dress before coming on deck, knowing now that there simply had not been time. The fate of her pal Evelyn King, and of Lt-Col Manson, worried her. They had all jumped together[a].

Savage and Malcolm heard a voice nearby. They called out. Malcolm wanted to get Sister Savage onto something more robust and supportive than their piece of decking. Pte Jim Coulsen answered, saying he and Tom Hobden shared a small raft but it had no room for any more. They heard a woman screaming. Malcolm thought the voice belonged to Sister Mary McFarlane, but could not be sure. Later he heard Fred Chidgey's voice. He shouted and Chidgey replied that he and several others were on a raft and would try to join up with them.

---

a. Able Seaman Ivan Cecich later reported he had seen Sister King in the water. She was hit by falling timber and killed.

Someone who did get tangled in the many snaking ropes was nightwatchman Frank Drust. After the horror of watching the pantry floor cave in beneath him he panicked, ran for the deck and dived overboard. Moments after coming to the surface he felt something curling around his leg. Like the tentacles of an octopus, whatever it was tightened, gripped, and pulled him down. Fortunately it cleared itself and released Drust, who popped back to the surface.

Greaser Bob Tierney, who had dived over the *Centaur*'s starboard side with his mate Mattie Morris, twice got sucked down. When he surfaced for the second time he hit some debris and broke his nose. He came across a barrel. He reached out to grab it, and saw another survivor on the other side doing the same thing. Before Tierney could exchange a word, however, the other man gave a sudden piercing scream and sank beneath the surface. Horror-struck, believing a shark had struck, Tierney swam away with extreme haste. A few minutes later he came across another lone figure clutching a hatchboard. Tierney reached out and grabbed the edge. He looked the man in the face and said, 'Dr Livingstone, I presume?'

Mattie Morris grinned and reached out to shake Tierney's hand. 'Now that's the sort of mate I like to have on a shipwreck!'[2].

When another engine room rating, Bill McIntosh, came to the surface after being sucked down, he was immediately struck on the head by debris. As his later descriptive narration to Jean Devaney explained:

> I came up with half a raft on one side of me and half a lifeboat on the other. They had split in two with the ship. I grabbed hold of the raft but I couldn't get onto it because it kept turning round on me so I let go and made for the piece of lifeboat. Then I found that there were already two men on that, Ross Downie and George Long, and I realised that three would be one too many. Oil was blinding me, running into my eyes out of my hair.
> I got my breath and settled down a bit, then shouted for a raft or boat. I got a hail from somewhere. "There's a raft here but we've got no paddles! Can you make it?"
> I shouted back: "I can't make it! I'm done!" My leg was now numb. Then they flashed a light from a lifebelt and I struggled to get to them, calling to Ross and George to follow me. Up till then we had kept our lights dark for fear of the Japs.
> I was pulled onto the raft by Colonel Outridge, a doctor. There I kept yelling for Ross and flashing my light . . . He didn't make it . . .
> George went down, too.

125

> We couldn't see anyone. I shook and shook. Not with cold, though
> it was midwinter. It was horror of what was going on in the water. I
> knew I was one of the lucky ones that night . . . No sound of the Japs
> . . . We were only fifteen miles out from land, you know. Could see the
> lighthouse flashing all the time[3].

The credibility of this account is enhanced by the fact that
McIntosh restrained himself from mentioning what he later
deputed before an inquiry — that a shark took Ross Downie.

After diving off the foredeck with Carter and Hegarty, Pte Fred
Chidgey's singular aim was to distance himself from the crippled
Centaur. He later compared his swimming speed with Johnny
Weismuller. There might have been a similarity in the effort put
into it, but not the pace. Chidgey, not a strong swimmer at the
best of times and now hampered by a bulky lifejacket, used a
stroke that could best be described as a cross between a crawl
and a dog paddle. In this way he paddled towards what he
thought was a piece of flotsam. He reached for it, touched it —
and the body rolled over slightly. The discovery startled him.
He instinctively pulled away, but then his basic training composed him. He checked the body for vital signs. The man's chest
did not move. Chidgey leaned over his face but could feel no
breath from either nose or mouth. He could find no pulse at the
wrist or the neck. He could not check the man's pupils, but knew
enough already to determine that he was dead. Chidgey could
do nothing more, so he abandoned the corpse and continued
his search for something to hold onto. After a while he came
across the large raft with several survivors on it, including Carter
and Hegarty.

Tom Hobden also eventually made his way to this raft, but
only after several hours of acute discomfort. When the *Centaur*
deserted him, as he put it, suction pulled him way down into
the depths. He felt sure he would drown. He had more or less
resigned himself to this fate when he suddenly shot to the surface. His lungs burned with pain as he gulped in air. Eventually
he caught his breath. The sea water stung his back, which had
been burned. He had also suffered a broken nose while the sea
tossed him about on the foredeck. He had perforated eardrums
and also spinal damage. He floated easily, and this surprised him;
as far as he knew he couldn't swim! His floundering took him
close to a makeshift raft made from four kerosene tins lashed
together. Another survivor appeared and together they tried to

clamber onto the flimsy contraption. It sank under their combined weight, but it gave some support. For the last few hours of darkness they lived in fear of a shark attack. They could hear threshing around them, and imagined the vultures of the deep feasting on the *Centaur*'s dead. Dawn brought some relief, when out of the half light emerged the welcome view of the large raft.

Tich Isherwood, who fractured his arm falling to the deck from his top bunk, managed to make it to the deck in time to be swept off by the surging sea. When he surfaced he found a piece of debris right alongside him. With his good arm he grabbed it. His life-support turned out to the boxed neon red cross sign from the funnel.

Like most who were swept off the ship, steward Ron Moate, who with fellow-stewards Jack Stutter and Charlie Carey had been helping Captain Murray free No. 2 lifeboat, was drawn down by suction. Unlike the others, Moate catapulted to the surface in a most unlikely vehicle — a huge bubble of air escaping from the plunging *Centaur*. Unfortunately the bubble also brought debris with it and something crashed against Moate's head. A hatchboard floated nearby and Moate got a hand to it, but he could not hold on. Soon after, a raft floated by. He quickly commandeered it. Jack Stutter joined him, and then the burned Sgt Bill Cornell. Not long afterwards greaser Stan Morgan came by on another raft. With him was a very badly burned ambulance driver, Pte Jack Walder.

Bob Westwood found himself floating in amongst a group of five or six men, the dim red lights on their lifejackets bobbing in the wallowing sea. The man nearest him suddenly disappeared beneath the surface without a sound. Westwood figured a shark had attacked and quickly paddled away from the group. He found a hatchboard and climbed aboard. It supported him, although his weight pushed it several inches underwater.

Two men, the stewards Mark Jonassen and Alex Cochrane, tried to distance themselves from the sinking *Centaur* by swimming under the spreading patch of floating diesel oil. They had to give up after a while, and then put their faith in a floating oil drum for support. Later they came across a small rubber raft.

Allan Pettiford, after being unceremoniously turfed out of the surging lifeboat, hit the water and was immediately tugged under by suction. Luckier than most, he quickly surfaced, but the suction had claimed its prize — Pettiford's underpants. He looked up at the ship. His last view of it was of a 'great red coal, going down'. Pettiford had surfaced close to the lifeboat that ejected him. He could see it was badly damaged. Believing it would probably sink, he abandoned it and swam away. Soon after he came across a raft supporting seven men, and climbed on board. A friendly voice said, 'Well, Pettiford, I'm pleased to see you.' Pettiford looked up and recognised his CO, Lt-Col Outridge[4].

Ron Bull, the ship's writer, also had his pants pulled off by suction when the *Centaur* sank. He somehow lost his false teeth as well. He managed to reach the big raft, but got his leg jammed while trying to climb aboard. It came clear as other survivors scrambled over him to get into the raft. He could see the raft was becoming crowded so swam away to take his chances on the monkey island.

Fourth Engineer Maurice Cairnie swallowed a lot of oil during his first few minutes in the sea. Feeling nauseous, he swam around for a while before coming across a wooden hatchboard, which he straddled. When he caught his breath he noticed at least two rafts floating nearby, both badly damaged. The sight angered him; those rafts should have released themselves when the ship sank, without being damaged. About half an hour later, still on his own and wondering who else had survived, Cairnie saw something about 100 metres off that alarmed him. He peered into the darkness, and made out a dark shape that looked like a submarine. He felt sure he could discern a conning tower and the two wire hawsers that span submarines from conning tower to bow and stern. Fearful of being seen, Cairnie turned his board away from the shape and paddled away as fast as he could. Not long afterwards he came across some other survivors: the 'porpoise watcher' Albert Taylor with L-Cpl Ken Murray and Pte Fred Millar of the 2/12th, all supported by bits of broken timber, mostly awning spars. Someone suggested they try to keep together. They did their best to lash the loose timbers to the raft. Cairnie contributed the sash of his pyjamas.

At least five other survivors later reported seeing a submarine on the surface within an hour of the sinking. Butchers Reid and Anderson together saw two lights about three to five metres above the water (though why a submarine would show lights is mystifying). They easily identified the outline of a submarine. Steward Sid Sandwell, on his own, reported the same. He could even discern two stubby masts. Ambulance driver Allan Dickson, sharing a hatchboard with fellow driver Les Horgan at the time, went even further. They were close enough, he said, to see the shape of a man in the conning tower. Young Bob Westwood saw a white light. None of these witnesses mentioned hearing any noise. The intruder might have been stopped or moving very slowly, but would not have been recharging batteries, which is a clangorous process.

Was it the assailant? But why? To administer a *coup de grace*? Surely self-satisfied eyes had watched the victim's final agony and death through a periscope lens? Was there a more sinister objective — like applying the dead-men-tell-no-tales technique? Could pangs of guilt be biting? Or maybe the spider was waiting for a new fly, attracted by the bait of these wallowing survivors.

Whatever the reason for its presence the silent caller soon left, neither contacting nor molesting anyone.

The survivors were once again alone. Scattered over a wide area in groups large and small they clung desperately to whatever would keep them afloat. They all wondered how many others had survived like them. They knew that some had; that much was evident from the isolated screams of pain and calls for help. It was an unnerving experience, for nothing could be done. Everyone simply peered into the darkness in the general direction of the piteous cries, until they stopped.

All they could do now was to wait for the first light of dawn.

Chapter Nine

A PITIFUL MUSTER

Dawn 14th May to 1400 15th May 1943

At daybreak on Friday 14th May 1943, at a spot on the ocean some 25 miles east of Moreton Island, the sun rose over a very melancholy scene indeed.

A greasy patch of diesel oil, pockmarked by wallowing debris and pitiful, oil-smeared humanity, lay over the sea like an unsightly stain. Within the perimeter of this black obscenity, perhaps as many as three score and ten human beings greeted the dawn with renewed hope, pushing aside the despair of the sombre hours of darkness. In some strange way, the rising sun symbolised a rebirth, a promise of liberation from the holocaust of the previous night, and surely eventual salvation.

Clusters of survivors dotted the dark patch. They clung tenaciously to a range of motley and innovative craft fabricated from debris left behind by the departing *Centaur*: a broken lifeboat, dislodged hatchboards, various spars, and a conglomeration of rafts of which some were intact, some damaged, others makeshift and many lethally precarious.

By analysing survivors' accounts, it is possible to piece together at least an overview of that tragic dawn scene. A totally accurate portrait is out of the question. Even reliable accounts conflict in some details, which is understandable, considering what their authors went through. Some survivors never made statements at all (or made them and they were subsequently lost). The sensationalised transcripts of some interviews by journalists had to be purged of dramatic license before being considered reliable[1].

In summary, the dawn revealed one main cluster of about 40 survivors, six other quite separate groups of a handful of men each, and two (possibly three) lone individuals. There may have been others; we will now never know. If there were, they lost the battle for survival.

As far as each of these groups were aware, they were the only ones to survive the sinking. They guessed from earlier calling voices and occasional screams of pain rending the night air that others had probably escaped the *Centaur*'s death plunge, but could not know for sure.

The main group had as its primary support vessel the only large drum raft dislodged from the *Centaur* in one piece. By first light, about 30 men packed tight on its decking, their weight almost forcing it beneath the water. Close by wallowed the wheelhouse roof (the monkey island) awash under the weight of seven men. Also close by was the lifeboat that Rippon, Banks, Smith and Sandwell had seized upon so eagerly, only to find it badly damaged.

Those on the monkey island were in a particularly dire state. They had to stand, while the sea swirled around their legs. They worked out an elaborate balancing act. One man stood, or sat, in the middle while the rest huddled around him as in a rugby scrum. Every so often the edge of the decking would dip into a wave, upset the equilibrium and pitch everyone into the sea. Amid much cursing the men would scramble back up and reform the scrum. Captain Detmers of the *Kormoran* would have appreciated the irony of their predicament.

Drifting not far away and now in sight of the main tri-fleet, Ellen Savage and Tom Malcolm greeted the dawn with immense relief. Their raft, the roof of the old hospital, gave them little support. In the dark hours voices calling out — among them Fred Chidgey's — had told them about the larger raft not too far away. Chidgey had even thrown a rope in the hope that it might reach them. Come daylight and visual contact, the voices said, someone would come and get them.

Some undetermined distance away from this main group, and seemingly entirely on their own, were five men on two rafts. Moate, Stutter and the burned Cornell on one raft, Morgan and Pte Walder on the other. Walder had been extremely badly burned. Charred flesh hung from his body in strips. No part of his skin had escaped the inferno. He lay in excruciating pain.

Also on their own were another four men, clinging to debris they had somehow joined up (using in part a pyjama cord) to keep them together. This gathering comprised Maurice Cairnie, Albert Taylor, Fred Millar and Ken Murray.

Other little separated groups scattered over the area included the greasers Morris and Tierney with young seaman Bob Westwood, all on hatchboards, Spud Jones with two other unknown men on a tiny raft, Cpl Keith Lange on a hatchboard, and Jonassen and Cochrane on two hatchboards.

Two men at least — seamen's cook Frank Martin, and AB Owen Christensen — were on hatchboards by themselves, apparently alone on the ocean with no-one else in sight. Pte Eric Taylor also started off this way.

Second Mate Gordon Rippon had already figured that he might be the senior surviving deck officer. The dawn, and a quick survey of oil-streaked faces confirmed it, at least for his group. He had no idea what other groups might exist. He knew he had to take charge and get things organised. The primary task, as he saw it, was to join the group together for security.

Rippon worried about the three men in the racked lifeboat. He had left them to it when he discovered the monkey island, but Smith, Banks and Sandwell were still holding their tenuous sitting positions in the waterlogged bow and stern.

Rippon cupped his hands and yelled out to the segregated groups, urging them to paddle their craft towards each other. They did so, using as paddles the two oars from the lifeboat and chunks of the timber red cross that had once adorned the monkey island. As they came together they used whatever lines they could find to lash their three craft into one unit.

Meanwhile those on the big raft had not forgotten their promise to send someone over to Sister Savage and Tom Malcolm. Storeman Jim Watterston set off with a rope tied around his waist to swim the 50 metres to the crude raft. He found Ellen Savage shivering in her thin silk nightdress. He took off his pyjama jacket and gave it to her. He could see she had a cut lip and a swollen eye. The men on the big raft began pulling on the rope. Savage and Malcolm paddled with their hands. When they joined up, willing hands gently transferred them onto the raft. Ellen Savage was pleased to see Dr Outridge there, and gratified to learn that he had salvaged a medical kit. She shivered. One man gave her his khaki trousers; another his army topcoat.

At that moment the grey fin of a shark — the first they had seen — cut ominously through the surface nearby.

By about 0930 they had the three craft secured together. Electrical cables still connected to the underside of the monkey island came in very useful as lashings. Rippon, ably supported by the competent and dignified figure of 3rd Mate Banks (who had been in this same predicament three times before), could now organise a united group. Ellen Savage suggested it was a fitting time to give thanks for their deliverance. Clutching her rosary beads she led the men in prayer. Tom Hobden noted that everyone joined in; even one man who had earlier so proudly boasted of his atheism.

The next task was to take stock of the situation; to check the injured, and the food and water supplies.

Few survivors had escaped unscathed. Most had swallowed oil, which burned their insides and induced vomiting. Some had skin burns, others physical injuries sustained during the sinking; mostly abrasions, lacerations and bruising. Sea water stung their wounds; diesel oil stung their eyes. They all suffered from varying degrees of shock; severe trauma compounded by grief at the loss of so many friends and colleagues, and apprehension about their survival. Added to this were the creeping effects of hypothermia, which would worsen the longer these lightly clad men — and one woman — remained immersed in cold sea water. Only about half of the survivors had lifejackets. Few were dressed. Most had left the ship in their night attire and not many had managed to hang on to even that. Most men were either naked or had but a singlet on. Driver George McGrath wore nothing but his watch, which had stopped at 0410.

With their scanty medical supplies Outridge and Savage began ministering to those most in need. Captain Jock Salt, badly burned about the face and hands, sat quietly without complaint. Percy Kelly had a wooden splinter right through his foot, from ankle to instep.

Tich Isherwood had fractured his arm. Dr Outridge, unfortunately, sat on the outer edge of the packed raft and could not get close enough to Isherwood to examine him. He could only ask questions and receive answers relayed by word of mouth. At Outridge's direction the men around Isherwood did their best to immobilise the arm and keep him comfortable. Another injured man was lifted onto the big raft and passed into the tender care of Sister Savage. (Who it was is now not known, but it was not Bob Westwood, as later widely reported.) She cuddled him, being as tender as she could, and shared the loaned greatcoat to keep him warm.

133

Ironically, other than Salt and Isherwood, the most seriously injured people in that group were the two senior medicos, Outridge and Savage. Outridge had severe burns. He treated himself, using the legs of his own ripped-up silk pyjamas as a dressing. Savage had mostly internal injuries, as already outlined, but she bore them stoically, asked for nothing, and none of the men around her even guessed at her condition.

As to sustenance, the lifeboat, although a wreck, was a godsend. As a source of food and also some flares, a sheet of canvas and two oars, it proved invaluable. Rippon ordered all the undamaged lifeboat rations transferred to the raft. Then they took stock. The inventory did little to cheer them up. They had two gallons (about nine litres) of water, 2,000 Ovaltine tablets, a small tin of malted milk tablets, a few tins of beef extract (but no tin opener), some prunes and raisins, and several bars of pemmican, an unpleasant-tasting but nourishing substance made from concentrated seal blubber. Of this victualling list, the more plentiful Ovaltine tables had become soaked in sea water and were not very palatable, and the beef extract tended to make everyone more thirsty. Sister Savage took charge of the rations. Based on the possibility of being adrift for a maximum of four days, she calculated a daily allowance per person of one lick of meat extract, a milk tablet, two prunes and a mouthful of water. 'Dinner' would be served in the evening. With luck, rain would augment their sparse supply of drinking water.

Although it did rain now and again, the weather became frustratingly variable, and subjected the survivors to the worst of both extremes. The early morning sun had been most welcome, bringing warm relief from the debilitating chills of night, but it soon became too much of a good thing, and skin already damaged by fire suffered yet again, this time from sunburn. Scantily clad survivors had no place to hide from the burning rays. Now and then the great golden orb disappeared behind a cloud formation, the air quickly cooled down, and a rain squall followed. Rain did relieve thirst and the effects of the sun's burning rays, but it also quickly chilled everyone, and those with burned skin suffered agony from the falling droplets. Then the rain stopped, out came the sun, and the whole cycle repeated itself.

As the morning progressed, the survivors discussed the chances of an early rescue. Rippon no doubt cautioned against false hopes.

He, more than most, knew that their immediate future was nothing short of bleak. He knew, because of strict radio silence, that no-one ashore would be concerned about not hearing from the *Centaur*. She could have steamed all the way to Cairns in blissful silence without raising the slightest query ashore. Their chances of a search and rescue mission therefore depended on some very tenuous and unlikely possibilities: 1 — that the duty radio operator (Eric Summers) had managed to send off a distress message (none of the three operators were in the group; in fact all had perished); 2 — that someone manning a shore radar screen noticed their sudden disappearance; 3 — that naval authorities would contact the ship with a message (which could only be one important enough to warrant breaking radio silence in response) and become suspicious when they received no answer.

The ship's officers at least had no illusions about their chances. They knew it was too early for any alarm bells to be ringing ashore, and that an early rescue depended almost entirely on a chance sighting by a passing ship or aircraft.

Ironically, that likelihood seemed most real soon afterwards. A few in the group thought they heard something and called for hush. They were right; the noise became more audible. It was the drone of aircraft engines. Then they saw it, in the distance to the north, flying eastwards at low altitude. A seaplane. Elated, all those who could yelled out at the tops of their voices and waved their arms madly above their heads. They lit flares. But the aircraft crew didn't see them. The plane lumbered on and slowly disappeared out of sight[a].

Not surprisingly, this incident dampened morale. Everyone realised then how difficult attracting a passing aircraft was going to be. At that point, Captain Jock Salt cheered them all up with some good old seafaring optimism. Having sailed along this coastline for the best part of 50 years, he could tell them that they were not too far from the shipping lanes. He said they would soon be intercepted by a ship of some sort. Salt knew that the *Centaur* had gone down on or near the 100 fathom line. This is where the south-bound ocean current is usually at its strongest, and ships often tracked along it to take advantage of the free push from nature. What he didn't tell them was that in wartime shipmasters had little freedom of movement. They moved as

a. This was probably the regular daily US flight from Brisbane to Noumea.

directed by Naval Control Officers, men who took scant regard for the commercial advantages of ocean currents. Nevertheless, Salt's assurances lifted the sagging spirits within the group. Eager eyes began scanning the horizon for just such a vessel.

About mid-day they sighted one, a large tanker. It seemed to be heading towards them, but at about five miles off it altered course to the north. Once again their flares went unseen. Heightened spirits once again crashed.

The flares they used came mostly from the sea, drifting among the debris. Many malfunctioned when fired and simply fizzled out. One that the group on the monkey island activated did go off as it should, but then fell onto Vince McCosker's leg and burned his knee. McCosker's leg soon began to stiffen. It also bled, prompting some wag to tease him about attracting sharks.

Well might he have jested, for as the morning wore on the scene became a focus of interest to these scavengers of the deep. Increasing numbers of tiger and grey nurse sharks were seen cruising around the rafts. Fred Chidgey observed their movements closely. They appeared to him to be in three size-groups swimming at different levels; small ones near the surface, larger ones slightly deeper, and deep down 'the big ones!'[2] The big fellows first made their presence felt by coming up under the rafts with a hefty nudge, no doubt hoping the movement would dislodge a meal. When this didn't work they became more aggressive, rushing the craft with wide, open mouths. One made such a vigorous charge it landed half out of the water on the edge of the monkey island.

All the survivors could do was beat the sharks off with the oars or other loose timber. The best weapon turned out to be timber pieces from the red cross that had once graced the monkey island deck. This merited 'three cheers for the Red Cross!' At one point, Rippon hurled a large empty biscuit tin at a monster that had ventured in a little too close for comfort. It took the tin in its mouth and ripped it in half with one clean bite. Everyone drew back with increased respect. Rippon remarked facetiously, 'if we had enough tins we could kill the bastards with indigestion!'[3]

During the day the group swelled in size. First to join, about mid-day, were Morris, Tierney and Westwood. Bob Westwood nursed a sore head caused by a blow from falling debris when the ship sank. Then came the twin-raft group comprising Moate,

Stutter, Morgan, Walder and Cornell. Walder was in a bad way and screamed in agony at every movement. Almost his entire body was burned and even the patter of light rain on his scorched skin drove him mad with pain. Most of the time he lay in a state of pain-induced unconsciousness. He occasionally awoke, but mercifully soon drifted off again. There was little Outridge, Savage, or for that matter anyone, could do. Outridge asked for a volunteer to go over to Walder's raft and comfort him. Jim Watterston went.

Late in the afternoon Jonassen and Cochrane, on their small raft, joined the main group.

Last to join the flotilla was Spud Jones with his two (unknown) mates. Jones had had quite a day. Before daylight he had drifted, relying for support on his trusty lifejacket. He remembered an officer telling him it would remain buoyant for only 24 hours, so rather than set off for the flashing light he could see in the distance (Cape Moreton light), he decided to hang around in the hope of coming across a raft of some sort. Daylight revealed a macabre sight; several motionless human figures, blackened with oil. He found a hatchboard and later a shattered raft, which gave more support. He began paddling towards the land. Sharks swam around him. 'I never knew such big sharks existed,' he later commented. 'I'm not a religious man but I prayed hard.' He was, however, a man with an uncompromising dread of the sea, which made his uncharacteristic serenity all the more remarkable.

Jones' paddling took him close to the black figure of another man on a hatchboard. His arms and legs were dangling limp in the water. Jones thought he might be dead. He paddled as fast as he could, reached the man, and lifted his head. The man opened his eyes, slowly and painfully, but said nothing. With no little difficulty Jones hauled him off the hatchboard and onto his own raft. It took a long while and the raft capsized three times before they were both safely aboard. Soon afterwards another survivor came by, a large man on a hatchboard. He insisted on transferring to the raft. Again it capsized, and Jones sent the third man packing, telling him to get his own plank. He pointed to a couple of specks he could see bobbing in the sea, and told the man that there was their destination. They paddled all day and reached it shortly before dark. The two specks Jones had seen were the main group of survivors. He joined his raft to the lifeboat by holding on to one of its grablines.

He told Rippon he had an injured man on board. Then he handed over a tin of biscuits he had come across during the day, to supplement the pool of food[4].

By late afternoon, after a couple more aircraft had flown blindly over, the group became very dispirited. They accepted the obvious, that no search party was out looking for them. Someone suggested a couple of fit men take one of the rafts and the two oars and row to the shore to get help. Sgt Dick Medcalf (an X-ray technician) offered to go on his own. They appreciated his good intentions, but talked him out of the idea. Captain Salt felt sure, from his observation of the loom of Cape Moreton light, that they were *at least* 27 miles offshore. Instead, they rigged the two oars and the sheet of canvas as a makeshift sail, hoping the wind would blow them to Moreton Island. Salt, Rippon and Banks all knew the attempt was futile, but at least it provided a welcome focus of attention and group activity, and in that sense had psychological merit.

Another ship passed by without seeing them, and four more aircraft passed frustratingly overhead. Morale plummetted. But then, as so often happens in times of adversity, strong characters came to the fore. Ellen Savage, ever the professional, rallied spirits with a vigorous sing-song. She led them into several old favourites, like *Roll out the Barrel* and *Waltzing Matilda*. Mattie Morris, too, the eternal optimist, figured he had an ideally sized group for a sweepstake. Each person had to forecast the time they would be rescued. Ten men were interested enough to buy in, at one shilling each. The winner stood to make the princely sum of ten bob! It was a psychological masterstroke; it got everyone thinking positively about eventual deliverance. Vince McCosker suggested each man think of and describe their favourite meals. Several youngsters responded enthusiastically, but soon everyone realised this was not a sensible thing to do. Hearing lurid details of epicurean feasts only made them all the more aware of their hunger. That game soon ceased.

Not much is known about what happened to the minor groups and individuals separate from the main gathering during that day. They no doubt shared the same privations, concerns, hopes, and in some instances agonies as their unseen fellow survivors. Owen Christensen, alone and naked on his hatchboard, suffered from cramps. Every time he felt one coming on he slipped off his board and set off on a brisk swim. At one stage he heard a plaintive cry for help from another man. Christensen answered, and began paddling towards him. He hoped the man might have a more substantial means of support, perhaps even a proper raft. His hopes were dashed when the man came into sight on no more than another hatchboard. The newcomer had likewise hoped that Christensen might have a raft. They talked, but after a while the stranger become delirious. He told Christensen he was going to get some fresh water, and paddled away. Christensen never saw him again.

At dusk, all hope of rescue that day evaporated. Everyone in their own way prepared themselves for a full night at sea.

After sunset the sea quickly radiated its warmth back into the atmosphere. Light rain fell, and chills soon began gnawing into tired, aching bones. Best served were those on the big raft. They soon appreciated that the clammy discomfort of tightly packed humanity during the heat of the day had its singular advantages at night. They huddled together for mutual warmth. Not so fortunate were those on the monkey island, with their tenuous rugby scrum. Around their shoulders they wrapped a strip of canvas recovered from the sea; another welcome item of flotsam. Although a soggy mess, it offered a modicum of protection from the cool night air. Rippon and Banks, commuting among the rafts, the monkey island and the lifeboat, organised a roster, swapping men around the craft to share more equitably the comforts and privations of each.

During the evening, a bald-headed corporal in the canvas-wrapped huddle on the monkey island coyly asked Rippon for permission to put an arm around his shoulder for additional warmth. Rippon agreed. A few minutes later, the corporal urinated over Rippon's leg. Rippon told the embarrassed soldier to forget about it; he had in fact welcomed the short-lived extra warmth it gave him. As things turned out, a few hours later Rippon repaid the compliment!

In the late evening, Vince McCosker, who could not take his turn sitting in the centre of the monkey island because of his stiffened leg, looked up to see an ocean liner with all her lights ablaze, heading straight towards them. Believing he was hallucinating he blinked his eyes, but could still see the ship. He later felt sure that others had seen it too and were yelling. He squinted, looked again . . . and it had gone! Disappeared! But it was so real! He would spend the rest of his life never able to come to grips with this mirage.

In the early hours of the following morning, around 0300, several survivors heard noises. Some thought they sounded like riveting, others whirring. Outridge felt sure it was an aircraft. AB Ivan Cecich made out a silhouette in the darkness that he thought might be a destroyer. Several others saw a dark shape. Some thought they saw a dark red light. Rippon and Smith had little doubt that what they could hear were the sounds of a sur-faced submarine. Someone, thinking it might be a rescue vessel, let off a flare. Almost immediately the noise ceased and everything became deathly quiet. Third Mate Monty Banks quickly called out to douse the flare. 'It's a submarine!' he hissed.

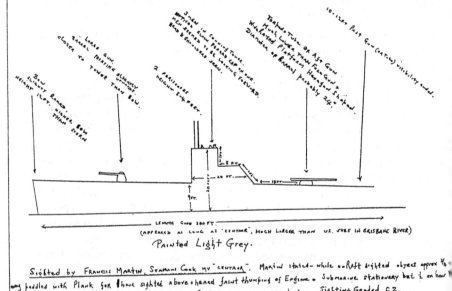

A naval artist drew this sketch from cook Frank Martin's verbal description of the submarine he saw the night after the Centaur *sank. Intelligence graded it C2, that is, a reliable report from an untrained observer.*

Hearts missed a beat. What if this was the submarine that had sunk the *Centaur*? What was it doing? Looking for survivors? If so, why?

One person in no doubt whatsoever about the source of the noise was the cook Frank Martin. Drifting by himself on a hatchboard, covered in oil and lying low in the water, he could plainly see a stationary submarine about 400 metres away from him. It had a well defined silhouette. He figured it to be about as long as the *Centaur* and larger than the US submarines he had seen. Its bow, about four metres high, was slightly raked. On the foredeck sat a large gun, its barrel pointing slightly upward. In the conning tower, which he estimated at about six metres above sea level, he could see two periscopes and also discern the heads and shoulders of three figures, even to the peaks of their caps. There was something abaft the conning tower, but he could not quite make it out. It might have been a large gun. The faint thumping of engines invaded the night stillness.

Martin quietly dipped his hands and slowly propelled himself away from the scene[5].

Everyone in the main group held their breath. They stayed silent for what seemed an excruciating length of time. Fear pumped adrenalin into their blood streams and hearts thumped wildly. Some were worried about the noise they felt sure their pounding hearts were making! Then the call 'Coo-ee!' rang out across the quiet sea. If it came from the submarine it failed in its objective. Seamen passed the message to ignore it. 'If they belonged to us, they'd shout *Ahoy!*'[6]

It became evident after a while that nothing was going to happen. Eventually, each survivor relaxed. About half-an-hour later, when the distant drone of a passing aircraft could be heard to the north, the noise of the submarine went away, much to everyone's relief.

One crewman had unknowingly been leaning against Sister Savage for some time. When he relaxed after the submarine left, and shifted his weight slightly, she whispered, 'Please don't lean on my side.'[7] For the first time the other survivors became aware that this gallant lady had internal injuries.

About an hour later Jack Walder passed away. Jack Stutter, who with Jim Watterston had been comforting him, called out to the big raft. 'He's gone.' His death was a merciful release[8]. Walder had suffered excruciating pain. Now and again he had regained consciousness. His head lolled from side to side. At one stage it fell over the edge of the raft and Watterston eased it back on. Walder smiled gratefully and said, 'I'm alright, Dig.' He had earned the admiration of all. Now his body lay at rest amongst them. By then emotionally drained and too exhausted to think rationally, they agreed to wait until morning before deciding what to do with him.

Come the dawn and once more the attention returned to Pte Walder. Opinion was divided. Some wanted to keep the body until they were rescued. But they were already into their second day and nobody could predict when that might happen. Medical logic swayed the argument. They agreed on a burial at sea.

Sister Savage insisted on a Christian ritual. Morris leaned over and removed one of the two identity tags and passed them to Dr Outridge. Ellen Savage led the sombre group in prayer. She conducted a simple, brief and very touching ceremony. It ended with a pause of respectful silence. Then the last remains of Private Jack Walder, driver of the 2/12 Field Ambulance, were eased over the side of the raft and committed to the deep. In silence they watched the body float away. Chidgey, among others, expressed a concern that it might be molested by sharks. Thankfully it was not. It slowly drifted off into the distance, and out of sight[9].

Afterwards, Rippon returned to the monkey island, allowing someone else to enjoy the comforts of the big raft. He found the monkey island waterlogged and the balancing act even more precarious than it had been before. Vince McCosker was still there, bone weary and very concerned about the slowly sinking platform he had been standing on for hours. His leg had stiffened up completely. Relief came only by standing all the time and taking most of his weight on his right leg. He knew he was stuck on the monkey island whether he liked it or not.

Another aircraft flew over. Like the others it kept on going. 'My God! Why don't they see us?', they muttered over and over again. So many had passed by! Deliverance was at hand — if only the aircrew would look down! But they didn't, and this chance, like the others, literally flew away. It created a wave of depression. Some survivors were beginning to show signs of stress. Patience began to wear thin, and tempers were easily lost, but fortunately the mood never deteriorated beyond general cursing or an expletive-sprinkled remark directed at blind aircrews.

Rippon had noted the sagging spirits and the despondency. He began to consider the likelihood of yet another night in these dreadful conditions. The thought appalled him. How long could the food last? How long could Pte McCosker remain standing on the monkey island? How long before all morale collapsed? It didn't bear thinking about, yet he had to. But not for too long. Salvation was on its way.

* * * * *

At 1040 that day, an Avro Anson belonging to 71 Squadron took off from Lowood Air Base to give anti-submarine support to northbound convoy SC648. Its pilot, Flying Officer O.Crewes, and navigator, Flying Officer J.Keith, had flown many similar patrols before. They regarded them as quite routine; almost mundane. As with the others, this patrol was uneventful. About 1340 they turned back to base. Soon after, one of the pilots spotted a warship escorting a cargo vessel east of Cape Moreton, and then almost immediately his attention was drawn to a flare in the sea, southeast of the two ships. Crewes circled to investigate. He and Keith were surprised to find an enormous oil slick about two miles in diameter, with several large pieces of debris in it. Their surprise turned to astonishment when they saw that the debris comprised lifeboats and rafts with clusters of living people on them. No reports were current about any ships lost in the area. Crewes turned towards the warship and flashed a signal: RESCUE SURVIVORS IN WATER AHEAD.[10]

Crewes then took his Anson down to sixty feet and flew over the scene. He flashed his morse lamp to the excited crowd below, transmitting WILL SEND HELP. He flew low past one man alone on a hatchboard, and waved: Owen Christensen waved back[11].

* * * * *

On the big raft, for the first time since the torpedo lanced into the *Centaur*'s side, Sister Ellen Savage burst into tears.

Chapter Ten

STARS AND STRIPES TO THE RESCUE
15th May

At dawn on 15th May, as the bedraggled and exhausted survivors of AHS *Centaur* paid their last respects to the mercifully departed soul of Pte Walder, 50 miles to the west at a Brisbane wharf a crew of smartly-uniformed and very fit young US sailors turned out to prepare their ship for sea. That day, naval command had detailed the US destroyer *Mugford* to escort a British freighter clear of Australian waters. The orders specified a rendezvous with the S.S. *Sussex* at 1030, outside Moreton Bay, near the pilot grounds off Caloundra.

Lt-Cmdr Howard S.Corey, USN[1], climbed the ladder to the bridge shortly before 0700 hours. His crew were already singling up the six manila moorings lines that secured the USS *Mugford* to No. 3 Newstead Wharf. The *Mugford* lay conveniently port side to, head downriver, which at high water flood made for a very simple departure. At Corey's command the shore linesmen tossed off the mooring lines, one by one. Corey ordered 'Dead Slow Ahead', and the *Mugford* moved slowly away from the berth and out into midstream[2].

Corey left the narrow bridge wing and moved into the wheelhouse. At the con, with the navigator at his elbow, he eased his ship into a smooth turn around Bulimba Point into Hamilton Reach. Ahead lay an hour-long winding passage downriver to Moreton Bay.

This Gridley class destroyer, pennant number *DD-389*, was commissioned into the United States Navy at the Boston Navy Yard on 16th August 1937[3]. She joined the Pacific Fleet later that year. When that 'day of infamy' came to Pearl Harbour in December 1941, she was there, on standby status[4]. Within ten minutes, her anti-aircraft guns had brought down two Japanese

bombers. During the lull between the first and second raids, and
while her engineering staff frantically raised steam, those on the
deck witnessed the USS *Oklahoma* turn turtle, the *West Virginia*
heel heavily to port, and the *Arizona* blow up. An hour later,
USS *Mugford* shot another aircraft out of the sky. She got under
way and steamed out of the harbour entrance, guns still blazing,
to fight another day.

In August the following year, after months of uneventful
convoy escort duties in the SWPA, more action came the
Mugford's way. On patrol off Lunga Point, Guadalcanal, she came
under enemy air attack. She shot down two twin-engined
bombers. After three near misses she suffered a direct hit with
a 100lb bomb near Number Three 5-inch gun. The blast caused
localised damage and heavy casualties: eight dead, ten missing,
17 wounded. The next day, on her way to join in the battle rag-
ing near Savo Island, she shot down another Japanese aircraft
and recovered its two-man crew. She arrived at Savo Island in
time to haul 400 survivors of the sunken US cruisers *Vincennes*
(CA-44) and *Astoria* (CA-34) from the water. During this action
she detected an underwater object and depth-charged it. Several
explosions followed, and oil floated to the surface.

This skirmish over, the *Mugford* went to Sydney. Over the
last three months of 1942, dockyard repair staff patched her up
and restored her to full combat readiness. In January 1943 the
refurbished *Mugford* went on patrol duty in the Coral Sea. Like
many other ships of the 7th Fleet at that time, the *Mugford*
adopted Brisbane as its base and often berthed at Newstead Wharf
between assignments[5].

Today's duty, escorting a ship into clear offshore waters, was
to the *Mugford*'s 200 crew-members just part of the daily grind.
Most no doubt hoped for a quiet trip and a swift return to
Newstead and the delights of Brisbane.

Also no doubt hoping for a swift — and safe — voyage were
the men on the escorted merchant ship. The S.S. *Sussex*, a New
Zealand Shipping Company cargo vessel of 11,063 tonnes, had
ahead of her a solo trans-Tasman voyage to New Zealand. To
get to the relatively safe open waters of the Tasman Sea she had
to run the gauntlet of the busy inshore shipping lanes so favoured
by predatory Japanese submarines. The crews knew well that
those undersea hunters had been actively menacing shipping in
recent weeks.

145

The *Mugford* cleared the Brisbane River entrance channel at 0849. Officer-of-the-Deck J.Shanahan noted in the log that she passed the Pile Beacon at a range of 1,000 yards. Corey secured the crew to 'special sea details' in 'condition of readiness III', and called for more revolutions from the two turbine-driven engines. The *Mugford* surged forward. At 26 knots, the outward passage through the channels of Moreton Bay went very quickly and the *Mugford* made her rendezvous with the *Sussex* on time. She took up station a mile ahead of the freighter and slowed to 17 knots, zig-zagging repetitively in front of her valuable ward. Her sonar gear probed the depths continuously for the tell-tale 'ping' of a hostile submarine. Her lookouts and her radar scanned the surface horizon[6].

An hour later, the *Mugford* led the *Sussex* through the narrow gap between Brennan Shoal and Cape Moreton, clearing the lighthouse by half a mile. Moreton Island gradually fell astern and once again the *Mugford* settled into a zig-zag pattern, this time along a base easterly course. She kept ahead of the *Sussex*, sweeping the seas in her path.

Shortly before 1400, one of the *Mugford*'s lookouts reported seeing what appeared to be a raft, bearing 140°[7]. A surprised R.Clodins, the *Mugford*'s OOD, immediately brought the destroyer around to that heading and increased speed to 20 knots. Clodins sounded General Quarters and Corey came quickly to the bridge to take command. As a precaution, should an enemy submarine be lurking nearby, Corey told Clodins to send a message to the *Sussex* to proceed independently away from the scene at maximum speed[8].

Ironically, after 34 hours of total isolation, the *Centaur*'s wreckage was detected simultaneously from both sea and air. The Avro Anson aircrew must have sighted the survivors' flares virtually at the same time as the alert *Mugford* lookout spotted the raft. By the time Crewes and Keith identified living humans amongst the debris and turned towards the nearby warship to send his rescue signal, the destroyer was already on its way[9].

The *Mugford* officers and lookouts intently scanned the sea for more debris. The crew responded to the General Quarters signal and scurried to their various battle stations. Corey, realising he had a rescue situation on his hands, sent a message to the Anson, asking it to cover the *Sussex*.

Crewes was low on fuel and could not stay long. Before leaving, however, he circled the debris field twice to give the

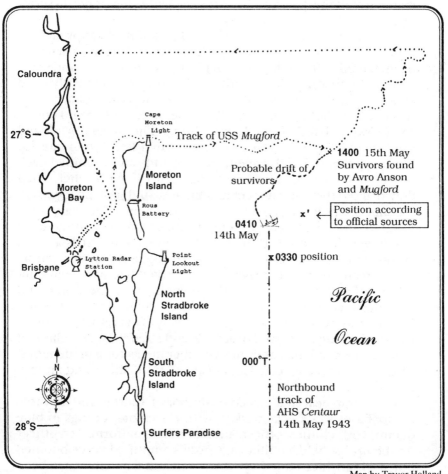

Map by Trevor Holland

Mugford an idea of its size, and dropped a flare near one of the smaller groups of survivors. He signalled to the *Mugford*: LEAVING X REPORT NUMBER OF SURVIVORS[10].

Corey quickly brought the *Mugford* towards the oil slick. Mindful of the likely presence of a submarine — and of the risk to his own ship — he had no choice but to vary his course and speed. He had already decided to proceed with a rescue operation without delay. By the time the destroyer entered the oil slick and slowed, the eagle-eyed lookouts had identified five separate groups of survivors. As slowly as he dared, Corey

147

manoeuvred the *Mugford* towards the gathering of nondescript rafts and oil-grimed humanity.

The effect that this weaving but unquestionably approaching camouflage-grey warship had on the *Centaur* survivors can well be imagined. After a day and a half of passing aircraft and ships seemingly treating them with total disregard, suddenly, and almost at the same instant, here came the white chargers of succour from both air and sea. This time there could be no doubt; rescue was at hand. Sister Savage clutched her rosary beads and gave thanks to God. Tears streamed down her drawn cheeks. The men cheered and waved, shook hands and thumped each other on the backs. Many cried unashamedly with relief. Then they realised that their hunger and thirst would soon be assuaged; the time for rationing had passed. 'Hey, where's that water tin?' What luxury, to gulp down a mouthful of water without guilt!

The warship nosed in through the oil slick towards a small group of men on makeshift rafts. Fourth Engineer Maurice Cairnie barely realised that the cavalry had arrived. He had been conscious off and on for most of this second day in the water, and lay exhausted on his hatchboard. Albert Taylor, Fred Millar and Ken Murray were similarly in a bad way. Several later reports emerged of one un-named orderly found straddling a hatchboard while he gripped the hands of two other men sitting in lifebuoys. This can only have been Albert Taylor, with Millar and Murray his two companions.

As the ship neared it turned to starboard. Cairnie and his three companions saw decks packed with US sailors; ratings in blue denim work-clothes, officers in smart khaki uniforms. An officer on the bridge held a bullhorn. Corey's amplified voice boomed out, asking which ship they were from and when they had been sunk. All four men instantly yelled back in excited unison. 'The Centaur! The Centaur! Yesterday morning!' they croaked, their voices suddenly firm with renewed faith.

No-one on the ship could sort through the jumbled yells[11]. 'What'd they say?' Corey asked around him, but saw only pursed lips and shrugged shoulders. He lifted the bullhorn and called again, and got the same result. He tried once more, asking that only one person answer. One did, and this time the message got through. Corey's reaction was not recorded, but can well be imagined. He lifted the bullhorn again.

'Have you seen the submarine?'

Top left:
S/Sgt Frank Mycock (lost).
Above:
Pte Bob Stubbs (lost).
Left:
*Driver Richard Cavanagh
(lost).*

(G. McGrath)

*Right: Ptes Les and Neville Clark,
brothers (both lost).*
(Mrs B.Jamieson)

Toshio Kusaka, captain of the I-180 . . . attacked the Ormiston and Caradale the day before the Centaur was torpedoed.

V-Admiral Hisashi Mito . . . issued the infamous secret order to execute all prisoners.
(US National Archives)

Hajime Nakagawa, captain of the I-177 . . . denied sinking the Centaur.   (US National Archives)

Japanese submarine I-176, sister

USN, captain of the USS Mugford when she rescued the Centaur survivors.

(Cdr P.A.Murray)

Right: Dr Bruce McCampbell, Mugford's Medical Officer ... examined each survivor.

(Cdr P.A.Murray)

Below: USS Mugford (DD-389)
(US National Archives)

USS Mugford *under way at speed . . . how the* Centaur *survivors would have seen their rescuer bearing down on them.*

("US Destroyers of WWII" Reilly, Arms and Armour Press)

USS Helm *(DD-388) . . . a futile search for more survivors.*

(US National Archives)

'Yes, early this morning!'

Corey spoke briefly to his officers. He raised the bullhorn again. His resonant voice told the four men to hold on while he picked up some of the other survivors. He assured them he would be back[12].

Then the *Mugford* went astern.

One of the grimy survivors cried out, 'Please don't leave us!' Seamen on deck watched pitifully as their ship pulled away from the four anguished, oil-streaked faces[13].

Observing these goings-on with great interest were the bridge crew of the *Sussex*. The *Mugford* had not explained what was happening, but the captain could judge from the order to 'beat it' that something was amiss. His course took him north of, but close to, the oil slick. His lookouts soon reported it, and the debris. He began to grasp what was happening when he saw the tattered collection of survivors floating in the water. Word spread rapidly throughout the ship and soon curious onlookers gathered. Anyone not on duty came on deck. The usual speculation ran rife; was it a submarine? A dreaded merchant raider perhaps? One young seaman, B.Middleton, told the authors he stood glued to the spot at the stern of the *Sussex*, mesmerised by the scene. He saw the *Mugford* moving in towards the survivors. A numbing fear took hold of him when someone mentioned seeing sharks. He felt a sense of guilt that a ship flying the Red Ensign could sail right by these pathetic survivors 'as if she didn't care!' But the *Sussex* had her orders to keep going, and could not help in the rescue[a][14].

Meanwhile Corey was zeroing in on a small clump of survivors farthest away from the main group. The *Mugford*'s Rescue-and-Repair gang cleared away sections of the side railings on the port quarterdeck. They rigged scrambling nets and a wooden-runged rope ladder. Fortunately destroyers have a small freeboard. The survivors would have less than three metres to climb. Seamen lined the rail ready to dive into the water if need be. Others, marksmen, stood by with rifles, ready to shoot at sharks[15]. The *Mugford*'s MO, Dr Bruce McCampbell, USN, stood at the rail, already casting his professional eye over the wallowing survivors. His pharmacist mates were at his side, ready for the casualties

---

a. The crew of the *Sussex* did not learn that the survivors were from the hospital ship *Centaur* until they reached New Zealand.

and with instructions to bring serious injuries to his immediate attention.

Corey deftly swung the aft port side of his ship alongside the three men. They were the stewards Alex Cochrane and Mark Jonassen, and another man. Despite a day and a half of exposure — and the surging, rolling destroyer's side — they clambered unassisted up the netting, happily accepting the outstretched hands at deck level. McCampbell and his men quickly checked them over, and then willing sailors took them below for attention.

OOD Clodins noted the time: 1410.

Corey turned the *Mugford* towards the main group of survivors. On the way he dictated an urgent message to Captain E.P.Thomas, NOIC Brisbane. It read:

> Am picking up many survivors of HMA Hospital Ship Centaur position 27 degs 03 mins South 154 degs 12 mins East at 0414z. Ship sunk at 0400k Friday. More details later[16].

Some ten minutes later, the *Mugford* approached the main group of survivors. What a pitiable bunch of miserable, oil-grimed humanity they were! A clinging cluster of near-naked, greasy torsos crammed together, using up much of a surge of new-found stamina to wave to their rescuers. Few had enough energy left to shout. Even so, many a grimy face cracked with a broad white grin of relief.

When within about 50 metres of the wallowing cluster, the seamen lining the *Mugford*'s decks were electrified to hear a strong female voice calling out. It came from the largest raft and shouted out a warning about the sharks. The Americans had already seen the sharks for themselves; it was hearing a woman's voice from the midst of this scene of devastation that shocked them![17] Then they saw her in a tight gathering on the raft. She wore barely any clothes. One leg was drawn up near her body, the other out straight in front of her. The sight of her in such a pathetic situation, a woman amidst the tragic consequences of war, ingrained itself on so many American memories. When asked fifty years later about that moment, they could recall it with total clarity, as if it had happened only a few weeks before[b][18].

---

b. Radioman Bill Records was so moved by her courage that he later corresponded with and became a firm friend of the Savage family.

Corey inched his way in, backing and filling and using his twin screws to best advantage to virtually berth the *Mugford* alongside the raft. The lady's voice called out again, calmly identifying herself and her fellow survivors, and their ship. Then the agonising transfer began. Some of the men forgot all their aches and pains in their determination to reach safety. They shinned up the netting or ladder and bounded onto the deck. Waiting were dozens of US sailors eager to shake hands and offer cigarettes. Tom Hobden was one of those with a burst of energy that an hour before he could not have imagined was still in him. He scrambled up the ship's side like a teenager. On deck an American seaman welcomed him on board and offered him a cigarette. The two became instant pals. Fred Chidgey and Tom Hegarty were close behind. Eager seamen desperate to help reached out to each man scaling the cumbersome nets to haul them onto the deck, then immediately offered cigarettes. Chidgey accepted readily. He lit up and inhaled deeply. Never had he appreciated a single cigarette so much and never had one tasted so good. He held it between his fingers, looking at it with a heightened awareness that he had not experienced before. He realised how much the smallest and simplest things in life suddenly meant to him. The sailors wanted all the survivors to go below for attention, but those who were able stayed on deck, watching anxiously to see who else might be rescued.

Others survivors, especially the burned, needed assistance. Without hesitation *Mugford* seamen climbed down the rope netting[19]. Some even took to the water[20]. Ellen Savage directed them to those survivors in most need of help. She refused to go up herself until the rescuers attended to them first, despite all urging that she precede them. Several *Mugford* seaman later remarked how cool and collected Ellen Savage was; totally in control of the situation.

The evacuation of the big raft went smoothly. Bill Cornell, not unexpectedly, slowed up proceedings. He was too badly injured to climb, even with assistance. The seamen lowered a wire stretcher over the side, lifted him into it, and hauled him aboard. However gentle they were, Cornell's blistered skin peeled off in strips. He screamed in agony, and fainted.

When Ellen Savage finally reached the deck of the *Mugford* she said, simply, 'It was horrible'[21]. She received an awed, almost reverential reception from the American seamen who milled around her. Her indelible strength of character, and the inspiration that she had clearly been to the other survivors, astounded them. That a woman could survive such a catastrophe amazed them. She appeared to be without serious injury. The moment she stepped on deck she lined up alongside Dr McCampbell and began assisting him with the other survivors, as if she were a nurse just coming on duty. She didn't fool McCampbell, however. He soon insisted that she stop and have her own injuries attended to[22].

One American sailor, machinist mate Alfred Alexander, stood mesmerised by the awesome figure of this magnificent lady. For some time he was under the misapprehension that she was a nun — because he heard survivors calling her 'Sister'. His confusion grew a few minutes later when one survivor already on board greeted another, 'Hey, Blue!' He could never understand why a man with red hair automatically acquired the nickname 'Blue'[23].

Mattie Morris, meanwhile, was enjoying a cigarette below deck when someone asked for the time. A seaman replied and Morris realised, much to his surprise, that he was the winner of his own sweepstake. He had picked the rescue time within half an hour. He was in no hurry to claim his winnings, but it added an extra sparkle to that sweet joy and relief at being alive and safe.

Relief was not one of the emotions Lt-Cmdr Corey experienced in those tense moments. Although the rescue was going well, he paced the bridge nervously, concerned about the vulnerability of his stopped ship. Every one of the crew not involved in the rescue was on full alert in case the predatory submarine returned. Silently, Corey urged the climbing survivors to greater efforts, willing them up and onto the deck so he could once again get under way. One can almost hear his American vernacular: 'C'mon, you guys, get the lead out! Let's get the hell outta here!'

And all the while that distinctive regular pulsing tone of the sonar punching out its probing sound rays into the depths pervaded the scene; 'Pinggg ... Pinggg ...' The bridge bristled with sharp-eyed lookouts penetrating every point of the compass. Inevitably, in their nervousness, lookouts reported spurious targets; apparent periscopes, disturbed water that might suggest the presence of a submarine, even torpedo wakes. Corey had to check out every one. None, to great relief, had any foundation, but he took no chances and restricted to the very minimum the time the *Mugford* lay stopped in the water. As an extra precaution, and possibly also because of the injuries he had seen, he ordered the engineers to flash up Nos.3 and 4 boilers. He wanted a fast trip back to Brisbane.

With the survivors from the main raft aboard, Corey sent word to the remainder of the group that he would move off and pick up the other survivors. He was becoming increasingly edgy about being stationary. As with Cairnie's group, he promised to come back for them later.

Rippon, on the monkey island roof, acknowledged. He and the rest of his group watched as the *Mugford*'s screws threshed the water. The great grey ship accelerated away from them.

At 1446 the *Mugford* drew alongside the lone figure of Owen Christensen, still drifting on a hatchboard no bigger than his own body. The now practised seamen had him on board in a trice. Corey turned the destroyer back for the last of the smaller groups.

This time the *Mugford* sailors had no choice but to go into the water to help[24]. Taylor had barely enough strength to hold onto his board. Seamen eventually lifted him out of the water in a sling. Cairnie and the others needed several seamen to give them a bunk-up. The marksmen on deck sent volleys of bullets into the sea to dissuade the sharks[25].

Frank Martin, seamens' cook, must have wondered when his turn would come. Eventually it did, at 1507 according to the *Mugford* log. The seamen had to handle him with extreme care; his arms and stomach were red raw from rubbing on a wet hatchboard.

Finally, at 1523, Corey kept his promise and returned to Rippon's group. Everyone on the monkey island, except Vince McCosker, easily made it up the rope netting to the deck, despite having been on their feet for several hours. McCosker, his knee stiff and painful, let the others go first. This gave him the distinction of being the last *Centaur* survivor to be hauled from the sea. The operation had taken one hour and twenty minutes[26].

Corey could not be sure he had rescued all the survivors. He ordered a criss-cross search pattern over the whole debris field. He sent an aide to find the *Centaur*'s senior surviving deck officer and ask that he come to the bridge to help in the search, if he was up to it. Rippon, who by this time had already savoured a stiff glass of scotch and was hoeing into some steaming tomato soup and coffee, readily agreed. Suddenly his legs, swollen, bruised and cut as they were, proved no obstacle to climbing several flights of stairs. Corey shook him warmly by the hand and offered him his commander's seat. He sent for more soup and cigarettes. While the search for more survivors continued (fruitlessly, as things turned out) Rippon gave Corey and his officers an account of the sinking. They searched until dark, then gave up. Corey had to do his best for anyone else who might have survived, but he also had several people on board in urgent need of proper medical attention. Their early transfer to hospital was essential. He darkened ship, set course due West, and increased speed to 30 knots[27].

Behind them they deliberately left the debris as it was. The rafts would make convenient markers for any later search parties. Something else they left behind was the floating body of Pte Walder. They had seen it once but then lost it.

Rippon enjoyed his experience on the bridge of this modern destroyer. The sudden surge in speed from 15 to 30 knots exhilarated him. Even the previous 15 knots seemed fast in comparison with the old *Centaur*'s at-best 12. Corey pulled out the chart and showed him where he had found the wreckage; 42 miles virtually due east of Cape Moreton. Rippon was amazed. He showed Corey where the *Centaur* sank. Over that day and a half in the water the survivors had drifted northeast for 20 miles!

Meanwhile, below decks, the crew of USS *Mugford* were treating their guests to some spontaneous hospitality and kindness[28]. They washed them, clothed them, and tended their injuries; all the while listening to detailed accounts of the loss of the *Centaur* and their efforts to stay alive in the sea. The Americans found it unbelievable that the Japanese could sink a hospital ship. Generous tots of Canadian rye whisky went round. Those survivors who could eat launched themselves into huge portions of steak and potatoes, but few oil-lined stomachs could hold the rich food for long. The sailors even gave up their bunks. They organised a 'tarpaulin muster' and collected £237/12/– (around $475)[29]. They were surprised at how much their guests appreciated such a seemingly insignificant item as a toothbrush, and the opportunity to clean their teeth. They were impressed with the Australians' friendliness and gratitude to their rescuers; and their genuine concern for their shipmates' well-being.

In an overflowing Sick Bay and in the Wardroom, Dr McCampbell's staff gave the injured every possible attention.

Those with burns were wrapped in rolls of gauze. Bill Cornell needed a blood transfusion; an American sailor donated the required blood. Bob Westwood's headwound was treated. Characteristically, Ellen Savage was in the thick of it, doing her job. Dr McCampbell once again ordered her to desist and look to herself. He persuaded her to lie down; she did so, reluctantly, sliding into a young ensign's bunk.

For the first time in 36 hours, everyone was warm and resting comfortably. Most had responded rapidly to the generous servings of food, fresh coffee, whiskey (from irregular sources) and American cigarettes, and were soon joking with their rescuers. One of the *Centaur's* seaman, wearing borrowed clothes, went on deck. He stood at the rail, watching the sea race by. A passing *Mugford* officer, Lt Pete Murray, stopped and asked how he was faring. The seaman said he owed his life to a good Lord and some good people. He asked Murray what speed the ship was making. Murray told him they were doing revolutions for 25 knots. The seaman's face broke into a toothy grin. '@#/%! Twenty-five knots! I've never been faster than fifteen knots in all my life!'[30]

Despite the euphoria of salvation however, there hung over these people an acute sense of loss. They could already tell, just by looking around, that many familiar faces would never be seen again. When word went round that the destroyer had saved only 64, they began drawing up their own sad inventories of lost colleagues.

Apart from close friends, colleagues, and in one instance a brother, there were several people whose deaths particularly saddened them all. Captain George Alexander Murray rated high on the list. Big, competent, friendly Captain Murray. Like in all good sea yarns, the captain had gone down with his ship. This relic of seagoing traditions just didn't seem right somehow. The last anyone saw of him he was frantically trying to release a lifeboat; doing all he could to care for the lives for which he had the ultimate responsibility. The same wave had overwhelmed Captain Murray, Moate, Stutter and Charlie Carey. Only Moate and Stutter lived through it. Chief Officer Harry Lamble, likewise, was last seen struggling with an unyielding lifeboat. Lt-Col Clem Manson, that lovable, happy-go-lucky C.O.Troops, jumped over the side with Sister Savage after gallantly holding back to help his girls up onto the rail — and he disappeared. Ellen Savage saw

Sisters Moston and King jump into the sea, but that was all. The last minutes of so many people went unseen by any of the survivors. No-one knew for sure what happened to the other nine lovely nurses; to the 18 other doctors; to Darwin Clark, the Red Cross representative, and his clerical cabin-mate Ernest Laverick; to all three radio operators. Many deaths were understandable, such as those in the engine room and the lower hospital deck, but others not so. No longer can it be estimated with any pretence of accuracy how many lives were snuffed out by the initial explosion and how many by drowning.

Grief did not lie easily with some. Mark Jonassen wept uncontrollably when he learned of the loss of two of his best mates. The wife of one was due to have a baby in June. The three pals had sat up thinking of possible names for the child that last evening on the *Centaur*[31].

Bob Westwood, the *Centaur*'s youngest, could not help but ponder about lady luck; how she had been so kind to him yet so brutal to his mate, Deck Boy David Abbot.

Surviving pals of L-Cpl M.J.O'Brien shook their heads in disbelief at the tragic irony of his passing. The three most important events in any man's life — his birth, marriage and death — had for O'Brien all fallen on the same calendar date, the 14th May.

Fred Chidgey thought back with acute sadness to a conversation with George Ockwell and Ray Hutchison on the *Centaur*'s last evening afloat. Ockwell had remarked how 'dead lucky' their group had been to survive this brutal war without anything serious happening. How poignant those words!

Maurice Cairnie was particularly saddened that Sister Rutherford had not survived. He admonished himself for not picking up her watch when he rushed out of his cabin; he could have given it to her family as a memento.

At 2110 the *Mugford* hove to off the Brisbane pilot steamer and embarked a pilot. Under his guidance she made her way across Moreton Bay via the North West Channel. She passed the Pile Beacon at 2245 and soon after entered the Brisbane River. An hour later she made her approach to berth starboard side to No. 3 Newstead Wharf. A surprisingly large crowd awaited.

OOD J.Shanahan noted in the log that the crew secured the last of the *Mugford*'s six manilla mooring lines at one minute to midnight[32].

It had been quite a day.

Chapter Eleven

THE SURVIVORS IN BRISBANE

When Lt-Cmdr Corey's first shock message reached Brisbane that mid Saturday afternoon, it not surprisingly prompted a flurry of activity. It went first to Captain E. Penry Thomas, the Naval Officer in Command (NOIC). Thomas must have felt a mild pang of *deja vu*. A year earlier, as NOIC Darwin, he had been the first official to receive confirmed word of the approaching Japanese aerial armada. It was he who sounded the sirens that alerted the anti-aircraft batteries. And now he was the first to learn of the most serious wartime merchant shipping tragedy to occur in Australian waters[1].

He knew this tragic event would shock Brisbane. Even though local residents knew about attacks on Darwin, on Townsville and even Sydney, this vicious assault right on their doorstep was bound to shatter any last residual complacency. It showed beyond doubt that war could be very close indeed.

Thomas had three immediate priorities: to organise an extended search for more survivors; to arrange medical attention for those coming in by the *Mugford*; and to notify all the appropriate authorities. He knew well that a disaster of this magnitude, with its obvious consequences for the navy, the army, the merchant service and indeed the US alliance itself, was destined to have profound repercussions at the highest military and political levels.

With the help of his chief staff officer, Lt-Cmdr J.C.B.McManus[2], Penry Thomas got things moving. The nearest warship to the search area was the USS *Helm*, another Gridley class destroyer, then *en route* from the Whitsunday Islands to Sydney. The *Helm* had rounded the tip of Fraser Island early that afternoon. She was promptly diverted to the search area[3].

157

To prepare for the inbound survivors, about whose medical condition he had little more than the sketchiest of details, Thomas, with the help of the Deputy Director of Navigation L.J.Burch, called in the army[4]. At that stage he had no idea how many survivors there were, nor of the ratio of army personnel to merchant crew. A message from the *Mugford* later that afternoon gave a figure of 54 men and one woman, but no departmental breakdown. Thomas assumed, rightly, that the army would look after its own. Members of the ship's medical staff and the 2/12 Field Ambulance would be taken care of by the Army Medical Corps. That the army would take responsibility for merchant seamen, on the other hand, could not be guaranteed. They were, after all, civilians. So he called on Padre Hoog of the Seamens' Mission. Hoog responded magnificently, and soon had a band of volunteers busily preparing bedding, food and other comforts[5].

Thomas' other concurrent priority was to notify the appropriate authorities. He informed his superiors in the Department of the Navy, who in turn immediately contacted the Department of Defence. The Secretary of Defence considered it serious enough to be taken right to the top — to the Prime Minister, the Right Honourable John Curtin. Unfortunately Curtin could not be reached. He had left Melbourne by car that morning *en route* to Canberra. All the Secretary of the Prime Minister's Department, Mr.Shedden, could do was leave instructions that someone inform the P.M. as soon as he reached the capital[6].

The other top-level notification was to the larger-than-life figure of General Douglas B.MacArthur, Allied Commander-in-Chief SWPA. Whatever the proprieties of the network of command and communication, it can be taken for granted that MacArthur got to know about the *Centaur* and the *Mugford* very promptly. GHQ SWPA acted swiftly, ordering all US naval personnel in Brisbane back to base. The recall order quickly spread. Movie theatres all over Brisbane flashed up the brusque message on their screens, without explanation[7].

That evening, army authorities put the nursing staff at 112th Army General Hospital Greenslopes on alert for a large number of casualties. They could expect them about midnight. No reason was given. Somehow the story spread that there had been a serious accident — an explosion — at a Brisbane wharf. Matron Grace Sheahan soon had her nursing staff and VADs preparing beds in Wards Three and Four, the surgical and medical wards. She arranged to move several patients in those wards to other parts of the hospital. Medical orderlies set to preparing a hot meal. Nursing staff on the evening shift were instructed not to undress when they finished their duty; they might be called on during the night[8].

USS *Mugford* berthed at Newstead Wharf at midnight that night. Her reception consisted of a variegate gathering of military and medical authorities, the Dalgetys agent, and a battery of military and civilian ambulances. A cameraman from Movietone News waited in the wings for a scoop. Only the authorities went on board, led by Lt-Cmdr McManus. They talked to the survivors and concluded they all needed medical attention and should be hospitalised. The merchant seamen, they decided, would be taken to Brisbane General Hospital at Herston[9].

Disembarkation began at 0045[10]. Most survivors were able to walk down the gangway to the waiting ambulances; some needed help. A few were stretcher cases. Pte Vince McCosker, his leg in a bad way, was one of them. As the stretcher bearers carried him across the dock McCosker heard shouts from a group of men nearby. He thought they were wharfies. 'You'll be sorry!' they bellowed, amongst other similar remarks. The taunts puzzled McCosker. He wondered what these men thought had happened. He wrote them off as 'brainless clots', and hoped their consciences would prick them when they found out the full story[11].

As Pte Fred Chidgey walked ashore to the waiting ambulances he pondered over the acute irony of the whole incident. A hospital ship had been destroyed, and a destroyer had become a hospital ship. And now members of a medical team had become patients, being given treatment in the very same manner that they themselves were trained to give.

At 0135 the last survivor stepped ashore. As Lt-Cmdr McManus quit the ship, a member of the *Mugford*'s crew handed over the money collected on board, entrusting him with spending it on the survivors' more immediate needs: clothing, cigarettes, soap, and so on. And with that final, thoughtful gesture by the *Mugford*'s officers and crew, the destroyer's role in the *Centaur* drama drew to a close. Soon afterwards, two ambulance convoys left Newstead Wharf; one bound for Greenslopes, the other for Brisbane General[12].

At Greenslopes, about 0200, and despite the wartime 'Brown Out', pensively waiting staff saw a line of lights coming from the direction of the city. Minutes later their incoming casualties arrived. All 34 military survivors — 20 ship's medical staff and 14 Field Ambulance — were quickly attended to. Greenslopes' doctors examined each arrival. All were suffering, with varying severity, from exposure, burns, ingested oil, sunburn and shock. All had bruises. Many had blisters. About two dozen men with burns were taken immediately to Ward Three, the surgical ward. Bill Cornell was so badly blistered the sisters had difficulty finding undamaged flesh into which they could insert a needle. They finally located two tiny areas free of blisters; in his upper arm, and near his instep.

The remaining, less-seriously injured men went to Ward Four, a medical ward. George McGrath remembers well that he ate a hearty meal; six eggs, six slices of toast, and six cups of tea. Afterwards nurses put him to bed and sedated him, and he did not wake up until the afternoon[13].

Lt-Col Outridge was allocated a private room in Ward Four.

Sister Ellen Savage, with deference to her calling, her rank and her sex, went to a ward reserved for sick nurses on the top floor of the nearby Nurses Home. After treatment she was tucked up in bed. She cried all that night.

The medical staff at Greenslopes toiled long and hard that night. One sister later spoke of the invaluable support given by the contingent of VADs. Everyone soon learned the truth about the 'accident on the wharf'. Army Intelligence had instructed the survivors to say nothing to anyone about the *Centaur*, but must have known the story would not stay bottled up for long. In no time the doctors and nurses realised that their patients were 'of the cloth', army medicos like themselves, and their tragic story could not thereafter have been contained. The news stunned the staff; not only because of the sheer magnitude of the disaster and the senseless loss of so many colleagues, but also because several of the *Centaur*'s staff had previously worked at Greenslopes and were personally very well known[14].

Meanwhile, at Brisbane General, hospital staff received the 30 merchant crew survivors in much the same way as any other incoming civilian casualties. Apart from Captain Salt, few were seriously burned, although most kept coughing up oil. They were well taken care of, even if their sheer numbers put a strain on the supply of beds. Steward Martin Pash suffered the embarrassment of being sent to the maternity ward!

At the Seamen's Mission, Padre Hoog — a little belatedly, the message did not reach him until 0230 — found out that all the seamen had gone to hospital. The authorities thanked him and his volunteers for their sterling efforts. The next morning, and despite his late night, Hoog went to the hospital to determine the seamens' needs. He wasn't the only one. Other officials were there: Messrs Smails and Barrett (local agents for Blue Funnel), a Mr Wong (Blue Funnel Engineering Superintendent), and Mr Burch from the Navigation Department.

The group interviewed each of the 20 seamen in turn. Hospital staff identified 13 men well enough to travel south to their home states, some for more treatment there. The remainder could be released as their medical conditions improved, and all should be fit for repatriation by the end of the month. Padre Hoog and the officials left the hospital in the early afternoon to begin making arrangements[15].

Second Mate Gordon Rippon had been subject to a more intense de-briefing, this time at the hands of Lt-Cmdr McManus, the naval intelligence officer. McManus also interviewed 3rd Mate Monty Banks, A.B. Cecich and the cook Martin.

Prime Minister Curtin, meanwhile, was still missing. By midday on this Sunday, urgent memos from the Secretary of Defence had begun to accumulate. The first amplified the initial message from the *Mugford* and informed the P.M. that the destroyer had picked up '54 men and one woman, including four seriously injured . . . ' This was of course a preliminary count; the exact total was 64. The memo added that 'H.S. Centaur was struck by one torpedo and sank in about two minutes. Warships and aircraft are continuing searching'[16].

The search at the wrecksite, both for more survivors and for the offending submarine, was indeed continuing.

First to reach the spot where the *Mugford* found the survivors was the USS *Helm*, DD-388, under the command of Lt-Cmdr W.Braun. When diverted that afternoon, the *Helm* had been heading 173° to pass about 20 miles off Cape Moreton on her run to Sydney. A course alteration of 20 degrees to port, to 153°, aimed the *Helm* at the *Centaur*'s drifting debris field. She reached the site around 2300. Lt-Cmdr Braun immediately began a systematic search pattern between the positions where the

Centaur sank and where the *Mugford* picked up survivors. Braun ordered the ship darkened and set 'Modified condition Affirm'. Anti-submarine sweeps continued incessantly. Sharpeyed lookouts found the first wreckage at 0026[17]. At dawn two small objects were seen and investigated: they turned out to be a wrecked lifeboat's buoyancy tanks. But that was all. Despite the most intense scrutiny while the *Helm* criss-crossed the area, her crew found neither survivors nor corpses. At noon Lt-Cmdr Braun received orders to discontinue the search and proceed south for other duties. By then other naval units had arrived to take over.

Helm's replacements were four motor torpedo boats and HMAS *Lithgow*, a Bathurst class minesweeper commanded by Lt-Cmdr Theo Haultain[18]. Over the previous few days the *Lithgow* had been at sea exercising with a US submarine doing a shake-down cruise after repairs in South Brisbane drydock. During that time the *Lithgow* picked up a strange asdic signal, and then unfortunately lost it. The *Lithgow* returned to Brisbane in the early hours of the 16th, but had barely finished tying up when orders arrived to proceed immediately to sea in the company of four torpedo boats. When Lt-Cmdr Haultain heard why, he reeled in shock. His sister was on the *Centaur*'s nursing staff. He and Helen Haultain (Cynthia, as her family knew her) had exchanged greetings only a few days earlier, during the *Centaur*'s last visit to Brisbane. Agonising at the brutally ironic coincidence that he should be called on to search for the survivors of his sister's ship, Haultain hastened to get the *Lithgow* under way. Ahead of him, were he to know it, were five days of anguish; five days and five sleepless nights of fruitless search before he had to concede — as had the commanders of the *Mugford* and *Helm* before him — that no more survivors could be found. Haultain could only reflect on the brutal prospect that the asdic signal the *Lithgow* had picked up a few days earlier had bounced from the hull of the *Centaur*'s attacker. The pangs of futile but recurring 'if only's' would not go away[19].

At this stage of the *Centaur* narrative, it might be useful to take brief leave from the chronological sequence of events; to examine what in a modern perspective might seem rather tardy and inadequate responses to the disaster. Astute, though lay readers might with cogent reasoning wonder why the authorities waited so long to launch these organised searches. They might ponder how a ship could be sunk for two days without being missed; and question why, given the reports by Mabel Hess and Lt Ward, the authorities took no action — not even a radio call to the ship. Now, fifty years on, we can answer these questions neither fully nor with ironclad assurances. Some aspects can be explained, and educated speculation offered about others, but gaps will remain. Perhaps at this juncture — while everyone is out looking for the Prime Minister — it might be fitting to address them in more detail.

First, that no-one gave a thought to the possibility of the *Centaur* meeting foul play can be attributed entirely to the ubiquitous wartime practice of radio silence. Unless under instructions to 'report in' at various places or times, Captain Murray would have authorised the use of the radio transmitter only for extremely important messages[a]. The only authorised method for passing intelligence to shore authorities was the Aldis signalling lamp, with ship's officers 'talking to' manned lighthouses. Reports also went in from reconnaissance aircraft, which overflew any ships they sighted to establish their identity. Most ships were equipped with a large, hinged name-board on the monkey island or bridge-wing. Normally stowed face down to hide the name, it would be swung face up for aircraft or vertically outwards for challenging warships — provided they were friendly! In these silent ways, at least some information found its way to the authorities, but by no means did they constitute a mandatory form of position-reporting. Whenever sighted, by whatever official means, a report certainly followed. The *Centaur* was seen and reported passing Coffs Harbour the evening before her demise. But that no-one saw her for more than 36 hours caused no alarm for her safety[20].

It could be argued that restrictive radio silence rules need not apply to hospital ships, immune — supposedly — from enemy attack. But maritime intelligence of any sort can be useful to an enemy. Although hospital ships eschew the cloak of anonymity — rather the opposite — their planned movements are nevertheless carefully guarded secrets, as evidenced by the withholding of the *Centaur*'s destination from most of her passengers and staff. An enemy can glean much direct and deduced information from details of a hospital ship's movements. RAN intelligence

---

a. On many ships the morse key was actually sealed, to prevent its use.

officer G.H.Gill, who later compiled the official war history of the RAN[b], was one official of the opinion that hospital ships *should* be allowed to send four-hourly position signals. He said this was the practice in the European war theatre, where Britain and Germany voluntarily submitted details of their hospital ships to each other. He observed with prescience that with such a system in place the absence of an official scheduled position message from the *Centaur* would have sparked an early search and rescue mission[21].

Was the *Centaur* not afforded aerial cover? No, she was not, and for a very good reason. Merchant convoys, certainly, enjoyed the umbrella of aerial cover, but to have extended the courtesy to AHS *Centaur* would have compromised her hospital ship status.

Interestingly, given her proximity to the coast, the Point Lookout early warning radar station should have detected her. After all, she sank only 24 miles away from it. If she had been, the operators — the US Army Air Corps — would have reported the contact to Fighter Sector in Brisbane, and through it to CDH. Moreover, a radar operator monitoring the *Centaur*'s progress across his screen could not help being puzzled by the sudden disappearance of what had been a strong radar target, and would surely have raised the alarm. That she passed undetected is attributed, amazingly enough, to nothing more than a faulty valve. Incredibly, that very morning one of the radar's transmitter valves blew. This was a common occurrence, usually and easily fixed by replacing the faulty component. But the technicians could not do this until the radar set cooled down, which took 40 minutes at least. For some reason the station did not report itself out of action. All this emerged after the event. When quizzed about not sighting the *Centaur*, the station replied that she must have entered the extreme radar range *after* the equipment had broken down, and been sunk *before* it came back on line[22].

This is interesting, considering the radar blip detected some three hours earlier by Mabel Hess at her Lytton Hill station. Her superiors discounted the report at the time, and others later expressed doubts about the possibility of it being the submarine *I-177*. Sceptics pointed to the interposing offshore islands and

---

b. See Bibliography.

doubted that the conning tower of a submarine on the other side could be detected by radar, especially at that range. A look at the chart, however, shows a fair gap between the southern end of Moreton Island and the northern tip of Stradbroke. In fact from Mabel Hess' radar site, an arc of ten degrees of clear surface horizon exists between the two islands, from 080° to 090°. When vectored seaward, this arc neatly encompasses the spot where the *Centaur* and the *I-177* made their fateful rendezvous. The range of more than 40 miles also drew scepticism, being about twice that normally expected for a surface target from a scanner only 50 metres above sea level. But atmospheric conditions could often extend effective range by quite phenomenal amounts. We are thankful for the reminiscences of Walter Fielder-Gill, the C.O. of 23 Radar Fort Lytton in May 1943, who in correspondence with us in July 1992 said he recalled this happening on several occasions. Both he and some of his operators — among them ACWs Pixie Woodward and Kaye Rae — reported unidentified surface vessels to seaward of Moreton Island. Fighter Sector classified these targets XI, i.e 'unidentified'. ACW Rae's report came during the evening of 13th May, only hours before Mabel Hess lodged hers. None of this offers any proof that Mabel Hess saw the Japanese submarine *I-177*, but it should have been enough to alert the authorities to the *possibility* that something lying virtually still in the water, something that suddenly appeared on a radar screen and equally as suddenly disappeared, might just be a submarine — especially as the submarine menace was at its peak at that time. Having said that, even had the authorities accepted the possibility of a submarine lurking off Moreton Island, realistically speaking there is little that they would have done that might have prevented the assault on the *Centaur*. They would have harboured no concern for the *Centaur*'s safety; to the best of their knowledge she was a good eighty miles farther out in the Tasman Sea.

So much for *before* the *Centaur* met her Waterloo; what about afterwards? Let us examine first the question of a distress message from the ship itself. Why wasn't one sent? After all, a radio operator (almost certainly Eric Summers) was on duty at the time. Only a few minutes earlier Gordon Rippon had handed him the 0400 position slip. Surely, in the *Centaur*'s obviously parlous state, he did not have to wait for authorisation from Captain Murray to at least punch out an SOS? No, but given the strictures of radio silence he might have hesitated, just for a few moments, expectant that Murray or one of the deck officers would appear with that authorisation. Even if he decided to act without it, whether he had *time* to do so (or for that matter was *able* to do so) is problematical and, frankly, unlikely. The radio aerials, bare wires strung from foremast to mainmast with a vertical connection to the top of the radio room, most probably came down with the first explosion. The shock of the blast could also have damaged the radio equipment. It is possible the blast killed or injured the radio operator himself. Those forlorn scenarios aside, the *Centaur*'s radio equipment was not the most modern and it needed at least a couple of minutes of aerial-tuning before it could transmit. It is doubtful that the Sparks even got started on this; within a few seconds of the explosion all main power ceased. He could switch over to emergency power, but in the sudden darkness would need some sort of lighting at least (possibly a torch) to help his groping hands find and engage the hinged knife-switch that brought battery power on line. Having done that, he then had to tune his aerials all over again. All this took time, which this hapless radio operator simply did not have. Somewhere along that process of activities, time ran out. The mainmast collapsed, pulling down any aerials that might still have been attached. Any remaining possibility of transmission collapsed with it. Seconds later the ship itself went. That this radio operator stuck to his post and paid the ultimate personal sacrifice is evidenced by the accounts of those survivors who made it to the boat deck; none mention seeing him.

Finally, what appears to be the most damning incident of all; the failure of CDH to heed the report of the fireball seen by Lt Ward and two others at the Rous Battery. One would rate the failure to at least investigate the likely source of a 'large, all-round orange glare' as totally inexcusable. Incredibly, the blame lay with one tiny, single-letter aural misinterpretation. Lt Ward's report emerged from the CDH telephonist who took down the message as a 'large, all-round orange *flare*'! This message, its meaning totally corrupted by just one letter, went to the duty naval officer. This gentleman took out the chart and laid off a bearing line 090° from Rous Battery. He noticed that if he projected the line far enough out — like 100 miles — it reached a currently gazetted anti-submarine exercise area. He came to the conclusion that Ward and the others had seen a flare dropped by an aircraft to indicate a submarine contact. Any doubts that a flare could be seen over a distance of 100 nautical miles did not seem to have entered his head. He took no further action. One would have thought that he should at least have *asked* Lt Ward exactly what he had seen[23].

But enough hypothesis and digression. Back to our story.

On Sunday evening the P.M. was still somewhere 'out in the sticks'. By this time, secretary Shedden had collected quite a pile of teleprinted messages, most of them from the Secretary of Defence (whom Brisbane sources were keeping fully informed). One Minute Paper from the navy gave a summary of the facts as then known. It came from an oral briefing by McManus, delivered via 'secraphone', and read:

1. Survivors stated attack took place at 0415K/14 May — 070 degrees True, 24 miles off Pt. Lookout. She was steering north at 12 knots in fine clear weather.
2. All lights were on. Except two floodlights right forward used for floodlighting the bows, these were switched off because they affected sight from the bridge.
3. Only one torpedo hit 'Centaur', striking her on the port side abaft number 2 hatch. She caught fire immediately and sank in two to three minutes. She made no signals and there was no time to launch any boats although two boats broke adrift from the ship.
4. Three of the survivors state that about 0330k/15th May, they saw the submarine on the surface near the ship's boats.
5. All survivors were on rafts spread over an area of about two miles, when they were picked up by 'Mugford' at about 1430K/15th May, in position approximately 20 miles NE of the scene of the attack.
6. Security Officer Brisbane gives the number of survivors as 25 merchant seamen, 31 military personnel (including one nurse). The attached list of survivors obtained from USS 'Mugford', however, shows in addition to the above, the names of Colonel English AAMC and Captain R.M.Salt (Torres Straits Pilot). The attached list will be further checked by Security Officer Brisbane.
7. From USS 'Mugford' and also from the survivors Security Officer Brisbane obtained the opinion that there was no chance of there being further survivors.
8. GHQ informed Security Officer Brisbane this morning that the news of the sinking would be published immediately. He has asked Commander Chesterman (RAN Liaison) to point out to GHQ that the procedure usually followed is to inform next of kin of missing persons before such an announcement is made. The result of that approach will be communicated to Navy Office. In the meantime Publicity Censors in Brisbane have been asked to prohibit any published reference to the sinking, and Press representatives have not been allowed to interview survivors[24].

A postscript explained that the list of survivors mentioned in 6 would not be attached, probably pending the security officer's review. This check was warranted because of the conflicting estimates of the number of survivors. The mention of a Colonel English is interesting, especially as by all accounts no such person embarked. As will be shown later the error probably occured during a re-transcript of the initial list of survivors; an understandable mistake, but one that did not prevent the enigmatic Colonel English becoming grist for the mill of contention.

One other message in Shedden's collection is worthy of note — the first from General MacArthur to Prime Minister Curtin on the subject of the *Centaur*. The secret memo said:

> I contemplate announcing in the communiqué on Tuesday the details with regard to the loss of the hospital ship "Centaur". This delay is to permit notification of the next of kin[25].

Notifying next-of-kin was already proving to be a difficult and melancholy task. Before the army authorities could begin sending out notification messages they had to be sure exactly who had sailed in the ship. Their base data came from the Nominal Roll, supplemented by naval information about the survivors. They had to double-check each name if they were to avoid sending a 'missing — believed drowned' notice to the relatives of someone not even on the ship, or fail to send a notice to the relatives of someone who was. We noted earlier a few comings and goings at sailing time; there may well have been others.

Private Clem Lynne was a prime example. He, it will be recalled, took it upon himself to join the *Centaur* in Sydney. He wasn't going to miss all the fun. How the army authorities found out about him is unclear, but they interviewed all 14 2/12th survivors to make absolutely sure he had sailed and, as it turned out, perished[26]. They had to consider that others of like mind might have copied him.

Army notification telegrams were wherever possible delivered personally to the addressee. Some were typed, some handwritten. Mrs Fred Fortier's read, 'It is with deep regret that I have to inform you that NXS7176 driver Frederick Lewis Fortier has been reported missing believed drowned and desire to convey to you the profound sympathy of the Minister for the Army'. A follow-up telegram the next day clarified that Fred Fortier, 'previously reported missing believed drowned is now

reported drowned by enemy action'[27]. Many 2/12th personnel
relatives must have been quite nonplussed at the 'believed
drowned' part; they had no idea that their menfolk had even
gone to sea! They put two and two together later, when news
of the *Centaur*'s loss hit the newspapers.

The missing merchant seamens' relatives were notified by
telegrams sent by Dalgety and Company, shipping agents for the
Centaur. These relatives, of course, well knew on which ship
their men served. Dalgety's cables, while nonetheless inescapably
brutal in their message, were slightly more informative and
sincere than their military equivalents. David Milligan's family
in Oakleigh received the following:[28]

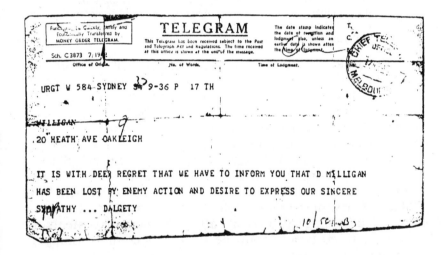

Sometime during the morning of the next day (Monday 17th
May), Prime Minister Curtin, now in Canberra, was at last briefed
on the *Centaur* incident. Discussing it with some colleagues he
must have authorised his Minister for Supply and Shipping,
J.(Jack) Beasley to make an unofficial statement at a press
luncheon in Sydney that day. About 100 women press correspondents from Sydney and Canberra heard Beasley's briefing, which gave the time and place of the sinking and the number
of casualties and survivors. For the women journalists, the
'scoop' was ephemeral; the ubiquitous censor came between

them and the presses, and they could do nothing but sit on this
tantalising piece of inside information for as long as he said.

For one woman in the group, however, the news came as a
chilling, personal shock. Her husband had sailed on the *Centaur*.
She had not at that stage received any official notification. Not
surprisingly, the way she heard the news distressed her a great
deal[29].

Not long after Beasley's briefing, MacArthur sent a memo to
Curtin marked 'Secret — Most Immediate'.

> Army authorities expect to clear notification to next of kin by nine
> a.m. Tuesday. For psychological reasons I believe it to be essential that
> the loss be announced by us before an announcement by the enemy.
> It will therefore without fail be carried in the official communique
> released by GHQ at 12 noon Tuesday. Press Relations report that
> announcement of loss was made in Sydney by Mr Beasley but the censors
> have been instructed to suppress all press stories until 12 o'clock Tuesday
> simultaneously with release of communique[30].

One could be forgiven for detecting a note of criticism about
Beasley's briefing, news of which reached MacArthur remarkably
quickly. Perhaps he did not approve of the announcement, or
of the manner in which it was made. Maybe he felt piqued that
Curtin had not consulted him first.

To make sure MacArthur did not get upstaged with his communique, Curtin immediately sent a cable to the British Secretary
of State for Dominion Affairs in London, Mr Attlee. He asked
for assurances that London would make no announcement before
MacArthur's. In the same cable, Curtin advised London that he
intended framing a protest and asked for the actual date that the
Swiss notified Japan about the *Centaur*'s commissioning as a
hospital ship[31].

A few minutes later Secretary Shedden informed his Prime
Minister that the army, despite its best efforts, might not be able
to notify all next-of-kin that day. He suggested Curtin ask
MacArthur to delay the communique[32]. MacArthur replied that
he wanted the notification task completed by 0900 Tuesday. He
deemed it vital that he head off any possible scoop announcement the Japanese might make for propaganda purposes. The
longer he waited, the higher that risk. 'It, therefore, without fail
will be carried in the official communique released from GHQ
at 1200 hrs Tuesday,' he replied, emphatically, if autocratically,
settling the matter[33].

Curtin wasn't the only one counselling a stay of proceedings. That night (Australian time) the British Chiefs of Staff discussed the *Centaur* incident. They recommended that 'as a temporary measure every means to suppress publication of this should be taken.' The First Sea Lord cabled the ACNB, urging the Board to do all it could to prevent publication[34]. MacArthur heard about it first thing the next morning (Tuesday 18th May). It reached him from at least two sources: Australian naval authorities and Secretary Shedden acting for the P.M. MacArthur responded promptly, decisively and, it might be said, a tiny bit sarcastically:

> In view of the fact that the press have had this news since its release by Mr Beasley yesterday afternoon in Sydney, it is impossible at this late hour to suppress it[35].

At exactly 1200 General MacArthur released GHQ SWPA Communique No. 401. Seven minutes later a copy reached the Department of Defence. The last item under the heading 'AUSTRALIA' gave details of the loss of AHS *Centaur*[36].

Soon afterwards Prime Minister Curtin rose to his feet in Parliament and read the following statement:

> It is with the deepest regret that the Commonwealth Government has learned of the loss of the Australian hospital ship "Centaur" and I know that the news will come also as a profound shock to the Australian people. The attack which took place within a few miles of the Queensland coast bears all the marks of wantonness and deliberation. Not only will it stir our people into a more acute realisation of the type of enemy against whom we are fighting, but I am confident also that this deed will shock the conscience of the whole civilised world and demonstrate to all who may have had any lingering doubts the unscrupulous and barbarous methods by which the japanese conduct warfare.
>
> To the next-of-kin of those who are lost the Government and nation extend heartfelt sympathy, which is the deeper since those persons were non-combatants engaged on an errand of mercy, and were by all the laws of warfare immune from attack.
>
> The full circumstances of the sinking of the "Centaur" are as follows:-
> The "Centaur" was at 4 o'clock in the morning of Friday 14th May a short distance off the Queensland coast. The weather was fine and clear, and the visibility was good. The ship was brightly illuminated in accordance with the Geneva Convention. Illuminations, in addition to the usual navigation lights, consisted of red crosses on each side of the hull, red crosses on each side of the funnel, a large red cross directed upwards on the poop, and rows of brilliant white lights along the sides of the hull to illuminate the characteristic green painted band — in this case five feet wide — which encircles hospital ships. On board the "Centaur" at the time were 352 persons, consisting solely of the ship's

crew and medical personnel, including twelve nurses. There were no wounded on board. In all there were only 64 survivors including one nurse. Remaining 288 persons, including members of the ship's crew, nurses and other medical personnel, lost their lives.

Notice of intention to use the "CENTAUR" as a hospital ship, together with particulars of her dimensions, markings, and appearance, was communicated by the Commonwealth Government to the Axis Powers early this year; in the case of Japan on February 5th. In addition, full publicity including photographs of the ship was given in the Press, and particulars were broadcast in news broadcasts from Australian radio stations.

There is therefore no reason to suppose that the Japanese Government and the Japanese naval authorities were not fully acquainted with the existence and purposes of this vessel. In all the circumstances, the Commonwealth Government is bound to regard the sinking of the "Centaur" as an entirely inexcusable act undertaken in violation of a convention to which Japan is a party and of all the principles of common humanity. An immediate and strong protest in these terms is being addressed to the Japanese Government, and the country may feel confident that the Government will do its utmost to establish right of redress and ensure that the war criminals responsible for this dastardly act are brought to justice[37].

The word was out. Press reporters and war correspondents rushed to their typewriters. Shock waves were about to encircle the globe.

Postscript: A startling claim that both the *Centaur* and its attacking submarine were tracked by radar emerged in March 1993, when the final printing of this book was about to commence. The *Toowoomba Chronicle* quoted a Robert Martin, who served at No.18 Radar Station on Stradbroke Island in May 1943. Martin remembered picking up a target that Air Defence Headquarters identified as the *Centaur*. When a second target emerged nearby, the navy identified it as hostile, but ADHQ said the *Centaur* was marked and lit according to the Convention and thus was in no danger.

Chapter Twelve

SHOCK WAVES

Bad news always travels fast. AHS *Centaur*'s death notice was no exception. The shock tidings reached the streets within a few hours of John Curtin's statement. One of the first off the presses with the story was the afternoon *Melbourne Herald*. Its bold headlines screeched:

HOSPITAL SHIP TORPEDOED!
Only 64 Saved Of 363
NO WARNING GIVEN: RED CROSS IGNORED

The story just about filled the front page. The *Herald* writers and staff had put together a creditably thorough coverage despite being limited to the information given in MacArthur's and Curtin's mid-day announcements. They even came up with a photograph of the *Centaur* and details of her early career and conversion to a hospital ship.

The Press clamoured for the nitty-gritty details. MacArthur and Curtin had let the genie out of the bottle, and an army of intrepid journalists and war correspondents sallied forth for information in time for the Wednesday dailies. They knew exactly where to go. In no time they had their hands on the preliminary casualty figures and were hot on the trail of the survivors.

At that stage, all the AAMC and 2/12th casualties were still at Greenslopes Hospital. For the most part they were recovering from their ordeal very well, although some contracted pneumonia after coming ashore. They were forbidden to speak to the Press, at least until interviewed by the Army legal branch. The branch must have cleared Lt-Col Outridge and Sister Ellen Savage fairly quickly; both made brief statements on that Tuesday afternoon and gave fuller interviews later. Some survivors

used their initiative to tell their families that they were alive,
mostly through concern that news of the *Centaur*'s loss might
break before the military got round to contacting next-of-kin.
A telephone in Greenslopes was the medium for most of these
illicit calls. Chidgey and Hegarty 'starred' in a Movietone
Newsreel about the *Centaur*, but it was not shown in the cinemas
until after the official news release[a].

The merchant seamen were apparently in a different category.
No-one had bound them to silence. By this time there were very
few left at Brisbane General. The four officers — Rippon, Banks,
Smith and Cairnie — were then in Turrawan Private Hospital
at Clayfield. At least 13 others had already gone south by train
to Sydney and Melbourne. Some were to be hospitalised for
further treatment; others could go straight home. They arrived
in Sydney early on Tuesday morning. Red Cross officials greeted
them at the station with a hearty breakfast. They took those who
were fit enough out to the shops and to the Red Cross stores,
and invited them to choose any clothing they might need. Others
went to hospital. By coincidence, some ended up in the same
hospital and same ward as the seaman George Lamb, the man
who missed sailing in the ship after hitting his head on a fan[1].

Wherever these seamen went, by mid-afternoon the Press had
them in their sights and soon zeroed in for a feast of dramatic
material for the printing press. Implacable journalists and
photographers hunted them down. They snared them at their
homes, at railway stations, and in hospital. For at least one war
correspondent, Rita Dunstan of the *Sydney Daily Telegraph*, the
task brought back poignant memories of her recent visit to the
Centaur. She and Hugh Dash (a Sydney reporter and war correspondent of some acclaim) caught up with some of the
Melbourne-based seamen on their way through Sydney. One of
them recognised her. 'And you said we had no news,' he said
with mild sarcasm. He made the comment without malice, but
it stung Dunstan[2]. The seamen described their experiences openly
and fully, and Dunstan and Dash scribbled furiously. Dunstan
asked about Corporal Joe Moss, the smiling New Hebridean
hospital attendant who the week before had caught the attention of photographer Jack Hickson.

a. To see it, the starring pair walked into Brisbane with Sgt Len Hooper. They had no
   money, and had to convince the cinema manager of their identity before he would
   allow them in without charge.

Alf Ramage answered. 'He was lost. He was the soul of kindness to every sick soldier he attended.'

Dunstan made a mental note to pressure her editor to run the photograph of Joe Moss, if only to commemorate this one man's sacrifice. It appeared in the next edition[3].

That evening, now well supplied with personal statements and transcripts of interviews with survivors, the Press put together a comprehensive account of the tragedy. Next morning (Wednesday 19th May) the newspapers revealed all, great screeds of information under headline banners that gave full vent to the depth of feeling this story was inevitably going to generate:

A FOUL ATROCITY AT SEA (*Melbourne Herald*)
WANTON AND DELIBERATE ATTACK (*Argus*, Melbourne)
HOSPITAL SHIP SUNK ON WAY TO N.G.; 299 LOST, 64
SAVED (*Sydney Daily Telegraph*)
HOSPITAL SHIP SUNK, 299 LIVES LOST NEAR BRISBANE
(*Brisbane Telegraph*)
TREACHEROUS NOCTURNAL ATTACK (*Cairns Post*)

Supporting the story were the casualty lists and a range of photographs: pictures of the *Centaur*, of survivors being interviewed in hospital, of some of those who had not returned.

By Wednesday afternoon, few Australians remained unaware of the loss of AHS *Centaur*.

Even the Allied Press overseas gave it a run:

LIMITLESS SAVAGERY (*Liverpool Echo*)
HOSPITAL SHIP SUNK (*The Times*, London)
HOSPITAL SHIP SUNK 299 DIE IN PACIFIC (*New York
Times*, New York)
JAP SUB SINKS HOSPITAL SHIP — 299 LOSE LIVES
(*Gazette*, Montreal)
JAPS SINK HOSPITAL SHIP OFF AUSTRALIA (*Montreal
Star*, Montreal).

The internationals gave the loss of AHS *Centaur* front page billing, although it had to compete for headline prominence with daring RAF bombing raids on two big dams in the Ruhr Valley. The censors encouraged newspaper editors to highlight good war news rather than bad, so it is understandable that the famed Dam Busters' spectacular successes in the very heart of Germany eclipsed the sad tidings of a hospital ship sunk in far-away Australia.

A leader in the London *Daily Telegraph* commented that by sinking the *Centaur* the Japanese had only added to the long series of 'foul outrages which have consistently disgraced their arms'. It stressed that the most effective form of protest must be to reiterate recent American warnings that 'both leaders and their minor accomplices ... will be brought to account'. The editorial closed with a few profound words:

> The case of the Centaur is not the least of many new strands in the shirt of Nessus, which will inexorably be fitted on the guilty[4].

To their credit, the coverage and detail of the Australian domestic newspapers the next day were remarkably thorough and mostly free of inaccuracies. The papers did err with the roll call of survivors and casualties, however. They quoted many varied computations; none correct. But the Press were not to blame; the fault lay much higher up. MacArthur's initial communique gave the total personnel on the *Centaur* as 363[5]. Colonel W.R.Hodgson (Secretary of the Department of External Affairs), noticed Curtin had quoted 352. He queried the figure with MacArthur, pointing out that the Prime Minister's information had come from the RAN in Brisbane[6]. MacArthur's reply caused some embarrassment; his advice had also come from the RAN in Brisbane![7] Hodgson sent an immediate memo to Shedden, asking for clarification[8]. It was most important; the figures would be included in an official protest to the Japanese Government (on which Hodgson was already working)[9] and in the interests of credibility had to be totally accurate. Shedden checked with the navy[10]. The navy came up with a third — but this time accurate — figure: 332. The estimate of 352 given to the Prime Minister, the navy explained, had come from army sources. Apparently it included an extra 20 men earmarked for late dispatch on the *Centaur*; men who for some reason did not embark. As to MacArthur's 363, the navy could offer no explanation[11]. General MacArthur, meanwhile, did his own checking. At last everyone agreed that 332 persons were on board AHS *Centaur* when she was torpedoed. MacArthur agreed to correct the matter in his next day's communique[12].

No such confusion occurred with the merchant seamens' statistics. Straight after Curtin's announcement, Dalgety's shipping manager, Mr Lorraine, told the Press the *Centaur* had 74 crew members, of whom 45 had lost their lives[13].

The true statistical breakup of personnel figures is as follows:

	Lost	Saved	Total
Merchant Crew[b]	45	30	75
Ship's Medical Staff	44	20	64
2/12 Field Ambulance	138	11	149
Attached Personnel	41	3	44
Totals	**268**	**64**	**332**

The shocking toll of Field Ambulance personnel is self evident from these figures. It has to be attributed to their concentration on the hospital decks. By contrast, the ship's medical staff, who mostly occupied berths either well forward or well aft in the lower decks, were spared the worst of the explosion and fire. At the same time, no sinister conclusions can be drawn from the much higher percentage of ship's crew among the survivors. They too were berthed in the extreme ends of the ship, but more importantly they were in a familiar environment, properly trained to deal with an emergency of this type. It is logical that the crew would be better equipped and prepared for survival, and not surprising that more than a third of them did. Something else in the crew's favour was the timing. Several were already wide awake, on duty, while those they had relieved only ten minutes earlier had not had time to fall into a deep sleep. When the torpedo struck, a fair proportion of the crew was awake, and took no time at all to work out what had happened.

Having disseminated the tragic news, the Press stood by for public and private reaction. It was not long in coming.

To a nation at war, newspaper headlines outlining grievous military news — however unwelcome — are an inevitable fact of life. In war, with competing sides armed and equipped to inflict damage on each other, military setbacks and casualties must be expected from time to time. They sometimes even have an element of glory about them. Readers absorb the news, shake their heads, and hope the paper will have better tidings tomorrow. But the callous rape of an unarmed hospital ship, an unprotected angel of mercy, well, this was something quite dif-

b. Including Captain Salt, the Torres Strait Pilot.

A contemporary cartoon highlights the Australian public's revulsion at the attack on the Centaur.   (I.Gall)

ferent. The public gasped in disbelief at the barbarism of the attack. There was something patently obscene about it, something akin to schoolyard bully-boy tactics; something beyond comprehension. Japanese atrocities were already well documented (although the worst excesses did not come to light until after the war), but here was an actual demonstration on the nation's very doorstep of the enemy's contempt for human suffering and of his uncompromising brutality.

Private responses to the *Centaur*'s sinking were not for the most part articulated in the newspapers. The official reaction certainly was. General MacArthur led the charge:

> I cannot express the revulsion I feel at this unnecessary act of cruelty. Its limitless savagery represents the continuation of a calculated attempt to create a sense of trepidation through the practice of horrors designed to shock normal sensibilities.
>
> The brutal excesses of the Philippines campaign, the execution of our captured airmen, the barbarity of Papua, are all of a pattern. The enemy does not understand — he apparently cannot understand — that our

invincible strength is not so much of the body, as it is of the soul, and rises with adversity.

The Red Cross will not falter under this foul blow. Its light of mercy will but shine the brighter on our way to inevitable victory[14].

Mr Artie Fadden, Leader of the Federal Opposition, railed against 'this dastardly act' and of 'the methods of warfare employed by an enemy which has no conception of decency'. The mercurial Billy Hughes, Leader of the United Australia Party, said the sinking of the *Centaur* 'will fill every Australian with horror. We are,' he went on, 'fighting against savages, not civilised men . . . ' Other politicians warmed to the theme, many exhorting their constituents to allow their rage redouble their war efforts[15].

Messages of sympathy tempered the expressions of fury. At 2130 on the Wednesday evening Curtin received the following cablegram from Mr Attlee, Deputy Prime Minister of Great Britain.

> My colleagues and I are greatly shocked at the sinking of the hospital ship Centaur. Please accept our deep sympathy with Australia in this tragic loss of life[16].

Both houses of parliament in NSW expressed sympathy, and as a mark of respect voted unanimously to adjourn for the day. The Prime Minister of New Zealand, Mr Fraser, sent a note of commiseration[17]. An outflowing of both compassion and controlled rage came from the Australian Red Cross Society, which particularly lamented the loss of its representative, Darwin Clark. The Society announced it would be making the strongest possible protest through its parent body, the International Red Cross in Switzerland[18].

People and organisations all over Australia expressed their sympathy. Some donated or pledged money. City councillors at Caulfield, a Melbourne suburb, voted to open a fund to replace the medical equipment lost in the *Centaur*, and launched it with £2,000. The 250 men who worked on the *Centaur* converting her to a hospital ship voted to contribute £1 each towards a replacement *Centaur*. Employees of Ansett Airways pledged to give one hour's pay towards the cost of fitting out a new hospital ship[19].

* * * * *

Before closing this chapter, a brief word on censorship. News about the *Centaur* was not exempt from censorship, despite her non-combatant status and her, if anything, highly conspicuous livery. On 12th March 1943, the day of the *Centaur*'s commissioning, the federal censor issued Directive K20. This prevented the publication of photographs of AHS *Centaur* until they had been submitted and passed by the Melbourne censor[20].

Not surprisingly, wartime censorship sparked some vigorous opposition from newspaper editors. Some adopted a rather less patriotic approach to the restrictions than others, and interpreted the rules in different ways.

Thus it was that the maverick tabloid *Smith's Weekly* published an extremely critical newsitem about the *Centaur* in its 29th May issue. Under its headline 'MUST TRAGEDY EVER PRECEDE REMEDY?', *Smith's* bluntly said the circumstances surrounding the *Centaur*'s loss 'reflect no credit upon Australian naval and air administrations'. The writer probed the issue of the survivors' 36 hours of torment before rescue, asking why air reconnaissance did not check the ship's progress along the coast. He also questioned the effectiveness of aircrew training, claiming pilots and observers were not trained to identify objects on the sea.

Some parts of this article appeared to cross censorship's carefully delineated but nevertheless invisible lines of propriety. Lt-Cmdr McManus, Penry Thomas' navy intelligence officer in Brisbane, wrote to Mr Horace H.Mansell (Victorian state publicity censor) about it. The article in *Smith's Weekly*, he asserted, was not only scurrilous but 'based on inaccurate information which was hitherto regarded as *most secret*'. By analysing the reporting of shipping movements, and by stating that 'a ship sunk in a recent convoy was a special type and one the loss of which would be especially severe to the Allies', *Smith's Weekly* could be guilty of infringing the censorship regulations[21].

McManus' letter highlighted the problems that confronted censors in locating and deleting information from articles, whether voluntarily submitted or not. It was the old dilemma; what appeared to be responsible journalism and good reporting by the Press was judged by the censor to be a breach of military security[22].

State censor Mansell ordered George M.Goddard, editor of *Smith's Weekly*, to submit to him any material intended for publication that contained any statements with respect to

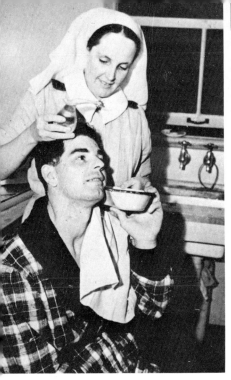

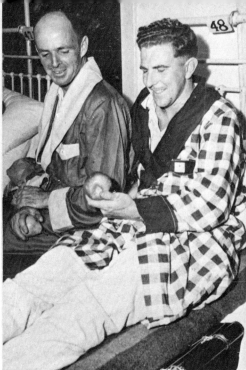

L-Cpl M.P.Thomas receiving treatment in Greenslopes Hospital.

(F.Chidgey)

Cpl Albert Blair and Pte Tom Hegarty in Greenslopes.

(F.Chidgey)

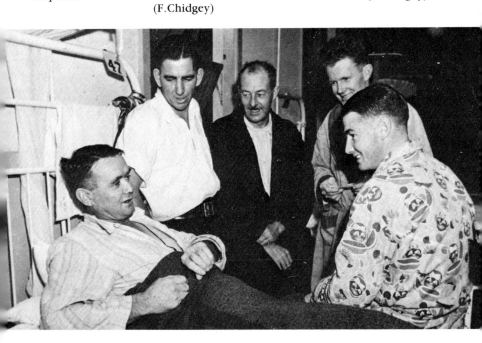

Pte Jim Coulsen tells his tale of survival to other patients in Greenslopes.

(F.Chidgey)

Extract from the front page of the Melbourne Sun, 19th May '43.

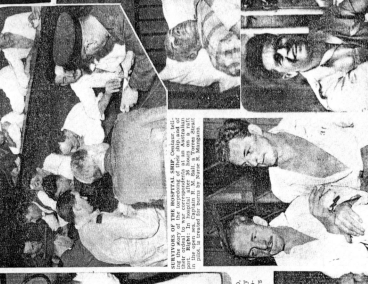

SURVIVORS OF THE HOSPITAL SHIP Centaur telling the story of the torpedoing of their ship and of their ordeal to war correspondents at an Australian port. **Right:** In hospital after 36 hours on a raft in the open sea, Captain R. M. Salt, a Torres Strait pilot, is treated for burns by Nurse R. Mangano.

BROTHERS WHO WERE RESCUED after the Centaur was hit by an enemy torpedo in the early hours on May 14, photographed at an Australian

TAKEN WHEN THE CENTAUR arrived at an Australian port from New Guinea on a previous trip, this picture shows Corporal Les Moss, of the New Hebrides, nock attendant, adjusting the pack of Private Keith

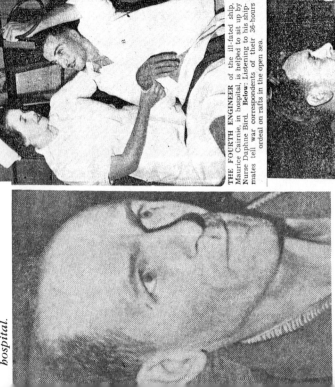

THE FOURTH ENGINEER of the ill-fated ship, Maurice Cairnie, in hospital, is helped to sit up by Nurse Daphne Bird. **Below:** Listening to his shipmates tell war correspondents of their 36-hours ordeal on rafts in the open sea.

Chief Engineer E. Smith in hospital.

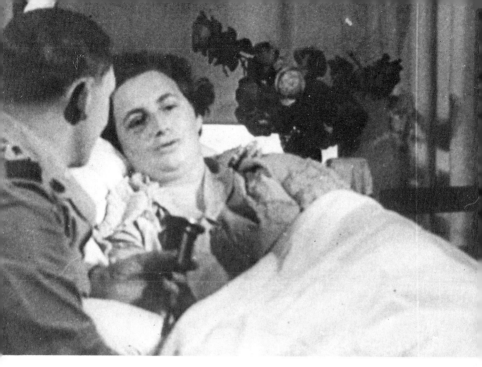

Sister Ellen Savage being interviewed in Greenslopes.

(F.Chidgey)

Left: US seaman Bill Records of the USS Mugford . . . *vivid memories of Ellen Savage on the raft prompted him to write to the family after the War.*

(W.Records)

Ellen Savage in later life.

General Douglas B. MacArthur and Prime Minister John Curtin. MacArthur described the sinking as 'limitless savagery'; Curtin spoke of 'unscrupulous and barbaric' conduct.

(Brisbane Courier Mail)

The Centaur *display at the Australian War Memorial. It was dismantled in 1992 to make way for a Vietnam display. Behind the model is the flare donated by Allan Pettiford.*

(A. Pettiford)

anything to do with any of the armed forces[23]. In reply, *Smith's* asked for more details of this 'punitive' action. What had they done? *Smith's* felt moved to remark that this sort of practice was remarkably similar to methods adopted by the Gestapo in Germany. 'We don't think Australia will stand for Nazism or Fascism.'[24]

Mansell assured *Smith's* that they 'need have no fear that censorship will do anything that is contrary to the principles of British justice'. The sole purpose of the order was to prevent breaches of security; merely to prevent the publication of uncensored material. *Smith's* could be assured that the censor would 'consider the material on its merits, just as if it had been submitted voluntarily'[25].

Smith's hedged yet again, asking to which security disclosures the censor objected. Earlier, *Smith's* had gone into print criticising the details of an official press release about a new reporting system for ships. The article drew criticism from the censor. *Smith's* averred that had the press release not been *officially* made they would have voluntarily submitted for censorship their own article on the topic. That the release *was* made suggested to *Smith's* that the newspaper was

> . . . free to discuss the matter of improving the method of reporting ships. Why not? Is there one law for the Minister and another for Smith's? I was convinced — and am still convinced — that nothing in the Centaur article as printed was of any value to the enemy[26].

Smith's editors had concluded, probably correctly, that this latest attack on them was a kneejerk reaction to the *Centaur* disaster.

But Mansell had the last word.

> The partial Order served on you is not intended to be punitive, but precautionary. You have merely been directed to do what other papers do voluntarily. It followed many warnings, including one from the Chief Censor on March 22nd that any further offence would automatically result in an Order to Submit.
> The Order should not affect the legitimate news value of any of your submissions, which will be treated on their merits as though submitted voluntarily. In the circumstances, further correspondence on the subject can serve no good purpose[27].

And you can't beat City Hall.

* * * * *

Australian newspapers, to their credit, were prompt in bringing to the world all the horrific details of the loss of AHS *Centaur*. It is probable, just the same, that first news of the *Centaur*'s loss came to most people either by word of mouth or by listening to radio news broadcasts. One group in the latter category were the staff of the hospital ship *Oranje*. As the ship entered Port Tewfik in Egypt (on or about the 18th May) loudspeakers throughout the ship blared out the latest short-wave news bulletins. To everyone's horror, the sombre newscaster announced that AHS *Centaur* had been sunk. The news was greeted with profound shock and almost universal disbelief. Like the staff at Greenslopes Hospital, so many on the *Oranje* had close friends on the *Centaur*. At least 27 of *Centaur*'s staff had previously served with them on the *Oranje*.

The announcement cast a pall of gloom over the entire ship. As soon as it could be arranged, a service of remembrance for those lost on the *Centaur* was held in the ship's lounge. Everyone the C.O. could possibly release from duty attended. As they stood with heads bowed in silent prayer, the faces of old colleagues who had likely paid the supreme sacrifice passed across their conscious minds[28]. They could not help pondering the fate of the popular Captain Bernie Hindmarsh; of Matron Jewell; of Sisters Adams, Rutherford, Walker, Haultain, King, Savage and McFarlane; of the orderlies Malcolm, Thomas, Chidgey, Coulsen, Hegarty, Isherwood, Jones, Kelly, Murphy, Burroughs, Cooke, Le Brun, Burrett, Hutchison, McLean, Ockwell and the Maynard twins. As they found out later, the tidings were not good. Only ten had survived.

Chapter Thirteen

THE WAR OF WORDS:
PROTEST AND COUNTER PROTEST

Some form of official protest to the Japanese Government over the sinking of AHS *Centaur* was inevitable. It was as much a priority in Curtin's and MacArthur's minds as those aspects demanding their more immediate attention: notifying next-of-kin, and the content and process of an official news release. The enemy could not get away with this cowardly attack on an innocent, unarmed, non-clandestine hospital ship without some international condemnation.

But international condemnation, to be realistic, is about all a protest would accomplish, no matter how acerbic the wording. By lodging an immediate protest the government reacted in advance to the inevitable public demand that 'something be done'. It provided a means of assuaging public fury. Not that anyone in government or the military expected anything substantive to come of it. Intergovernmental protests, particularly about crimes against civilians, were all part of the psychological warfare between combatant nations. Their main purpose was to publicise the misdemeanours of the enemy, thereby stiffening home resistance and encouraging a greater war effort. Their architects had little expectation of tangible redress, or even of an apology.

As for this protest, it would have been wishful thinking indeed to expect the Japanese to respond with an admission of guilt, a heartfelt apology, or an offer to compensate the families of the victims.

Regardless of the probable outcome, Prime Minister John Curtin had resolved to lodge the strongest complaint possible, and without delay. At his very first briefing on the loss of the *Centaur* — a briefing delayed by his country meanderings —

Curtin asked for information from the navy, army and Department of External Affairs to help him frame the protest[1]. He conferred with MacArthur. He worked on the draft of the protest concurrently with that of his statement to parliament[2].

Naval advisers told Curtin the Japanese had not formally acknowledged the *Centaur*'s conversion[3]. They knew that all enemy powers had been notified, because the Italians had requested more information. Curtin needed a date to quote in the protest, so he cabled Dominion Affairs in London and asked for the exact date that the Swiss informed the Japanese[4]. The prompt reply said 5th February[5]. Curtin had the protest ready to go to London soon after his parliamentary statement, but Colonel Hodgson delayed its transmission when he noticed discrepancies in the casualty statistics. It did not get sent until the 19th May[6]. Curtin directed Stanley Bruce, Australia's High Commissioner to London and representative on the War Cabinet (and a former Australian prime minister), to deliver it to the Foreign Office for communication to the Japanese via the Swiss Government.

Meanwhile, whether it be entirely coincidental or part of an attempt to gain the high moral ground in anticipation of international censure, the Japanese went on the air at 1830 on Saturday 15th May (38 hours after the *Centaur* sank) to denounce the Allies for repeated attacks on Axis hospital ships in the Pacific and Mediterranean. They claimed the Allies had attacked every one of the 40 Italian hospital ships and sunk eight[7]. Two days later, a Radio Berlin broadcast quoted a Mr Horii of Tokyo protesting about Allied air attacks on the hospital ship *Mizuho Maru* near Rabaul on 27th April[8]. And on 18th May, only a few hours before the release of General MacArthur's communique, Tokyo broadcast:

> Enemy America has repeatedly revealed its tendencies toward inhumanitarianism in the Greater East Asia War. They have bombed or attacked our hospital ships, carrying clearly visible red cross insignias. Although they have become hysterical with each successive defeat, the American practices, which defy humanity, cannot be hated enough[9].

It is the *timing* of these tirades that is significant. If they *were* a deliberate attempt to deflect international denunciation, and not simply a coincidence, then they strongly suggest that Imperial General Headquarters already knew about the *Centaur* sinking.

It is not difficult to imagine the Japanese embarrassment over the *Centaur* incident. They were thrown onto the back foot in the propaganda stakes. This unjustifiable act left them nowhere to go but on the defensive.

In fairness, the Japanese had issued several earlier complaints about attacks on hospital ships, dating back to the alleged sinking of the *Harbin Maru* by submarine in the South China Sea in January 1942. Australian intelligence monitored five such broadcasts in April alone[10]. It is also now known, thanks to US intelligence (SRNS 0406), that on 3rd May Foreign Minister Shigemitsu forewarned his minister in Berne about pending protests over attacks on Japanese hospital ships. The Japanese Government later officially protested to the British and the Americans (via the Swiss) about several specific Allied attacks on six named Japanese hospital ships. Moreover, the Japanese had been quick to point out their own restraint in this regard. In February, Japanese broadcasters announcing the attack on Darwin claimed that their aircraft had respected the status of a hospital ship in the harbour (the *Manunda*). Apart from the work of one rogue bomber pilot (out of more than 150) this was undeniably correct. Again, in Milne Bay, the warships *Tenryu* and *Arashi* had to their credit studiously avoided hitting the *Manunda*, even though she lay a sitting duck in their sights. RAN intelligence officer G.H.Gill observed at the time that the attack on the *Centaur* seemed in strange contrast to previous Japanese recognition of the Red Cross. He quoted several examples of Japanese restraint[11].

Now it was time for the Japanese to be on the receiving end of an extremely forthright protest. As a *MOST IMMEDIATE* telegram it went first to Mr Bruce at Australia House in London[12]. His staff transcribed it into official letter form, and typed it on paper bearing the insignia and title 'Commonwealth of Australia'. Bruce dated it 19th May 1943 and addressed it to The Right Hon. Anthony Eden MC MP, at the Foreign Office[13]. His staff delivered it the next day. Foreign Office staff put it on that evening's Cabinet agenda as a topic for discussion. They sent a copy to the Admiralty, which had earlier sought the opportunity to comment on any protest regarding the *Centaur*. Their Lordships of the Admiralty were 'anxious that their interests should not be disregarded[14]'.

Foreign Office staff began checking through the document. The two-page letter began with a request to ask the Swiss to protest strongly to the Japanese government. Then followed a resume of the incident with emphasis on the ship's markings and illumination in compliance with the Hague Convention. Curtin had stressed the publicity given to the *Centaur*'s conversion and pointedly reminded the Japanese that they had been officially notified on 5th February. The final paragraph contained the bite:

> ... Australia most emphatically protests to the Japanese Government against this wanton attack in disregard not only of the Hague Convention and of international law but also of the principles of common humanity accepted by all civilised nations. The Commonwealth Government demands that those responsible for the attack should be punished immediately and demands an assurance from the Japanese Government that there will be no repetition ... of such an incident in violation of international law and practice. The Commonwealth Government reserves the right to claim full indemnification and redress for the losses...[15]

One line of this paragraph raised a few Foreign Office eyebrows. Dour officials pondered over the demand that *'those responsible for the attack should be punished immediately...'* This struck them as being a very strong protest indeed, as it made a demand 'which we have never made in any protest of this kind on our own behalf[16]'. They wondered how the Admiralty would react. They soon found out. The First Sea Lord, said the Admiralty, did not want the protest sent in its present form.

> It is in our interest to ensure, even at some cost, that the Conventions protecting hospital ships are generally respected and to avoid any unnecessary action which might provide an excuse for the Japanese to denounce these Conventions[17].

Of primary concern to the Admiralty was the likely reaction of the Japanese to Curtin's demand for punishment. The Japanese had protested strongly over alleged attacks on six of their hospital ships but had made no demands for punishment — and the Admiralty wanted to avoid putting that idea into their heads. Their Lordships particularly feared the follow-on effect; that if the Japanese demanded punishment and failed to get satisfaction, they might take reprisals on other prisoners. This, apparently, had been the reasoning behind the combined Chiefs-of-Staff call for suppressing the announcement a few days earlier.

The Admiralty also made the point that the Americans had 'a definite interest in the matter and may have reason to regret any ill-considered protest which might be made[18]'.

Mr Stewart took the Admiralty's comments on board, but replied that the Australian Government had very strong feelings on the issue. He did not think the British could delay the protest on their own responsibility.

Nevertheless, the Foreign Office decided to make a low-key approach to Mr Bruce. Perhaps the Australians would agree to the deletion of the offending sentence. The next day Bruce listened to Anthony Eden's arguments. He agreed to discuss the matter with Curtin. Bruce was probably sympathetic to the British view; he had been in other issues of wartime disagreement between Britain and Australia. He cabled External Affairs in Canberra[19]. He put the argument cogently, making the additional point that while the Japanese *might* take reprisals on other prisoners, the Australians certainly would not. He urged a prompt reply, as the issue delayed the protest's lodgement with the Swiss[20].

Curtin's reply next day, 22nd May, was brief and to the point:

We agree in circumstances to omission of the words mentioned[21].

Then things got moving. Bruce notified the Foreign Office. The Foreign Office contacted its man in Berne, Mr Norton. Norton contacted the Swiss Government[22]. The Swiss Government contacted its Minister in Tokyo. The Minister contacted the Japanese Government.

Advice later filtered backwards through the same network that the protest had finally passed to the Japanese Government on 29th May[23]. As well, the International Red Cross Committee in Geneva had served a stern protest on the Japanese Red Cross, in response to an outcry from the Australian, British, New Zealand, South African and US Red Cross Societies. The ICRC demanded a reply.

From there on everyone had to wait.

In the meantime, the British still had to prepare a response to the protest the Japanese had slapped on them. It gave details of attacks on six of its hospital ships. Briefly, they were:

Arabia Maru — bombed near Rangoon 4th January 1943; slight damage,

America Maru — bombed and strafed near Rabaul 30th January 1943; little damage,

Manila Maru — attacked by two torpedoes east of Mindanao 4th March 1943; no damage (vessel took evasive action),

> *Ural Maru* — bombed near Rabaul 3rd April 1943; considerable damage and loss of life,
> *Huso Maru* — bombed on three occasions near Shortland Island (New Guinea) 15th April 1943; no damage. Bombed and strafed the next day; slight damage,
> *Buenos Aires Maru* — torpedoed *en route* to Hong Kong 25th April; slight damage, seven wounded.

The Admiralty noted dryly that 'if, as is not impossible, there is any truth in these charges, some of the attacks could only have been made by American pilots[24]'. It suggested a coordinated response with the Americans. As all the alleged attacks had occurred in the Far East, Mr Attlee (Dominion Affairs) sent a copy of the protest to the Australian Government[25]. He sought Curtin's help with information, particularly about the alleged attacks in the SWPA. Curtin referred the matter to General MacArthur[26].

MacArthur agreed to investigate the charges. He did make the suggestion that the *Centaur* could have been sunk as a retaliatory act for an unfortunate incident on 3rd April near Rabaul, when US aircraft bombed a Japanese vessel that turned out to be a hospital ship (the *Ural Maru*). Aircrews were adamant that no hospital ship markings were visible[27].

MacArthur's report landed on Curtin's desk on 1st June[28]. MacArthur rejected out of hand the alleged attacks on the *Arabia Maru*, *America Maru*, *Manila Maru* and *Buenos Aires Maru*. Unfortunately the claims about the *Ural Maru* and *Huso Maru* had some foundation.

On 3rd April, an American aircraft flying a mission to attack enemy shipping lanes near Kavieng and Rabaul spotted what turned out to be the *Ural Maru*. From 6,000 feet the ship appeared 'sort of white', but the aircrew could see no conventional hospital ship markings. When the bombardier observed and reported what he took to be a canvas-covered gun on the foredeck, the pilot decided to attack. MacArthur examined a series of five photographs taken during the action. He noted that in only one could he distinguish the hospital ship insignia, and then only by magnifying glass. In defence of the US aircrew, he asserted that no insignia was visible from overhead and the ship flew no Red Cross flag. Furthermore, the object on deck that looked like a gun only gave additional support to the pilot's judgment. MacArthur laid the blame for the attack squarely on the Japanese, for failing to identify the ship properly.

The *Huso Maru* incident was different. Two Avenger aircraft carried out a night strike on four cargo vessels, three patrol craft and two destroyers known to be near the Shortland Island. One pilot attacked a large vessel. After an unsuccessful bombing run he returned and strafed the ship. He then identified his target as a hospital ship, and immediately abandoned the attack. Visibility was not good at the time and the vessel's hospital ship markings could not be discerned from above 2,000 feet. MacArthur accepted the attack took place, but stressed that the pilot pulled out the moment he realised his mistake. However, the pilot may well have been fully entitled to attack the ship. It was 'in the vicinity of an engagement' and thus, under the Hague Convention, was 'acting at its own risk and peril'[29].

Curtin relayed MacArthur's report to Dominion Affairs, London, on 13th June[30]. The Japanese were still biding their time answering the *Centaur* protest. They were in no hurry. Why should they be? While their allegations diverted attention from the *Centaur* and put the Allies on the defensive, the psychological edge in this propaganda battle was very much to their liking.

During these diplomatic waltzes other things were happening in relation to hospital ships. In short, the Allies were mutually and confidentially giving voice to their doubts about the effectiveness of the Hague provisions. They had knowledge of several breaches of the rules in recent months; too many to ignore. Examples were the improper use and marking of Japanese hospital ships, the accidental US attack on an Italian hospital ship on 13th May, the *Centaur* incident one day later, and then the First Sea Lord's statement on 27th May that Axis forces (admittedly over a period of time) had attacked 19 British hospital ships, sinking four. The Hague rules were written nearly half a century earlier, after all, and were proving unwieldy, open to varying interpretation, and very much out of kilter with the then modern context.

The US Chiefs-of-Staff took the lead. They came up with a modern interpretation which they submitted to the combined Chiefs-of-Staff for approval.

In Australia, meanwhile, the curtain was rising on a farce that added another dimension to the already confused debate. It began on 20th May, six days after the *Centaur* sank. On that day the Secretary for the Department of Defence sent the following to the Chief of the General Staff for 'necessary action':

> The question has arisen as to the sailing of the hospital ship 'Manunda'
> and whether she should proceed —
>> (a) displaying lights and unescorted, in accordance with convention;
> or
>> (b) blacked out and escorted, contrary to convention . . .[31]

Not surprisingly, the loss of AHS *Centaur* had raised doubts about the immunity of hospital ships. Had Japan 'moved the goal posts'? Would the *Manunda* go the same way as the *Centaur*? Relevant and profound questions. The Chief of General Staff consulted his top military chiefs and also General MacArthur. The First Naval Member supported the first option. He suggested AHS *Manunda* be escorted by a naval vessel trailing well astern, 'whilst Japanese policy is uncertain[32].' The others didn't agree. The final view was that the *Manunda* should sail escorted and blacked out with 'No, repeat No, Red Cross markings[33].' Orders went out to remove all AHS *Manunda*'s hospital ship livery.

Before the work began, however, Prime Minister Curtin received a pertinent, if imprudent, memo from his Chief of Naval Staff. The letter in part warned of the possible implications of withdrawing the claim of immunity for hospital ships. Curtin responded that the subject was an operational, rather than policy, matter; one that MacArthur would handle. In other words, 'be careful, you are treading on sensitive toes'[34]. Curtin had to clear his yardarm with MacArthur. He told the C-in-C he regarded this as an operational matter for McArthur's determination. The Chief of Naval Staff did not heed the warning. He wrote to the Department of Defence with a recommendation that the government confer with UK, US and NZ authorities on the matter. He also revealed that he had asked for the Admiralty's views[35]. MacArthur took exception to this; the Navy had unquestionably exceeded its authority. He made it clear to Curtin that such a recommendation should properly only come from his office. Seriously embarrassed, Curtin wrote him another, this time more detailed, message of explanation, reiterating MacArthur's authority. Not surprisingly, the Minister of the Navy, Makin, copped a blast[36].

Regardless of the continuing disagreements behind the scenes — and with hindsight it must be said that the Chief of Naval Staff was right in his judgement, if not in his observance of the political niceties — on 14th June 1943 conversion work began on AHS *Manunda* in Sydney. This didn't stop the issue simmering on. On 28th June Major-General Burston, DGMS, wrote to the

Adjutant General. Removing the *Manunda*'s hospital ship markings, he declared, was tantamount to admitting that the Geneva Conventions did not hold good. He noted that the *Manunda* would be the first hospital ship altered after its declaration as a non-combatant. He strongly recommended the work be cancelled[37].

Burston unknowingly had a few allies around the world. In London, the Admiralty were not about to renounce the Hague Conventions without a fight. On that same day Their Lordships sent a long cable to the attention of the Australian and New Zealand naval boards, and other authorities[38]. The message relayed verbatim a 9th June message from the US Joint Staff Mission to its British counterpart, and the reply. It gave details of areas of agreement among the Allied Chiefs of Staff on the topic of hospital ships. Briefly, these were:

— that immunity of hospital ships from attack should be maintained;

— that US and British interpretations of the conventions must be consistent;

— that if hospital ship markings are not adequately illuminated at the time of an attack, then no complaint about the attack can be made. Hospital ships have the right to darken ship, but they do so at their own risk;

— that while deceptive manoeuvring is unwise (because it might confuse attacking forces), it may be necessary to avoid compromising an operation;

— that escorted hospital ships must not be deliberately attacked, though they must accept the risk of accidental attack by virtue of their nearness to legitimate targets[39].

One paragraph was particularly relevant and is worth quoting in full:

> Arising out of the "Centaur" sinking, the Australian Commonwealth Naval Board reports that it has suggested that the abandonment of special markings for hospital ships in favour of camouflage should be considered. We have heard of no Japanese attack other than that on the "Centaur", and it is conceivable that the latter may have been the act of an irresponsible commander. Unless other evidence is available, we feel strongly that it would be better to wait until further incidents have occurred. If the Japanese give unmistakable evidence of the intention to attack hospital ships, we fully agree that any reprisals against the Japanese should not be extended to Germany or Italy unless they show solidarity with Japan[40].

Curtin sought General MacArthur's views[41]. MacArthur recommended that the Australian Government agree with the interpretation[42]. Curtin accepted the advice and notified Dominion Affairs on 26th July[43].

Three days later, the navy notified the Department of Defence that it had removed all AHS *Manunda*'s hospital ship insignia. She was now painted grey and defensively armed[44]. But by now the thinking at the top had changed. It took a while, but finally, on 10th August, the navy was told to undo all it had done; to repaint the *Manunda* as a hospital ship and remove her armament[45]. This was done and on 30th August, resplendent once more as a hospital ship, the *Manunda* left Sydney for Brisbane. The total cost of her conversion and reconversion came to £12,500[46].

Finally, in December 1943, more than half a year after the *Centaur* sank, the first signs of a response to the Australian protest emerged. In a brief radio broadcast from Tokyo on 2nd December, the announcer denied that a Japanese submarine had attacked the *Centaur*. The Japanese Government, he said, rejected the Australian protest[47].

The Hon. F.M.Forde (Minister for the Army) dismissed this as 'subtle propaganda'. Japan had realised that world public opinion condemned her cowardly action, he said, and it was too silly for words to suggest that the Allies would sink their own ship[48].

A week later, the International Red Cross was graced with a reply to its protest. An in-depth inquiry, the JRC said, had concluded that the alleged attack had never taken place.

Then, on 16th December, the Swiss Minister in Tokyo received a communication from the Japanese Minister for Foreign Affairs[49]. The Swiss passed it on to the British Foreign Office for retransmission to the Australian Government via Stanley Bruce[50]. It arrived in Australia on 26th December. It began:

> Australia addressed to Japan a protest concerning the loss of hospital ship "Centaur" alleging the ship was torpedoed by Japanese submarine in Queensland waters on May 14th, 1943. Thorough enquiry by the Japanese Government has revealed no facts justifying Australian allegation. Japan therefore categorically states she cannot approve Australian protest and that she can take no responsibility for any Australian claims[51].

The document went on to counter protest about alleged attacks on nine Japanese hospital ships by enemy planes and submarines. MacArthur had already investigated five of these charges. Three were new: *Takasago Maru*, *Muro Maru* and *Mizuho Maru*.

Three days later, Curtin's office received from London its copy of the separate Japanese protest on these new alleged attacks. The Japanese, full of vitriol and righteous indignation, demanded the British 'guarantee that deeds of this kind will not be repeated in the future'[52].

The next day Dominion Affairs told Curtin that they were still discussing the matter with the Americans, whom the Japanese had also targeted. Their eventual response went to the Swiss, for transmission to the Japanese, on 19th January 1944[53]. It did not mince words.

'His Majesty's Government', it said, 'most emphatically rejects the contention of the Japanese Government that His Majesty's Forces have deliberately and culpably attacked Japanese hospital ships.' It respectfully but forcefully reminded the Japanese that 'during and after an engagement, they (hospital ships) act at their own risk and peril', and no responsibility could be accepted for accidental damage done to a hospital ship 'in the vicinity of a legitimate military target, whether in port or on the high seas'. Moreover, 'it is extremely difficult for aircraft always to identify the markings of a hospital ship at the heights from which bombing is often carried out'.

The lecture continued, pointing out as if to a recalcitrant shoolchild that hospital ship safety depended on 'adequate and clearly visible markings and illuminations', for which the Convention placed specific obligations on those countries operating hospital ships. Photographic reconnaissance had 'given His Majesty's Government the most serious reasons for doubting whether the Japanese Government have taken steps to place adequate and clearly visible markings and illumination upon their hospital ships'. While the British Government admitted and regretted that some accidental attacks had occurred, it accepted no responsibility for them; they were due either to inadequate markings and illuminations or to the ship's proximity to legitimate military targets, or both.

The British stressed they would continue to respect the immunity of hospital ships, but in a final patronising but telling warning, pointed out that the markings prescribed in the convention should be considered the *minimum*. British hospital ships, as British diplomats had informed the Japanese in December 1942, had been given additional markings — and the Japanese would be well advised to do the same[54].

MacArthur, meanwhile, investigated the *Takasago Maru*, *Muro Maru*, *Mizuho Maru* and *America Maru* allegations. He identified attacks on all but the *Mizuho Maru*, and disclaimed responsibility in all instances[55].

The Japanese — surprise, surprise — didn't care much for the British response to its complaint. They protested — perhaps with all the ardour of those who 'protesteth too much' — that the British had either acted with 'malicious motive' or with 'lack of due care', and 'the most distinct markings of hospital ships and the best illumination therefore could be no safeguard'. Keeping the pot boiling, the Japanese insisted the British Government 'conduct a thorough re-investigation of the matter and admit all responsibility for unlawful attacks on hospital ships'[56].

These exchanges were becoming tedious. Hoping to put the matter to rest once and for all, the British Foreign Office rejected emphatically that any British or Allied Forces had attacked a Japanese hospital ship either maliciously or from want of due care. It also expressed once again the expectation that the Japanese would instruct its hospital ships to make their markings sufficiently plain[57].

It seemed that the Japanese wanted the last word. Annoyingly, they replied on 29th September, still spitting forth invective and indignation. They refuted the claim that their ships were near military objectives or were improperly marked or illuminated, and 'reserved their rights relating to unlawful attacks made on "Arabia Maru" and five other hospital ships'[58].

By this time the British had had enough. They were getting nowhere. On 14th November, the Dominion Office told Curtin that 'nothing can usefully be added to the previous communication to the Japanese Government on the subject'[59]. They decided to make no further response.

And that should have been that ... *should* have.

About a month later, intelligence from POWs recovered from Japanese hands caused them to change their minds. The POWs brought reports that the Japanese were making questionable use of some of their hospital ships[60]. The scribes got busy and on 24th February 1945 handed the Swiss a fresh communication for the Japanese Government[61]. The British note began by reaffirming that its forces scrupulously respected the immunity of hospital ships, then went on:

His Majesty's Government at the same time wish to notify the Japanese Government that SIBERIA MARU and BUENOS AIRES MARU, whilst still hospital ships, are known to have been loaded with guns and ammunition. Reliable reports indicate that these two ships are now painted grey and are being used as military transports . . . (we therefore) assume that these ships have been withdrawn from hospital ship service and request . . . (confirmation) . . . that this is the case . . . (and wish to be notified) whether any other ships, previously notified as hospital ships have been withdrawn from that service[62].

The archival file contains no reply to this request.

Chapter Fourteen

UNDER THE LEGAL MICROSCOPE

Since the moment the first news of the *Centaur*'s loss reached the public — and despite the constrictions of wartime censorship — a lively debate raged. Exactly how had the *Centaur* met her end? If, as claimed, a Japanese submarine was the culprit, what could possibly have motivated its commander to attack a brilliantly lit and internationally-recognised non-combatant? As so often happens when the authorities cannot, or will not, give clear-cut answers, a sceptical public finds its own. When that happens, any tiny snippet of 'inside information', be it true or mischievously false, adds fuel to the flames of rampant speculation.

Rumours about the *Centaur* abounded; some fanciful, some pertinent, and some very close to the truth. We will discuss them all in the next chapter, when we take a close look at not only how but why the *Centaur* was attacked and sunk. Suffice to say at this stage that the most prevalent rumour had the *Centaur* carrying fighting troops and munitions — and widespread sentiment had it that should this be correct then it was no wonder the Japanese had sunk her.

The first opportunity to lay some of the wildest speculation to rest came in late 1944, when War Crimes Commissioner Sir William Flood Webb began an inquiry into the loss of the *Centaur*[1].

Webb, the Chief Justice of Queensland, had begun his career in war crimes investigation in June the previous year. H.V. Evatt, Attorney General and Minister of State for External Affairs, asked him to investigate and report on Japanese atrocities or breaches of the rules of war in Papua and New Guinea. This became known as the Japanese Atrocities Commission[2]. Then in June 1944 the

196

government set up the Australian War Crimes Commission, with Webb again as commissioner[3]. The AWCC had much broader terms of reference than the JAC. Its function was to investigate Japanese war crimes against any military and non-military persons who were Australian residents before the war began. It produced periodic reports of evidence, and sent them to the United Nations Commission for the Investigation of War Crimes.

In the AWCC's terms of reference, the Attorney General listed 32 classifications of war crimes. They ranged from 'murder and massacres — systematic terrorism', to 'poisoning wells'. The 24th detailed the 'attack and destruction of hospital ships'[4]. With this inclusion it became inevitable that the AWCC would examine the *Centaur* incident.

This first formal investigation into the attack on the *Centaur* began in the second week of August 1944. Between then and late October, Commissioner Webb presided over hearings at Melbourne, Sydney, Yungaburra and Brisbane[5]. He heard and recorded the testimony of 37 witnesses, 34 of whom were *Centaur* survivors. From the merchant crew came Cairnie, Cullum, Davidson, McIntosh, Morris, Rawlings, Reid, Sandwell, Stutter, Westwood, and Captain Salt; from the medical staff Argent, Bidmead, Blair, Carter, Cornell, Hegarty, Hooper, Johnson, Jones, Malcolm, Medcalf, Murphy, Sister Ellen Savage and Taylor; and from the 2/12 Field Ambulance Bayly, Dickson, Isherwood, Jonassen, Jones, McGrath, Murray, Lt-Col Outridge and Taylor[6].

Each faced much the same line of questioning. AWCC secretary John Brennan did most of the examining, with Webb breaking in as he saw fit. After establishing each witness's status on the *Centaur*, Brennan led them through their recollections of the ship's markings and illumination, their activities during that last evening at sea, how they first became aware of the explosion and how they escaped the doomed ship and found some means of support. Brennan asked each in turn if they remembered any sounds or lights that might indicate the presence of a submarine. Lastly, he asked them to estimate the value of their personal losses[7]. Each examination closed with a warning that defence authorities had classified the inquiry 'Most Secret'[8].

Webb also examined Major A.S.MacKinnon[9]. MacKinnon headed 'Q' Branch in 1943, his job being to direct the movement of cargo and personnel around Australia. Under questioning, MacKinnon confirmed that he gave the order to transport the ambulance unit on the *Centaur*. It comprised solely medical personnel. He also confirmed that the ASC men had their rifles and ammunition, and that this conformed with the convention, as interpreted by the army's legal experts. He had given orders to load about eight tonnes of equipment. This did not include unit vehicles, which were prohibited.

Another witness was Lt-Cmdr A.V.H.Dalzell, RNVR, an expert on mines and torpedoes[10]. Brennan questioned him about the possibility that the *Centaur* had struck a mine. Dalzell ruled out magnetic or acoustic mines; he said he had no evidence of any being found in Australian waters. He also discounted the likelihood of the *Centaur* striking a moored mine. The depth where the *Centaur* sank, he said, is over 100 fathoms; too deep for a moored mine. Moreover, he had never heard of a ship striking a moored mine anywhere but near the bow. Asked about Australian-laid magnetic mines, Dalzell said they were effective only in shallower waters and in any event the *Centaur*'s degaussing equipment would have protected her. He added that damage from magnetic mines is invariably felt most in the after section of the ship. Webb dropped this issue, but as we shall see it later became the subject of vigorous debate.

Webb's report — on all aspects of his inquiry, not just the *Centaur* case — went to H.V.Evatt in October that year. Within this 109-page 'most secret' document, 25 pages were devoted to *The Sinking Of The H.M.A.H.S. "Centaur"*[11].

In summary, Webb noted that the *Centaur* had been fully accredited, marked, and illuminated as a hospital ship. Although none of the witnesses had given sworn testimony that she flew the Red Cross flag when attacked — something hardly likely in the middle of the night (flags on well-run ships are always lowered at sunset) — Webb concluded, sensibly, that after dark the illuminated red crosses were the only effective substitute. For some reason that has little relevance to the *Centaur* incident, Webb concluded that because the lifeboats might not have been painted with hospital ship markings (i.e. green band and red crosses), this denied them immunity if used. However, in his opinion it did not deprive the *Centaur* of her immunity.

Neither, in his opinion, did the 52 rifles and 2,000 rounds of ammunition on board compromise the *Centaur*'s immunity. They were, he said, reasonably required for the preservation of order and the protection of the wounded and sick, although he still wanted some clarification of this practice from a high-ranking officer.

Sir William concluded that the *Centaur* was entitled to protection under the convention. He found she had been sunk by an enemy submarine, but stressed he could not state whether a German or a Japanese vessel had committed the crime. He recommended the government submit the *Centaur* case to the United Nations Commission, and it was[12].

The scene now moves to Japan, to the SCAP (Supreme Command Allied Powers) investigations. As an adjunct to the main game, the Tokyo trials of Imperial Japan's defeated leaders, the Yokohama War Crimes Trials addressed the misdeeds of hundreds of subordinates, most of them accused of atrocities. These hearings began in 1945. One of the many incidents examined was the sinking of AHS *Centaur*. Over the best part of three years, investigators collected, checked and verified a vast amount of information connected with the loss of this hospital ship. They interrogated and re-interrogated several Japanese; mostly former naval officers. At various stages of the investigation a total of five case officers were attached to it. They included the son of one of the world's wealthiest men and an English RNVR intelligence officer fluent in oral and written Japanese. These men wrote fifteen separate 'Reports of Investigation' before SCAP closed the *Centaur* file in December 1948[13].

In an evolutionary way, rather than by design, the *Centaur* investigation passed through four stages. First, gathering information; second, mystery about the loss of submarine *I-178*; third, confusion about the dates of submarine *I-180*'s various attacks; and fourth, the coalescing of evidence that finally pointed the finger of suspicion in the right direction.

Unfortunately the investigation got off to a poor start.

On 8th October 1945, Col F.P.Munsen, the Assistant Chief of Staff G-2, GHQ SCAP, wrote to Mr K.Nakamura of the Imperial Japanese Second Demobilization Ministry, formally asking for his cooperation with an inquiry into the *Centaur* sinking. Unfortunately, Munson's letter said the *Centaur* was sunk 'off Sydney Harbour', instead of Brisbane, and gave the year as 1942, instead of 1943! How he could mistake Sydney for Brisbane, and why he failed to give the exact and correct date, is now hard to believe.

It mattered little whether the IJSDM was aware or not of the facts of the *Centaur* sinking; it could now happily investigate an alleged attack on a hospital ship outside Sydney in 1942 without fear of contradiction. Nakamura replied on 3rd December, obsequiously apologising for not being able to offer a satisfactory answer. He gave a most full account of the activities of all Japanese submarines off the Australian east coast during 1942, and of course none of the ships known to be sunk were hospital ships. Nakamura explained that '... all of the related documents as well as all reports received from these submarines have been lost through fire and other causes'. His reply of necessity relied solely on the 'memories of those survivors who took part in the submarine operations ... ' Nakamura closed with the following paragraph:

> We would like to state at this juncture that the Imperial Japanese Navy, throughout the war, not only strictly prohibited the attacking of hospital ships but also drove this point thoroughly to all submarine commanders; and also although there were several instances of our submarines having abandoned the attack of a target which was found in the course of the approach manoeuvre to be a hospital ship, we have never received a report of any of our submarines having attacked a hospital ship even by mistake[14].

In February 1946 the *Centaur* investigation began in earnest. SCAP assigned it 'Investigation No. 563'[15].

Its first task was to acquire all the relevant evidence given at Webb's hearings. SCAP asked the Australian Army for copies of the affidavits. Over the next two months the data flowed in: certified copies of departmental cablegrams, details of the *Centaur*'s routeing, technical details of hospital ship markings and insignia, a photograph of the *Centaur*, the nominal roll of all AMF personnel on board, and finally the evidence of thirteen witnesses who testified before Webb. The file on the *Centaur* soon began to bulge.

SCAP assigned Case 563 to 1st Lt George F.Getty, an investigating officer attached to its legal section. Getty, the 22-year-old son of John Paul Getty, was a graduate of Princeton University and a former 2nd Lt on active service in the Philippines and Malaya[16].

Getty approached the Central Liaison Office of the Imperial Japanese Government, an administrative body set up to respond to SCAP requests for Japanese documentation. He wanted a list of all Japanese submarines stationed off the east coast of Australia between 25 °S and 35 °S for the period 1st May to 31st May 1943. He asked for details of their route patrols and the names and present whereabouts of their squadron and submarine commanders[17].

Mr Katsube (chief of the Liaison Section, CLO), who replied to Getty's request on 24th June, may well have been to the same school as Nakamura. His letter almost mimicked Nakamura's fobbing off of Col Munsen. He stressed that the CLO was happy to provide the information sought, but regrettably a detailed report was impossible because '. . . most of the interested records were destroyed by fire and a number of submarines engaged in the operation were lost in action'. In consequence, the CLO could only submit a report '. . . based only upon the memory of certain personnel concerned'[18].

Just how deliberately evasive this response was cannot now be determined. It was not totally worthless, however. Katsube did identify several naval officers. They were: Rear Admiral Katsumi Komazawa (Commander 3rd Submarine Squadron), Captain Tsuneo Shichiji (Submarine *I-11*), Captain Hidejiro Utsuki (*I-178*), Captain Toshio Kusaka (*I-180*) and Captain Hajime Nakagawa (*I-177*). All except Utsuki had survived the war. The loss of his submarine (*I-178*) became the subject of detailed scrutiny, as we shall see.

Getty summoned Komazawa, Shichiji, Kusaka and Nakagawa to report for interrogation as soon as possible[19]. In early July he questioned them, separately, in room 824 of the Meiji Building in Tokyo.

Shichiji appeared first. His evidence was sketchy, to say the least. His submarine, *I-11*, had been the flagship of the 3rd Submarine Squadron based at Truk under Komazawa's command. From early April to mid-May 1943 *I-11* made an uneventful patrol along the east coast of Australia. Its patrol area stretched from Bass Strait north to Sydney. He returned to Truk in the middle of May. Shichiji could remember only *I-11*, *I-177* and *I-178* as being members of the 3rd Squadron. The numbers of the other submarines escaped him. He denied ever hearing about an Allied hospital ship being sunk off the Australian coast[20].

Admiral Komazawa came next. He corroborated Shichiji's fragmentary evidence. Komazawa said that from January to August 1943 he commanded the 3rd Submarine Squadron, which formed part of the Sixth Fleet based at Truk. This comprised the flagship (*I-11*), the 22nd Flotilla (*I-177* and *I-178*[a]) and occasionally other Sixth Fleet submarines. In April the squadron left Truk for the east coast of Australia.

Komazawa said submarine *I-178* did not return from this April/May patrol and he presumed it lost in action. From the reports of the other submarine commanders, he calculated the squadron sank about six Allied ships. None of the commanders, he added, reported sinking a hospital ship. Komazawa insisted he had given all commanders strict orders prohibiting them from attacking hospital ships[21].

Then Hajime Nakagawa, captain of the *I-177*, came before Getty. This was not Nakagawa's first interrogation at the hands of Allied investigators. He had previously been interviewed about his conduct in relation to prisoners-of-war in the Indian Ocean in February 1944 (of which, more later). Nakagawa was reasonably fluent in the English language. He could read English newspapers and even write in English, but had limited ability in conversation. He told Getty he arrived at Truk in the *I-177* in early April. He left one week later, heading south to a new patrol area between Sydney and Brisbane. Sometime between the 20th and 25th of April he attacked a convoy about 30 to 50 miles east of Cape Byron. He said he fired a torpedo at a 4,000 tonne cargo ship[b]. He heard two hits followed by an explosion. He submerged to 250 feet (80 metres) when a destroyer escort launched a depth charge attack. After patrolling for 20 days the *I-177* returned to Truk.

When asked about the other submarines on this patrol, Nakagawa could recall only the *I-178* and *I-180*. He agreed there may have been others but could not remember them. He said that the *I-178* did not return to Truk from this patrol.

In other parts of his testimony, Nakagawa told Getty that he left the *I-177* at Rabaul because of illness and returned to Japan, that two months later he took command of the *I-37* and went to the Indian Ocean, and that in early 1945 the *I-177* left its base in Japan and was lost[22].

Getty managed to track down Toshio Kusaka, the fourth man on his list, during the following week. Kusaka, formerly captain of the *I-180*, then had a job as master of the repatriation

---

a. And also the *I-180* which he forgot to mention.

b. The *Limerick*.

ship *Shinko Maru No. 2*, and rarely came to port. Kusaka confirmed much of the basic information Getty had gleaned from the other three. According to Kusaka the submarines left Truk at four day intervals. First the *I-11*, then his *I-180*, then *I-178* and finally the *I-177*. Kusaka's assigned area stretched from Sydney northward to Brisbane. He explained that during the day he patrolled submerged, about three miles off the coastline. At night he moved seaward about 100 miles to surface and recharge batteries. He made three attacks during the patrol. He described them as follows:

> The first ship was sunk about noon on 29 April 1943 near Cape Byron. At that time the *I-178* was the closest submarine to my position. The second was sunk on 5 May 1943 in the same area. The *I-177* was the nearest submarine to my position at that time. The third ship was hit on *15 or 16 May 1943* (our emphasis) south of Brisbane. It was travelling in convoy, and the *I-11*ᶜ was depth charged for about two hours after this attack. There were no submarines near to my position at the time as they had all left the area and were going back to Truk. The other submarines sank about one ship apiece during the operation[23].

With his next comment Kusaka in almost the same breath first created a neat spot for himself at the top of the list of suspects, and then vigorously declared his innocence.

> On 14th May 1943 I was cruising alone off Brisbane. However, I did not sink any hospital ship in that area at that time, or at any time. I saw a hospital ship off Sydney in 1942, and I know what the markings of the ship are. I had no documents on my submarine containing identifications of various Allied hospital ships. Since the ship was new and had not been completely equipped with documents, *I only had a document notifying me not to attack hospital ships*[24]. (our emphasis).

After this first round of interrogations Getty pinpointed several inconsistencies in the evidence. On 23rd September 1946 he filed two requests. He asked for the names and addresses of all officers, petty officers and ratings aboard the *I-180* during its April-May patrol. And he sought the re-interrogation of Nakagawa.

On 9th October Hajime Nakagawa reported once again to the Meiji Building[25]. Through interpreter Paul Hayami, Getty asked Nakagawa to go over his testimony once more. Nakagawa did so, giving much the same information as before. This time he gave more detail. Now he could remember that all four submarines of the 3rd Squadron went to Australia. Nakagawa could

---

c. He no doubt meant *I-180*.

Centaur

not recall exactly when he left Truk, although he felt sure his was 'not the first . . . and also not the last submarine to leave'. He though it was 'on about 10th April', being more specific than his previous 'mid-April' estimation. He also recalled that he arrived off Brisbane 'about 20th April'. Whereas he could previously only recall his attack on the convoy in vague terms, now Nakagawa said it happened 'some 30 or 40 miles' east of Cape Byron at 'about 0100 in the morning of about 27th April'. His earlier description of firing 'a torpedo at a 4,000 ton cargo ship' became 'four or six torpedoes at the second ship in the western file of the convoy'. Originally he recalled hearing 'two hits and an explosion'; now it was 'two or three hits'.

After patrolling for about 20 days, said Nakagawa, the *I-177* returned to Truk, arriving 'on or about 20th May'.

Nakagawa admitted that Allied officers had told him a hospital ship was sunk by a Japanese submarine off the east coast of Australia in mid-May 1943. He denied emphatically that he had any 'knowledge as to the identity of the submarine or the submarine officer who committed this act'[26].

Getty dismissed Nakagawa at that point, although he brought him back two days later to sign a one-page typed deposition of the interrogation. He asked Nakagawa to note any errors or omissions. Nakagawa read the report. With three pen strokes he deleted the words: 'On returning to Truk Island, I was the first submarine to enter the harbor. In a week's time both the "I-11" and the "I-180" came into the harbor'. He initialled the deletions, writing 'HN' in English characters. At the bottom of the document he signed his name in English cursive longhand, followed by the three vertical characters of his name in Japanese.

Getty filed a request to have Nakagawa's name placed on the Watch List of the Civil Censorship Detachment, GHQ, for the next 45 days. This would intercept all letters to and from Nakagawa.

A week later, on 14th October 1946, George Getty typed up his first report on Case 563. He headed it 'H.M.A.H.S. CENTAUR'. He had a lot to say about Hajime Nakagawa.

> (Nakagawa) is suspected of being involved in the unlawful sinking of HMAHS CENTAUR on 14 May 1943 . . . As (he) is aware that Allied authorities are investigating his complicity in the sinking . . . it is thought that he may attempt to write some of his former naval associates and advise them of this fact so that together they could concoct some story

204

whereby they could postpone the discovery of the part they played in the sinking of this hospital ship[27].

Getty doubted Nakagawa's claim that he arrived back at Truk on 20th May. It seemed too pat. If true, it effectively cleared him of a crime committed less than a week earlier 2,400 miles away. That return date was the linchpin of Nakagawa's alibi. While these interrogations were in progress, Getty continued to amass material from Australia for his *Centaur* file. From the Australian Navy he requested details of the names, dates, types, and positions of all Allied merchant ships sunk off the eastern coast of Australia during April and May 1943. He asked for the same details about Japanese submarines sunk in the area, plus the whereabouts of any Japanese survivors, if known.

Naval sources identified nine ships either sunk or damaged: *Recina* (11th April); *Kowarra* (24th April); *Limerick* (26th April); *Lydia M Childs* (27th April); *Woolongbar* (29th April); *Fingal* (5th May); *Caradale* (12th May); *Ormiston* (12th May); and *Centaur* (14th May). They added that no Japanese submarines were sunk off the east coast, thereby ruling out the possibility of interrogating any survivors[28].

Meanwhile, from sources within SCAP, Getty obtained more information about Japanese submarine activity. He got a list of all known submarines sunk between Truk and Australia. The details of one of them caught his eye: *I-178*, said to have been sunk on 25th August 1943 by the USS *Patterson*. Something was awry here. Both Komazawa and Nakagawa had said the *I-178* failed to return to Truk in late May. So where was the *I-178* between late May and 25th August? It would have had to put into port somewhere, if only for fuel and provisions. Patrols longer than eight weeks were exceptional; this one would have lasted four and a half months! Something didn't ring true. The disappearance of the *I-178*, a submarine that — if the protestations of innocence gushing from the other 3rd Squadron commanders could be believed — could well have sunk the *Centaur*, seemed too neatly coincidental.

Getty asked for proof that *I-178* had been sunk by the USS *Patterson*. He also asked if there were any survivors[29].

The reply came from the War Crimes Office in Washington, DC. Apparently the IJSDM had given an approximate date for the loss of the *I-178* as 'August 1943, in the Solomons Area'[30].

205

As the *Patterson* had sunk an unidentified submarine in that area on 25th August, the Americans assumed it must have been the *I-178*.

Intrigued, Getty lodged a demand with the Japanese the next day for full details of the circumstances surrounding the loss of *I-178*[31]. Two weeks later the Japanese informed him that the *I-178* was 'Missing and presumed lost during the period from late in May to mid-June 1943 in the sea off the eastern coast of Australia; the exact date and area of loss are unknown'[32]. Curiouser and curiouser. This didn't square with the *Patterson* theory. The rest of the information repeated much of what Getty already knew; that the *I-178*, commanded by Hidejiro Utsuki, formed part of the 22nd Flotilla, 3rd Submarine Squadron, under Rear-Admiral Katsumi Komazawa. Interestingly, a new name popped up; Captain Kozo Nishino, commander of the 22nd Flotilla.

By now Getty had resolved to get to the bottom of all this. He issued the Japanese another demand, this time for a 'certified true extract of the portion of the Second Demobilization Ministry Report of 11 September 1945 that lists the date and area of loss of the submarine I-178'[33].

In its response on 10th December, the IJSDM told Getty that, regrettably, it could not find the report[34]. It did, however, submit a copy of Captain Utsuki's death certificate. The IJN had sent this to the Mayor of Oyama-machi (presumably Utsuki's home town) so his name could be removed from the census register. The man who authorised its dispatch was none other than Rear Admiral Hisashi Mito, the man who sent that infamous secret directive to his submarine commanders about annihilating Allied survivors[d]. The date, time and place of Utsuki's death were given as '4th August 1943, time unknown, on the sea east of Australia'. A different date again, this time 21 days earlier than the *I-178* had been reported sunk!

By this time, Getty's tenure as an investigator was drawing to a close. His discharge from the army neared. It must have irked him to quit without getting to the truth about the *Centaur* and the strange demise of the *I-178*. He told his successor, Lt William Salter, RNVR[35], he believed that 'for some unknown reason the information offered by the CLO was distorted and incorrect'[36].

d. See end of Chapter Four.

Lt Salter took charge of the *Centaur* case file in January 1947. From earlier investigations into atrocities committed against British merchant seaman in the Indian Ocean in 1944, Salter was already familiar with Nakagawa, Kusaka and Admiral Mito.

Salter also had a good idea why Getty would believe that the CLO's information was distorted and incorrect. Only two months earlier, the British had complained about Japanese frustration of their efforts to prosecute submarine personnel charged with crimes against British ships. The IJSDM's Tokyo Bureau had been distinctly evasive and had shown total disregard for some SCAP directives. Surprisingly and annoyingly, and for some strange reason, US authorities seemed less than enthusiastic about dealing with these evasions[37].

It seemed clear that officials at this bureau (the vice-chief of which was Vice Admiral Mito) were reluctant to take action against anyone who might give evidence potentially damaging to themselves. They allegedly arranged convenient disappearances for some wanted men, then blandly claimed they could find no trace of them. In one instance, British investigators found out that two wanted former submarine officers had avoided arrest. The dilatory manner of the police sent to arrest one of them was so blatant that SCAP demanded the arrest of the bureau chief, Rear Admiral Yamamoto. G-2 countermanded the arrest order. Yamamoto, the Americans declared, was 'indispensable' to the demobilization process[38]. Without the wanted man, the trial of a submarine commander and two junior officers charged with executing merchant survivors proved impossible. The frustrated British then asked for Mito's arrest, so he could be interrogated about his notorious secret directive. Once again the Americans refused, on the grounds that Mito, like Yamamoto, held too important a position in the bureau[39].

Political pragmatism eventually held sway. London told its investigators in Tokyo they had to weigh one thing against the other. The smooth demobilization of the Japanese armed forces might well outweigh the importance of prosecuting those responsible for outrages. They had to look at the 'big picture'.

All this might seem to be getting away from the hunt for the *Centaur*'s attacker, but it illustrates the frustrations experienced by SCAP investigators.

Lt Salter still wanted to clear up the mystery about the date the *I-178* sank. On the evidence accumulated so far, the *I-178* was his most likely culprit for the *Centaur* attack. It took a lot more probing, but eventually he got an answer from the CLO. Its earlier statement, that the *I-178* was lost near the Solomon Islands, apparently had been written in haste. It had based the statement on personal recollections and very scanty data. A later analysis concluded the *I-178* sank between late May and mid-June somewhere off eastern Australia. If true, this meant she had been sunk much earlier than 4th August, the date of Utsuki's assumed death, so where did that date come from? The CLO explained that practices varied when it came to deciding which actual day lost naval personnel fell in battle. Sometimes they chose the date the vessel sank, if known; otherwise they took the date that naval officials officially recognised the loss of that vessel. They had made that decision about the *I-178* on 4th August[e].

Salter realised the futility of this line of inquiry. He still had no idea where or when the *I-178* sank. The *Centaur* investigation appeared to have gone nowhere. It would have been easy for Salter to conclude that the *I-178* was the culprit, close his file, and get on with something else; but he didn't. Instead he reviewed the entire case. He went through all the evidence and testimony, combing for new leads. He remained far from satisfied with CLO explanations[40].

Soon the time came for Salter, like Getty before him, to move on. In July 1947 he handed over Investigation 563 to Major B.B. Rogers, JAGD (Judge Advocate General's Department).

Rogers brought a fresh approach to the probe. He focussed his attention on the other three submarines, intending to work through them one by one, exonerating each only when satisfied that they *did not* attack the *Centaur*. By now Rogers had a reasonably complete picture of the 3rd Squadron's command structure for this crucial April/May patrol[41]:

---

e. This also happened with the *I-177*. It was not until November 1944 that the IJN decided she had been lost, although the actual date was in September.

3RD SUBMARINE SQUADRON — TRUK
Commandant: Rear Admiral KOMAZAWA

— Senior Staff Officer: IKEZAWA

I-11 — Flagship. Commander: SHICHIJI

22nd Submarine Flotilla Commander: NISHINO

I-180 — Flagship. Commander: KUSAKA

I-177
Commander: NAKAGAWA

I-178
Commander: UTSUKI

Note: Komazawa and Ikezawa accompanied Shichiji on the *I-11*. Nishino accompanied Kusaka on the *I-180*.

Salter eliminated the *I-11*, which had not operated in the area where the *Centaur* sank. As the *I-177* had reportedly already left there by the date of the sinking, the obvious first candidate for re-examination was Kusaka and his *I-180*. Kusaka, foolishly or truthfully, had openly admitted his presence in the area on 14th May.

Before he brought Kusaka in, however, Rogers arranged for the interview of eleven surviving former *I-180* officers and ratings. All were on board during this contentious patrol. The list of names that Getty had asked for ten months earlier had finally arrived. All these men lived on Kyushu, so they were assembled in Fukuoka by another investigator, J.F.Sartiano. Sartiano grilled the men between 25th and 29th August 1947. Their testimony seemed to agree on most points. Sartiano sent Rogers a summarised report[42].

According to these men, the *I-180* sank only three transport ships during the patrol, all in daylight hours. Naturally they based this on information given them by Kusaka at the time. The *I-180* remained submerged after each attack, so picked up no survivors. The crew never even saw any. Asked about the last victim, they recalled Kusaka telling them it had been one ship in a convoy. They mostly agreed on the date for that attack as 12th May. They made no mention of sinking a hospital ship. A key witness was the torpedo officer, Petty Officer Etsuzaki. He said the sinkings took place on 29th April, 5th May and 12th May 1943. Sartiano immediately picked up the discrepancy with Kusaka's first deposition. Kusaka said then that 'the third ship was hit on 15th or 16th May, south of Brisbane'.

Rogers asked to interview Captain Nishino, commander of the 22nd Flotilla[43]. He now knew (no thanks to Kusaka who had omitted to mention the fact) that Nishino used the *I-180* as his command ship and accompanied Kusaka on the patrol. Sartiano probably picked this up during his interrogation of the crew. Another example of Japanese procrastination? A lapse of memory perhaps?

Nishino said he remembered when the first two ships were sunk. The first occurred on the Emperor's birthday, 29th April, and the second on the Japanese Boy's Festival, 5th May. He thought the third had happened on 14th May, but conceded that if several of his crew had stated it was 12th May then they were probably right and his memory was faulty.

Rogers then questioned Kusaka in detail about this third attack. His crew were right about the date. From Kusaka's description of the location, the convoy, the ship and the attack, it was clear to Rogers that Kusaka was talking about the *Ormiston*, torpedoed on 12th May. No other submarine had been identified as the *Ormiston*'s attacker.

The *I-180* now seemed to be off the hook. Lacking any solid information about the *I-178*, all Rogers had left to work on was Nakagawa and his *I-177*.

Before confronting Nakagawa again Rogers made yet another request to the CLO to locate and produce Captain Ikezawa, the 3rd Squadron's former senior staff officer. Getty had issued the first request back in October 1946. Rogers thought Ikezawa might be useful, as he had assisted Admiral Komazawa on training and operational matters, He also drafted the operational plan for the April/May patrol. At last, in September 1947, the indolent Japanese produced him. It had taken them the best part of a year to track him down.

Ikezawa's evidence certainly gave more detail, but turned up little that was new[44]. Instead, it seemed more like an opportunity for him to regurgitate the common creed; denying any knowledge of orders to eliminate survivors, and reiterating that

Admiral Komazawa repeatedly warned his commanders not to attack hospital ships. It sounded so boringly hollow and trite. Ikezawa did, however, reveal that each submarine commander met with Admiral Komazawa before they left Truk. He said Komazawa wanted to make sure each man understood his designated patrol area. Their task was simple; to maintain radio silence and sink all enemy shipping encountered. They were to report their results orally on their return to Truk. Komazawa expected the patrols to last between 40 and 45 days, with about 15 days allotted for the round trip to Australia and back.

Rogers was not much more the wiser after Izekawa's contribution.

Rogers re-interrogated Komazawa in mid-November 1947, but again learned nothing new[45]. The only conclusion he could draw was that the *I-11* had clearly — and impotently, by all accounts — operated south of Sydney. This confirmed his former view, and effectively absolved Komazawa and Shichiji of any blame for the *Centaur*.

Now only the *I-177* remained. Nakagawa, by process of elimination, became the prime suspect.

Once more the *I-177*'s commander was hauled before his inquisitors. Once more he went through his story. This time he was much more talkative; more prepared to go into detail. This uncharacteristic loquaciousness must have surprised Rogers[46].

Nakagawa spoke in detail about written orders from Komazawa dividing the destination area into three sectors for the first ten days of the patrol. Komazawa had set the *I-177*'s southern limit at 30 °S, with its primary task to cover the port of Brisbane. The admiral left to the discretion of the individual commanders how best to cover their assigned sectors.

Nakagawa said he entered his patrol area on 20th April. Seven days later, at 1000, when 30 to 40 miles off Cape Byron, he sighted a six-ship convoy heading north with a destroyer escort. At a range of about 3000 metres Nakagawa fired six torpedoes on the second (middle) ship in the westerly file. After hearing two hits followed by an explosion he submerged; the destroyer escort had begun dropping depth charges.

This, he persisted, was the only attack he made during this patrol.

In early May he moved about 100 miles away from his coastal patrol position, hoping to intercept shipping bound to and from

Brisbane and other East Australian ports. He returned to Truk on 20th May 1943. He particularly remembered the date as the 20th, because it was a whole week before Japanese Navy Day (although the association of ideas seems a bit tenuous). The *I-11* had already arrived. The *I-180* had not; it returned on the 24th or 25th of May.

On arrival Nakagawa had reported to Admiral Komazawa to explain that he had come back in 40 days rather than 45 (and with six torpedoes still on board) because the morale of his crew was low. He had only 14 or 15 experienced men aboard; the rest being young recruits on operational duty for the first time. They were making serious, potentially lethal, mistakes.

Once again, Nakagawa denied having sighted a hospital ship, and recalled that Admiral Komazawa had lectured him just before sailing about not attacking hospital ships. The Admiral had mentioned that the Allies had sunk a Japanese hospital ship at Singapore, but 'we should not take like action'.

Nakagawa could produce no supporting evidence such as letters, photographs, a diary or personal records to back up his alibi. He did, just the same, give SCAP the name of his gunnery officer on that patrol of the *I-177* — Lt Hajime Obori. As far as he knew, Obori was the *I-177*'s only surviving officer[47].

On 12th December 1947 Rogers put in a request for Obori to report for interrogation. A month later he had still not appeared[f].

The investigation continued. Time passed, and 1947 merged into 1948, but still there was no firm answer to the question — who sank the *Centaur*? In January, Major Rogers compiled a progress report[48]. He drew up a chart plotting all the ships sunk in the area during the 3rd Squadron's patrol. He could account for every ship except one — the *Centaur*. The most encouraging thing he could say was, 'Further investigation discloses that the I-177 was assigned to and operated in the area in which the CENTAUR was sunk'. However he had to admit that the *I-177*'s commander denied sinking the *Centaur*. Nakagawa denied even being in the area on that day. And Rogers couldn't prove otherwise. So where could he go from there?

Back to the interrogation transcripts.

---

f. More will be said about Mr Obori in the next chapter.

Nakagawa's alibi depended on his claim that he arrived back at Truk on 20th May. If true, and with 2,400 miles separating Brisbane and Truk, he had to have left Australian waters before the 14th May, the day the *Centaur* went down. It seemed as watertight as his submarine.

Yet something in the last interrogations of Nishino and Kusaka knocked a big dent in it. Both men insisted that the *I-180* returned to Truk on the 24th or 25th of May, and both observed that the *I-177* came in *a day or two later*. This changed the whole complexion of Nakagawa's defence!

Something else emerged, this time from Nakagawa's own testimony. At his first interrogation, talking to Getty about the *Limerick* attack, Nakagawa said he fired 'a torpedo'. At the second interview this had become 'four or six torpedoes'. By the time he told Rogers this story, the tally had grown to a quite definite six. Rogers knew that submarines closing on convoys often did fire several torpedoes — a fan shot, as they called it — in the hope that even if the primary target escaped, one of the other ships would get in the way. But he could not help but wonder if Nakagawa was trying to account for a few extra torpedoes that he used against some other target; a target he would rather not talk about.

Rogers tried to follow through on this. He contacted the Australian Army. Subsequently, on 16th February 1948, in Canberra, the army asked the Australian Navy for certain information 'urgently required for war crime investigation'[49]. Referring to the list of merchant ships sunk off the east coast of Australia, the army asked if it were possible to calculate the number of torpedoes fired by attacking submarines, counting hits and misses. The navy said no. It had figures for the number of torpedoes that had found their targets, but obviously not for the number actually fired[50].

It had been a wild card, but Rogers' attempt to identify the *Centaur*'s attacker by torpedo accounting drew a blank.

Rogers inserted a succinct conclusion to his part in the *Centaur* investigation: '. . . this agent believes Nakagawa to be lying'[51].

SCAP's probe into the loss of AHS *Centaur* came to an official end later that year. Captain Robert E. Miller took over Case 563 from Major Rogers. He discussed it with Lt Salter and a Major Kyte of the British Division. They decided to turn it over to the British Division, for future investigation. Salter told Miller he did not need the case folder at that time (perhaps another measure of political pragmatism?). Miller sat down and typed up a final report. He concluded: 'Case transferred to British Div. Case Closed'[52].

On 7th June Salter once again took responsibility for the *Centaur* case, this time as part of the British Division. He checked through the case file one more time[53].

Four days later Nakagawa surrendered himself to the authorities at Sugamo prison. He was a suspected B-class war criminal, charged with atrocities committed in the Indian Ocean in February 1944.

On 14th December 1948, SCAP's three-year war crimes investigation culminated in the sentencing of four former admirals and 11 other subordinate officers of the Imperial Japanese Navy[54]. Collectively, SCAP found them responsible for more than 800 deaths. They went to jail for terms varying from one to 20 years. On 23rd December, in the early hours of the morning, seven Class-A war criminals went to the gallows at Sugamo[55].

None of the charges laid had related to the *Centaur*.

On that same day, Salter put the case file aside. Possibly he could no longer find the drive to pursue the matter further. He knew he lacked direct proof, and that Nakagawa had the element of reasonable doubt in his favour. All the evidence was indirect and inferential. Salter had seen several other war criminals aquitted from evidence far more damning than he had against Nakagawa; he knew his case would be thrown out of court[56].

Neither the British nor the Australians, nor for that matter the Americans or the Japanese, opened the *Centaur* case again. But to the many naval historians already collating the plethora of material the War had so kindly brought them, the *Centaur* incident was one of those unsolved mysteries they simply could not leave unsolved.

Perhaps the first person to take a close look at it was Lt-Cmdr G.Hermon Gill, the official RAN historian. In Volume II of his *History of the Royal Australian Navy (1942-45)*, published in 1968, Gill came to the conclusion that either the *I-178* or *I-180* had done the dirty deed, with *I-178* the more likely candidate. His findings probably brought some comfort to certain ex-submariners still living in Japan. Gill might have fallen for the three-card trick (a comment that will be clarified in the Conclusion).

At the same time, a German professor, Dr F.Rohwer, while researching for his book *Die U-Boot-Erfloge Der Achsenmachte*, conducted an extensive collaborative correspondence with Rear Admiral Sakamoto of the Japanese National Defence College. Sakamoto was recognised as the leading historian on Japanese submarine warfare. They exchanged information on Allied losses by Axis submarines in the Pacific and Indian Oceans. Both men concluded that AHS *Centaur* must have been sunk by Nakagawa in the *I-177*. Rohwer said as much in his *Chronology of the War at Sea*, published in 1972. When asked by co-author Chris Milligan for the basis of this information, Rohwer replied that the *I-177* had in fact reported sinking a ship on 14th May 1943 at a spot near where the *Centaur* had sunk.

Finally, in June 1979, Sakamoto said so too; in his official *History of Submarine Warfare*[g].

Without going into too much speculative depth at this stage — this chapter is for historical fact, the Conclusion will deal with deliberation — we can take it that the Japanese would never, even after what might seem a respectable period of 36 years, have admitted guilt for sinking the *Centaur unless they had actually done so.* They probably — with a high degree of probability, one would suspect — knew very well what Nakagawa had done all along, but, well, if the victorious Allies couldn't prove it, why own up? Sakamoto probably persuaded the new Japanese Navy, either by argument or by simply including the information in his manuscript, to allow him (and, *de facto*, the IJN, as his was an official work) to concede the issue, if only to tidy up the loose ends for his book.

Establishing the identity of the man who sank AHS *Centaur* had taken 36 years. By then it was too late to make him pay for his misdeed. No-one suggested it. Perhaps they should. Nakagawa's only penance for snuffing out 268 innocent lives was living with his troubled conscience — if he had one.

---

g. Shenshisosho Volume 98 Sensuikan shi, published by Boeicho Kenshujo Senshishitsu, June 1979.

CONCLUSION

In this chapter we focus attention on the answers to several fundamental questions: how the *Centaur* met her end; what the Japanese did afterwards; how Nakagawa got away with his crime; and lastly what made him commit it.

First we examine the progress of the 3rd Submarine Squadron's contentious April/May patrol. This summary reflects the mutual view of co-author Chris Milligan and Lt-Cmdr David Stevens, RAN, an expert on Japanese submarine activity on Australia's east coast in 1942-43. The pair analysed immense research material; data from such eminent sources as N.Polmar, J.Rohwer and D.Jenkins (three acknowledged experts in wartime naval history), CINCPAC daily intelligence bulletins, National Security Agency Record Group 457 (SRN) and CNO summaries of radio intelligence, and all the depositions and records of interviews at the AWCC and SCAP investigations; in short the most impeccable sources available.

This summary, as far as it affects the *Centaur* story, is as follows:

> 10th April 1943: all four submarines leave Truk bound for Australia's east coast[1].
> 26th April: *I-177* sinks *Limerick* off the northern NSW coast.
> 26th/27th April: *I-180* arrives off Brisbane.
> 27th April: *I-178* sinks *Lydia M Childs* off Sydney.
> 29th April: *I-180* sinks *Wollongbar* off Newcastle.
> 5th May: *I-180* sinks *Fingal* off Coff's Harbour.
> 7th/8th May: *I-11* leaves the area to return to Truk.
> 12th May: *I-180* attacks *Ormiston* and *Caradale* off Coffs Harbour, then departs for Truk.
> 14th May: *I-177* sinks *Centaur*. After the attack, *I-177* surfaces briefly.
> 15th May: *I-177* surfaces once more among the *Centaur* survivors, then departs immediately for Truk.

23rd May: *I-177* arrives at Truk[2].
24th/25th May: *I-180* arrives at Truk[3].

We conclude, from the evidence available to us, that Nakagawa sank the *Centaur*. His motivation for doing so will be examined later in this chapter. What we don't know is exactly *how* or *why* he did it. We don't even know his preferred technique for attacking ships at night. We will probably never know. The authors compiled the word picture painted in the Preface to this book using material from various published sources, a contemporary intelligence assessment of Japanese techniques, and the advice of a Royal Naval wartime submariner, Captain George E.Hunt DSO* DSC* RANR(Ret). Captain Hunt assessed it as arguably the most accurate depiction possible of the assault on the *Centaur*.

Having sunk the *Centaur*, what did Nakagawa do? What went on behind the scenes afterwards? What was the reaction of his superiors, from Komazawa to the higher echelons of the Imperial Japanese Navy and indeed the War Cabinet and Government itself? Again, we are unlikely ever to know for sure. Our research gives us a good idea, however, and without making any specific accusations, we offer the following scenario:

Sometime after his attack on the Centaur *— possibly while on the surface among the survivors — Nakagawa notified Truk that he had sunk a hospital ship. Reporting successful attacks, especially of significant targets, was standard practice[4]. Vice Admiral Komazawa had not yet returned; he was still on his way back in the* I-11. *Whichever officer was in command there, aware of the implications, informed the naval hierarchy in Japan. Word passed to the War Cabinet. It no doubt caused quite a stir, and perhaps some embarrassment. The government had been complaining to the Allies about alleged attacks on Axis hospital ships[5]; to have one of their own submarines guilty of the same crime could rob them of their high moral ground.*

The War Cabinet decided to make no comment on the incident and to parry the inevitable Allied denunciation with an absolute and unequivocal denial. Deny, deny, deny. Let the enemy prove otherwise — if he could. In the meantime the Japanese repeated and amplified their earlier accusations of attacks on Axis hospital ships. The propagandists and radio newswriters got busy.

Meanwhile Nakagawa waited around the area of the sinking, hoping to snare other vessels that might come to the rescue. Truk ordered him to check out the scene during the next night. Nakagawa did, and reported hearing several voices and seeing a flare. The stubborn survivors were refusing to succumb. Nakagawa was instructed to return quickly to Truk.

Nakagawa reached Truk on 23rd May. The voyage took almost eight and a half days. He had to travel on the surface during the day whenever circumstances permitted.

Japan took note as news of the Centaur's *loss reverberated around the world. It steeled itself for a vigorous protest from the Allies. One soon arrived. By then the Japanese strategy of uncompromising denial was firmly in place. Deny everything; admit nothing — and turn up the heat on the adversary. Attack is the best form of defence.*

It worked. The stream of hysterical Japanese claims about other incidents deftly diverted attention from the attack on the Centaur. *As they predicted, the Allies toiled assiduously to refute the Japanese allegations — and all the while their efforts merely thickened the smokescreen over the* Centaur *episode.*

The Japanese were in no hurry to respond to the official protest. Eventually they did, and the disbelief that greeted their emphatic denials hardly surprised them. From then on they were happy to let the issue degenerate into a hollow exchange of correspondence that soon got off the subject of the Centaur *and back onto Allied attacks on Japanese ships. Inexorably they wore their antagonists down. The Allies finally decided this frustrating see-sawing exchange of puerile diplomatic notes had achieved nothing — and moreover was unlikely ever to bear fruit. The Allies dropped the matter, as Japan hoped they would.*

The issue remained dormant until the end of the war. When the victorious Allies arrived in Japan hauling case files bulging with evidence of atrocities, the cagey Japanese military greeted them in a submissively cooperative manner; apparently helpful, but effectively a hindrance. Records requested by investigators that might be damning or incriminating 'were lost in a fire'. Former personnel who might say more than they should under interrogation sadly 'disappeared'. Former submarine commander Zenji Orita (who coincidently served as captain of the I-177 after Nakagawa), in his book I-Boat Captain *published*

*in 1976, says that one of his primary tasks at War's end was
to destroy all the documents he could lay his hands on[a].*

*The Japanese gambled that political pressures in Washington
and London would soon wind these investigations down. In
the meantime they could procrastinate.*

Former submariners soon learned that the assault on the
Centaur *was one of many maritime crimes on the list. It seemed
the official Japanese denial of culpability had cut no ice with
the Allies. But how much did the Allies know?*

*Nakagawa and his former commanding officer, Komazawa,
got together. Both knew they were in the firing line on this issue.
They decided to play it cool, hoping their interrogators were
short on evidence. To their advantage, most of the crew of the
I-177 at the time of the* Centaur *incident lost their lives when
the submarine was later sunk, so the folio of potential witnesses
was small. Nakagawa and Komazawa set their strategy: say
as little as possible and deny any blame for the* Centaur. *They
decided to take advantage of the I-178's loss, which by then was
well known. By testifying that Utsuki's boat did not return to
Truk after the patrol, they could drop a subtle hint that he was
the guilty party. They could not make a direct suggestion to
that effect; that would be too obvious. For if Utsuki in the I-178
had sunk the* Centaur *it would have been more in character for
them to do their best to clear their comrade, especially as he
had later paid the supreme sacrifice. It was very subtle —
perhaps too subtle as things turned out — but they hoped it
might persuade the Allies to draw back the blowtorch.*

*At his first interview, with 1st Lt George F.Getty, Nakagawa
said very little. He hoped this would be his first and last interrogation about the* Centaur. *He denied sinking her. He stressed
that Vice Admiral Komazawa had particularly cautioned all
his submarine commanders not to attack hospital ships. He
casually mentioned that the I-178 did not return from patrol.*

*Komazawa said much the same at his interview, including
the throw-away line about the I-178 not returning.*

*When called a second time Nakagawa knew that Getty was
not going to be fobbed off with vague recollections. Before the
interrogation, he and Komazawa got together again. Maybe
the ploy to implicate the I-178 had failed? Getty hadn't taken*

a. Page 310.

the bait, despite the CLO's convenient recollection that the I-178 *was sunk much earlier than August, somewhere between Australia and Truk. They then concocted Nakagawa's alibi that he returned to Truk on 20th May. At the interrogation Nakagawa tried to appear cooperative but knew he had to be careful; the more he said, the more he created opportunities for Getty to knock holes in his story. This time he was more specific about his attack on the* Limerick — *he could afford to be* — *and maintained that he left the patrol area 'after patrolling for about 20 days' (i.e. about 10th May) and returned to Truk on 20th May.*

A year passed. Nakagawa had begun to think SCAP had dropped the matter when Major B.B.Rogers called him in again. Rogers now had circumstantial evidence implicating the I-177. *Nakagawa knew he had to be on his toes. He again denied responsibility for the* Centaur. *This time he claimed he splurged six torpedoes on the* Limerick. *To create another alibi he told Rogers he moved about 100 miles away from the coast in early May and eventually left from there to Truk. He insisted he arrived back at Truk on 20th May. When asked why he had returned early, he attributed this to lack of morale on board.*

This was Nakagawa's last interrogation about the Centaur. *No charges were ever laid. He had got away with it.*

Nakagawa was closer to being nailed than he could have imagined. We noted in the previous chapter that Rogers didn't believe him. Rogers' gut feeling about Nakagawa was correct. If only Rogers had known then about an Allied decryption of one particular Japanese radio message, he would have had Nakagawa on toast; perhaps even been able to secure a confession. The transmission reported: 'I-177 new sub entered Truk from south May 23rd'[6]. Lt-Cmdr David Stevens came across this all-important message in 1990 amongst CINCPAC daily intelligence bulletins from ULTRA sources. Co-author Chris Milligan confirmed it in 1991 while foraging through a labyrinth of unedited and unindexed ULTRA records in Washington DC. It showed that the *I-177* could easily have been off Brisbane on 14th May, and thus effectively demolished Nakagawa's alibi.

When Rogers asked Nakagawa for some documentary evidence to support his alibi, the former commander gave none. He did give Lt Obori's name, but as we have seen the Japanese were 'unable' to produce him. In 1981, however, a *Brisbane Courier*

Mail journalist tracked down both Obori and Nakagawa, thanks to some clever investigative work by a press agency in Tokyo. Journalist Ken Merrigan's primary target was Nakagawa, then living in Shizuoka City. Nakagawa politely but resolutely refused Merrigan's request for an interview. Nakagawa's daughter told Merrigan her father held the view that the War was over and nothing could be gained by resurrecting it. She commented that those who won can talk about what they wish, adding that she had no doubt American submarines would have sunk Japanese hospital ships if they felt they were losing.

Merrigan followed up the lead to Obori. The retired weapons officer was more talkative than his former commander, although guarded about the *Centaur*. He did not deny that the attack took place. Although he could not remember the incident clearly he did manage to recall (with amazingly selective recollective powers, it would seem) that he left the bridge before the approaching ship was identified. Obori remained adamant that Nakagawa would not have sunk the *Centaur* had he known it was a hospital ship. Interestingly, Obori said that after the War he voluntarily presented himself to Allied headquarters for interrogation, and was allowed to leave[7]. This contradicts the records, but is not surprising; so many slipped through the net. He also said that the *I-177*'s crew respected Nakagawa highly. He described the crew as 'high spirited', which is at variance with Nakagawa's claim of low morale.

In 1991 the authors got in touch with Hajime Obori. He was very guarded. To us he denied all knowledge of the *Centaur* and admitted only that the *I-177* sank a ship in late April[b]. Significantly, his recollection was that *Nakagawa* used four torpedoes on that ship, not six. When asked if Nakagawa had any prior intelligence about a hospital ship, Obori recalled that they 'could expect to meet one'. Whether that referred to one specific hospital ship — as distinct from a general warning to expect hospital ships at any time — is not clear. A second and then a third letter from us, in which we sought his help in getting to the truth of the *Centaur* incident, came back unopened. Stamped on the envelope was 'Retour Refuse'. We were, it would seem, getting too close. It is difficult to avoid the conclusion that someone had ensured certain mouths were kept shut.

---

b. Obviously the *Limerick*.

We invite readers to make up their own minds.

Before leaving this quest to determine which submarine sank the *Centaur*, we need to clarify — if possible, given the conflicting source material available — the possible role of the *I-178*. The reader could be forgiven for wondering why we have paid so much attention to it; after all, did not Sakamoto ascribe Nakagawa's *I-177* to the *Centaur*? Yes, but the possibility still exists that *I-178*, and not the *I-177*, sank the *Centaur*. The issue is clouded by the assertion that she did not return from the April/May patrol (when there are almost impeccable sources saying otherwise), and further by the mystery surrounding her eventual demise. The significance of her return — or otherwise — to Truk is that if she had sunk the *Centaur* Captain Utsuki *would have personally reported it to Komazawa*. By asserting that Utsuki did not return, Komazawa could wash his hands of anything the *I-178* might have done while on patrol. Allied prosecutors could hardly take Komazawa to task for a subordinate's actions — if he had no knowledge of those actions. Komazawa knew he was on reasonably safe ground; by the time he reported in for interrogation, the loss of the *I-178* was beyond doubt. No ghosts should return to haunt him.

So what was the story of the enigmatic *I-178*? We have wildly conflicting data. To briefly summarise what we know, it seems almost certain that the *I-178 did* return to Truk, on 18th May, and took part in navigational exercises there on 2nd June[8]. All the prominent post-War historians we consulted agreed that the ULTRA intercepts, the source of this information, can be trusted as accurate. Yet on 29th May, east of Espiritu Santo, the US subchaser *SC669* engaged a submarine[9]. Some historians concede that this was the *I-178*. Again, as we saw in an earlier chapter, the Japanese Navy acknowledged on 4th August 1943 that they had lost the *I-178* — yet the Americans claimed that their USS *Patterson* sank the *I-178* northwest of Espiritu Santo 21 days later, on 25th August![10] Orita, in his book, strongly refutes the *Patterson* theory[11]. He says the *I-178* was sunk three months earlier, which tends to support the *SC669* claim. In late 1992 an Australian historian, Hugh MacMaster, professed to have discovered the wreck of a submarine off the Queensland coast. He believes it to be the *I-178*, although he gives no evidence to support this. He may well be right. Perhaps the truth about the *I-178* is yet to surface — maybe even the submarine itself!

Something we must also deal with is the theory that the *Centaur* was not torpedoed at all, but rather struck a mine. This became the subject of a vigorous debate pursued mostly in the letter columns of the *Canberra Times* in September 1988[12]. The theory seems to have stemmed from research material stating that in April 1943 HMAS *Gympie* exploded an acoustic mine about six miles northeast of Caloundra Head. Post-war research revealed that in March 1943 the submarine *I-6* laid several mines in that vicinity, ejecting them through torpedo tubes. Perhaps too much credence was given to the proximity of this area to the spot where the *Centaur* exploded; they were, in fact, well apart[13]. Moreover, acoustic mines were ineffective in deep water; the *Centaur* sank in 1,000 fathoms (about 1,800 metres). On this topic, the reader might also recall Lt-Cmdr Dalzell's examination at the AWCC, when he dismissed with cogent logic the likelihood of a mine being responsible[14].

Perhaps the most telling argument against the mine theory came, in a contrary way, from the Japanese themselves. Surely if they felt they could attribute the loss of the *Centaur* to a mine — even one of their own — they would have done so very quickly.

Having removed almost any doubt that Nakagawa sank the *Centaur*, we turn now to his motivation for the crime; to ponder what went through his mind that mid-May, pre-dawn morning as he gazed through his night-sight at a brilliantly lit hospital ship — and gave the order to fire. What drove him to give that fateful command? Was it a spur-of-the-moment response, a cold, calculating, hateful and deliberate act — or specific instructions from superiors?

If the rumours, speculation and innuendo that dotted the Australian press at the time — and occasionally right through to the present day — are anything to go by, it was the last-mentioned. Contemporary wisdom in Australia had it that the army had loaded the *Centaur* with fighting troops and munitions in flagrant violation of the Geneva Convention, that some fifth columnist had passed this on to the Japanese, and it was no wonder they sank her.

The damaging speculation quickly took root. As early as 18th May, the day of MacArthur's communique and Curtin's parliamentary announcement, Captain J.Armstrong, RAN, writing to the Director of Naval Intelligence on the subject of shipping censorship, wrote in part:

> Rumours are very prevalent in Sydney regarding armed troops being carried in "Centaur", but I am assured that the only arms carried were by AASC Ambulance personnel who are justified in doing so under the provisions of the Geneva Convention, as interpreted by Navy Office Letter 09232 of 12th February, 1943, paras. 2(b) and 3(b).[15]

There can be little doubt that the rumour about munitions stemmed from that minor altercation over rifles and sidearms on the wharf in Sydney. It was a good story, easily embellished, and it spread wildly once news of the *Centaur*'s loss hit the headlines.

That rumours should arise about fighting troops is hardly surprising. Both 2nd Mate Rippon and 4th Engineer Cairnie commented to the authors about the *Centaur*'s decks being thick with soldiers when leaving Sydney. A teeming mass of green fatigues. Anyone watching from Sydney's foreshores could easily draw the conclusion that the military was using her as a troopship. Official press releases after the event were not entirely blameless either. On 16th May the Commander-in-Chief directed that 'reference will be made only to the Medical personnel, NOT to units (2/12 Fd Amb)'[16]. Astute analysts of the casualty figures were quick to do their sums and soon worked out that even if all the ship's regular medical staff and its crew had perished they could not make up the huge number of recorded deaths. There were no wounded on board, so who made up the difference? It was not difficult to conclude that the *Centaur* carried troops; an analysis that official silence seemed to confirm.

To combat this rumour, the army decided to give the Press a statement that *some* medical personnel had embarked on the *Centaur* besides her usual complement. Notification went to the censors, orally at first, then in writing. However, much to the annoyance of the military authorities, on page 10 of the *Sydney Morning Herald* on 27th May, in the Roll-of-Honour column, the following memorial appeared:

Marshall, John Bruce,
2/12 Fd. Amb. Missing
Hospital Ship Centaur.[17]

That cat at least was well and truly out of the bag.

Meanwhile, authorities in Brisbane had to move quickly to cap leaking information which they traced to Corporal Albert Blair of the *Centaur*'s medical staff. While under treatment with the other survivors at Greenslopes, Blair apparently told a wardsman that when an ASC unit boarded the *Centaur* the ship's crew refused to put to sea. The wardsman passed it on. Army intelligence officers interviewed Blair at 101 Convalescent Depot. Blair told them about the events on the wharf in Sydney on 11th May. This was the first his questioners had heard about this incident. They asked Lt-Col Outridge to verify it. Blair was cautioned that if he repeated the story he would breach the Security Regulations[18].

This incident illustrates the misconceptions harboured by even those on board the *Centaur*. We mentioned earlier the letter John Maynard wrote to his wife shortly before sailing. There were other similar instances. Paymaster Sergeant Len Hooper told the authors a radio operator remarked to him before sailing that Tokyo Rose had predicted the *Centaur* would not reach its destination[c]. Second Mate Rippon heard one of the medical staff spouting a similar tale. Under questioning, the man admitted it to be no more than scuttlebutt, and Rippon warned him about the dangers of spreading rumours.

Even Captain Murray came in for some posthumous criticism. By electing to follow a route of his own, rather than the one specified by the navy, his critics asserted he had compromised the *Centaur*'s hospital ship status. Incorrect. Murray had a right to decide whichever route he thought suitable. Even if Nakagawa had somehow *known* that the *Centaur* was off its designated track, that knowledge gave him neither reason nor justification to launch an attack.

It is no wonder that rumours grew on rumours, and when officialdom seemed reluctant to 'come clean' then wild conjecture quickly assumed the mantle of proven fact.

These rumours persisted despite intense damage-control. Citizens began to express their feelings. One Andrew Gerrand wrote to John Curtin after he authorised a war loan poster depicting the *Centaur*[19]. He thought the Prime Minister should know '. . . that there was a breach of the Geneva Convention

---

c. Nothing material should be read into this. The said lady was known to predict similar dire consequences for many ships at that time.

in that a Field Unit fully equipped was on board . . . the Captain raised objection to this portion of the cargo and had to be ordered to sail by the authorities . . .[20]'

Curtin checked it out. The army soon assured him of the regularity of the embarkation. Movement Section, LHQ Melbourne, told him 'The Captain did not at any time raise any objection to this Group or STO or so far as can be ascertained, to anyone, nor did he make any comment at all on the matter. It is untrue he had to be ordered to sail . . .'

Citizens wrote to their MPs. One letter to the Rt Hon. P.C.Spender said in part:

> I saw a brawl on a bus on Saturday night when a soldier made a state-ment that the 'Centaur' was taking fighting troops to New Guinea and deserved to be sunk. The woman, who took to the soldier, said she lost two sons on the 'Centaur' and was mad with grief and rage . . . I have heard the rumour before and since, and what is more the rumour per-sists that it is a general procedure for hospital ships to return with fighting troops and arms . . .[21]

Spender passed this on to John Curtin, who directed the Minister for the Army to look into the matter and 'favour me with advice as early as is practicable'. He subsequently received copies of Advisory War Council Minutes. One noted that this was not the first time an Australian hospital ship had carried arms; medical units sent to the Middle East had been similarly equipped[22].

Over later years rumours about munitions and troops periodically resurfaced. As recently as 1988 a former sapper named John Clifton from West Bathurst stated that he and several other soldiers at an army base near Liverpool were taken to the *Centaur* in the middle of the night to load cases of ammunition[23]. Attempts by the authors to contact Mr Clifton failed. He may well have been right; it seems impossible now to prove it either way. One possible explanation is that he might have confused crates of field rations for crates of ammunition. L-Cpl Ron 'Spud' Jones said that before leaving Cowra he packed food rations into dozens of crates and drums. He remembered thinking that the crates looked like ammunition boxes and the drums like petrol drums. As well, there can be little doubt that had the wharfies heard about soldiers loading cargo during the night (and they could easily tell if someone had used the wharf) an instant stop-page would have resulted. Again, cargo work could hardly have gone on during the night without the knowledge of the ship's officers, and both Rippon and Cairnie vehemently dispute the suggestion. As Rippon commented to the authors, after the *Centaur*'s conversion only the space between the floored-off ironstone ballast and the top of the hold could be used for cargo. There simply wasn't *room* for anything more than that being loaded by the wharfies. Admittedly one seaman survivor, in a taped interview, insisted that automatic rifles were hidden beneath spare mattresses in the accommodation, but all the others we asked emphatically rejected the notion of the ship carrying armaments.

It may be instructive to quote the remarks of Gordon Rippon in a letter to Chris Milligan (dated 31st January 1980), when he commented on the incident with the rifles at the Sydney wharf. He said, 'Remember we had experienced four years at sea in wartime, many of us in North Atlantic convoys (and with) the attendant dangers and discomforts of blackouts at sea. Now we were on to "a good thing" and were determined not to let any incident jeopardise it.'

Another post-sinking theory had it that the *Centaur* was a marked ship after earlier carrying 15 Japanese POWs from New Guinea to Australia for interrogation. The author of this assertion said the Japanese were not wounded, and one of them — a high-ranking officer — told him the ship would be sunk once it left Port Moresby. That this did not happen was attributed to bad weather in the Coral Sea. Certainly some Japanese POWs did travel on the ship's first Moresby voyage, but the records confirm that they were wounded.

That the *Centaur* carried troops *before* her last voyage is the claim of a former Brisbane lines-launch hand in a very lucid letter to the authors. He is certain he saw troops embarking on the *Centaur* at Hamilton Wharf, marching onboard through her sideport doors and never appearing on deck again. Soon after this happened, a local Italian was arrested as a fifth columnist. He had been taking notes about ships in the river and transmitting details to the Japanese. Our correspondent suggests, not unreasonably, that this spy told Tokyo about the *Centaur* carrying troops, and Japanese submarines were then authorised to sink her if the chance arose.

Another story had it that members of a commando squadron masqueraded as field ambulance personnel on that last voyage.

Centaur

The seaman who raised the arms-under-mattresses allegations said he saw men on board with commando double-diamond shoulder patches. Adding fuel to this rumour were the inclusion of the names English and Gellurray on the list of survivors rescued by the *Mugford*. The authors contacted Noel Bedford, president of the M-Z Queensland Commando Association. Mystified, he checked his records and reported back that he could find no commando connection with the *Centaur*. He very kindly canvassed his members, just in case, but none replied. A pertinent point here is that commando units had their own medical corps members, whose presence on the *Centaur* would not breach the Convention. They could have been medical orderlies travelling on the ship to rejoin their commando unit after a spell of leave or illness. Be that as it may, the surviving 2/12 Field Ambulance men we spoke to discounted the commando theory. Theirs was a closeknit organisation; they had been together for some time and they would have been well aware of any last minute 'ring-ins'.

This Colonel English puzzled us for some time. His name on the list of survivors — indeed, at the very top — became the seed from which most of rumours about commandoes and armed troops germinated and grew. But who was he? And who was K. Gellurray? Neither name matched up with any on the nominal roll. Army archival repositories denied all knowledge of the enigmatic pair. This didn't necessarily prove anything: if both men *were* commandoes, and their presence on the *Centaur* was secret, then we would hardly expect the military to admit as much, even today. With logical progression we wondered if other men in this category had travelled — and perished — on the *Centaur*. This was a mystery we simply had to solve.

At first we figured that English and Gellurray were merely clerical corruptions of Outridge and K.G.Murray. 'Gellurray' from 'K.G.Murray' could be explained thus, but 'Outridge' to 'English' was perhaps drawing too long a bow. The riddle deepened when Chris Milligan obtained a copy of the *Mugford*'s log from Washington. Attached was a list of survivors drawn up while the destroyer headed back to Brisbane. Neither English nor Gellurray appear. So how did the two names make it onto the list the navy later compiled in Brisbane — particularly as it was based on the *Mugford* data? Milligan made a critical comparison of the two lists. He reached some startling, if logical, conclusions that because of the importance of the topic are worth explaining.

The *Mugford* list reads as follows (complete with spelling mistakes; we have marked merchant seamen with an asterisk):

MALCOLM, T.C. CPO VX29354
SAVAGE, E. Sister A.A.N.S.
DRUST, F. Steward VX56247
KELLY, F.G. NX83583
WESTWOOD, Robert. Ord Seaman *
CHRISTENSEN, Owen. A.B.Seaman *
PATON, R. Pte NX48936
DAVIDSON. A.F. Butcher *
MOATE, L.C. Chief Pantryman *
WALTERSTON, Assist. Storeman *
THOMAS, M.P. VX64860
TAYLOR, E.G.W. NX47368
CECICH, F. A.B. Seaman *
MORRIS, M.A. Greaser *
CHIDGEY, F.B. Pte NX97247
BAYLY, J.L. NX52791
HORGAN, L.J. NX52791
McGRATH, G. NX33029
MILLAR, S.P. Pte NX31460
SANDWELL, S. Steward *
COCHRANE, A. Steward *
McCOSKER, V. Pte QX37971
JOHNSTON, J.C. QX42608
HOGGINS, T. Cook *
HOGGINS, M. Baker *
MURPHY, G. NX73722
DICKSON, A.R. NX52733
BULL, R.D. *
McINTOSH, W. *
BANKS, E. 3rd Officer *
HEGARTY, T.C. NX83273
REID, Frank, Butcher *

SMITH, E.D. Chief Engineer *
STUTTER, J.D. Steward *
CARTER, G.R. VX104834
HOOPER, L.R. Sgt NX10974
PETTOFOOD, QX24620
ARGENT, J.H. NX80674
BLAIR, CPO
HOBDEN, T. JX4911
BAMAGE, A. A.B. Seaman *
MORGAN, S. Donkeyman *
RAWLINS, J. Cook *
BIDMEAD, T. VX90953
JONES, C.G. QX23837
RAVENSCROFT, E.L. NX47509
TEIRNEY, W.H. Greaser *
CAIRNSE, M. 4th Engineer *
LANGE, K. CPO NX66150
COULSEN, J. QX23135
RIPPAN, C.C. 2nd Mate *
MEDCALF, D. S/Sgt NX150851
CULLUM, S.J. A.B. Seaman *
JONASSEN, M. Steward *
TAYLOR, A.J. NX51175
SALT, R.M. Captain *
CORNELL, W. Sgt
JONES, R.
ISHERWOOD, Ronald
MARTIN, E. *
MURRAY, K.G.
OUTRIDGE, L.U.
PASH, M. SC *
WADDINGTON, A. *

This list was complete, albeit it with a few forgivable spelling errors. The names were taken at random, the compiler having no concerns about alphabetical listing or military/civilian ranking. They were all survivors to him. The authorities in Brisbane, on the other hand, needed an accurate military/civilian breakdown. And they wanted it as soon as the ship docked, to sort out who would go to Greenslopes and who to Brisbane General.

It is not difficult to imagine the scene at Newstead Wharf that night. Perhaps not chaotic, but certainly very busy and confused. Staff Officer (Intelligence) Lt-Cmdr McManus was no doubt grateful to receive the *Mugford*'s comprehensive list. He most likely passed it promptly to an aide to sort out military personnel from merchant crew. Sometime afterwards this aide would have telephoned the list through to HQ for typing up. It is in this transliteration that several crucial mistakes were made. We look now at the list as compiled by the navy (again with spelling errors):

ARMY PERSONNEL:
Colonel ENGLISH
Sister E.SAVAGE
T.C.MALCOLM
F.DRUST
P.G.KELLY
R.PASON
K.GELLURRAY
M.P.THOMAS
E.G.W.TAYLOR
F.B.CHIDGEY
I.L.BAYLY
L.J.HORGAN
G.McGRATH
S.P.MILLAR
V.McCOSKER
J.C.JOHNSON
G.MURPHY
A.R.DICKSON
T.C.HEGGARTY
G.R.CARTER
L.R.HOOPER
- PETTOFOOD
J.H.ARGENT
C.P.O. BLAIN
T.HOBDEN
T.BIDMEAD
C.G.JONES
E.RAVENSCROFT
K.LANGE
J.COULSEN
D.MEDCALF
A.J.TAYLOR

MERCHANT SERVICE:
R.M.SALT (Pilot)
M.JONASSEN
S.J.CULLUM
C.C.RIPPAN
M.A.CAIRNSE
W.H.TEIRNEY
J.RAWLINS
S.MORGAN
A.RAMAGE
J.D.STUTTER
E.D.SMITH
Frank REID
E.BANKS
W.McINTOSH
R.D.BULL
M.HOGGINS
T.HOGGINS
A.COCHRANE
S.SANDWELL
M.A.MORRIS
F.CECICL
- WALTERSTON
L.G.HOATA
A.F.DAVIDSON
O.CHRISTENSEN
R.WESTWOOD

Comparing the two lists, it seems very likely that the aide, reading the *Mugford* list over the telephone, perhaps to a stenographer, picked out the military names first. Being a gentleman, he put Ellen Savage before Tom Malcolm. He then read out the military names in their order. When he reached the name W. Cornell he noticed that none of the last seven names had any rank or status. Confused, he mumbled 'Cornell — Jones

— Isherwood', which the stenographer interpreted as 'Colonel English' and, in deference to the rank, put him top of her list. The aide then decided to leave the last seven names for the time being and began reading out the merchant crew. For some reason he started at the end of the *Mugford* list, with R.M. Salt, and proceeded in back order to R.Westwood. It will be noted that the last eight names on the *Mugford* list, from Cornell to Waddington, are missing on the navy list. That mistakes did occur is evidenced by the number of spelling errors *additional to* those made on the *Mugford*, i.e. Pason, Blain, Cecicl and Hoata. K.Gellurray is explained as a shorthand mistake from K.G.Murray. No doubt the aide and stenographer were under pressure to get this list prepared as soon as possible.

It seems reasonable to suggest that this puts the Colonel English myth to rest. If he did exist, he was clever enough to prevent the *Mugford* clerk blowing his cover yet inept enough to allow his own authorities to do so, which seems absurd.

As an interesting aside, a Lt-Col J.C.English *did* exist. And by coincidence he commanded a Field Ambulance during WW2! When asked about this in 1992, he was adamant he never set foot on the *Centaur*. Ironically, he would have had a perfect right to be there!

Rumours and innuendo about the *Centaur* continue to the present day. The authors have heard a variety of stories. Tales of naval ships seen conducting underwater explosions off Point Lookout (no doubt to destroy what remains of the *Centaur*, and with her any evidence of a cargo of munitions); of private diving parties being warned off the wrecksite (one even said a naval helicopter swooped down over his boat to warn him away); and of jittery official responses to formal requests for information about the ship. When the authors tracked down one diver reputed to have physically dived on the wreck, he refused to speak about it over the phone. It might, he said, be bugged!

So many people seem to *know* that there is a cover-up regarding the *Centaur*, and that no-one will be allowed to get to the truth. We have heard of an envelope in the Melbourne office of the Australian Archives that cannot be opened for fifty years; our natural curiosity makes us wonder what could possibly be in it. We also have information about remarks allegedly made by a Red Cross representative not long after the *Centaur* disaster; that the ship carried prohibited personnel and equipment and

Centaur

the authorities were aware of this. A Melbourne historian told the authors that a retired army officer, known well to him, once mentioned a certain (now deceased) brigadier associate who 'had the task of covering up the "*Centaur*" mess at the highest political and military levels'. If true, this brigadier did a superb job, because we have to say that in all our dealings with officialdom we met neither intransigence nor evasiveness.

This is not to say that a cover-up, a very effective one, is *not* in place. It may well be. We can only tender the evidence that came our way, and assure the reader that we listened, noted and investigated to the best of our ability every allegation put to us. It there was a cover-up, however, we think its architects would hardly resort to crude strong-arm tactics like blowing up wrecks from chartered dive-boats or using helicopters to scare people away. Surely it would have been much more subtly and efficiently orchestrated.

Armed with all this conjecture, we can now work through a list of possible motives that Nakagawa had for sinking the *Centaur*.

First we must consider the possibility that the *Centaur* did have munitions on board, or non-medical troops, or commandoes, or a combination of all these, and/or was guilty of transporting non-wounded Japanese POWs. If this information was transmitted by fifth columnists, either straight to the *I-177* or via Japanese naval intelligence, it gave Nakagawa all the justification he needed to deny the *Centaur* her hospital ship immunity. Perhaps a spy's observation of the *Centaur* leaving Sydney, her decks thick with soldiers, was enough.

That Japanese agents did transmit information of this type from Australian shores cannot be dismissed as woolly thinking[24]. The military must have suspected it. The investigation into the telephone call made by greaser Bill McIntosh shortly before sailing highlights the degree of counter-espionage surveillance in place at the time. When he returned to Sydney after the sinking, McIntosh found himself under intense questioning. Fortunately for him he had nothing to fear; his call had been of a legitimate domestic union nature[25].

So it is possible, under those circumstances, that the Japanese considered the *Centaur* fair game — nay, more, genuinely deserving of attack. She was, they could assert, sheltering behind her hospital ship immunity for blatant combatant military purposes[d]. And so Nakagawa sent the torpedo in her direction quite deliberately, as if administering punishment for her duplicity. This relies on much supposition. Was the *I-177* lying in wait for the *Centaur*? If so, how did Nakagawa know she would take the inshore route? A wild guess? Admittedly the *I-180* could have been looking for her farther offshore. Likewise, the squadron might have been authorised to destroy the *Centaur* *if* it came across her.

Putting that conjecture aside, let us now look at the more likely possibility that Nakagawa had no prior knowledge of the *Centaur*'s northbound voyage and was as surprised as his lookouts when the brightly lit ship loomed into view.

First, let us discount for all time the notion that Nakagawa could have mistaken AHS *Centaur* for anything other than what she was. The night was dark, moonless and clear and the *Centaur*, as Outridge succinctly put it, was 'lit up to glory'. Vice Admiral Sakamoto, who wrote the official history of the Japanese submarine war (and in whose book appeared the admission that *I-177* sank the *Centaur*), suggested that in the half light of dawn the *Centaur*'s floodlights might not have been clear. Unconvincing. At four o'clock in the morning at that time of the year, at the spot where the *Centaur* sank, it is still pitch black. The sun did not rise until 0621 that morning, more than two hours after the attack. At the usual attacking range of about one mile, and at a time when the submarine is virtually on its target's beam, the proposition that the floodlit *Centaur* could be mistaken for a general cargo ship — which would be totally blacked out — is beyond belief.

Assuming Nakagawa knew with what he was dealing, then something particular, something out of the ordinary, drove him to pursue the attack. It was no knee-jerk reaction; it took some time to set up the approach, to line up in readiness to launch the poisonous dart. By the time he gave that fateful order he had had more than enough time to reflect on what he was doing. There can be little doubt that by then his resolve was rock solid.

What made him do it?

There are several possibilities.

---

d. They would have been neither surprised nor shocked by this. Enough evidence came to light after the war to show that they played this game to its fullest extent themselves. Italian hospital ships were similarly used.

It might have been no more than his interpretation of the patrol orders, which directed him to 'carry out attacks on enemy naval vessels and . . . sever the supply lines . . .' Did Nakagawa merely classify a hospital ship as a naval ship in another guise?

Nakagawa might have taken the view, as the commander of one U-boat did in WW1, that as this nearing hospital ship was heading *towards* the war theatre it did not have wounded on board. Thus, he erroneously reasoned, it could not strictly speaking claim immunity as a hospital ship, and it was fair game for attack.

David Jenkins, in his book *Battle Surface*[e], offers the opinion that the *Centaur* gave Nakagawa the opportunity to put himself in a more favourable light with his superiors, some sort of sweetener for having sunk only one ship during the patrol. He would soon have to return to Truk, and had not much to show. If so, he needn't have worried: some of the other submarines had enjoyed no success at all.

More likely is that Nakagawa responded to a recent shift in IJN policy on the rules of naval warfare. It came about as a result of a meeting in Berlin between Reich Foreign Minister Ribbentrop and Japanese Ambassador Oshima in March[26]. Ribbentrop wanted the Japanese to toughen up their submarine warfare, as the Germans had done. Hitler himself had decreed an end to humanitarian practices. U-boats were ordered to sink ships without warning. Survivors in lifeboats were to be machine-gunned. Hitler's strategy was to make it very difficult for the Americans to recruit seamen, of which he knew they already had an acute shortage. If the Japanese adopted a similar policy, Ribbentrop avowed, Germany would make a gift of two of its new type submarines. The Japanese accepted the offer. What followed that pivotal meeting was the Naval General Staff's infamous *Gunki* (ultra-secret) operational order to the 6th Fleet about the treatment of survivors from torpedoed ships[27]. The order flowed down to the commanders of the three submarine squadrons: 1st, 3rd and 8th. We know that at least one of these commanders, Vice-Admiral Mito[f], sent it to all his submarines. Article 4 is worth repeating:

e. Random House, Sydney, 1992.
f. See end of Chapter Four.

Conclusion

> Do not stop with the sinking of enemy ships and cargoes; at the same
> time that you *carry out the complete destruction of the crews of the
> enemy's ships* (authors' emphasis), if possible seize part of the crew and
> endeavour to secure information about the enemy.[28].

Although we have no direct evidence, this order almost certainly went to other submarine squadrons. From the post-War
testimony of Rear Admiral Hisashi Ichioka, former commander
of the 8th Submarine Squadron, it is clear that Nakagawa was
aware of it. Ichioka said, 'After the termination of the War I heard
it at Sugamo . . . (from) Nakagawa . . . (he) was the one — one
of many from whom I had heard this. They said that they had
seen the written order'[29]. Another wartime submariner, former
Lt Motohide Yanaba, an engineer on the *I-8* (part of the 8th
Squadron), testified that his captain, Ariizumi, told him the order
had come from Naval General Staff[30].

We can now only speculate how much this new hard-line (or
harder-line) policy influenced Nakagawa. How did it square with
those alleged pious warnings by the naval hierarchy that hospital
ships were not to be molested? Perhaps in the early part of the
War, when Japan bathed in success after success on the battle-
front, these cautions were genuine. But when defeat loomed as
the more likely outcome they became hollow, tongue-in-cheek
allusions. Orita, who followed Nakagawa in command of the
I-177, tells us in his book that when he passed up an opportunity
to sink a hospital ship a high-ranking officer roundly and
hysterically censured him[31].

It is interesting that, having sunk the *Centaur*, Nakagawa held
back from slaughtering the survivors. He probably had few personal qualms about such an outrage, if his conduct later in the
War is any indication. Was it simply the extent of the task —
the survivors were spread over a broad area and there were many
of them — or because he knew that the staff of hospital ships
were classified inviolable under the Convention? If it was the
second, it at least shows that Nakagawa knew very well he had
sunk a hospital ship.

Whatever went through his mind at the time, however,
whatever mental excuse he drummed up to legitimise his attack
on an unarmed, non-combatant ship of mercy, there can be no
doubt that *he knew very well what he was doing*.

Even so, and accepting any or all his possible excuses, it is
still reasonable to ask 'why did he do it?' What could he possibly

hope to gain by such a brutal and senseless act? Surely he must have anticipated the outcry of Allied condemnation, the opprobrium that his actions would bring him, his crew, his squadron, his navy and indeed his nation?

The authors' considered opinion is that Nakagawa acted on his own initiative; he took advantage of the chance meeting with the unsuspecting *Centaur*, and sank her. His motivation: vengeance. Vengeance for the Bismark Sea incident[32]. Vengeance for the alleged recent Allied attack on a Japanese hospital ship at Rabaul. Vengeance for the Japanese hospital ship that Komazawa had told him had been sunk near Singapore.

He had grounds aplenty for revenge.

Moreover, we also believe that he did not expect to be chastised for sinking a hospital ship, but on the contrary, praised.

In conclusion, as horrific, as blatant and as callous as the attack on the *Centaur* was, we should put it in perspective. Throughout the history of hospital ships, unprovoked assaults have been by no means rare. Statistics for British Empire hospital ships in both world wars show that they were common. In the First War the enemy torpedoed eight, five of which sank. In the second conflict, nine were bombed and three torpedoed; eight sank. The enemy too, suffered hospital ship losses; even the victorious Allies had taints of guilt in that regard[33]. Zenji Orita made a profound comment on this subject in his book. He said, 'I have thought of the comparison between events in the Indian Ocean and what took place in the Bismark Sea slaughter. I suppose 'war atrocities' are committed only by the losing side'[34].

EPILOGUE

What is left of AHS *Centaur* rests in peaceful tranquillity on the bottom of the sea, a thousand fathoms deep. Unseen and untouched for half a century, the shattered, twisted and burnt-out hulk almost certainly still lies where it first came to rest on the sea-bed that early morning in May 1943.

Exactly where that is, like many other features of the *Centaur* story, has remained a matter of contention over the years since. It became of critical importance to those who alleged that the *Centaur* carried munitions. If the wreck could be located and dived on then the truth — however embarrassing or politically unpalatable it might be — would come out.

Only one survivor could give anywhere near an accurate estimation of the *Centaur*'s position; the man who held the bridge watch until 10 to 15 minutes before the torpedo struck — 2nd Mate Gordon Rippon. Rippon told naval authorities the *Centaur* sank 24 miles ENE of Point Lookout lighthouse. Although the depth contours on the then current chart were less than precise, there could be little doubt the *Centaur* had gone down on the edge of the continental shelf, outside the 100-fathom line[a]. If Rippon's position was correct, the wreck of the *Centaur* lay well out of reach of any inquisitive or acquisitive divers.

To be truthful, there is one thing that could throw doubt on Rippon's position — the apparent drift of the survivors during their agonising day and a half in the water. The USS *Mugford* picked them up 40 miles due east of Cape Moreton, some 20 miles northeast of the spot where Rippon said the *Centaur* sank.

---

a. The latest edition of the chart shows a depth in this position of about 1,800 metres, roughly 1,000 fathoms.

Along this section of the southern Queensland coast, however, and especially outside the 100-fathom line and at that time of year, the East Australian Current runs with some predictability in a southerly direction. Rates of up to five knots are not uncommon. How could the survivors drift against such a force? Being low in the water they had virtually no windage. We asked the CSIRO. George Cresswell at the CSIRO's Division of Oceanography told us that occasionally the core of the EAC drifts seaward, creating clockwise-rotating eddies between it and the continental shelf. The accounts of some of the survivors tend to suggest that this happened. One mentioned seeing just one light from the elevation of the *Centaur*'s upper decks before the sinking, while others talked of seeing two lights when on the rafts. The first light was Point Lookout, just abaft the port beam when the torpedo struck; the other was identified by Captain Salt as Cape Moreton. From this it seems likely that the survivors drifted in a clockwise direction, first closer inshore, then north-wards and eastwards away from the coast.

We, the authors, have little doubt that the wreck of the *Centaur* lies near where Rippon states. Rippon was the *Centaur*'s navigating officer; if anyone should know, it is him. He was on the bridge from midnight to 0400, taking regular bearings of shore lights. He plotted the ship's position every 30 minutes. When he could see two lights he used cross bearings; when only one, he fell back on the traditional 'running fix' or 'four-point-bearing'. At 0330 Point Lookout light on the northeastern tip of North Stradbroke Island was abeam to port, distance 23 miles. Rippon later remembered this with clarity, as it was the position he wrote on the chit for the duty radio operator. Thirty minutes later, at 0400, when Harry Lamble came up to relieve him, he plotted the position again. He cannot now be sure, but by then he might also have had the loom of Cape Moreton light to work with, which would have improved the accuracy of the position. Had the *Centaur* been much farther inshore, or farther seaward, than he had estimated at 0330, his 0400 fix would have shown it up straight away. Certainly, had he been so inclined, Rippon could have given the authorities a bogus position. Assuming he wanted to (and we cannot imagine why), he had first to get together with 3rd Mate Monty Banks on the rafts and prepare the story. This seems unlikely; by then they had more impor-tant, life-threatening matters to deal with than conspiracies.

Hindsight, that most exact of all sciences, does raise the possibility that Rippon could have made an error in his estimation of the ship's speed over the ground. He was not expecting a northward-setting current; rather the reverse. The survivors' drift suggests that the ship was influenced by an eddy. She was either drifting inshore (which would have shown up in the chartwork), or she was going faster than Rippon thought. By making no allowance for this extra speed — which Rippon admits — his charted position at 0330 was possibly *inshore* of the ship's actual position. If so, the *Centaur* is in fact farther seaward, in even deeper water than 1,800 metres.

Interestingly, an entry about the *Centaur* in the War Diary Situation Report on 14th May (Washington time) 1943 gave her position as, quote: 'Latitude 27°17'S, Longitude 154°05'E (50 miles east of Brisbane)' unquote. This is to the east of Rippon's position — seven miles farther east in fact — but it became accepted as the true position. It appeared in Lloyd's 1947 typescript register of war losses, and in both Sakamoto's and Rohwer's books. But where did it come from? We could find no foundation for it. We wondered why the military would not accept the position given by the most authoritative surviving source, 2nd Mate Rippon? We think we now know. We think they did accept it, but when converting Rippon's quoted bearing and distance into latitude and longitude they made a mistake. It was an understandable error. Rippon, it will be recalled, and based on his recollection of passing Point Lookout at 23 miles, told Lt-Cmdr McManus that the *Centaur* sank 24 miles ENE of Point Lookout. McManus would have passed this on in his report, using the same terminology. To give the military and political chiefs a rounded-off idea where the *Centaur* sank, he probably added '50 miles east of Brisbane', not intending his '50 miles' to be taken literally. It seems likely, however, that more importance was given to his estimate of 50 miles from Brisbane than the more authoritative 24 miles from Point Lookout. For the position that appeared in the War Diary is precisely ENE from Point Lookout and almost exactly 50 miles from Brisbane!

Interested divers could do little but take the given position at face value. Even if the *Centaur* did lie closer inshore, in shallower water, they still had not the faintest idea where to start looking. Theirs was a lost cause either way.

Centaur

This frustration might have fuelled the gestating rumour that the *Centaur was* closer inshore, in a diveable depth, and that military authorities knew the *Centaur*'s position very well and were deliberately suppressing it. Cover-up rumours are the most virulent of all, especially when they have the potential to fulfil prophecies.

So it was no wonder that the headline CENTAUR FOUND! in *The Sydney Sun* on 5th March 1974 pricked a few receptive ears. Two skindivers, Mike Hatcher and Paul Rand, announced to an astonished diving fraternity and a fascinated general public that they had not only found the *Centaur* but had dived on her. Not surprisingly, they were less than forthcoming about the position. 'About 40 miles east of Brisbane' was as precise as they were prepared to be. They said the wreck lay in 60 metres of water. Hatcher and Rand had all the right motives. They hoped to put the munitions rumour to rest. They also wanted to establish beyond doubt that the ship was torpedoed and not mined. They were confident they could do this, despite being limited to only ten minutes on each dive. They intended bringing up the *Centaur*'s bell and lamps, to present to the Australian War Museum. They also hoped to find a suitable souvenir for Ellen Savage, whose fortitude and diligence had captured their imagination.

Diving sources in Brisbane told the authors that the Hatcher/Rand wreck lies about six miles east of Point Lookout. Others told us of an intense naval survey off the southern Queensland coastline that took place after Hatcher and Rand went public (not that there is anything sinister in that; more likely coincidental). One other diver mentioned hearing about a private vessel (chartered by the navy) moored over Hatcher's wreck, conducting 'underwater operations'. The clear inference was that the military has made sure this wreck is destroyed, whether or not it is the *Centaur*.

In 1992 we located Mike Hatcher. He told us his wreck lies about five to six miles ESE of Point Lookout. He said neither he nor Rand brought anything to the surface from it. They did not pursue the venture because several organisations pilloried them for 'disturbing a war grave'. Hatcher said he bases his belief that it was the *Centaur* on its size. Whatever it is, Hatcher believes it got there through being torpedoed. There is a large hole in the side, its steel edges bent inwards. (The *Centaur*'s two

240

butchers, Davidson and Reid, said they saw the jagged edges sticking *outwards*.)

The identity of this wreck has yet to be established. An interested group plans more diving parties, but in late 1992 were having trouble relocating it.

On the topic of torpedoes, there is a remote chance that the one used to sink the *Centaur* was not itself destroyed by the explosion but was recovered from the sea in a trawl net, and is today in private hands in Ipswich, west of Brisbane. This astonishing possibility stems from the fact that after the War a prawn trawlerman named Joe Berger recovered something resembling a torpedo east of Moreton Island. It had no casing, but did have a long shaft and a propeller and moreover was imprinted with Japanese characters. For many years it sat on display at Jack Evans' Porpoise Pool at Tweed Heads. When Evans closed down, the strange device passed to explosives expert Bill Hookway of Southport. Hookway found a serial number. He wrote to Japan, asking the IJN to confirm that it was a torpedo, and seeking the identity of the submarine to which it had been supplied. He received no reply. Hookway later gave the contraption away, although he kept the guidance mechanism. He told the authors he would not rule out the possibility that this was the actual torpedo that struck the *Centaur*. It just might, he suggested, have hit the ship, exploded its warhead, and yet for the most part remained intact. He based this on his experience of some very strange effects of underwater explosions.

To suggest that this is the torpedo that struck the lethal blow might be drawing too long a bow. For one thing, fishermen don't trawl in 1,800 metres of water. For another, a month after the *Centaur* sank, the *I-174* expended four torpedoes at a ship in the same area, but closer inshore. All missed their target, so are somewhere around there, on the seabed. It is possible, again if remotely so, that Hookway's relic could be the *second* torpedo fired by Nakagawa. Perhaps the explosion caused by the first torpedo damaged it before it reached its target. Maybe it hit the ship, failed to explode, and sank to the bottom. The speculation is interesting, if nothing else.

Will the wreck of the *Centaur* ever be found? Possibly yes. The recent *Titanic* and *Bismark* successes by Dr Ballard of the Woods Hole Oceanographic Institute (WHOI) show that the technology exists to locate wrecks at that depth. A more important question would be — does finding the *Centaur* warrant the expense? The *Titanic* and *Bismark* were obvious, high-profile targets; the *Centaur* much less so. However, all may not be lost. Ballard's team has recently been to the Southwest Pacific, to Savo Island near Guadalcanal where it located among others the wreck of HMAS *Canberra*, sunk by Japanese bombers in August 1942. And there are tentative plans for WHOI to come to the Indian Ocean and join a search for both the *Kormoran* and HMAS *Sydney*. We, the authors, hope this expedition might make a clean sweep of that *Kormoran/Sydney* incident by finding the ship that brought the *Kormoran* survivors to Carnarvon — the *Centaur*. Time will tell.

Fears about the eventual discovery of the *Centaur*, and its plunder by souvenir hunters, persuaded a group of Queenslanders to seek the ship's classification as an historic wreck. Leading the push was Lt-Cmdr T.F. Roberts Retd, who for several years stressed the significance of the *Centaur* as a war grave. Another diligent urger was Mr Bernie Robert of Nambour. The government was reluctant, but persistence eventually prevailed. In October 1990 the government declared the *Centaur* henceforth protected under the *Historic Shipwrecks Act 1976*. Diving on the wreck, should that ever become a practical reality, is permitted, but interference is strictly prohibited. Once again, the position quoted in the declaration was not Rippon's, but the mythical spot farther east.

Flushed with success, Lt-Cmdr Roberts persuaded the Royal Queensland Yacht Squadron to organise a special celebration at the wrecksite. On 20th April 1991 TSMV *Taslander* took several interested people out to the spot. During a short service they cast wreaths on the sea.

Coincidently, there is another sunken *Centaur*, also an historic wreck. It lies off the West Australian coast. In February 1870 the 188-tonne brig *Centaur* loaded a cargo of Galena ore from the Narra Tarra mine near Geraldton to take to Fremantle. She grounded not long after leaving port, broke up, and sank without loss of life.

Perhaps while delving this far back into historical chronicles it might be appropriate to mention the British Royal Navy's affection for the name *Centaur*. Several warships have held the name; substantial and important vessels, too, like a 74-gun frigate in the 18th century and, more recently, a fleet aircraft carrier.

Back on this side of the chronological ledger, the name *Centaur* has graced the bows of at least two other vessels. The first, no more than fitting, appeared on a Blue Funnel vessel. Blue Funnel Line fared badly during WW2. Of the 94 ships on its list at the outbreak of hostilities, 51 succumbed to enemy action: a disproportionate share of disaster. In the immediate post-War years, the company struggled to find tonnage to renew its traditional trades. By good fortune the *Charon* and *Gorgon* (the latter despite being bombed in New Guinea waters) had survived. They quickly and efficiently slotted back into the Fremantle/Singapore run. Soon everything had returned to normal, as if nothing had happened. The two sisters gave sterling service through the remaining 1940s, all the 50s, and on into the 60s. By then they were showing their age. Blue Funnel decided the time was right to replace them. It placed an order with John Brown's Clydebank yard for a new, 8,000-tonne passenger/cargo ship; it's name — *Centaur*.

In many ways the new *Centaur* was special.

When she emerged from John Browns her futuristic design shocked the purist Holt traditionalists, but delighted everyone else. Of the three-island profile so typical of Holt steamers since the turn of the century there was no sign. Her bow was raked and stylish. From her raised focsle a long cargo deck swept sternwards in an aesthetic sheer, all the way back to a tall, streamlined after-superstructure housing the passenger and crew accommodation. The twin B&W engines were aft, their exhausts directed into the atmosphere via a dainty, squat funnel — so different from the towering, vertical stacks of old. Like her predecessor the new *Centaur* was a hybrid, designed to handle with ease whatever shipping business the Fremantle/Singapore trade brought her way; be it passengers, general cargo, or live cattle and sheep. Again like the old *Centaur*, her hull had been strengthened to take the bottom at ports with high tidal ranges. But there the physical comparisons ended. The new *Centaur* could carry perhaps twice the cargo of the old. She had accommodation for almost twice the number of passengers, in cabins designed at the highest conventional level of comfort. And at 20 knots service speed she was almost twice as fast.

She acquired one special feature of the old *Centaur*; she became as popular. She remained on the Fremantle/Singapore trade for almost 20 years. Only once did she leave it; for a voyage

around Asia and Australia as a floating trade fair. Once she called at Brisbane; an unscheduled stop, her stabilisers needed repair.
While in dock members of local nursing groups went aboard.
They talked to Captain Williams about the previous *Centaur* and
her significance to nursing. Captain Williams agreed to hold a
brief service over the wreck on his way to Sydney. True to his
word, he brought the new *Centaur* to a halt over the top of the
old. Wreaths given by the nurses were cast on the sea.

In 1979, on her 252nd round voyage from Fremantle, *Centaur*(3) had a very special passenger: former chief engineer of
AHS *Centaur*, Ernie Smith.

Blue Funnel Line withdrew *Centaur*(3) in late 1982. She spent
the next three years on charter, running mostly between
Plymouth and South Africa. In 1985 a Chinese company bought
her and renamed her *Hai Da*[b].

That same year, almost as if someone lamented the name's
passing, it appeared again. This time, however, its custodian was
by no means as grand a vessel. Ansett Transport Industries gave
the name *Centaur* to a new landing barge built for work among
the Whitsunday Islands of central Queensland. Interestingly, like
all previous *Centaur*s, this was a passenger/cargo vessel. With
historical aptness it was built at Brisbane, a mere 50 miles from
the wreck of a gallant predecessor.

Getting back to our *Centaur*, it was primarily the controversy
surrounding her loss that triggered a long-overdue review of
hospital ship rules, in particular for the transport of formed units.
New guidelines now specify that:

> . . . the personnel of a complete military medical unit may be carried
> by a Hospital Ship as a formed unit, notwithstanding that certain per-
> sonnel (e.g. AASC attached within WE) do not, as individuals, fall within
> the categories who may be carried. Such a formed unit may be carried
> on either the outward or homeward voyage.

The section dealing with 'WEAPONS OF PERSONNEL' became
more specific:

> 11. For the purpose of maintaining order and for defending the sick and
> wounded, personal weapons may be carried on a hospital ship by
> (a) the ship's crew and staff;
> (b) an armed guard where special approval for a guard for enemy
> prisoners of war has been given;

---

b. She was still in service in 1992.

(c) all personnel travelling as passengers who are entitled to the protection of the Red Cross convention, including combatant
personnel posted within the W.E. of a formed military medical
unit being conveyed as a unit[1].

While AHS *Centaur* became the last Allied hospital ship to be
sunk by enemy action (perhaps we should add 'so far'), her
passing did not mark the end of the hospital ship era, although
for many years it might have seemed that way. The war in Korea
was notable for the development of the evac helicopter to
transport wounded troops direct from the combat zone to field
hospitals. The military chose not to use hospital ships. Their place
in history, many thought, had passed. Not so. They made a surprising comeback role in the conflicts in Vietnam, the Falklands
and the Persian Gulf. Helicopters and hospital ships working
together forged a most effective partnership, clearing casualties
away from the battlefield to a modern, safe hospital and then
eventually back to their home bases. An interesting British con-
cept emerged during the recent Gulf War against Iraq; the
Primary Casualty Receiving Ship. The British converted a Royal
Fleet Auxiliary aviation training vessel, RFA *Argus*, into a 'highly
versatile, self-defending and helicopter-capable PCRS'. They took
full advantage of a spacious hangar, which became hospital
accommodation, and a long flat upper deck already used for
helicopter operations. The *Argus* was ideally suited to a hospital
ship role, yet she retained her naval livery and her defensive
capability, and thus enjoyed no immunity under the Geneva Convention. A 'fighting hospital ship' the International Red Cross
called it, with obvious concern. The IRC counselled caution and
urged recognition of the well-documented worth of the
traditional hospital ship[2]. The British had obviously decided to
take their chances in that respect. Evidently the Americans preferred the traditional system. In the mid-1980s the U.S.Navy
invested some US$341 million in two hospital ships. Both were
deployed in the Gulf during the Iraq war, but interestingly were
always escorted by a warship. Technically, this might have
annulled their immunity, but as the main threat to surface craft
in that conflict were mines and missiles — which are totally non-
discriminatory — obviously some defensive protection was
necessary.

Hospital ships are extremely expensive ships to create (either
by building or converting) and to run. Few nations in the world

could afford the luxury of the likes of the two U.S. ships standing by just waiting for a call to duty. Even if they could, it seems clear from what happened to the *Centaur* and *Manunda* that despite a review of the rules they are still open to interpretation — and abuse. The temptation to take advantage of a hospital ship's immunity will always be hard to resist, and in turn the suspicion that one's enemy is giving in to that temptation will make it so much harder for a bomber pilot or submarine commander with a hospital ship in his sights to take his finger off the trigger. Perhaps the answer is a UN-sponsored Hospital Ship Service. It could comprise a small fleet of fast, modern, internationally-manned hospital ships scattered around the world, on stand-by to heed the call to any trouble spots; not only areas of conflict but also regions suffering from natural disasters. These ships, surely, would enjoy total immunity. To prevent attacks due to mistaken identity, they could emit strong radio signals, constantly alerting military forces to their presence. It's just a thought.

While on the subject of ships, we should take a look at the fate of the two other vessels that played so critical a role in this story: the *I-177* and the *Mugford*.

After sinking the *Centaur* the *I-177* survived another year and a half of the war in the Pacific. She never sank another ship. Her class, however, is credited with some momentous successes against US warships.

Three weeks after returning to Truk, both the *I-177* and *I-180* left again for the Australian east coast to resume their interceptive duties against Allied shipping. Before reaching their patrol areas, however, new orders diverted them back to the Solomons, the scene of a renewed Allied offensive. Action there was followed by several months of outpost transport duties. Like underwater freighters they hauled much-needed supplies from Rabaul to various New Guinea bases to help sustain beleaguered forces reeling from Allied assaults. On one occasion the *I-177* picked up 278 survivors from a Japanese troop transport sunk by US naval units. In early 1944 the *I-177* returned to offensive duties, heading north to the Aluetian Islands. In mid-year she returned to the Yokosuka Naval Base for a refit.

Lt-Cmdr Hajime Nakagawa remained with the *I-177* until 29th August 1943. On that date, at Rabaul, and for health reasons, he stepped down. Lt-Cmdr Zenji Orita took over. Orita stayed

with the *I-177* until February 1944, when 1st Lt Masaki
Wantanabe replaced him. Wantanabe had the misfortune to be
in command later in the year.

There are two accounts of the *I-177*'s demise. Both agree
approximately on the position, while differing on the date and
on the engagement details. The most strongly supported view
by post-War historians has the *I-177* leaving Kure on 24th
September to patrol the area between Palau and Mindanao. On
the night of 3rd October, when about 60 miles northwest of
Palau, she was radar-detected by the US destroyer escort *Samuel
S. Miles*[3]. The *I-177* submerged, but the US warship locked on
to her with sonar and began a depth charge attack. A large
explosion followed and the dawn revealed a great deal of floating
debris. The other account suggests she was depth-charged on
19th November, outside the Kossol Channel, about 100 miles
west of Palau. Two US destroyer escorts, *Conklin* and *McCoy
Reynolds* claimed the kill[c4]. Either way, and with poetic justice,
the *I-177* joined its two earlier victims as a shattered wreck on
the bottom of the sea (in her case, some 2,500 fathoms down).
Unlike those two victims, the *I-177* left no survivors.

All the same, the *I-177* outlived her Pacific base on Truk Island.
Truk had been the headquarters of the Combined Pacific Fleet
since early 1943; a vital, strategic naval outpost. Japanese air
superiority, which once gave the island base its impregnability,
eventually succumbed to superior Allied forces, and Truk became
vulnerable. In mid-February 1944 an Allied air attack (code-
named 'Hailstorm') caught the fleet napping. The IJN lost two
cruisers, four destroyers and 325 aircraft. Admiral Koga had no
option but to shut up shop and withdraw.

By contrast with the *I-177*, a more illustrious and exciting wartime career and a peaceful, if ignominious, fate awaited the USS
Mugford.

After her starring role in the *Centaur* incident, the *Mugford*
left Brisbane the very next day to join up with a naval task unit
forming at Townsville. Over the next two years she saw more
action around the SWPA than even the most munificent producer
in Hollywood would consider putting on film. Action followed
action for the *Mugford* in New Guinea waters as Allied forces

c. More likely, they had sunk the *I-37*, which by an amazing coincidence had also been
commanded by Nakagawa.

wrested island after island from their entrenched and fanatical Japanese occupiers. She supplied bombardment support for the landings at Woodlark, Lae, Finschhafen, Buna, Arawe, Cape Cloucester and Saidor. Day after day Japanese aircraft attacked, causing several casualties. *Mugford* became the victim of a successful Kamikaze bomber attack in the battle for the Philippines, but survived, and went on to experience several other near misses. The *Mugford*'s wartime service earned her seven Battle Stars. At war's end, the *Mugford* escorted the hospital ship *Haven* into Nagasaki to repatriate Allied POWs to Okinawa. Not long afterwards the USN withdrew her from service. She was decommissioned and stripped. She had been earmarked for a new role, one by no means as sheathed in glory as wartime service, but in those early days of the nuclear age one of importance; she went to the Pacific for decontamination experiments during the Bikini atomic tests. Afterwards, on 22nd March 1948, about one month after Salter had finally relegated the *Centaur*'s case to the archives, the navy scuttled the shell of the *Mugford* off Kwajalein Island. A sad end for a valiant ship. She too ended her career on the sea-bed, although she at least went there without malicious intent[5].

Whatever her eventual fate, the memory of the USS *Mugford* — and all who served in her in May 1943 — would remain fondly and firmly entrenched in the hearts of 64 people back here in Australia. For the one woman and 63 men she delivered from the horrors of explosion, fire, shipwreck, exposure and marauding sharks, the image of that charging white knight (well, camouflage-grey anyway) galloping to their rescue across the waves left an indelible imprint on their memories. She was their saviour, and they could never forget.

Second Officer Rippon especially, and despite exposure and exhaustion, enjoyed his few short hours on the *Mugford* immensely. Relief and physical restoration aside, he revelled in the attention that he, as the senior surviving *Centaur* officer, received from the *Mugford*'s personnel. Being taken to the bridge for a briefing with Corey, and invited to sit in the commander's seat while the *Mugford* cut through the water at more than 30 knots, was an experience he would never forget. He almost regretted reaching Brisbane.

When the *Mugford* docked, Rippon went to the Brisbane General Hospital with the other merchant survivors. The hospital staff found it difficult to cope with a sudden influx of 30 patients. Some seamen were given early releases and allowed to travel south to their homes. A day or so later Dalgetys arranged the transfer of Rippon, Banks, Ernie Smith and Maurice Cairnie to Turrawan Private Hospital in the nearby suburb of Clayfield.

Rippon was lucky. Other than exhaustion and exposure, his only injury amounted to a large bump of clotted blood beneath one knee. Turrawan released him after a couple of weeks. He then took advantage of a week's survivor's leave in Melbourne, courtesy of Blue Funnel Line. Afterwards, as Extra-2nd Mate on a Blue Funnel ship, he returned to England and resumed his sea-going career. Promotion to captain came in due course, followed by many years in command. He retired from Blue Funnel in 1974 at the age of 60, and with his wife enjoys his retirement in North Yorkshire.

That old sea-dog Captain Jock Salt never went to sea again. Not even the desperate Pilot Service secretaries would dare ask him to do another trip. After initial treatment to his burns in Brisbane, he transferred to a Sydney hospital. He eventually recovered, although an injury to his ankle, a legacy of the *Centaur* sinking, plagued him for the rest of his life. One medical specialist recommended the climate of Western Australia and treatment in cold water; another suggested Queensland and warm water. Neither worked.

Chief Engineer Ernie Smith's triumphant return home to Cottesloe in WA was tarnished by the loss of Captain George Murray. Their families had become close friends over the years. Smith retired from the sea in 1967. He passed away in 1987, aged 89.

Maurice Cairnie continued his career as a Blue Funnel engineer. Less than a month after the *Centaur* sank he signed the Articles of M.V. *Charon*, the *Centaur*'s old trade sister. He was back on the Fremantle/Singapore trade, and he stayed there until he swallowed the anchor in 1948 to become manager of an engineering firm. He retired in 1976. He and his wife live in East Fremantle.

Third Mate Monty Banks eventually went back to South Africa. He attained his command and later became a harbour pilot in Durban. He passed away in 1990.

Most of the other merchant crew survivors returned to sea; some within a couple of weeks of the *Centaur* sinking. Seamen were scarce in those difficult times. Some, like fireman Bill McIntosh, swallowed the anchor. He still liked the smell of the sea in his nostrils, all the same; he became a waterside worker.

Turning to the nursing staff; it was perhaps not surprising that the media focussed its attention, both immediately after the sinking and over the half-century since, on Ellen Savage. As the sole surviving woman, Ellen — as much as she personally wished it otherwise — found herself thrust into the limelight. This was unfortunate. It tended to dilute the accounts of her fellow survivors' heroism and fortitude; to nudge into the background the abundant gallantry and mateship that characterised those horror-filled 36 hours in the sea. Being singled out for special laudatory treatment embarrassed Ellen. Characteristically, she regarded her actions as no more than that which her profession demanded of her. As her sister Kathleen told the authors: 'The tributes Ellen received she accepted gracefully for her shipmates, those who survived and those who perished'.

All the documentation, both direct and anecdotal, show beyond doubt that during those traumatic 36 hours in the water she played a paramount role in boosting morale. She gave medical care, she displayed immense personal courage, and she sustained hope in eventual rescue. It was only fitting that her courage and fortitude should be recognised. In 1944 Ellen was awarded the George Medal.

After the War she received a Florence Nightingale Scholarship and went to the Royal College of Nursing in London to study nursing administration. She later became Matron of the Rankin Park Chest Hospital (part of the Newcastle Hospital), where she remained until her retirement in 1967. Ellen Savage kept up her contacts with *Centaur* survivors and retired AANS members. Every year, on 14th May, like all the survivors who could make it, she attended a remembrance ceremony at Sydney's Cenotaph. She never missed an Anzac Day reunion with her wartime mates. On Anzac Day 1985, she attended the usual hospital ship reunion lunch at the Sydney Hospital. She made a speech and had a wonderful time renewing old acquaintances. Afterwards, while waiting for a taxi in the street, Ellen collapsed and died. She was 72 years old. She found her final resting place in Sydney's Northern Suburbs Cemetery. Death rarely comes at a suitable moment, but for Ellen Savage, Anzac Day must surely be a most fitting day to depart this life.

Aptly, her name lives on. In her memory the John Hunter Hospital in Newcastle named its chapel after her. Her portrait hangs in the Australian War Memorial in Canberra.

Ellen Savage was just one of 3,477 women who served in the AANS during WW2. Of these, 55 received decorations, 82 were Mentioned in Despatches, and 53 lost their lives to enemy action: 41 in Malaya, one in the *Manunda*, and 11 in the *Centaur*.

The loss of eleven Nursing Sisters in such a tragic and senseless act of barbarism — and so close to our shores — shocked all Australians. A year after the sinking, the public gave strong support to a fund-raising appeal for a suitable war memorial for nurses. Swelling the coffers were the proceeds from a small booklet about the *Centaur*, published by the AANS. Titled *Lest We Forget*, the 28-page volume sold for two shillings. In Melbourne on Empire Day alone, volunteers collected over £2,000 when donations poured into 350 boxes scattered around the city. Some surviving *Centaur* crew members helped out by selling buttons.

Two years later, in 1948, Queensland nurses created a new fund, the aptly-named *Centaur Memorial Fund for Nurses*. At its core was the Australasian Trained Nurses Association of Queensland, formed back in 1904. The ATNA leased rooms in Exton House in Brisbane's Queen Street. On 4th November that year, at a meeting chaired by Senator (later Dame) Annabelle Rankin, it created a *Centaur*-oriented fund. The *Brisbane Telegraph* agreed to launch and sponsor the appeal. The public reacted magnificently, opening their hearts in gratitude to the War's unsung heroines. The response exceeded all expectations. In no time the fund swelled to £48,000, in those days a staggering sum. It was enough to actually buy Exton House, the building the ATNA formerly tenanted. The CMFN renamed it *Centaur House*. One large meeting room became the *Ellen Savage Room*.

Centaur House fulfilled a special and jealously-cherished role for nurses. It became a place all nurses could call their own; a venue for convivial meetings; a residence, where nurses from out of town could stay in inexpensive lodgings. It became the emotional heartbeat of nursing in Queensland.

Fund-raising continued by various means, one of the more remunerative being a Wheel-of-Fortune at Brisbane's annual

EKKA[d]. Another event was an annual Queen of the Nurses Quest. The nurse raising the most money for the CMFN earned herself a cash reward. In the early 50s, an already-legendary Sister named Sadie MacDonald won the quest. She sacrificed her prize to fund a commemorative sandstone bas-relief tablet. The exquisitely crafted plaque, which depicts the *Centaur* and the profile of a nurse (thought by some nurses to be that of Sadie MacDonald herself), graced the foyer at Centaur House for many years.

In 1971 the CMFN sold Centaur House. The proceeds were used to buy land in Wickham Terrace and erect a new building; a new Centaur House, complete with Ellen Savage Room and sandstone plaque. In 1979 this building too was sold.

Today the CMFN still exists. Its aims are to promote the welfare and well-being of the nursing profession, mostly through nursing education. It achieves this through scholarships and bursaries, and assistance to former nurses in need. The fund relies for its revenue on judicious investments. Long-term secretary Rodney Gibson believes the fund's unbroken longevity is perhaps its greatest triumph, considering the many dramatic changes to the nursing profession in the last half century.

Queensland nurses were not the only ones perpetuating the *Centaur* memory. In Victoria the nursing fraternity funds an annual Centaur Nurses Memorial Education Trust Scholarship.

Playing a parallel and complementary role to the *Centaur*'s nursing sisters were the AAMC members. Unfortunately, not a great deal is known about the later lives of the 19 other surviving medical staffers.

Some, like Tom Hobden, Tom Hegarty and Fred Chidgey, took up where they left off. They served out the rest of the war on a hospital ship (the *Wanganella*). Others, like Vince McCosker, went to the steamy jungle battlefields of New Guinea. Vince McCosker became a relative by marriage of fellow-survivor and friend Eric Taylor; he married Eric's sister Dorothy in 1946. After the war Vince and his sister, Daphne, worked hard to maintain the emotional *Centaur* ties among survivors and relatives of those who perished. Each year until the 70s, Vince organised a 14th May remembrance service at Brisbane's Anzac Shrine. One year Ellen Savage attended. Vince and Daphne had a dream; to

d. Brisbane's annual Exhibition. This Wheel-of-Fortune continues to the present day.

build a memorial to the *Centaur* at Point Lookout. Every year, Daphne organised a concert party to raise funds. Sadly, she left Brisbane for England in 1954. Her annual concert parties — and her dream of a memorial — ended. What money she and Vince had raised went to the CMFN.

Very little remained of the 2/12 Australian Field Ambulance after the *Centaur* disaster. Nakagawa's torpedo had culled 93% of the unit's manpower in one foul blow. Of the 193 men who embarked, only 14 came ashore, including the lone officer survivor, Lt-Col Outridge. Most survivors left Greenslopes after a week, went to a convalescence depot for two weeks, then took two weeks home leave before returning to what was left of their camp at Corrimal. Surprisingly, despite the unit's near obliteration, the army elected to reform it by amalgamation with the 4th Light Field Ambulance. Six months after the sinking, a revamped 2/12th set off from Wollongong to Atherton in North Queensland to complete the mission it had begun in May. This time it took the train. After beach landing training the unit went to New Guinea and later Borneo. It set up field hospitals in support of the Allies' progressive, successful, but still bloody island-by-island assaults. By November 1945, the fifth anniversary of the unit's formation, elements of the 2/12th were scattered over 1,800 square miles of the SWPA.

These days, former members retain their connections through a very active 2/12 Australian Field Ambulance Association.

Lt-Col Outridge did not return to the 2/12th. On his return to full health the army gave him command of the 2/8 Field Ambulance. Like the men of the 2/12th, Outridge went to New Guinea. He was Mentioned in Despatches. At war's end he set up a private practice in Gympie, Queensland. He retained his links with the army in an honorary capacity.

Many survivors kept contact with each other in the post-war years, though mostly on a regional basis. Surprisingly, given the unique bond that set them apart from other surviving casualties of the war at sea, they formed no association. Something like the Turtle Club, one would think, would have been most germane; its membership restricted to those who shared this one tragic experience; a unique eliteness. But they did not; perhaps deliberately so, in view of the disturbing rumours. Possibly no-one thought of it at the time. Some in fact went on with their lives without ever making contact again with any others. This dispersion made it difficult to track them all down. Some were easily found, others not so; and some emerged from their quiet existences of their own accord, lured out into the limelight by renewed public interest in the tragedy as its 50th anniversary nears.

In early 1993, as this book goes to press, there has been recent contact with Gordon Rippon, Maurice Cairnie, Ron Moate, Rupert Paton, Mattie Morris, Robert Westwood and Martin Pash of the merchant crew; Tom Hobden, Dick Medcalf and Tom Malcolm of the AAMC; and Allan Pettiford, Len Hooper, George McGrath, Edwin Ravenscroft, 'Spud' Jones and B.Trigg from the 2/12 Field Ambulance — 16 in all. Others, hopefully, are still around.

An event that might bring them out of the woodwork is the unveiling of a Centaur Memorial on 14th May 1993.

Arguably no other wrecked ship in Australian waters has inspired as many emotional and physical legacies as the *Centaur*.

They began to manifest themselves soon after news of the *Centaur* disaster reached a dumbfounded world. The first memorial service took place two weeks after the tragedy. On 28th May hundreds of mourners gathered in Sydney's St. Andrew's Cathedral. Archbishop Mowell officiated before a packed church. So many attended that for the first time in the cathedral's history a *Standing Room Only* sign had to be posted outside.

'Such outrages as this do not fill us with dismay, much less frighten us,' said Archbishop Mowell in his sermon, 'but make us redouble our determination that good shall triumph over evil and right over wrong.'

Afterwards, NSW Premier William McKell laid a wreath at the Cenotaph. Other politicians, medical officers, nurses, and merchant seamen followed suit.

Two days later the residents of Corrimal rallied spontaneously in a memoriam service to the *Centaur*'s dead. They remembered especially the 179 men of the 2/12 Field Ambulance, until so recently bivouacked nearby. Clerics and army chaplains conducted the service in the local Princess Theatre. They had hastily prepared and printed an order of service. It included a roll of honour.

From 1943 on, at dawn on each 14th May, *Centaur* survivors and relatives of victims gathered at the Cenotaph in Sydney and the Anzac Shrine in Brisbane (and no doubt in other places as well) to pay their respects to their lost comrades. The event drew the support of returned servicemens' organisations, nursing groups, and especially seafarers. The Seamens' Union of Australia never failed to remember its fallen.

Time inevitably took its toll and the number of survivors dwindled, as did the attendance at these remembrance services. The stalwarts held their last parade at the Sydney Cenotaph in 1973. Anzac Shrine reunions in Brisbane ceased at much the same time.

Many other remembrance services have taken place over the years, several connected with the unveiling of plaques and memorials.

We learned about so many physical *Centaur* memorials during our research for this book that we can but wonder how many others there are in existence of which we know nothing. The loss of the *Centaur* is portrayed and perpetuated in displays, monuments, plaques, books and paintings in places all over the nation.

First off the mark to donate one was Blue Funnel Line. The company presented a model of the *Centaur* to the Australian War Memorial in Canberra. Showing the *Centaur* in hospital ship livery, it became the centrepiece of a permanent display[e]. The AWM has other *Centaur* relics. Lt-Col Outridge somehow managed to souvenir a liferaft distress light. His wife donated it after his death. Another Queensland survivor, Allan Pettiford, gave the AWM a flare he had brought ashore. Tom Hobden and George McGrath donated their wristwatches; George McGrath's watch had stopped at 0410. Other relics held by the AWM include a lifejacket and whistle, and the scissors, scalpel and tweezers from the medical kit.

The loss of the *Centaur* struck a compassionate chord in the Victorian port city of Williamstown, home to the ship during her conversion to a hospital ship. At St Nicholas Seamen's Church, the visit by so many *Centaur* officers and men was recalled with sadness. Someone (identity now unknown) donated a missal, a mass book, dedicated to those who lost their lives. Both the bible the visiting *Centaur* seamen signed, and the missal,

---

e. In 1992 this display was dismantled to make room for an exhibition on Vietnam.

can be seen in the new St Nicholas Church at Flagstaff Hill, Warrnambool.

Plaques either dedicated to the *Centaur* or listing names of *Centaur* victims, are manifold. The first appeared in Sydney in May 1944, donated by the officers and crew of the *Charon*. They chose the Missions to Seamen as its home. *Centaur* survivor Maurice Cairnie and the incumbent Padre jointly unveiled the plaque, on the north wall of the congregation hall. More plaques were on their way. In the early post-War years almost every town and city in Australia unveiled memorial tablets listing home-town heroes who paid the supreme sacrifice, and many included *Centaur* victims. The Sydney Memorial lists the *Centaur* dead. The names of the eleven Sisters appear on a memorial outside the Nurses Memorial Centre in Melbourne. There is a Centaur Memorial rose garden at the Heidelberg Repatriation Hospital in Victoria, and on the chapel wall a plaque commemorates the three Victorian Sisters: O'Donnell, Rutherford and Walker. Sister Joyce Wyllie's name appears on Bundaberg's War Memorial. Sergeants Paul Bracken and Kevin Williams are both memorialised in stone outside the Ambulance Office of their hometown in Yass, NSW. Private Robert Stubbs is remembered on a plaque next to a tree planted in his honour in Sydney's Botanical Gardens (of which he had once been a staff member). The list goes on.

In Brisbane, the sandstone bas-relief tablet that for many years adorned the foyers of two successive Centaur Houses is now permanently displayed in the Anzac Hall of Memories. The CMFN considered this a fitting home after the sale of its Wickham Terrace premises. The tablet was unveiled there on Anzac Day, 1989, the last official act of long-term CMFN president Eileen 'Bindy' Walker[f].

In Melbourne, in the grounds of the Nurses Memorial Centre, there stands a ship's mast commemorating the nurses who lost their lives on the *Centaur*.

On 15th September 1968, Queensland Premier Sir Francis Nicklin unveiled a monument to the *Centaur* on a grassy headland at Wickham Point, Caloundra. Vince McCosker, Dr

---

f. Bindy Walker was president of the CMFN for so long her name became synonymous with the *Centaur*. She had been a patient in Greenslopes the night the survivors were brought in, and gave up her bed for Ellen Savage; something of which she remained immensely proud.

Outridge, and other survivors attended. Simultaneously, seamen on board HMAS *Adroit* cast a wreath on the sea at the wrecksite, and a flight of Canberra bombers roared overhead. The robust concrete cairn was a project of the Caloundra Rotary Club, initially proposed by member (and *Centaur* enthusiast) Mannie Comino. On its face a plaque outlines the story of the *Centaur* and gives the ship's name to the surrounding park. Not far away is the Centaur Memorial Nursing Home, opened in October 1992. Its first patient, Mr Alan Pitcher, served as an engineer of the *Centaur* before the War.

In 1990 the most ambitious *Centaur* memorial project yet came to fruition. A NSW-based AHS Centaur Memorial Window Committee, with retired naval officer John Jeppesen, OAM, RFD, at the helm, raised some $16,000 for an ornate, stain-glass window in Concord Repatriation Hospital. The late Rear Admiral Sir David Martin, KCMG, AO, Governor of NSW, unveiled the memorial window on 13th May. The guestlist ran into the hundreds and included five *Centaur* survivors: Tom Hobden, Ron Jones, George McGrath, Edwin Ravenscroft and James Rawlings. Tom Hobden recited the Ode of Remembrance.

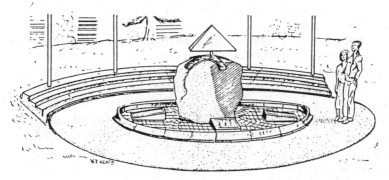

An artist's impression of the Danger Point Centaur *Memorial ... to be unveiled by the Australian Prime Minister on 14th May 1993, the 50th anniversary of the sinking.* (W.Keats)

There appears to be no end to the public's interest in the *Centaur*. Even as this book goes to print, the plans of a group of *Centaur* enthusiasts at Tweed Heads to build a memorial at Danger Point on the NSW/Queensland border are well advanced. The $60,000 memorial, which includes a concrete cairn and a walk of remembrance with plaques listing every ship sunk in

Australian coastal waters in WW2, will be unveiled on the 50th anniversary of the tragedy. The current Prime Minister has expressed a willingness to officiate (his political circumstances permitting). If the support shown at merely the site dedication on 17th May 1992 is any indication, this ceremony will be extremely well attended. Some 350 people turned up in atrocious weather. *Centaur* survivors Allan Pettiford and Tom Malcolm attended.

The Danger Point memorial is an initiative of the Merchant Navy War Service League, an organisation dedicated to securing repatriation benefits (to which members of the armed services automatically qualify) for merchant seamen who served in WW2. One in every eight Australian merchant seamen lost their lives during the War; the armed forces lost one in 30. Drawing support from several groups (including the RSL, AANS, RN Association, Red Cross and others), and under the auspices of the Lower Tweed River Historical Society, the League formed a Centaur Commemoration Committee in July 1991. Donors were many and diverse. Ocean Steam donated £5,000, an astonishing contribution.

To boost its fund-raising effort, the committee organised a Centaur Memorial Concert. Vince McCosker and sister Daphne would have been thrilled. Held in Brisbane's City Hall on 13th October 1992, the WW2-nostalgia concert was compered by local thespian identity Wilson Irving. Irving had his own connection with the *Centaur*. As an army officer based in Brisbane at the time of the sinking, he remembers taking a search party to the coastal beaches to look for bodies. He found none.

Another fund-raiser was a booklet on the *Centaur*, entitled *Three Minutes of Time*. Committee historian Alan Smith compiled the work, which the federal Minister for Veterans' Affairs, Ben Humphreys, later launched.

Another book released in 1992 with content about the *Centaur* was Dr Rupert Goodman's *Hospital Ships*. It is a comprehensive history of hospital ships, with detailed coverage of the role of Australia's gallant four: *Manunda*, *Wanganella*, *Oranje* — and *Centaur*.

Rupert Goodman has been the proud owner of two oil paintings of the *Centaur*. They were two of three painted by Queensland marine artist the late Dick Wills, all of which depict the *Centaur* in hospital ship colours. One of Dr Goodman's now hangs in Brisbane's Victoria Barracks. Wills himself donated the third to the Broken Hill Hospital.

And finally, another, perhaps more abstract memorial to the *Centaur* will appear in April 1993, the month before the 50th anniversary of this tragic event. It will be a memorial that should span the nation; one with the potential to find its way into every corner of the globe — a postage stamp. Australia Post announced the four-stamp issue in January. The *Centaur* and three other WW2 ships of note have been chosen for the theme.

$1.20 AUSTRALIA

Hospital Ship: Centaur

It is morbidly fascinating that all this interest, this emotional homage, memorial-building, inspirational artistry, even the motivation to write this book, stem from the consequences of a single, spontaneous decision by one man; by his deliberate act of barbarism; by the whim that crossed his mind that early morning in mid-May 50 years ago when a non-combatant ship with its non-combatant crew unwittingly and innocently crossed his path.

What about him, this Hajime Nakagawa? Did fate ascribe a punishment to fit the crime? *Is* there a suitable punishment for such an act of villainy?

We need to go back to early 1947. On 14th January the International Military Tribunal heard evidence about attacks on the survivors of torpedoed British merchant ships in the Indian Ocean[6]. After sinking the tanker *British Chivalry*, it was alleged, Japanese submariners took her master prisoner and forced him to watch as they machine-gunned his crew, killing several men. Likewise, after sinking the *Ascot*, they machine-gunned lifeboats holding 52 survivors, and killed all but eight. Surviving crewmembers of another victim, the *Sutley*, became the target of small arms fire while clinging to rafts and wreckage. The prosecutors, who included Lt Salter, gave other examples; evidence that over 100 seamen — British, Dutch, Indonesian, Australian and American (a Red Cross nurse) — were murdered in cold blood. The lucky ones met their deaths from pistols and machine guns; the remaining unfortunates succumbed to sledgehammers and samurai swords.

The three British ships singled out for special mention had been sunk by the one submarine, the *I-37*. And the captain of the *I-37* at the time? None other than Hajime Nakagawa.

At that time Salter was concurrently still pursuing his *Centaur* investigation. He had no personal doubt of the identity of the man responsible — but immense difficulty proving it. So he must have taken great delight when his prime *Centaur* suspect turned up at Sugamo Prison on 11th June 1948 for confinement as a suspected war criminal.

By then Salter had the goods on Nakagawa; if not for the *Centaur*, then at least for his brutal treatment of British seamen in the Indian Ocean. Unfortunately for Nakagawa, some seamen from all three ships survived the massacre. They gave detailed evidence of being raked with machine gun fire and rammed by the *I-37*. Salter's case looked strong.

Nakagawa entered Sugamo carrying nothing more than the clothes he stood up in; no currency or other valuables, no toilet articles, no books[7]. The duty jailer at the time, a Pte Goodrich, escorted Nakagawa to an examination room and told him to strip naked. Medical Officer Lt R.J.O'Neil gave him a physical. Nakagawa stood 5 foot 4½ inches tall (160 cms), weighed 139 lbs (63 kilos), had brown eyes, ruddy skin and black hair. His blood pressure and pulse rate were normal. He checked negatively for signs of syphilis. His body had no distinguishing marks or unusual characteristics. Prison staff took his fingerprints, then led him to a disinfecting room to dust him and his clothes with DDT powder. They told him to get dressed. They photographed him; front and profile. They assigned him prison number 2594. Military Police then took him to his holding cell; Red West, Block Three, tier C, room three. He later moved to Red East, Block Six, tier B, room three.

Nakagawa waited in Sugamo for a month before his trial began. One wonders if he reflected much about the orders he gave on those three separate days in February 1944, in the Indian Ocean. No doubt he contemplated acquittal. Why not? Had he not merely been following orders? The instruction to leave no survivors had come from the highest naval level; the Naval General Staff itself. On the other hand Nakagawa knew he could not rule out a guilty verdict, and possible execution. He and the other

M.A. HOSPITAL SHIP "CENTAUR"

LOST AT SEA THROUGH ENEMY ACTION
14th MAY, 1943

In Memory of
THE OFFICERS AND CREW

G. A. MURRAY	MASTER		J. CAPPER	CH. STEWARD
H. E. LAMBLE	1st MATE		A. J. MORRIS	2nd STEWARD
E. J. SUMMERS	PURSER			
W. D. CUTHILL	2nd ENG		J. C. BUCK	BARMAN
C. ALEXANDER	3rd ENG			
H. R. HALL	4th ENG		V. LOCKHART	STEWARD
K. SYKES	ELECT		C. E. J. CAREY	STEWARD
T. V. MORRIS	2nd R.OPR		A. RAYNER	STEWARD
R. M. LAIRD	3rd R.OPR		F. SIDDONS	STEWARD
			W. A. WARNER	STEWARD
D. R. McLEAN	PRINTER			
R. J. SPENCE	CARPENTER		D. COCKERILL	COOK
G. BRANDIN	BOSUN		F. J. GANNON	COOK
			S. LONGDEN	COOK. CH.
D. ABBOT	A.B.		W. McKINNON	COOK
F. W. FOX	A.B.		S. L. STRACK	COOK
R. R. HART	A.B.			
T. S. HUGHES	A.B.		S. O. PEARL	BAKER
L. KAKI	A.B.		T. E. PRITCHARD	BAKER
M. J. LEE	A.B.			
J. LE BLANC	A.B.		T. BEHAN	GREASER
G. LONG	A.B.		J. O. BOWDEN	GREASER
J. LYON	A.B.		C. CLARK	GREASER
D. MILLIGAN	A.B.		W. R. DOWNIE	GREASER
E. C. PAGE	A.B.		J. GALLAGHER	GREASER
E. B. SIMPSON	A.B.		R. GRAINGER	GREASER

ERECTED BY OFFICERS AND CREW OF THE SISTER SHIP M.V. "CHARON"

"Greater Love hath No Man Than This"

The first Centaur *memorial plaque, donated by the officers and crew of the* Charon *(Centaur's trade sister ship) to the Seamens' Mission in Sydney. Here* Centaur *survivor Maurice Cairnie, 4th Engineer, assists the Mission Padre unveil the plaque on 14th May 1944.*

Survivors Bill Cornell and Les Horgan head a wreath-laying march to Sydney's Cenotaph from St Andrew's Cathedral. Bill Cornell suffered shocking burns when the Centaur *exploded.*

(Mrs E.Cornell)

AT THE GOING DOWN OF THE SUN AND IN THE MORNING
WE WILL REMEMBER THEM

Sandstone plaque in Brisbane's Anzac Hall of Memories. It previously adorned the foyer of Centaur House, home to the Centaur Memorial Fund for Nurses.

(D.McMillan *Words & Pix*)

The Centaur *memorial at Centaur Park, Caloundra . . . unveiled by* Premier Sir Frank Nicklin *in 1968.*

(J.Foley)

The remains of what is thought to be a Japanese torpedo, retrieved by a trawler off Point Lookout after the War.

(J.Evans)

Centaur *(III), built in 1962 for the Fremantle/Singapore service . . . her futuristic design shocked the Blue Funnel Line purists.*
Below: SNAP! M.V. Centaur *passes HMS* Centaur, *a British aircraft carrier, on her entry into Hong Kong harbour as an Australian Trade ship in 1964.*

(A. Diack)

prisoners charged with Class B and C war crimes paid close attention to the progress of the Class A trials in Tokyo, no doubt pondering the likely effects on their own hearings.

On 14th July 1948, the 'Ichioka Case' began in Yokohama's District Courthouse before a six-man Military Commission. On trial were 43 former IJN personnel, ranging from petty officers to vice admirals, all charged with violating the laws and customs of war. They included Hajime Nakagawa, Toshio Kusaka (*I-180*)[8], and Vice Admiral Mito. All pleaded not guilty.

On the bench, with prosecutor Thomas C.Fisher, sat Lt William Salter.

Unfortunately for the prosecution, some deft manoeuvring by the defence nullified much of the evidence against the accused. Perhaps relying too heavily on affidavits, Fisher had decided against calling some witnesses to give evidence, as they were then back in their own countries (and probably, being seamen, already back at sea). Defence counsel Sol Brinsfield successfully convinced the Commission that for most of the accused the evidence as presented did not support the charges. Twenty three men walked free. This was galling, especially to Salter, who had put a lot of effort into the case. Fortunately Nakagawa was still in the dock, although on the next sitting day he and seven others (including Kusaka) were acquitted of two of the three specifications to the charge. Then Brinsfield, possibly recognising the unlikelihood of total acquittal for these men — and perhaps through some early form of 'plea bargaining' — persuaded his clients to change their pleas to guilty on the last remaining charge.

Commission president Colonel Henry Lyon wanted to hear it from the lips of the accused. 'If the plea is made voluntarily by the accused, it will be permitted[9].'

He addressed each man in turn, eventually getting to Nakagawa.

'Nakagawa, do you understand specification two as changed today by the prosecution with certain deletions, and read to you this afternoon?'

(Through an interpreter) 'Yes.'

'And do you understand by changing your pleas from not guilty to guilty you admit the elements of the offence?'

'Yes.'

'How do you now plead to specification two of the charge?'

'I plead guilty.'

'You may be seated.'

Lt Salter, who dearly wanted Nakagawa brought to justice, at least now had the satisfaction of seeing him convicted. He guessed Nakagawa would escape execution, but predicted a lengthy prison term.

The Court gave Nakagawa eight years hard labour.

Interestingly, it gave Mito the same punishment. It seems the Commission drew no distinction between the transgressions of administrator and subordinate; the law viewed them equally culpable.

Salter no doubt thought Nakagawa had got off lightly. He took some minor comfort from the fact that Nakagawa was at least a convicted war criminal. And even though Nakagawa had got away with the *Centaur* outrage, he had not been cleared of it. Salter knew that if he persisted with a case against Nakagawa an acquittal might well be the outcome; in his view a totally unacceptable result.

Salter wasn't the only one to consider these sentences too lenient. In March 1949 trial reviewer Paul Spurlock commented that the court had found the accused guilty of

> some of the most heinous, barbaric, sadistic and brutal mistreatment of prisoners in the history of war crimes . . . Wilful and wanton murders were committed by some of them under the orders of others . . . Crimes of this type are so foul that it does not require rules of conventions to implant it in the mind that they are wrong.'[10]

Nakagawa worked at several tasks in prison; at common labour, on a hydroponic farm, in the hospital grounds. In 1951 he applied for parole. He said he wanted to return to his family in Shizuoka-shi, where his wife Sawko and two children were struggling financially without him as a breadwinner. As to his trial, he made the comment, 'the order to execute the crew of the torpedoed enemy ship was truly issued by the Chief of the General Staff . . .' The parole board denied his application[11].

Former Vice Admiral Mito also applied for parole. He insisted that no cruelties by his subordinates could be traced back to the order he issued in 1943. The parole board noted the inconsistency of this statement with Nakagawa's. It denied Mito's application as well.

Nakagawa walked away from Sugamo on 2nd October 1954. He had served almost six years of an eight year sencence. He was 52 years old. He lived a very quiet life thereafter, rarely communicated with his former naval colleagues, and passed away on 27th May 1986 at the age of 84.

Co-author Chris Milligan made an attempt to communicate with Nakagawa in 1980, soon after he began researching the *Centaur* story. He found out Nakagawa's address and wrote to him. He hoped to obtain a comment on the *Centaur* incident, and offered Nakagawa the opportunity to refute the accusation that he was responsible. Nakagawa did not respond personally, but made it clear through an intermediary that he had no wish to communicate.

The silence of a man who literally did get away with murder speaks volumes.

Unfortunately for the *Centaur*, posterity will not remember her short career as a hospital ship for the service she gave, nor for the potential she offered, but more for her sudden, violent end, and for the rumours associated with her loss.

AUTHORS' ACKNOWLEDGMENTS

At the outset we are duty bound to proclaim a mighty thanks to everyone who helped us with the mammoth task of putting this story together. We trust we might be forgiven for not expressing here our personal thanks to each one; the list would run into hundreds and occupy more space than some of the chapters in this book. Special thanks are unquestionably due to certain people, and will be given; but if we have omitted the name of someone who contributed even the tiniest snippet of information or advice, please rest assured that this is not by design, but purely in the interests of brevity.

Our primary and most sincere thanks has to go to all those *Centaur* survivors, and relatives and descendants of *Centaur* personnel, who so graciously and enthusiastically reacted to Chris Milligan's worldwide appeal for information. Chris sent each of them a long and detailed questionnaire — and they responded magnificently. They gave freely of their knowledge, their recollections, and their opinions. Many sent photographs priceless in family sentimental value.

This blanket vote of thanks also goes to those respondents with a more peripheral role. This includes those having a link with the ship at the time; to former *Centaur* staff, to *Mugford* personnel, the army, navy and Blue Funnel Line, to several ex-servicemens' and nursing associations, 23 Radar Station Fort Lytton, 71 Squadron, and to many former doctors and nurses. It also includes people who became connected more recently through their employment or membership of various societies, and those merely entranced by the sheer fascination of the story. In this context we must pay special tribute to Rod Gibson (secretary, Centaur Memorial Fund for Nurses), Cmdr John Jeppesen, OAM, RFD, RAN (Retd) (chairman, Concord Centaur Memorial Window Committee), Warren Keats (chairman, Centaur Commemoration Committee), Tony Matthews (Greenapple Media), Ron Mierendorf (secretary 2/12 Fld Amb Association), and Charles Medcalf (Nestorian Association).

Lt-Cmdr David Stevens, RAN, deserves our special gratitude. His detailed research and his assessment of Japanese submarine activity in the western Pacific in 1943 proved invaluable. His enthusiastic collaboration enabled us to piece together an accurate assessment of the *I-177*'s movements before and after the *Centaur* sinking. This background, it would be fair to say, became crucial to any informed speculation about the guilt of the *I-177*, and IJN efforts to conceal that guilt.

We must acknowledge the help of the staffs of archival offices and libraries in several countries. In Australia we drew on the sources of the Commonwealth Archives, various state archives, the Australian War Memorial, Army Records Office, the Mitchell Library in Sydney and Oxley Library in Brisbane. In Canada we found the McLennan Library at McGill University, Montreal, most helpful and useful. In the United States we were assisted by the United Nations Archives Library in New York City; the Nimitz Library at the US Naval Academy, Annapolis, MD; and the Navy Dept Library at the Washington Navy Yard. At the National Archives, Suitland Reference Branch, MD — a particularly fruitful source of information — Assistant-chief Richard Boylan identified pertinent records of the Investigation Division, Legal Section, GHQ, SCAP. The Military Reference Branch in Washington, DC, houses boxes of wartime messages intercepted by ULTRA. Barry Zerby helped identify those associated with submarine movements. The National Archives in Washington, DC, which houses hundreds of cardboard boxes full of wartime messages intercepted by ULTRA, was a rich source of information about Japanese submarine movements. The service details of several former IJN officers were obtained from the National Institute for Defence Studies in Tokyo, courtesy of Lt-Cmdr Hidetoshi Itoh, of the Military History Department. In England we were helped by Ocean Archives, the Public Record Office, and Greenwich Maritime Museum.

Our special gratitude goes to Professor Geoffrey Blainey, who very kindly penned this book's Foreword. Professor Blainey is not only arguably Australia's most respected and read historian;

he is also a very busy man. We are humbled and honoured by his contribution.

We are indebted also to Captain Ian Smith of Brisbane, who edited the MS. His frank review of the draft, his advice and his refreshing candour, were of inestimable value. Nothing passed his eagle eye. Ian came well credentialled. His mastery of the finer points of the English language, complemented by his awesome knowledge of matters nautical and military (especially WW2), rendered him most suitable for the task. His extensive seafaring experience added cream to the cake. Ian's career at sea began in 1939. He spent the entire War-years serving in British merchant ships. He is a professional colleague of co-author John Foley; a pilot of the Queensland Coast and Torres Strait Pilot Service.

Thanks are also due to Stephen S.Bloomer of Montreal, who painted the stunning watercolour on the cover of this book, and to Mary Milligan who designed the jacket titles.

This book is the result of a trans-Pacific collaboration: Chris Milligan in Montreal; John Foley in Brisbane. Communication between the authors has of necessity been affected by distance, time and the inordinate cost of postage and telecommunications. Individually, we had to research aspects of the story in our respective countries, and thus we now have separate lists of people to whom our personal gratitude is due. What follows is a brief comment from each of us.

CHRISTOPHER MILLIGAN:

I always instruct elementary Social Studies students to teach history in the classroom from the 'bottom up' i.e. starting with the individual. To practice the approach, each member of the class is required to produce a personal history. The act of interviewing relatives, reading precious family letters, decoding old photographs and locating personal family treasures (artefacts) never fails to ignite individual enthusiasm for the project. By the time these young teachers report back to the class about their personal history detective work they are well on their way to understanding the importance and the impact behind making history real and meaningful. Few encounter any difficulty in transferring this enthusiasm for history to children during classroom practice.

Authors' Acknowledgments

Little did I realise in 1978 that my own interest in family history (let's practice what we preach) of an uncle I never knew, who had died in WW2 before I was born, would begin an investigation that was to continue for the next fourteen years of my life! It would result in: McGill University-funded research in London, Liverpool and Whitby, as well as in Washington, DC, and Suitland, Maryland; an examination of Japanese war crime trials in general and the Yokohama War Crime Trial of Vice Admiral Hisashi Ichioka in particular; the analysis of Sugamo Prison files, certain Japanese WW2 ULTRA intercepts and Japanese submarine activity off the Australian eastern seacoast and culminate in the collaboration between a Social Studies Professor in Montreal and a Torres Strait Pilot in Brisbane, to produce a book about the torpedoing of a WW2 Australian hospital ship.

Why bother? A few years ago the Canadian government officially apologised to its citizens of Japanese ancestry for gross injustices perpetrated against them. For the duration of the war, members of this community were interned *en masse* in Canadian concentration camps. Accompanying the government apology was a compensation package. At the same time Canada was finally rectifying a dreadful miscarriage of justice, Canadian Hong Kong POWs who survived Japanese slave labour camps during WW2 were still seeking 'just' compensation from Japan. They are still waiting!

Japan, unlike other WW2 Axis powers, encounters difficulty accepting responsibility for certain of its war-time actions and policies. Modern day Japan still prefers its sanitised version of history when it comes to WW2. One Japanese professor puts it this way, 'Japan only talks about half of its history — the half where it is the victim'. It is only through the recent efforts of a few Japanese academics and researchers that the Japanese general public learned of wartime acts of cannibalism by Japanese Imperial Army soldiers against Australian troops, Asian labourers and indigenous people in Papua New Guinea. Researchers were also able to embarrass the Japanese Government into publicly acknowledging for the very first time that tens of thousands of women from the Korean peninsula, China, Taiwan, the Philippines, Indonesia and Japan itself had been forced into prostitution and sex slavery as 'comfort women' for Japanese soldiers during WW2.

Centaur

Why not just forget? Prof. Saburo Ienaga has long maintained that Japan suffers from 'collective amnesia' about WW2. He believes that Japanese students have to know all about 'the horrors of war' in order to fully appreciate what is meant by a free and peaceful society. Otherwise, he adds, 'a generation raised on sugar-coated history would be likely to repeat the errors of the past'. For the longest time the *Centaur* sinking was part of the 'amnesia'. In 1979 it received only passing footnote-type treatment in the Official History of Japanese Submarine Warfare. The sinking of the *Centaur* has more meaning than can fit in a footnote. What is offered here is not a sugar-coated accounting. Hopefully the lessons we learn from this tragedy will help make the world a better place for all of us to live in.

I am duty bound to again thank all those acknowledged in the original 1981 monograph. Space constraints do not permit me to reprint their names here, so please accept this as my special thanks to each and every one of you. However, two of the survivors, Fred Chidgey and Tom Hobden, require a few additional lines of thanks. Fred shared with us his meticulously-documented photographic records of war service onboard Australian hospital ships, particularly the *Centaur*. Unfortunately, Fred died in 1983, but his superb eye for detail and description can still be heard on two audio tapes he made concerning the *Centaur*. Tom is an avid world traveller who has visited me twice in Montreal. He too has clear and detailed recollections of his time onboard *Centaur*. During his last visit I videotaped him reminiscing about the *Centaur*.

McGill University has been a source of much support. The research in England and Washington, for example, was partly funded by grants from the Faculty of Graduate Studies and Research. Also, colleagues have offered encouragement and advice over the years. A few have been highly supportive with their time, suggestions and assistance. The are: Dr David C. Smith (my former Dean of Education); Dr A.E.Wall (my present Dean) who understands the importance of 'magic carpets'; Prof. A.K.Maconochie (a fellow geographer and my military expert) whose knowledge, insights, interpretation and continual support I value dearly; Dr Tom Eišmon, whose kindness greatly simplified my research trip to Washington, DC; Peter Blaney (Acquisitions Editor, McGill-Queen's University Press) who took time out of a busy schedule to read the manuscript and offered

268

sound feedback and publishing insights; Jim Harris (Manager, Educational Media Centre) who via computer wizardry bridged the Macintosh and IBM worlds between Montreal and Brisbane (I'm still not sure how Jim does it — but it works!); the EMC crew — Debbie Metchette, Dave Lacroix, Lewis Wosu and Mike Roberge — whose individual skills have been invaluable to me; Sean Huxley (Technical Services, Division of Instructional Services), another computer wizard and a software magician; and the Reference Desk and Inter-library Loan Dept at McLellan Library, who were challenged by a number of esoteric requests and always came through magnificently — please accept this as my heartfelt thanks.

I am grateful to Prof. Peter Glasgow, Concordia University, Montreal, who supplied information about the classical origins of Centaurs.

Finally, John Foley first contacted me in September 1989 concerning his own interest in the *Centaur* story. His love of the ships, respect for the sea; feel for the ordinary individual in history, and an interest in just telling the story as it unfolded were important elements that led to our collaboration. The rationale was simple: a cooperative approach combining both of our resource materials, writings and respective expertise would produce a more authoritative book about the *Centaur* than either one of us could produce alone. John is a dedicated, talented and creative team player. I have the utmost respect for my co-author.

My last vote of extra special thanks goes to my wife Mary, for her love, artistic advice and support, and then to our sons Andrew, Thomas and Mark.

It seems important to end with the following observation about family history process. I started this project before Mark was born. Interestingly, he helped in the final indexing of the manuscript. Now the entire family understands why a great-uncle died years ago, during WW2, off the coast of eastern Australia.

JOHN FOLEY:

My primary vote of thanks must go to my co-writer, Chris Milligan. When I first began researching the *Centaur* with a view to writing a book, the name Milligan soon cropped up. I learned about the monograph that Chris released in 1981, and I took early steps to secure a copy. Then someone told me that with the nearing 50th anniversary this Chris Milligan had plans to expand his monograph into a book. I doubted there would be room for *two* authoritative works on the *Centaur*, so I wrote to him. He replied candidly, but without animosity, explaining his personal interest in the story. Later, when I better understood his deep-seated attachment to the *Centaur*, I realised how devastating my letter must have been to him; how much he must have wanted to tell me to 'shove off — this story is mine!'. To his credit he didn't. He simply remarked how nice it was that so much interest was being shown in the *Centaur*. Acknowledging his depth of research — some 12 years of it — and the minimal possibility of my being able to cover the same ground, *and* write the book, in time for the 50th anniversary in 1993, I pulled aside, leaving the field clear for him. The idea of a collaborative effort came from him, and that sacrifice — offering to share 12 years' work with a potential literary rival — must have wrenched his stomach. I take my hat off to him.

Captain Sam Southey, a retired stevedore of my long-term acquaintance, and Dr Murray Anderson, a chiropractor whom I have also known for more years than I care to remember, were both responsible for getting me going on the *Centaur*. Separately, but by coincidence within a day or so of each other, both men suggested I write a book on the topic. (There have been odd times in the past two years when I have wondered if they deserve my thanks or not!) At the time I was happily settling back into a biography of Lt Charles Jeffreys[a]. I had put the Jeffreys book on ice once before, while I produced *'The Quetta — Queensland's Worst Disaster'*, and I was enjoying being back into it. Even so, the *Centaur* tempted me. It was a logical progression from the *Quetta*. But if I was going to do it, it had to be then. The pending 50th anniversary of the sinking became a clear objective. All reservations evaporated when I noticed the parallels between the *Centaur* and *Quetta*. Both were Queensland tragedies of immense proportions: both ships sank within three minutes; in both incidents two (damaged) lifeboats surfaced after the ship

a. This book, to be entitled *Crown and Anchor*, details the life of Lt Charles Jeffreys, who commanded HMS *Kangaroo* on the Australia station from 1813 to 1818. Jeffreys was a lovable larrikin who flouted authority — particularly that of NSW Governor Lachlan Macquarie — and yet is credited with finding a full-length shipping channel inside the Great Barrier Reef.

sank; and both ships had a Torres Strait Pilot on board (something of special interest to me). Even more remarkable, the number of *Centaur* casualties was exactly double that of the *Quetta*, 268 to 134. I was hooked.

Charles Jeffreys went back on ice. I think he's getting used to it.

Once serious research and writing got under way, I was fortunate enough to make the acquaintanceship of several people for whose generous help I remain in eternal debt.

Alan Smith, historian for the Centaur Commemoration Committee, comes first. While researching for his booklet *Three Minutes of Time*, Alan was able to draw on his own wide knowledge, his extensive personal library, and a network of MNWSL contacts across the nation. He came across a lot of information and several potential sources of information; all of which he unselfishly passed on to me. Many items were invaluable; particularly contacts with several survivors and survivors' relatives. Alan became a very helpful sounding-board on many aspects of this manuscript. He read it through in the draft stages and made several most pertinent comments based on his personal experience of life at sea on the Australian coast during WW2.

Dr Rupert Goodman, a prolific writer of military medical history, also most charitably shared with me the fruits of his personal research into the *Centaur*. As he was at the time writing a book that encompassed the *Centaur* story[b] — and could justifiably have branded me a hostile literary rival — his unselfishness is thus all the more remarkable.

I must not forget to record the willing and enthusiastic help of Joff Case (Sister at 112 AGH Greenslopes the night the injured survivors arrived there), Gordon Rippon, Maurice Cairnie, and Allan Pettiford (the sole remaining Queensland *Centaur* survivor), whose brains I often and unashamedly picked for advice about many aspects of the project.

Many, many others deserve my thanks. People who responded to my letters, or wrote to me unsolicited. People I telephoned, or who telephoned me; helpful conversations all. I wish I could amplify all their contributions. They all know they have my gratitude. They include the following, in alphabetical order, but even this list is by no means exhaustive:

b. Released in April 1992 under the title *Hospital Ships* (Boolarong, Brisbane).

Pixie Annant, Mrs Vicki Argent, Noel Bedford, Maj.(USA) Bill Bentson Rtd, Mary Biggs, John Brown (QNU), Burl Burlingame, Dr Bill Cammack, Captain Mike Carolyn, Mrs Enid Charters, Captain Harold Chesterman, M.Chihaya, Neville Crouch, David Jeanes, Captain Arthur Diack, George Dudeck, Michael Elliott, Vaughan Evans, Walter Fielder-Gill, Brigadier R.Fullford, Mrs Fran Gardner, Joan Godfrey, Bert Hannaford, Captain Graham Haultain, Captain Basil Helm, Mrs B.Hindmarsh, Rob Hindmarsh, Bill Hookway, Captain Jim Howatson, Doug Hubbard, George Hunt, Wilson Irvine, Warren Keats, Stephen Kentwell, Tom Malcolm, Mrs V.McCosker, George McGrath, Doug McMillan, Bill Muller, Bill Oakley, Hajime Ohori, Hiroshi Osedo, Mrs Barbara Outridge, Roger Pineau, Lt-Cmdr T.F. Roberts, Phil Ryan, Bartz Shultz, Kit Skehan, Doug Smith, Charles Taylor, Garry West, Robert Westwood, Bob Williams, Paul Wilson, Barbara Winter.

Finally, I must record my appreciation of the forebearance of my dear wife, Denice. How she puts up with me, I'll never know.

APPENDIX A

"CENTAUR" — PERSONNEL STATISTICS

(BY ALPHABETICAL, DEPARTMENTAL, AND SURVIVAL STATUS)

ALPHABETICAL:

NAME	RANK	DEPT	L/S	HOME	AGE
Abbot, David	Deck Boy	MC	L	Vic	16
Adams, A.T.	Private (Driver)	FA(AP)	L	NSW	
Adams, Margaret L.	Sister	SMS	L	Vic	30
Aitchison, G.F.	Private	SMS	L	Qld	
Alexander, George M.	Third Engineer	MC	L	Sco	26
Alexander, J.R.	Private (Driver)	FA(AP)	L	NSW	
Anderson, Fred W.C.	Private	FA	L	NSW	
Annis-Brown, James	Private	FA	L	NSW	
Annis-Brown, Reginald	Private	FA	L	NSW	
Argent, Jack.H.	Private	SMS	S	NSW	
Bailey, W.H.	Private	FA	L	NSW	
Banks, Ernest 'Monty'	Third Mate	MC	S	NSW	29
Barlow, T.D.H.	Staff Sergeant	FA	L	NSW	
Barnes, W.E.C.	Private	FA	L	NSW	
Bayley, A.N.	Private	FA(AP)	L	NSW	
Bayley, John L. 'Jack'	Driver	FA(AP)	S	NSW	
Bedkober, Lincoln L.	Captain (dentist)	FA	L	NSW	28
Behan, Tom	Engine Wiper	MC	L	Qld	36
Benton, K.E.	Private	FA	L	NSW	
Bidmead, L.E.O. 'Leo'	Private	SMS	S	Vic	
Black, W.C.	Corporal	FA	L	NSW	
Blackman, R.McG.	Private	FA	L	NSW	
Bladen, H.A.	Private	FA	L	NSW	
Blair, Albert E.	Corporal	SMS	S	Vic	
Bond, S.R.	Driver	FA(AP)	L	Vic	
Bourchier, K.P.	Private	FA	L	NSW	
Bowden, John O.	Steward	MC	L	NSW	32

Centaur

NAME	RANK	DEPT	L/S	HOME	AGE
Bowen, David L.	Private	FA	L	Qld	
Boyd, A.	Private	FA	L	NSW	
Bracken, John W.	Private	FA	L	NSW	
Bracken, Paul J.	Sergeant	FA	L	NSW	
Brandin, Gustav	Boatswain	MC	L	Swe	50
Brewer, Bertram W.H.	Private	FA	L	NSW	
Brown, A.V.	Private	FA	L	NSW	
Browne, Jack McG.	Private	FA	L	Qld	
Buck, John C.	Storekeeper/Barman	MC	L	WA	54
Bull, Ronald D.	Steward/Writer	MC	S	Vic	34
Burns, W.R.	Private	FA(AP)	L	NSW	
Burrett, William E.	Private	SMS	L	NSW	
Burroughs, S.P.	Corporal	SMS	L	NSW	
Bush, George F.	Private (Driver)	FA(AP)	L	NSW	30
Bush, George R.	Corporal	FA	L	NSW	
Butt, W.J.	Private	FA	L	NSW	
Cairnie, Maurice A.	Fourth Engineer	MC	S	WA	29
Capper, James	Chief Steward	MC	L	NSW	49
Carey, Charles E.J.	Assist. Steward	MC	L	Vic	28
Carey, William R.	Private	FA	L	Qld	41
Carter, George R.	Staff Sergeant	SMS	S	Vic	
Cavanagh, Richard C.	Driver	FA(AP)	L	SA	
Cecich, J.'Ivan'	A.B.	MC	S	NSW	29
Chadwick, Leslie N.	Lieutenant	FA	L	NSW	
Chapman, E.A.	Private	FA	L	NSW	
Chidgey, Fred B.	Private (Dental Asst)	SMS	S	NSW	24
Christensen, Owen N.	A.B.	MC	S	Vic	26
Clark, Charles 'Nobbie'	Fireman's attendant	MC	L	NSW	54
Clark, J.M.	Private	SMS	L	Qld	
Clark, Leslie S.	Private	FA	L	NSW	
Clark, Neville S.	Private	FA	L	NSW	
Clark, W.F.Darwin	Mr (Red Cross rep.)	SMS	L	SA	51
Claydon, J.A.	Private	FA	L	NSW	
Clegg, Percy L.	Private	SMS	L	Qld	
Cochrane, Alex S.	Steward	MC	S	WA	35
Cockerhill, David	Third Cook	MC	L	Vic	43
Colefax, B.Douglas	Private (Driver)	FA(AP)	L	NSW	
Colemane, W.J.	Private (Driver)	FA(AP)	L	NSW	
Collins, H.S.	Corporal	FA(AP)	L	NSW	
Collins, L.F.	Private	SMS	L	Qld	
Cooke, A.J.	Lance Corporal	SMS	L	Vic	
Cooley, Geoffrey G.	Major	SMS	L	NSW	

274

NAME	RANK	DEPT	L/S	HOME	AGE
Corbett, K.N.	Corporal	FA(AP)	L	NSW	
Cornell, William T.C.	Sergeant	FA	S	NSW	
Coulsen, Jim	Private	SMS	S	Qld	
Cripps, Leslie J.	Private	FA	L	Qld	
Cross, H.R.T.	Corporal	FA	L	NSW	
Cullum, Sammuel J.	A.B.	MC	S	Vic	57
Cummings, M.H.	Private	FA	L	Qld	
Cuthill, William D.	Second Engineer	MC	L	Sco	41
Davidson, A.Francis	Second Butcher	MC	S	NSW	30
Denne, F.J.	Private	FA	L	NSW	
Dickson, Allan R.	Driver	FA(AP)	S	NSW	
Doherty, J.P.	Private	FA	L	NSW	
Donohoe, H.M.	Private	FA	L	NSW	
Downie, Walter Ross	Engine Wiper	MC	L	NSW	29
Drust, Frank	Nightwatchman	MC	S	WA	44
Dutfield, C.C.	Warrant Officer I	FA	L	NSW	
Etheridge, G.R.G.	Private (Driver)	FA(AP)	L	NSW	
Evans, John K.	Corporal	FA(AP)	L	NSW	28
Evans, W.A.	Corporal	FA(AP)	L	NSW	
Fawcett, G.	Private	FA	L	NSW	
Fehrenbach, H.S.	Private	FA	L	NSW	
Ferrow, J.W.	Sergeant	FA(AP)	L	NSW	
Findlay, R.W.	Private	FA	L	NSW	
Fishwick, Charles E.	Private	FA	L	NSW	
Foley, Stephen D.	Captain	FA	L	NSW	
Forrest, Jack M.	Private	FA	L	Qld	
Fortier, Alan D.	Driver	FA(AP)	L	Qld	26
Fortier, Fred L.	Private (Driver)	FA(AP)	L	NSW	30
Fowler, C.A.	Driver	FA(AP)	L	Tas	
Fox, Frank W.	Ordinary Seaman	MC	L	NSW	18
Friedrich, Victor	Private	FA	L	Qld	
Gallagher, John	Engine Wiper	MC	L	Eng	46
Galvin, S.G.	Private (Driver)	FA(AP)	L	NSW	
Gannon, Frank J.	Scullion	MC	L	NSW	31
Garbutt, Don R.	Private	FA	L	NSW	
Garfit, W.D.	Private	FA	L	NSW	
Geaghan, W.T.	Private	FA	L	NSW	
Goffett, Charles A.	Private	FA	L	NSW	
Gordon, C.T.	Private	FA	L	NSW	
Gore, W.H.	Private	FA	L	NSW	
Grainger, Robert	Greaser	MC	L	NSW	51
Gunning, A. 'Dick'	Acting Corporal	FA	L	NSW	

Centaur

NAME	RANK	DEPT	L/S	HOME	AGE
Hall, Harry R.	Fourth Engineer	MC	L	Eng	32
Hart, Roger F.	Deck Boy	MC	L	NSW	16
Haultain, Helen F.J.C.	Sister	SMS	L	NSW	
Haynes, Keith R.	Sergeant	FA	L	NSW	
Hayward, C.E.	Private (Driver)	FA	L	NSW	
Hayward, T.H.	Private (Driver)	FA(AP)	L	NSW	
Hegarty, Thomas C.	Private	SMS	S	NSW	
Hembrow, J.H.	Private	FA	L	NSW	
Henderson, Leslie J.	Private	FA	L	Qld	
Hewison, R.J.	Private	FA	L	NSW	
Hindmarsh, Bernie F.	Captain	SMS	L	NSW	44
Hoare, J.W.	Private	FA	L	NSW	
Hobden, Tom	Corporal (Male Nurse)	SMS	S	Tas	28
Hodgkinson, N.A.	Private	FA	L	NSW	
Hogan, K.F.	Private (Driver)	FA(AP)	L	NSW	
Hoggins, Mark	Third Baker	MC	S	Vic	32
Hoggins, Trevor	Assistant Cook	MC	S	Vic	37
Holland, L.	Major	SMS	L	NSW	
Holloway, Sam G.	Private	FA	L	Qld	
Hooper, Leonard R.	Sergeant (paymaster)	SMS	S	NSW	36
Horgan, Leslie J.	Driver	FA	S	NSW	
Howson, A.	Private	SMS	L	Qld	
Hughes, T. Stanley	A.B.	MC	L	Vic	37
Hutchison Raymond R.	Private	SMS	L	NSW	
Isherwood, Ron C. 'Tich'	Private (Staff Orderly)	SMS	S	Vic	25
Jackman, Vincent M.	Private	FA	L	Qld	
Jewell, Sarah A.	Matron	SMS	L	Vic	
Johnson, A.E.	Lieutenant	SMS	L	Vic	
Johnson, James C.	Warrant Officer II	SMS	S	Qld	
Johnston, Richard C.	Captain	FA	L	NSW	
Johnston, S.R.	Private	FA	L	NSW	
Jonassen, Mark	Steward	MC	S	NSW	45
Jones, Clifford G.	Private	SMS	S	Qld	
Jones, Gorden.R.	Temporary Major	FA	L	NSW	
Jones, Ron 'Spud'	Lance Corporal	FA	S	NSW	
Kaki, Laurie	A.B.	MC	L	Vic	53
Kelly, Percy G.	Private	SMS	S	NSW	
Kemp, A.Roy	Private	FA	L	NSW	
Kerr, J.A.	Private	SMS	L	Qld	
Key, Jack J.R.	Private	FA	L	Qld	
King, Evelyn	Sister	SMS	L	NSW	
Laird, Robert M.	Third Radio Operator	MC	L	Sco	20

276

NAME	RANK	DEPT	L/S	HOME	AGE
Lambert, Charles	Private	FA	L	NSW	
Lamble, Henry E.	First Officer	MC	L	Eng	32
Lange, Keith	Corporal	FA	S	NSW	
Laverick, Ernest G.	Chaplain/Captain	SMS	L	Vic	
Law, R.	Lance Corporal	SMS	L	Qld	
Lawson, William T.	Private (Driver)	FA(AP)	L	NSW	
Le Blanc, James	A.B.	MC	L	Can	46
Le Grand, Peter M.P.	Private	FA	L	Qld	
Leask, Alexander R.	Private	FA	L	NSW	
Leask, Harold M.	Private	FA	L	NSW	
Leask, Henry H.	Private	FA	L	NSW	
Lebrun, C.R.	Lance Corporal	SMS	L	Vic	
Lee, Michael J.	A.B.	MC	L	Vic	44
Lee, T.A.	Acting Corporal	FA	L	NSW	
Lesnie, Norman M.G.	Warrant Officer II	FA	L	NSW	
Lillas, R.L.	Private (Driver)	FA(AP)	L	NSW	
Loader, James J.J.	Acting Corporal	FA	L	NSW	32
Lockhart, Vincent	Second Pantryman	MC	L	WA	42
Long, A.	Driver	FA(AP)	L	NSW	
Long, George E.	A.B.	MC	L	Den	36
Longden, Sammuel	Chief Cook	MC	L	NSW	44
Lotze, E.L.	Corporal	FA(AP)	L	NSW	
Lowe, H.H. 'Lofty'	Private	FA	L	Qld	
Lucas, Joe	Private	FA	L	NSW	
Lynagh, F. Jack	Private	FA	L	Qld	
Lyneham, H.L.	Private (Driver)	FA(AP)	L	NSW	
Lynne, Clem E.	Private	FA	L	NSW	39
Lyons, John	A.B.	MC	L	NSW	40
Lyttleton, Sidney F.	Private	FA	L	NSW	
MacLean, Donald R.	Printer	MC	L	NSW	26
McCaskie, T.E.	Private	FA	L	NSW	
McCosker, V.	Private (Orderly)	SMS	S	Qld	20
McDougall, W.O.	Acting Sergeant	FA	L	NSW	
McFarlane, Mary H.	Sister	SMS	L	SA	
McGrath, George W.	Driver	FA(AP)	S	NSW	
McGuire, H.J.	Private	FA	L	NSW	
McGuire, C.P.	Private (Driver)	FA(AP)	L	NSW	
McIntosh, William	Fireman	MC	S	NSW	34
McKay, C.S.	Lance Corporal	FA	L	NSW	
McKinnon, William J.	Third Cook	MC	L	Vic	24
McLean, N.	Private	SMS	L	NSW	
McSkimming, S.G.	Lance Corporal	FA	L	NSW	

Centaur

NAME	RANK	DEPT	L/S	HOME	AGE
Malcolm, Thomas C.	Corporal	SMS	S	Vic	
Mansfield, J.K.	Private (Driver)	FA(AP)	L	NSW	
Manson, Clem P.	Lt.Colonel	SMS	L	Vic	
Marshall, John B.	Private	FA	L	Qld	
Martin, Francis	Seamens' Cook	MC	S	Vic	38
Maynard, Alan F.	Private	SMS	L	Qld	23
Maynard, John C.	Private	SMS	L	Qld	23
Medcalf, Richard	Staff Sergeant	SMS	S	NSW	
Melbom, E.E.	Private	SMS	L	Qld	
Miles, R.W.	Lieutenant	FA	L	NSW	
Miley, Thomas H.	Private	FA	L	Qld	
Millar, Fred S.P.	Private	FA	S	NSW	
Miller, C.O.	Private	FA	L	NSW	
Milligan, David I.	A.B.	MC	L	Vic	40
Moate, Ronald G.	Chief Pantryman	MC	S	Vic	28
Montgomery, C.G.	Private	FA	L	NSW	
Moore, D.W.	Corporal	SMS	L	Qld	
Moran, Jack O'N.	Private	FA	L	NSW	
Morgan, Stanley	Donkeyman	MC	S	Vic	43
Morris, Albert J.	Second Steward	MC	L	NSW	46
Morris, Matthew A.	Greaser	MC	S	Vic	23
Morris, Thomas V.	Second Radio Operator	MC	L	Eng	32
Mort, R.F.	Private	FA	L	NSW	
Moss, Leslie 'Joe'	Corporal	SMS	L	NSW	
Moston, Merle	Sister	SMS	L	NSW	
Murphy, G.G.	Private (Driver)	FA(AP)	L	NSW	
Murphy, George S.	Private	SMS	S	NSW	
Murray, George A.	Captain	MC	L	WA	53
Murray, Kenneth G.	Lance Corporal	FA	S	NSW	
Mycock, Frank J.	Staff Sergeant	FA	L	Qld	
Newell, E.L.	Sergeant	FA	L	NSW	
O'Brien, M.J.	Lance Corporal	FA	L	Vic	
O'Connor, Richard	Corporal	FA	L	NSW	
O'Donnell, Alice M.	Sister	SMS	L	Vic	
O'Neill, Thomas W.	Private	FA	L	Qld	
O'Sullivan, J.C.	Corporal	SMS	L	Qld	
Oakley, H.V.	Private	FA	L	NSW	
Ockwell, L.George	Private	SMS	L	NSW	
Outridge, Leslie McD.	Lt.Colonel	FA	S	Qld	42
Overett, H.H.	Private	FA	L	NSW	
Owens, E.L.V.	Private (Driver)	FA	L	NSW	
Page, Elijah C. 'Ron'	A.B.	MC	L	Vic	44

278

NAME	RANK	DEPT	L/S	HOME	AGE
Pain, R.A.	Private (Driver)	FA(AP)	L	NSW	
Palmer, V.A.	Private (Driver)	FA(AP)	L	NSW	
Pash, Martin L.	Printer	MC	S	Vic	21
Paton, Rupert	Private	FA	S	NSW	20
Pearl, Sidney O.	First Baker	MC	L	Eng	53
Perrett, E.R.	Private	FA	L	Qld	
Perry, N.E.	Private	SMS	L	Qld	
Pettiford, Allan A.	Private	FA	S	Qld	22
Phillips, N.E.	Sergeant	SMS	L	Qld	
Povey, A.R.	Private	FA	L	NSW	
Power, Edward J.	Private	FA	L	Qld	
Pritchard, Thomas E.	Second Baker	MC	L	NSW	45
Ramage, Alfred	A.B.	MC	S	Vic	27
Ravenscroft, E.Laurie	Private	FA	S	NSW	31
Rawlings, James A.	Cook/sculleryman	MC	S	NSW	39
Rayner, Albert	Assistant Steward	MC	L	Vic	19
Reid, A.	Private	FA	L	NSW	
Reid, Frank T.	Butcher	MC	S	NSW	27
Richardson, C.	Private	FA	L	Qld	
Richardson, H.F.	Private	FA	L	Qld	
Rippon, Richard G.	Second Mate	MC	S	Eng	29
Roberts, H.O.	Private	FA	L	NSW	
Robinson, C.M.S.	Private	FA	L	NSW	
Robinson, Ray L.	Lance Corporal	FA	L	NSW	
Rutherford, Ellen M.	Sister	SMS	L	Vic	
Salmon, Len J.	Private	FA	L	NSW	
Salt, Richard M.	Torres Strait Pilot	MC	S	NSW	67
Sandwell, Sidney C.	Linenkeeper	MC	S	WA	34
Savage, Ellen	Sister	SMS	S	NSW	30
Sender, I.H. 'Dick'	Major	FA	L	NSW	
Shaw, Edna A.	Sister	SMS	L	NSW	
Sheard, H.E.	Private (Driver)	FA(AP)	L	NSW	
Shepherd, G.P.	Private (Driver)	FA(AP)	L	NSW	
Siddons, Fred	Head Waiter	MC	L	NSW	34
Simpson, E.J.	Driver	FA(AP)	L	Vic	
Simpson, Ernest B.	A.B.	MC	L	NSW	36
Skafte, L.R.	Private	FA	L	NSW	
Smellie, M.A.	Private	SMS	L	Qld	
Smith, Ernest D.	Chief Engineer	MC	S	Sco	45
South, A.E.	Private	FA	L	NSW	
Spence, Robert J.	Carpenter	MC	L	WA	21
Stanley, Jack E.	Private	FA	L	NSW	

Centaur

NAME	RANK	DEPT	L/S	HOME	AGE
Stephens, Harold Britt	Private	FA	L	NSW	
Stevens, J.A.	Private	FA	L	NSW	
Stewart, J.	Private	FA	L	NSW	
Strack, Stanley L.	Second Cook	MC	L	WA	35
Stubbs, Robert G.	Private	FA	L	NSW	22
Stutter, Jack D.	Steward	MC	S	Vic	47
Summers, Eric J.	1st Radio Operator	MC	L	WA	32
Swan, L.R.	Private	FA	L	NSW	
Sweeney, S.E.	Private (Driver)	FA(AP)	L	NSW	
Swinburn, Richard	Private	FA	L	NSW	
Sykes, Keith	Electrician	MC	L	Vic	33
Taggart, J.	Private	FA	L	NSW	
Taylor, Albert J.	Corporal (Dental Tech.)	FA	S	NSW	37
Taylor, Eric G.W.	Private	SMS	S	NSW	
Taylor, J.	Staff Sergeant	FA	L	Qld	
Thelander, Charles E.	Temporary Major	FA	L	Qld	
Thomas, Allan K.	Warrant Officer II	FA(AP)	L	NSW	26
Thomas, Gethyn L.	Captain	SMS	L	Vic	29
Thomas, J.V.	Private	FA	L	NSW	
Thomas, M.P.	Lance Corporal	SMS	S	Vic	
Thompson, Don L.	Private	FA	L	NSW	
Thompson, Hedley W.	Private	FA	L	Qld	
Thorpe, James	Corporal	FA	L	NSW	
Tierney, Walter H.	Greaser	MC	S	SA	21
Trigg, B.S.	Driver	FA(AP)	L	SA	
Upton, George H.	Private	FA	L	Qld	
Vincent, Edward C.M.	Private	FA	L	Qld	
Waddington, Arthur	Assistant Steward	MC	S	Vic	21
Walder, Jack J.	Driver	FA	L	NSW	
Walker, N.L.	Acting Corporal	FA	L	Qld	
Walker, W. 'Jennie'	Sister	SMS	L	Vic	24
Warner, William A.	Assistant Steward	MC	L	NSW	43
Watterston, James	Assistant Storeman	MC	S	Vic	20
Wattus, E.O.	Private	FA	L	NSW	
West, W.C.	Lance Corporal	FA	L	NSW	
Westendorf, R.H.G.	Private	FA	L	NSW	
Westhorp, S.B.	Lieutenant	FA(AP)	L	NSW	
Westwood, Robert K.	Ordinary Seaman	MC	S	Vic	16
Wheeler, N.E.W.	Lieutenant	FA	L	NSW	
Williams, Alan H.	Private	FA	L	NSW	
Williams, D.Kevin	Staff Sergeant	FA	L	NSW	
Williams, E.F.	Private	FA	L	NSW	

NAME	RANK	DEPT	L/S	HOME	AGE
Williams, L.L.	Warrant Officer II	SMS	L	Vic	
Williams, M.A.	Corporal	SMS	L	Qld	
Wilson, A.	Private	FA	L	NSW	
Wilson, G.A.T.	Private (Driver)	FA(AP)	L	NSW	
Winder, G.A.	Corporal	FA(AP)	L	NSW	
Winterflood, A.A.	Private (Driver)	FA(AP)	L	NSW	
Wood, Allan	Private	FA	L	NSW	
Wood, L.S.	Private	FA	L	NSW	
Woods, C.	Private	FA	L	NSW	
Wright, G	Private	FA	L	NSW	
Wyllie, Doris Joyce	Sister	SMS	L	NSW	26

DEPARTMENTAL:

NAME	RANK	NAME	RANK

MERCHANT CREW:

NAME	RANK	NAME	RANK
Abbot, David	Deck Boy	Grainger, Robert	Greaser
Alexander, George M.	Third Engineer	Hall, Harry R.	Fourth Engineer
Banks, Ernest 'Monty'	Third Mate	Hart, Roger F.	Deck Boy
Behan, Tom	Engine Wiper	Hoggins, Mark	Third Baker
Bowden, John O.	Steward	Hoggins, Trevor	Assistant Cook
Brandin, Gustav	Boatswain	Hughes, T.Stanley	A.B.
Buck, John C.	Storekeeper/Barman	Jonassen, Mark	Steward
Bull, Ronald D.	Steward/Writer	Kaki, Laurie	A.B.
Cairnie, Maurice A.	Fourth Engineer	Laird, Robert M.	Third Radio Operator
Capper, James	Chief Steward	Lamble, Henry E.	First Officer
Carey, Charles E.J.	Assistant Steward	Le Blanc, James	A.B.
Cecich, J. 'Ivan'	A.B.	Lee, Michael J.	A.B.
Christensen, Owen N.	A.B.	Lockhart, Vincent	Second Pantryman
Clark, Charles 'Nobbie'	Fireman's attendant	Long, George E.	A.B.
Cochrane, Alex	Steward	Longden, Sammuel	Chief Cook
Cockerhill, David	Third Cook	Lyons, John	A.B.
Cullum, Sammuel J.	A.B.	MacLean, Donald R.	Printer
Cuthill, William D.	Second Engineer	McIntosh, William	Fireman
Davidson, A.Francis	Second Butcher	McKinnon, William J.	Third Cook
Downie, Walter Ross	Engine Wiper	Martin, Francis	Seamens' Cook
Drust, Frank	Nightwatchman	Milligan, David I.	A.B.
Fox, Frank W.	Ordinary Seaman	Moate, Ronald G.	Chief Pantryman
Gallagher, John	Engine Wiper	Morgan, Stanley	Donkeyman
Gannon, Frank J.	Scullion	Morris, Albert J.	Second Steward

Centaur

NAME	RANK	NAME	RANK
Morris, Matthew A.	Greaser	Siddons, Fred	Head Waiter
Morris, Thomas V.	Second Radio Operator	Simpson, Ernest B.	A.B.
Murray, George A.	Captain	Smith, Ernest D.	Chief Engineer
Page, Elijah C. 'Ron'	A.B.	Spence, Robert J.	Carpenter
Pash, Martin L.	Printer	Strack, Stanley L.	Second Cook
Pearl, Sidney O.	First Baker	Stutter, Jack D.	Steward
Pritchard, Thomas E.	Second Baker	Summers, Eric J.	1st Radio Operator & P
Ramage, Alfred	A.B.	Sykes, Keith	Electrician
Rawlings, James A.	Cook/sculleryman	Tierney, Walter H.	Greaser
Rayner, Albert	Assistant Steward	Waddington, Arthur	Assistant Steward
Reid, Frank T.	Butcher	Warner, William A.	Assistant Steward
Rippon, Richard G.	Second Mate	Watterston, James	Assistant Storeman
Salt, Richard M.	Torres Strait Pilot	Westwood, Robert K.	Ordinary Seaman
Sandwell, Sidney C.	Linenkeeper		

SHIP'S MEDICAL STAFF:

NAME	RANK	NAME	RANK
Adams, Margaret L.	Sister	Johnson, A.E.	Lieutenant
Aitchison, G.F.	Private	Johnson, James C.	Warrant Officer II
Argent, Jack.H.	Private	Jones, Clifford G.	Private
Bidmead, L.E.O. 'Leo'	Private	Kelly, Percy G.	Private
Blair, Albert E.	Corporal	Kerr, J.A.	Private
Burrett, William E.	Private	King, Evelyn	Sister
Burroughs, S.P.	Corporal	Laverick, Ernest G.	Chaplain/Captain.
Carter, George R.	Staff Sergeant	Law, R.	Lance Corporal
Chidgey, Fred B.	Private (Dental Asst.)	Lebrun, C.R.	Lance Corporal
Clark, J.M.	Private	McCosker, V.	Private (Orderly)
Clark, W.F.Darwin	Mr (Red Cross rep.)	McFarlane, Mary H.	Sister
Clegg, Percy L.	Private	McLean, N.	Private
Collins, L.F.	Private	Malcolm, Thomas C.	Corporal
Cooke, A.J.	Lance Corporal	Manson, Clem P.	Lt.Colonel
Cooley, Geoffrey G.	Major	Maynard, Alan F.	Private
Coulsen, Jim	Private	Maynard, John C.	Private
Haultain, Helen F.J.C.	Sister	Medcalf, Richard	Staff Sergeant
Hegarty, Thomas C.	Private	Melbom, E.E.	Private
Hindmarsh, Bernie F.	Captain	Moore, D.W.	Corporal
Hobden, Tom	Corporal (Male Nurse)	Moss, Leslie 'Joe'	Corporal
Holland, L.	Major	Moston, Merle	Sister
Hooper, Leonard R.	Sergeant (paymaster)	Murphy, George S.	Private
Howson, A.	Private	Ockwell, L.George	Private
Hutchison Raymond R.	Private	O'Donnell, Alice M.	Sister
Isherwood, Ron C. 'Tich'	Private (Staff Orderly)	O'Sullivan, J.C.	Corporal
Jewell, Sarah A.	Matron	Perry, N.E.	Private

282

E	RANK	NAME	RANK
ips, N.E.	Sergeant	Thomas, M.P.	Lance Corporal
erford, Ellen M.	Sister	Thomas, Gethyn L.	Captain
ge, Ellen	Sister	Walker, W. 'Jennie'	Sister
, Edna A.	Sister	Williams, L.L.	Warrant Officer II
lie, M.A.	Private	Williams, M.A.	Corporal
or, Eric G.W.	Private	Wyllie, Doris Joyce	Sister

FIELD AMBULANCE:

erson, Fred W.C.	Private	Dutfield, C.C.	Warrant Officer I
s-Brown, James	Private	Fawcett, G.	Private
s-Brown, Reginald	Private	Fehrenbach, H.S.	Private
ry, W.H.	Private	Findlay, R.W.	Private
w, T.D.H.	Staff Sergeant	Fishwick, Charles E.	Private
es, W.E.C.	Private	Foley, Stephen D.	Captain
ober, Lincoln L.	Captain (dentist)	Forrest, Jack M.	Private
on, K.E.	Private	Friedrich, Victor	Private
k, W.C.	Corporal	Garbutt, Don R.	Private
man, R.McG.	Private	Garfit, W.D.	Private
en, H.A.	Private	Geaghan, W.T.	Private
chier, K.P.	Private	Goffett, Charles A.	Private
en, David L.	Private	Gordon, C.T.	Private
l, A.	Private	Gore, W.H.	Private
ken, Paul J.	Sergeant	Gunning, A. 'Dick'	Acting Corporal
ken, John W.	Private	Haynes, Keith R.	Sergeant
er, Bertram W.H.	Private	Hayward, C.E.	Private (Driver)
vn, A.V.	Private	Hembrow, J.H.	Private
vne, Jack McG.	Private	Henderson, Leslie J.	Private
, George R.	Corporal	Hewison, R.J.	Private
W.J.	Private	Hoare, J.W.	Private
y, William R.	Private	Hodgkinson, N.A.	Private
twick, Leslie N.	Lieutenant	Holloway, Sam G.	Private
man, E.A.	Private	Horgan, Leslie J.	Driver
, Leslie S.	Private	Jackman, Vincent M.	Private
, Neville S.	Private	Johnston, Richard C.	Captain
don, J.A.	Private	Johnston, S.R.	Private
ell, William T.C.	Sergeant	Jones, Gorden.R.	Temporary Major
es, Leslie J.	Private	Jones, Ron 'Spud'	Lance Corporal
s, H.R.T.	Corporal	Kemp, A.Roy	Private
nings, M.H.	Private	Key, Jack J.R.	Private
e, F.J.	Private	Lambert, Charles	Private
rty, J.P.	Private	Lange, Keith	Corporal
hoe, H.M.	Private	Le Grand, Peter M.P.	Private

283

Centaur

NAME	RANK	NAME	RANK
Leask, Alexander R.	Private	Richardson, C.	Private
Leask, Harold M.	Private	Richardson, H.F.	Private
Leask, Henry H.	Private	Roberts, H.O.	Private
Lee, T.A.	Acting Corporal	Robinson, C.M.S.	Private
Lesnie, Norman M.G.	Warrant Officer II	Robinson, Ray L.	Lance Corporal
Loader, James J.J.	Acting Corporal	Salmon, Len J.	Private
Lowe, H.H. 'Lofty'	Private	Sender, I.H. 'Dick'	Major
Lucas, Joe	Private	Skafte, L.R.	Private
Lynagh, F.Jack	Private	South, A.E.	Private
Lynne, Clem E.	Private	Stanley, Jack E.	Private
Lyttleton, Sidney F.	Private	Stephens, Harold Britt	Private
McCaskie, T.E.	Private	Stevens, J.A.	Private
McDougall, W.O.	Acting Sergeant	Stewart, J.	Private
McGuire, H.J.	Private	Stubbs, Robert G.	Private
McKay, C.S.	Lance Corporal	Swan, L.R.	Private
McSkimming, S.G.	Lance Corporal	Swinburn, Richard	Private
Marshall, John B.	Private	Taggart, J.	Private
Miles, R.W.	Lieutenant	Taylor, Albert J.	Corporal (Dental Tec)
Miley, Thomas H.	Private	Taylor, J.	Staff Sergeant
Millar, Fred S.P.	Private	Thelander, Charles E.	Temporary Major
Miller, C.O.	Private	Thomas, J.V.	Private
Montgomery, C.G.	Private	Thompson, Don L.	Private
Moran, Jack O'N.	Private	Thompson, Hedley W.	Private
Mort, R.F.	Private	Thorpe, James	Corporal
Murray, Kenneth G.	Lance Corporal	Upton, George H.	Private
Mycock, Frank J.	Staff Sergeant	Vincent, Edward C.M.	Private
Newell, E.L.	Sergeant	Walder, Jack J.	Driver
Oakley, H.V.	Private	Walker, N.L.	Acting Corporal
O'Brien, M.J.	Lance Corporal	Wattus, E.O.	Private
O'Connor, Richard	Corporal	West, W.C.	Lance Corporal
O'Neill, Thomas W.	Private	Westendorf, R.H.G.	Private
Outridge, Leslie McD.	Lt.Colonel	Wheeler, N.E.W.	Lieutenant
Overett, H.H.	Private	Williams, Alan H.	Private
Owens, E.L.V.	Private (Driver)	Williams, D.Kevin	Staff Sergeant
Paton, Rupert	Private	Williams, E.F.	Private
Perrett, E.R.	Private	Wilson, A.	Private
Pettiford, Allan A.	Private	Wood, Allan	Private
Povey, A.R.	Private	Wood, L.S.	Private
Power, Edward J.	Private	Woods, C.	Private
Ravenscroft, E.Laurie	Private	Wright, G	Private
Reid, A.	Private		

AME	RANK	NAME	RANK

12 FIELD AMBULANCE, ATTACHED PERSONNEL:

NAME	RANK	NAME	RANK
dams, A.T.	Private (Driver)	Hogan, K.F.	Private (Driver)
lexander, J.R.	Private (Driver)	Lawson, William T.	Private (Driver)
ayley, A.N.	Private	Lillas, R.L.	Private (Driver)
ayley, John L. 'Jack'	Driver	Long, A.	Driver
ond, S.R.	Driver	Lotze, E.L.	Corporal
urns, W.R.	Private	Lyneham, H.L.	Private (Driver)
ush, George F.	Private (Driver)	McGrath, George W.	Driver
avanagh, Richard C.	Driver	McGuire, C.P.	Private (Driver)
olefax, B.Douglas	Private (Driver)	Mansfield, J.K.	Private (Driver)
olemane, W.J.	Private (Driver)	Murphy, G.G.	Private (Driver)
ollins, H.S.	Corporal	Pain, R.A.	Private (Driver)
orbett, K.N.	Corporal	Palmer, V.A.	Private (Driver)
ickson, Allan R.	Driver	Sheard, H.E.	Private (Driver)
heridge, G.R.G.	Private (Driver)	Shepherd, G.P.	Private (Driver)
vans, John K.	Corporal	Simpson, E.J.	Driver
vans, W.A.	Corporal	Sweeney, S.E.	Private (Driver)
rrow, J.W.	Sergeant	Thomas, Allan K.	Warrant Officer II
ortier, Alan D.	Driver	Trigg, B.S.	Driver
ortier, Fred L.	Private (Driver)	Westhorp, S.B.	Lieutenant
owler, C.A.	Driver	Wilson, G.A.T.	Private (Driver)
alvin, S.G.	Private (Driver)	Winder, G.A.	Corporal
ayward, T.H.	Private (Driver)	Winterflood, A.A.	Private (Driver)

URVIVAL STATUS:

OST:

NAME	RANK	NAME	RANK
bbot, David	Deck Boy	Benton, K.E.	Private
dams, A.T.	Private (Driver)	Black, W.C.	Corporal
dams, Margaret L.	Sister	Blackman, R.McG.	Private
itchison, G.F.	Private	Bladen, H.A.	Private
lexander, George M.	Third Engineer	Bond, S.R.	Driver
lexander, J.R.	Private (Driver)	Bourchier, K.P.	Private
nderson, Fred W.C.	Private	Bowden, John O.	Steward
nnis-Brown, James	Private	Bowen, David L.	Private
nnis-Brown, Reginald	Private	Boyd, A.	Private
ailey, W.H.	Private	Bracken, John W.	Private
arlow, T.D.H.	Staff Sergeant	Bracken, Paul J.	Sergeant
arnes, W.E.C.	Private	Brandin, Gustav	Boatswain
ayley, A.N.	Private	Brewer, Bertram W.H.	Private
edkober, Lincoln L.	Captain (dentist)	Brown, A.V.	Private
ehan, Tom	Engine Wiper	Browne, Jack McG.	Private

NAME	RANK	NAME	RANK
Buck, John C.	Storekeeper/Barman	Ferrow, J.W.	Sergeant
Burns, W.R.	Private	Findlay, R.W.	Private
Burrett, William E.	Private	Fishwick, Charles E.	Private
Burroughs, S.P.	Corporal	Foley, Stephen D.	Captain
Bush, George F.	Private (Driver)	Forrest, Jack M.	Private
Bush, George R.	Corporal	Fortier, Alan D.	Driver
Butt, W.J.	Private	Fortier, Fred L.	Private (Driver)
Capper, James	Chief Steward	Fowler, C.A.	Driver
Carey, Charles E.J.	Assist. Steward	Fox, Frank W.	Ordinary Seaman
Carey, William R.	Private	Friedrich, Victor	Private
Cavanagh, Richard C.	Driver	Gallagher, John	Engine Wiper
Chadwick, Leslie N.	Lieutenant	Galvin, S.G.	Private (Driver)
Chapman, E.A.	Private	Gannon, Frank J.	Scullion
Clark, Charles 'Nobbie'	Fireman's attendant	Garbutt, Don R.	Private
Clark, J.M.	Private	Garfit, W.D.	Private
Clark, Leslie S.	Private	Geaghan, W.T.	Private
Clark, Neville S.	Private	Goffett, Charles A.	Private
Clark, W.F.Darwin	Mr (Red Cross rep.)	Gordon, C.T.	Private
Claydon, J.A.	Private	Gore, W.H.	Private
Clegg, Percy L.	Private	Grainger, Robert	Greaser
Cockerhill, David	Third Cook	Gunning, A. 'Dick'	Acting Corporal
Colefax, B.Douglas	Private (Driver)	Hall, Harry R.	Fourth Engineer
Colemane, W.J.	Private (Driver)	Hart, Roger F.	Deck Boy
Collins, H.S.	Corporal	Haultain, Helen F.J.C.	Sister
Collins, L.F.	Private	Haynes, Keith R.	Sergeant
Cooke, A.J.	Lance Corporal	Hayward, C.E.	Private (Driver)
Cooley, Geoffrey G.	Major	Hayward, T.H.	Private (Driver)
Corbett, K.N.	Corporal	Hembrow, J.H.	Private
Cripps, Leslie J.	Private	Henderson, Leslie J.	Private
Cross, H.R.T.	Corporal	Hewison, R.J.	Private
Cummings, M.H.	Private	Hindmarsh, Bernie F.	Captain
Cuthill, William D.	Second Engineer	Hoare, J.W.	Private
Denne, F.J.	Private	Hodgkinson, N.A.	Private
Doherty, J.P.	Private	Hogan, K.F.	Private (Driver)
Donohoe, H.M.	Private	Holland, L.	Major
Downie, Walter Ross	Engine Wiper	Holloway, Sam G.	Private
Dutfield, C.C.	Warrant Officer I	Howson, A.	Private
Etheridge, G.R.G.	Private (Driver)	Hughes, T.Stanley	A.B.
Evans, John K.	Corporal	Hutchison Raymond R.	Private
Evans, W.A.	Corporal	Jackman, Vince M.	Private
Fawcett, G.	Private	Jewell, Sarah A.	Matron
Fehrenbach, H.S.	Private	Johnson, A.E.	Lieutenant

NAME	RANK	NAME	RANK
Johnston, Richard C.	Captain	McGuire, C.P.	Private (Driver)
Johnston, S.R.	Private	McKay, C.S.	Lance Corporal
Jones, Gorden.R.	Temporary Major	McKinnon, William J.	Third Cook
Kaki, Laurie	A.B.	McLean, N.	Private
Kemp, A.Roy	Private	McSkimming, S.G.	Lance Corporal
Kerr, J.A.	Private	Mansfield, J.K.	Private (Driver)
Key, Jack J.R.	Private	Manson, Clem P.	Lt.Colonel
King, Evelyn	Sister	Marshall, John B.	Private
Laird, Robert M.	Third Radio Operator	Maynard, Alan F.	Private
Lambert, Charles	Private	Maynard, John C.	Private
Lamble, Henry E.	First Officer	Melbom, E.E.	Private
Laverick, Ernest G.	Chaplain/Captain	Miles, R.W.	Lieutenant
Law, R.	Lance Corporal	Miley, Thomas H.	Private
Lawson, William T.	Private (Driver)	Miller, C.O.	Private
Le Blanc, James	A.B.	Milligan, David I.	A.B.
Le Grand, Peter M.P	Private	Montgomery, C.G.	Private
Leask, Alexander R.	Private	Moore, D.W.	Corporal
Leask, Harold M.	Private	Moran, Jack O'N.	Private
Leask, Henry H.	Private	Morris, Albert J.	Second Steward
Lebrun, C.R.	Lance Corporal	Morris, Thomas V.	Second Radio Operator
Lee, Michael J.	A.B.	Mort, R.F.	Private
Lee, T.A.	Acting Corporal	Moss, Leslie 'Joe'	Corporal
Lesnie, Norman M.G.	Warrant Officer II	Moston, Merle	Sister
Lillas, R.L.	Private (Driver)	Murphy, G.G.	Private (Driver)
Loader, James J.J.	Acting Corporal	Murray, George A.	Captain
Lockhart, Vincent	Second Pantryman	Mycock, Frank J.	Staff Sergeant
Long, A.	Driver	Newell, E.L.	Sergeant
Long, George E.	A.B.	O'Brien, M.J.	Lance Corporal
Longden, Sammuel	Chief Cook	O'Connor, Richard	Corporal
Lotze, E.L.	Corporal	O'Donnell, Alice M.	Sister
Lowe, H.H. 'Lofty'	Private	O'Neill, Thomas W.	Private
Lucas, Joe	Private	O'Sullivan, J.C.	Corporal
Lynagh, F. Jack	Private	Oakley, H.V.	Private
Lyneham, H.L.	Private (Driver)	Ockwell, L.George	Private
Lynne, Clem E.	Private	Overett, H.H.	Private
Lyons, John	A.B.	Owens, E.L.V.	Private (Driver)
Lyttleton, Sidney F.	Private	Page, Elijah C. 'Ron'	A.B.
MacLean, Donald R.	Printer	Pain, R.A.	Private (Driver)
McCaskie, T.E.	Private	Palmer, V.A.	Private (Driver)
McDougall, W.O.	Acting Sergeant	Pearl, Sidney O.	First Baker
McFarlane, Mary H.	Sister	Perrett, E.R.	Private
McGuire, H.J.	Private	Perry, N.E.	Private

Centaur

NAME	RANK	NAME	RANK
Phillips, N.E.	Sergeant	Taggart, J.	Private
Povey, A.R.	Private	Taylor, J.	Staff Sergeant
Power, Edward J.	Private	Thelander, Charles E.	Temporary Major
Pritchard, Thomas E.	Second Baker	Thomas, Allan K.	Warrant Officer II
Rayner, Albert	Assistant Steward	Thomas, Gethyn L.	Captain
Reid, A.	Private	Thomas, J.V.	Private
Richardson, C.	Private	Thompson, Don L.	Private
Richardson, H.F.	Private	Thompson, Hedley W.	Private
Roberts, H.O.	Private	Thorpe, James	Corporal
Robinson, C.M.S.	Private	Trigg, B.S.	Driver
Robinson, Ray L.	Lance Corporal	Upton, George H.	Private
Rutherford, Ellen M.	Sister	Vincent, Edward C.M.	Private
Salmon, Len J.	Private	Walder, Jack J.	Driver
Sender, I.H. 'Dick'	Major	Walker, N.L.	Acting Corporal
Shaw, Edna A.	Sister	Walker, W. 'Jennie'	Sister
Sheard, H.E.	Private (Driver)	Warner, William A.	Assistant Steward
Shepherd, G.P.	Private (Driver)	Wattus, E.O.	Private
Siddons, Fred	Head Waiter	West, W.C.	Lance Corporal
Simpson, E.J.	Driver	Westendorf, R.H.G.	Private
Simpson, Ernest B.	A.B.	Westhorp, S.B.	Lieutenant
Skafte, L.R.	Private	Wheeler, N.E.W.	Lieutenant
Smellie, M.A.	Private	Williams, A.H.	Private
South, A.E.	Private	Williams, D.Kevin	Staff Sergeant
Spence, Robert J.	Carpenter	Williams, E.F.	Private
Stanley, Jack E.	Private	Williams, L.L.	Warrant Officer II
Stephens, Harold Britt	Private	Williams, M.A.	Corporal
Stevens, J.A.	Private	Wilson, A.	Private
Stewart, J.	Private	Wilson, G.A.T.	Private (Driver)
Strack, Stanley L.	Second Cook	Winder, G.A.	Corporal
Stubbs, Robert G.	Private	Winterflood, A.A.	Private (Driver)
Summers, Eric J.	1st Radio Operator & Purser	Wood, Allan	Private
Swan, L.R.	Private	Wood, L.S.	Private
Sweeney, S.E.	Private (Driver)	Woods, C.	Private
Swinburn, Richard	Private	Wright, G	Private
Sykes, Keith	Electrician	Wyllie, Doris Joyce	Sister

SAVED:

Argent, Jack.H.	Private	Bull, Ronald D.	Steward/Writer
Banks, Ernest 'Monty'	Third Mate	Cairnie, Maurice A.	Fourth Engineer
Bayley, John L. 'Jack'	Driver	Carter, George R.	Staff Sergeant
Bidmead, L.E.O. 'Leo'	Private	Cecich, J. 'Ivan'	A.B.
Blair, Albert E.	Corporal	Chidgey, Fred B.	Private (Dental Asst.)

288

ME	RANK	NAME	RANK
~ristensen, Owen N.	A.B.	Millar, Fred S.P.	Private
~chrane, Alex	Steward	Moate, Ronald G.	Chief Pantryman
~rnell, William T.C.	Sergeant	Morgan, Stanley	Donkeyman
~ulsen, Jim	Private	Morris, Matthew A.	Greaser
~llum, Sammuel J.	A.B.	Murphy, George S.	Private
~vidson, A.Francis	Second Butcher	Murray, Kenneth G.	Lance Corporal
~ckson, Allan R.	Driver	Outridge, Leslie McD.	Lt.Colonel
~ust, Frank	Nightwatchman	Pash, Martin L.	Printer
~garty, Thomas C.	Private	Paton, Rupert	Private
~obden, Tom	Corporal (Male Nurse)	Pettiford, Allan A.	Private
~ggins, Mark	Third Baker	Ramage, Alfred	A.B.
~ggins, Trevor	Assistant Cook	Ravenscroft, E.Laurie	Private
~ooper, Leonard R.	Sergeant (paymaster)	Rawlings, James A.	Cook/sculleryman
~rgan, Leslie J.	Driver	Reid, Frank T.	Butcher
~nerwood, Ron C. 'Tich'	Private (Staff Orderly)	Rippon, Richard G.	Second Mate
~hnson, James C.	Warrant Officer II	Salt, Richard M.	Torres Strait Pilot
~nassen, Mark	Steward	Sandwell, Sidney C.	Linenkeeper
~nes, Clifford G.	Private	Savage, Ellen	Sister
~nes, Ron 'Spud'	Lance Corporal	Smith, Ernest D.	Chief Engineer
~lly, Percy G.	Private	Stutter, Jack D.	Steward
~nge, Keith	Corporal	Taylor, Albert J.	Corporal (Dental Tech.)
~cCosker, V.	Private (Orderly)	Taylor, Eric G.W.	Private
~cGrath, George W.	Driver	Thomas, M.P.	Lance Corporal
~cIntosh, William	Fireman	Tierney, Walter H.	Greaser
~alcolm, Thomas C.	Corporal	Waddington, Arthur	Assistant Steward
~artin, Francis	Seamens' Cook	Watterston, James	Assistant Storeman
~edcalf, Richard	Staff Sergeant	Westwood, Robert K.	Ordinary Seaman

289

APPENDIX B

EXTRACTS FROM THE *CONVENTION OF THE ADAPTATION OF THE PRINCIPLES OF THE GENEVA CONVENTION TO MARITIME WARFARE*

(Italicised emphasis in the extracts is the authors')

Article 1.   Military hospital ships, that is to say, ships constructed or assigned by States specially and solely with a view to assisting the wounded, sick, and shipwrecked, the names of which have been communicated to the belligerent Powers at the commencement or during the course of hostilities and in any case before they are employed, shall be respected, and can not be captured while hostilities last.

Article 4.   The ships . . . shall afford relief and assistance to the wounded, sick and shipwrecked of the belligerents without distinction of nationality.

The Governments undertake not to use the ships for any military purpose.

These vessel must in no wise hamper the movements of the combatants.

During and after an engagement they will act at their own risk and peril.

Article 5.   Military hospital ships shall be distinguished by being painted white outside with a horizontal band of green about a meter and a half in breadth.

The boats of the ships above mentioned, as also small craft which may be used for hospital work, shall be distinguished by similar painting.

All hospital ships shall make themselves known by hoisting, with their national flag, the white flag with a red cross provided by the Geneva Convention . . .

Article 8. The fact of the *staff of the said ships and sick wards being armed* for maintaining order and for defending the sick and wounded, and the presence of wireless telegraphy apparatus on board, *is not a sufficient reason for withdrawing protection.*

Article 10. The religious, medical, and *hospital staff of any captured ship is inviolable*, and its members cannot be made prisoners of war.

APPENDIX C

M.V. *CENTAUR* — CONSTRUCTION DETAILS

Builder:	Scotts Shipbuilding & Engineering Co., Greenock
Year Built:	1924
Length:	315.7 ft (96 metres)
Beam:	48.2 ft (14.7 metres)
Depth:	21.5 ft (6.6 metres)
Gross tonnage:	3,222
Net tonnage:	1901
Engine:	4-stroke, 6-cylinder, oil-fired, blast-injected Burmeister & Wain
Decks:	2 tween decks and upper 'shade' deck
Holds/hatches:	4
Grain space:	240,000 cu ft (6,800 cu metres)
Bale space:	220,000 cu ft (6,200 cu metres)
Livestock capacity:	450 head
Passenger capacity:	72
Official number:	147275

BIBLIOGRAPHY

PUBLISHED ARTICLES, MONOGRAPHS, AND
RECOLLECTIONS:

Alden, J.D. Japanese Submarine Losses in World War II. *Warship International*. 1985, No. 1

Cameron, R.A. Singapore-Fremantle Service. *Bulletin of the Blue Funnel and Glen Lines*, Liverpool. July 1960, 239-256.

Conway, C. Canada's First Hospital Ship. *Canadian National Magazine*. 29(5), May 19 1943, 4-5,17.

Fielder-Gill, W. Notes On Radar Station Surface Vessel Sightings — Particularly 23rd Radar and 'The Centaur Story'. (mimeo) Chatswood, Sydney, N.S.W., 1992.

Graf, Lt. F.A. Knowing the Law, *Proceedings*. June 1988, 58-61.

Foxwell, D & Jolly, R. The RFA Argus: a gas-tight, floating field hospital. *International Defense Review,* 2/1991.

H.J.M. Sinking of Hospital Ship "Centaur" Recalled. *Reveille*. May 1 1963, 5,34.

Hobden, T. The Sinking of the Centaur. Recollections (mimeo) 4 pages.

Jeffrey, V. Sinking of the Centaur, *Ships Monthly,* May 1987, 36-37.

Jeffries, Col. J.H. Law of War Trivia, *Proceedings*. June 1988, 57

Long, G. The Six Years War. *AWM*. 1973, 291-292.

Milligan, C.S. Land, Sea and Air Roots! *History and the Social Science Teacher*. 1980:2, 130-135.

Milligan, C.S. *Australian Hospital Ship CENTAUR*. (monograph) Montreal: McGill University, 1981.

Minto, T. Account of Darwin Air Raid 1942, *Seamen's Journal*. March/April 1990, 96-97.

O'Sullivan, G.J, *Unit War History, Fifth Birthday Celebration Booklet.* 2/12 Field Ambulance Association: Kuching, 22 Nov. 1945.

Records, Bill. The Timely Rescue. Recollections 1992 (mimeo) 3 pages.

Scott's Shipbuilding & Engineering Co. *Two Hundred and Fifty Years of Ship Building by Scotts at Greenock.* (mimeo) Private circulation.

Simmond, E. & Smith, N (Eds.,) *Radar Yarns.* (year unknown)

Smith, A.E. World War II Comes to Australia, *MNWSL*, Brunswick, 1992.

Centaur

Spurlock, P.E. The Yokohama War Crimes Trials: The Truth About a
Misunderstood Subject, *American Bar Association Journal*. May
1950, 387-389,436-437.
Unknown. Atrocity That Shocked The World. *Parade*. July 1956,
28-29.
Unknown. War's Worst Sea Crime, *The Seamen's Journal*. June
1943, 2.

BOOKS:

Baty, S. *Ships that Passed*. Sydney, N.S.W.: Reed Books, 1984.
Beesly, P. *Very Special Intelligence*. London: Sphere Books, 1978.
Bergamini, D. *Japan's Imperial Conspiracy*. New York: William
Morrow and Company, 1971.
Blair, C. Jnr., *Silent Victory — the US Submarine War Against Japan*
(Vol I) New York, Lippencott, 1975.
Blair, J. & Blair, C.Jnr, *Return from the River Kwai*. New York: Simon
& Schuster.
Brittin, B.H. *International Law For Seagoing Officers*. Annapolis:
Naval Institute Press, 1986 (5th. ed).
Cahill, R.J. *The Seamen's Union of Australia 1872-1972*. Sydney,
N.S.W.: Seaman's Union of Australia, 1981.
Caidin, M. *The Ragged, Rugged Warriors*. New York: Ballantine Books,
Inc, 1968.
Carpenter, D. & Polmar, N. *Submarines of the Imperial Japanese
Navy*. Annapolis: Naval Institute Press, 1986.
Detmers, Theodor. *The Raider Kormoran*. London: William Kimber,
1959.
Dower, J.W. *War Without Mercy — Race and Power in The Pacific
War*. New York: Pantheon Books, 1986.
Drea, E.J. *MacArthur's ULTRA Codebreaking and the War against
Japan, 1942-1945*. Lawrence, Kansas: University Press of Kansas,
1992.
Dull, P.S. *A Battle History Of The Imperial Japanese Navy
(1941-1945)*. Annapolis: United States Naval Institute, 1978.
Durand, A. *Histoire du CICR De Sarajevo a Hiroshima*. Ch. IX, Section
2, p. 406; and Section 6, pp. 465-466.
Edwards, B. *Blood and Bushido: Japanese Atrocities at Sea 1941-1945*.
Upton-upon-Severn, Worcs: The Self Publishing Association Ltd.,
1991
Foley, J.C.H. *Reef Pilots; The History of the Queensland Coast and
Torres Strait Pilot Service*. Sydney, N.S.W.: Banks Bros. & Street,
1982

— *The Quetta: Queensland's Worst Disaster.* Brisbane, QLD: Nairana Publications, 1990.

Gill, G.H. *Royal Australian Navy 1942-1945. Australia in the War of 1939-1945 Series, Australian Navy.* Vol II. Canberra: Australian War Memorial, 1968.

Gibson, R. *My Years in the Communist Party.* Melbourne: International Bookshop, 1966.

Goodman, R. *The AANS in Australia.* Brisbane, QLD: Boolarong, 1985.

— *Hospital Ships.* Brisbane, QLD: Boolarong, 1992.

— *Queensland Nurses — Boer War to Vietnam.* Brisbane, QLD. Boolarong, 1992

Hanayama, S. *The Way of Deliverance — Three Years with the Condemned Japanese War Criminals.* New York: Charles Scribner's Sons, 1950.

Hashimoto, M. *Sunk: The Story of the Japanese Submarine Fleet.* London: Cassell, 1954.

Hosoya, C; Ando, N; Onuma, Y; and, Minear, R. (Eds.,). *The Tokyo War Crimes Trial — An International Symposium.* New York: Harper and Row, 1986.

Howlett, L. *The Oranje Story.* Wollongong, N.S.W.: Oranje Hospital Association, 1991.

Hunt, F. *The Untold Story Of Douglas MacArthur.* New York: Manor Books, 1954.

ICRC. *Report of the ICRC on its Activities during the Second World War.* Part I, Vol. I, 173-178. Part II, Vol. I, 213-215.

Ienaga, S. *The Pacific War, 1931-1945 — A Critical Perspective on Japan's Role in World War II.* New York: Panthon Books, 1978

Jenkins, D. *Battle Surface.* Sydney: Random House, 1992

Jentschura, H; Jung, D. & Mickel, P. (Translated by Preston, A. & Brown, J.D.). *Warships of the Imperial Japanese Navy, 1869-1945.* Annapolis: Naval Institute Press, 1977, 1982 (3rd. Ed).

Kennedy, P. *Pacific Onslaught 7th Dec. 1941 / 7th Feb. 1943.* New York: Ballantine Books, 1972.

Kodama, Y. *Sugamo Prison.* Japan: Radiopress, 1960

Lockwood, D. *Australia's Pearl Harbour.* Adelaide: Rigby, 1966.

Masanori, I. *The End of the Imperial Japanese Navy.* London: 1962.

Mayo, L. *Bloody Buna.* New York: Doubleday, 1974.

McClement, F. *Guns In Paradise: The Saga of the Cruiser Emden.* Markham,ON: PaperJacks, 1968.

Minear, R.H. *Victors' Justice — The Tokyo War Crimes Trial.* Princeton, NJ: Princeton University Press, 1971.

Montgomery, M. *Who Sank the Sydney?* Australia: Cassel, 1981.

Morison, S.E. Breaking the Bismark's Barrier, 22 July 1942 — May 1944. Vol. VI *History of the United States Naval Operations in World War II.* Boston: Little, Brown and Company. 1950

— *The Two-Ocean War; A Short History of the United States Navy in the Second World War.* Boston, MA: Little, Brown and Company, 1963.

Muggenthaler, K. *German Raiders of World War II.* London: Pan Books, 1980

Odgers, G. *Air War Against Japan 1943-1945 Canberra.* A.C.T.: Australian War Memorial, 1957

Orita, Z. with Harrington, J.D. *I-Boat Captain.* Canoga Park, California: Major Books. 1976

Pritchard, R.J. & Zaide, S.M. (Eds.,). *The Tokyo War Crimes Trial.* (Multiple Volumes). New York & London: Garland Publishing Inc. 1985.

Reilly, J.C. *United States Navy Destroyers of World War II.* Poole, Dorset: Blandford Press. 1983

Rohwer, F-J. *Die-U-Boot Erfolge Der Achsenmachte 1939-1945.* Munchen: J.F. Lehmanna Verlag, 1968.

Rohwer, F-J. and Huemmelchen, G. *Chronology of War at Sea 1939-1945.* Vol.s I & II. New York: Arco Publishing, 1972 & 1974.

Roling, B.V.A. & Ruter, C.F. (Eds.,). *The Tokyo Judgment — The International Military Tribunal for the Far East (I.M.T.F.E.) 29 April 1946 — 12 November 1948.* (Vol.I — Vol.V) Amsterdam: APA-University Press Amsterdam BV, 1977

Roscoe, T. *Pig Boats.* New York: Bantam Books, 1982 (originally Roscoe, 1949).

— *United States Destroyer Operations in World War II.* Annapolis: United States Naval Institute, 1953.

— *US Submarine Operations In World War II.* Annapolis: U.S. Naval Institute, 1949.

Roskill, S.W. *A Merchant Fleet In War.* London: Alfred Holt, 1962.

Russell (of Liverpool), Lord. *The Knights of Bushido — A Short History of Japanese War Crimes.* London: Cassell and Company Limited, 1958.

Sakamoto, K. History of Submarine Warfare. *Military History Series,* Vol. 98, National Defence College (Sensuikan shi). Tokyo: National Defence Agency, War History Section (Boeicho Kenshujo Senshishitsu), 1979.

Smith, A.E. *Three Minutes of Time: The Torpedoing of the Australian Hospital Ship "Centaur".* Queensland: The Lower Tweed River Historical Society, 1991.

Spector, R.H. *Eagle Against the Sun* New York: Vintage Books, 1985

— (Ed.) *Listening to the Enemy. Key Documents on the Role of Communication Intelligence in the War with Japan.* Wilmington, Delaware: Scholarly Resources, Inc. 1988

Thomas, D.A. *Japan's War at Sea, Pearl Harbor to the Coral Sea.* London: Andre Deutsch, 1978

Underwood, P. *The Reflections of an Old Grey Mare.* Rockhampton: Self-published, 1987.
U.S. Army Far East Command. *The Imperial Japanese Navy in World War II; A Graphic Presentation of the Japanese Naval Organization and List of Combatant and Non-Combatant Vessels Lost or Damaged in the War.* Tokyo: Military History Section, Special Staff, General Headquarters, Far East Command, 1952.
U.S. Navy Department. *Dictionary of American Naval Fighting Ships.* (Vol. IV). Naval History Division, Washington: Office of the Chief of Naval Operations, 1969.
U.S. Navy Department. *U.S. Navy At War 1941-1945. Official Reports to the Secretary of the Navy.* Washington, DC: US Navy Dept, 1946.
U.S. Naval History Division. *United States Submarine Losses World War II.* Washington, DC: Office of the Chief of Naval Operations, 1963.
Walker, Allen S., et. al., Australia in the War of 1939-1945. *Medical Services of the RAN and RAAF, Series V.* Canberra: Australian War Memorial, 1961.
Wellesley-Smith, A. & Shaw, E.L. *Lest We Forget.* Melbourne: AANS, 1944
Winter, B. *H.M.A.S. Sydney — Fact, Fantasy and Fraud.* Brisbane: Boolarong Publications, 1984.

NEWSPAPERS:

Australian:
Bathurst, *Western Advocate*
Brisbane, *Courier-Mail*
Brisbane, *Telegraph*
Hobart, *Saturday Mercury*
Melbourne, *Age*
Melbourne, *Argus*
Melbourne, *Herald*
Perth, *Daily News*
Sydney, *Daily Mirror*
Sydney, *Daily Telegraph*
Sydney, *Sun*

Canadian:
Montreal, *Gazette*
Montreal, *Montreal Star*

American
Boston, *Boston Post*
New York, *New York Times*
Washington, *Washington Post*

British
Liverpool, *Liverpool Echo*
London, *The Times*

Others
Royal Australian *Navy News Pictorial*
Daily Commercial News
The Weekend Australian

Centaur

TAPED REMINISCENCES:

Albert John Taylor — Reminiscences of the CENTAUR.
Fred Chidgey — Centaur Story Part 1 & 2.
Doug Wight — Reminiscences of David I.Milligan.
Richard G.Rippon — Reads letter to father.
Ron Moate — taped reminiscences
Tom Hobden — videotaped recollections

CHAPTER NOTES

Archive Abbreviations
The following abbreviations simplify the identification of general archive sources within footnotes.

AAB	Australian Archives, Brighton (Melbourne), Vic.
AAD	Australian Archives, Dickson, A.C.T.
AAS	Australian Archives, Sydney, N.S.W.
ANU	Australian National University, A.C.T.
IMT	International Military Tribunal — The Tokyo War Crimes Trial.
JAG	Judge Advocate General
Log	Official Navy log, deck log, war diary of a vessel
OTT	Ocean Transport and Trading Limited, Liverpool, England.
PRA	Public Records Office, (Admiralty Records), London.
PRO	Public Records Office, (Foreign Office), London
SCAP	Supreme Commander for the Allied Powers
SPR	Sugamo Prison Records
SRN	Japanese Naval Messages
SRNS	Summaries of Radio Intelligence, Japanese Naval Attache Messages

A code number consisting of the aforementioned abbreviations and a number are used to identify parent archive files, records, or documents. Exact location of source is given at the right of each code number.

Code No.   **ARCHIVES**
Documents in Australian Archives, Brighton (Melbourne), Victoria.

MP 121 Department of Shipping and Transport, Marine Branch: Correspondence Files, Multiple Number Series with "M" and Year Prefix, 1912-1951

Centaur

AAB-121   file: M43/543/763 "Casualties-Preliminary Enquiries-Loss of HMA Hosp. Ship Centaur."

           MP 138 (Navy) Corres'ce. Files, Multiple Nos series with 201 secondary INFIX, '23-'50:
AAB-259   file: 603/292/259 "Conversion of Centaur."
AAB-410   file: 603/292/410 "Takeover of Centaur, fitting out, crew pay etc . . ."

           MP 729/6, CA 19 Defence (II) 1936-1939; CA 36, Department of the Army 1939-1945: Secret Correspondence Files Multiple Number Series (Class 401), 1936-1945
AAB-729   file: 59/402/6 "Centaur" Report No. 1. (Manson Report); 59/402/36 Sinking of Centaur.

           MP 742:
AAB-361   file: 336/1/1506 part 1 "Ships plans before and after conversion."

           MP 742; CA 36 Army: Correspondence Files Multiple Number Series 1943-1951
AAB-362   file: 336/1/1506, part 2. "War Crimes Inquiry re Sir William Webb."

           MP 742 DEPT. CA 36 Army: Correspondence Files, Multiple Number Series, 1943-1951
AAB-299   file: 299/3/39 "Carrying of Firearms on Hospital Ship Centaur."

           MP 1185/8 Department CA 2456, Navy Office (III) to 1939: CA 38, Navy (II), Navy Office (III): Secret and Confidential Correspondence Files Multiple Number Series, 1923-1950
AAB-858   file: 2026/13/1858 "Sinking of Hospital Ship 'Centaur'."

Documents in Australian Archives, Dickson, A.C.T.:

           CRS. A649; CA 68,Department of the Treasury, Defence Division: Correspondence Files, Multiple number series (unclassified) 1942-1962:
AAD-135   item: 52/600/135 "Mercantile Marine-Pens'n etc.-benefits for crew of 'Centaur'" '42-43.
AAD-197   item: 20/600/1197 "H.S. 'Centaur' Admission of Expenditures Without Supporting Receipts" Sept-Oct. 1944

CRS A816; CA 46, Department of Defence Co-ordination. Correspondence files, multiple number series, (Class 301) (Classified) 1935-1957.

AAD-396   item: 40/301/396 "Protest of Japanese Gov't Regarding Attacks On Hosp. Ships" '43-'45.

AAD-399   item: 40/301/399 "Integration of Int'l Convention Relating To Hospital Ships" 1943-1944.

CRS A 989; CA 18 Department of External Affairs (II). Correspondence Files, multiple number series with prefix 1943-1944.

AAD-989   item: 44/43/925/1/26/1 "Treaties-Red Cross-Prisoners of War — Hospital Ship 'Centaur' 1943-1944.

CRS A 2663: (located at Aust. War Memorial, Canberra)

AAD-409   file: 409/7/5 "Instructions, Centaur Voyages, April 1943."

AAD-883   file: 883/2/11 "Investigation of rumours concerning Centaur."

CRS A2670 CA 1468, War Cabinet Secretariat. War Cabinet Agendum. 1939-1945:

AAD-157   item: 157/1943 "Statement of Urgent Defence Measures Approved Under War Cabinet Minutes Nos. 1573 & 2144" 1943, April 30. at Melbourne.

AAD-270   item: 270/1943 Statement of Urgent Defence Measures (Army) Approved Under War Cabinet Minutes Nos. 1573 and 2144" 1943, July 13. at Melbourne.

CRS A2684; CA 495 Advisory War Council, Minute Files, 1940-1945. (Attachment)."Sinking Of Hospital Ship 'Centaur' 14th May, 1943." (Formerly CRS A816, 40/301/400) item: 1203

AAD-684   "Sinking Of Hospital Ship 'Centaur' 14th May, 1943."

Documents in Australian Archives, Sydney, N.S.W.

SP 106/1:

AAS-243   item: PC 243 Office of the State Publicity Censor, N.S.W. 'Casualties and Hospital Ship Publicity, Returned Personnel, etc.,' 1942-1944.

AAS-37   item: PC 37 Office of the State Publicity Censor N.S.W. 'Smiths Weekly' (Batch 2), 1942-1943.

Documents in Australian National University, A.C.T. Archives of Business and Labour, Research School of Social Sciences.

ANU-8   100/3/111/8 August 1935 — December 1940. Shipping Registers and Diaries.

ANU-9   100/3/111/9 January 1941 — June 1945. Shipping Registers and Diaries.

Documents in Ocean Transport and Trading Limited, Liverpool, England.

OTT-963   (OA = Ocean Archives) OA.696/3. Cameron, R.A. 1960. Singapore — Freemantle Service. *Bulletin* Blue Funnel and Glen Lines. 239-256.

OTT-964   OA.696/4/261. 'Flash Jack'. (19——). An Aboriginal Painting. *Bulletin* Blue Funnel and Glen Lines. 261.

OTT-697   OA.697/1.. (1969). Centaur Memorial and Park. *Ocean.* January, 19——

OTT-921   OA.792a. M.V. CENTAUR -- Extract from A Voyage Report, October 1936, and abstract from a December 1936 issue of Lloyd's list.

OTT-923   OA.792b. CENTAUR 2 -- Description of ship details including brief history.

OTT-261   OA.826a. "Diesel Machinery Data Book" (Office copy extract) -- construction, engineering and mechanical information.

OTT-262   OA.826b. "Diesel Machinery Data Book" (Office Copy extract) -- Dry Dockings from 1937 — 1942 and mechanical data from Voyage No. 87 (February 1938) and Voyage No. 120 (28 February and 21 April 1942).

OTT-263   OA.826c. Extracts -- mechanical and engineering data for Voyage Nos. 79 (Feb/Apr. 1937), 93N and 94S (Dec.'38 - Jan. 1939), 119 (Nov/Dec 1941), 120 (Dec '41 — Jan '42), 121 -123 (May '42 — Aug '42).

OTT-986   OA.986/42. List of Merchant Crew members on CENTAUR 27.4.42.

OTT-380   OA.1380. Centaur-Merchant Marine Casualties List.

OTT-536   OA.1536. S.W. Roskill. *A Merchant Fleet In War 1939-1945.* London: Collins, 1962.

OTT-826   OA.1826/20. Centaur Notes From Admiralty -- Rippon's Report of Loss of Hospital Ship (dated 20 May 1943).

OTT-931   OA.1931. "CENTAUR" General Arrangement Scale: 1/16 = One Foot. Drawing No. A 5404.

Documents in The Public Records Office Archives, Great Britain.

PRA   *Admiralty Records:* ADM 199/2145 6818 (Docket: M010693/43, 24 May '43, 128A-128B -- TORPEDOING OF H.M.A.H.S. "CENTAUR".

Foreign Office Records, FO. 371: 36573 X/K 6940: GENERAL — W:

PRO-479	1479, 26 Jan. 1943
PRO-723	1723, 29 Jan. 1943
PRO-478	4478, 19 Mar. 1943

Foreign Office Records, FO. 371: 36574 X/K 6940: GENERAL — W:

PRO-567	5567, 09 Apr. 1943
PRO-759	6759, 04 May. 1943
PRO-432	7432, 18 May. 1943
PRO-462	7462, 19 May. 1943
PRO-731	7731, 24 May. 1943

Foreign Office Records, FO. 371: 36576 X/K 6940: GENERAL — W:

PRO-812	11812, 14 Aug. 1943
PRO-949	11949, 18 Aug. 1943
PRO-455	17455, 18 Dec. 1943

Foreign Office Records, FO. 371: (*) XC 009934: WAR CRIMES — U:

PRO-037	9037, 15 Nov 1945, (*51050)
PRO-041	8041, 21 Nov 1946, (*57429)
PRO-106	6106, 27 June 1946, (*57611)

Documents in the U.S. National Archives, Record Group 24, Records of the Bureau of Naval Personnel

Log	USS *Greenling* (SS213)
Log	USS *Helm* (DD388)
Log	USS *Patterson* (DD392)
Log	USS *Mugford* (DD389)
Log	USS *Nicholas* (DD449)
Log	USS *SC669*

Documents in U.S. National Archives, Record Group 153, Records of the Office of the Judge Advocate General (Army), War Crimes Case Files

JAG-455	Box 1455, Review of Trial; Exhibit Statements
JAG-456	Box 1456, Clemency Petitions (Toshio Kusaka) To Record of Trial -- U.S. vs Ichioka, et al.
JAG-459	Box 1459 & 1542, Case File No. 67-186-1, Case Docket No. 339 Record of Trial of *U.S. vs Hisashi Ichioka et al*, Yokohama, Japan, 14 July 1948 — 28 December 1948

Documents in U.S. National Archives, Record Group 331, Records of Allied Operational and Occupation Headquarters Supreme Commander for the Allied Powers (SCAP)

SCAP-97	Box 997, "The sinking of the H.M.A.H.S. "Centaur" (Officially known as the 2/3rd Australian Hospital Ship 'Centaur'". *A Report of War Crimes Against Australians Committed by individual Members of the Armed Forces of the Enemy. Oct. 1944.* (52-77).
SCAP-98	Box 998, File No. JA-27 Information Re Sinking of Merchant Ships in the Indian Ocean.
SCAP-781	Box 1781, File No. 503 Japanese Submarine Secret Operational Orders.
SCAP-782	Box 1782, File. 520 (S.S. Br. Chivalry); File. 521 (S.S.Sutlej); File. 522 (S.S. Ascot).
SCAP-783	Box 1783, Investigation No. 563 Re Centaur, includes Reports of Investigation Division; Interrogations; Correspondence; and, Additional information including — authenticated true copies by Lt-Col. Thomas F.Mornane AMF of official evidence given before His Honour, Sir William Webb, in the course of the "Inquiry into the sinking of H.M.A.S. Centaur".

Documents in U.S. National Archives, Record Group 338, Records of US 8th Army Command, Sugamo Prison Records, 1945-52, Paroled Prisoner 201 Files.

| SPR-222 | Box 222, Hajime Nakagawa; Hisashi Ichioka; Hisashi Mito (et. al.) - Sugamo Prison File |

Documents in U.S. National Archives, Record Group 457, Records of National Security Agency/Central Security Service.

| SRN | Japanese Naval Messages 6204 to 6383 (Box 8); 6854 to 7169 (Box 9); 7344 to 7707 (Box 10). |
| SRNS | Summaries of Radio Intelligence, Japanese Naval Attache Messages - 353 to 718 (Box 2). |

Chapter One — THE GOOD LIFE

1. Scotts' Shipbuilding & Engineering Co. *Two Hundred and Fifty Years of Ship Building by Scotts at Greenock.* (mimeo) Private circulation, 19--.
2. R.A.Cameron, "Singapore Fremantle Service", *Bulletin of the Blue Funnel and Glen Lines.* Liverpool. July 1960, 239-256. (same as OTT-963)
3. OTT-923
4. OTT-921; OA-931.
5. OTT-931.
6. AAB-361 (same as OTT-931); After -- Two Sheets 1943 "Centaur" Conversion to Hospital ship — scale 1″ = 8 feet); OTT-964, p.261.
7. OTT-261; OTT-262; OTT-263; OTT-931
8. Lloyds List, December 1936.
9. AAB 259, Minute Paper (4 pages) 25 March 1943 "Extra Galley Equipment" (p.2), Accommodation (p.7); AAB-410 — See for example 'List of Officers (41 European) and Crew (29 Asiatics)' for Voyage No.127; AAB-361
10. ABB-259, for details of 'Equipment and Cargo Gear' and 'Electrical Equipment' see B.P.Fielden's 1 Feb 1943 Lloyd's Register of Shipping Survey. pp.8-13; OTT-931.
11. Cameron, 246.
12. OTT-921
13. Cameron, 246.
14. Lloyd's Captains' Registers, Guildhall Library, London.
15. Unknown. "Atrocity That Shocked the World", *Parade.* July 1956. 28-29; Correspondence with Ernest Smith, 30 May 1979.
16. OTT-262.

Chapter Two — A MERCHANT SHIP AT WAR

1. S.W.Roskill, *A Merchant Fleet In War* (London: Alfred Holt, 1962) is the definitive history of the Holt fleet during W.W.II. (same as OTT-536)
2. Ibid., 152, 280 operating from Australian waters.
3. Cameron, 247.
4. Roskill, 23.
5. A.E.Smith, "World War II Comes to Australia", *MNWSL*, Brunswick, 1992
6. Correspondence with Maurice Cairnie, 1991
7. AAB-410, Minute Paper: 19 Feb 1943 gives the gunners' rates of pay.
8. Barbara Winter, *H.M.A.S. Sydney — Fact, Fantasy and Fraud* (Brisbane: Boolarong Publications, 1984), 148-149.
9. Ibid., 165.
10. Ibid., 166-167

11. Correspondence with Ernest Smith, 8 August 1980.
12. Correspondence with Capt. Gordon Rippon, 1991.
13. Winter, 254. 'Appendix 3: Kormoran survivors' — 103 German survivors reached land; 26 were picked up by *Aquitania*, 25 by *Trocas*, 31 by *Koolinda*, 61 plus 1 Chinese by *Centaur*, and 70 plus 2 Chinese by *Yandra*. Total 316 plus 3 Chinese.
14. Theodor Anton Detmers. (b) 22 August 1902, Witten i. Rhur (d) 4 Nov 1976. For additional biographical information see Winter, 251.
15. Winter, 167.
16. Theodor Detmers, *The Raider Kormoran* (London: William Kimber, 1959), 196.
17. Winter, 168 (note: photo p.168 of Centaur lifeboats P2 and P4 lowered for Kormoran survivors).
18. see photo in Winter, 180 (Kormoran lifeboat picked up by Centaur).
19. Detmers.
20. Ibid.
21. *New York Times*. 4 December, 1941 'Hitler Honors Commander of Raider That Sank Cruiser'.
22. Winter, 165-179
23. Roskill, 76 (footnote).
24. *The Times*. 3 Dec 1941. 'Sunk Raider's Career'. For additional details refer to Winter 1984; and, Detmers, 1959.
25. for additional information on German Raiders refer to Roskill, Ch 4. 'Actions with German Surface Raiders 1939-1942', 88; K. Muggenthaler, *German Raiders of World War II* (London: Pan Books, 1980).
26. for an intelligence perspective see Patrick Beesly, *Very Special Intelligence* (London: Sphere Books 1978), 131-132; *New York Times*. 4 Dec 1941. Quoting sources in Berlin 'No Precedent, Nazis Say' — "An encounter without precedent in the annals of naval warfare".
27. For this WWI encounter refer to Fred McClement, *Guns In Paradise: The Saga of the Cruiser Emden* (Markham ON: Paper-Jacks, 1968).
28. ANU-9, Oct 1942, 1-13: "Voyage 119S — Capt. Dark — 30 Nov 1941 1.40am Berthed B. Shed . . . 60 German Prisoners 40 Guard X Canarvon ex German Raider Cargo"; Cameron, 247-248; Roskill, 88; and Winter, 178-179.
29. Cameron, 248
30. Ibid.,
31. AAB-410, List of Officers and Crew — Voyage 127.
32. ANU-9, p.11 Voyage 122N — Capt. Murray — 5 June 1942; OTT-262; Cameron, 248-249.

33. Correspondence with Maurice Cairnie, 1991; ANU-9, 11-13 (Voyages 122N/S, 123S/N, 124S & 125E); AAB-410, Letter: 4 Jan 1943 to Navy from Sir Thomas Gordon; Letter: (ref. 2265) 12 Jan 1943, to Sir Thomas Gordon from Navy.
34. Cameron, 249; ANU-9, 11-12.
35. Lida Mayo, *Bloody Buna* (New York: Doubleday, 1974); Paul Kennedy, *Pacific Onslaught 7th Dec 1941/7th Feb 1943* (New York: Ballantine Books, 1972) 136-153; Frazier Hunt, *The Untold Story Of Douglas MacArthur* (New York: Manor Books, 1954) 282-288; and Roskill, 19-33, 155-173, 279-285.
36. AAB-259, Note: Proposed New Hospital Ship — General Requirements and Queries (undated); Memo: from Army to Navy 14 Dec 1942.
37. for additional information on Australian Hospital Ships refer to Rupert Goodman, *Hospital Ships — MANUNDA, WANGANELLA, CENTAUR, ORANJE*. (Brisbane: Boolarong 1992); Lorna Howlett, *The Oranje Story* (Wollongong: Oranje Hospital Association, 1991); Allen Walker, *Medical Services of the R.A.N. and R.A.A.F.* (Canberra: Australian War Memorial, 1961).
38. Rupert Goodman, *Hospital Ships*, Boolarong, 1992.
39. See for example Howlett (1991) for shipboard life on *Oranje*.
40. For an eyewitness account by the Chief Officer of H.M.A.H.S. *Manunda*, see Thomas Minto. "Account of Darwin Air Raid 1942", *Seamen's Journal*. March/April 1990, 96-97; Correspondence with Thomas Minto, 28 May 1990.
41. John Foley, *Reef Pilots* (Sydney: Banks Bros & Street, 1982) 100-101
42. AAB-259, Letter: 14 Dec 1942 Army to Navy
43. AAB-259, Memorandum: 14 Dec 1942 for Navy from Army.
44. AAB-259, Minute Paper: 14 Dec 1942 from Dir of Naval Engineering — suggests Centaur.
45. Official movement log for M.V. *Centaur*, September 1939 to May 1943.
46. AAB-259, Minute Paper: 9 Feb 1943 par.1a; AAB-410, Minute Paper: 19 Feb 1943 from Director of Navy Accounts — for rates of pay (note: 2nd Mate £53 per month).
47. AAB-410, Letter: 4 Jan 1943 --To Navy from Sir Thomas Gordon; Letter: (ref. 2265) 12 Jan 1943, To Sir Thomas Gordon from Navy; Letter: 16 Jan 1943 — From Dalgety to Navy.
48. AAB-259 — Fielden's 13 page Report of 1 Feb 1943; Valuation sheet: dated 3 Feb 1943.
49. AAB-410.
50. Hansgeorg Jentschura, Dieter Jung and Peter Mickel (translated by Antony Preston and J.D.Brown), *Warships of the Imperial Japanese Navy, 1869-1945* (Annapolis, MD: Naval Institute Press, 1977, 1982 (3rd. Ed)), 172.

51. Ibid; Correspondence with Saburo Toyama, Japan Defence Academy, Hashirimizu, Yokosuka, 20 Sept and 10 Dec 1979; Kaneyoshi Sakamoto, "Vol.98 History of Submarine Warfare", *Military History Series*, Vol. 3 (National Defence College (Sensuikan shi). Tokyo: National Defence Agency, War History Section, Boeicho Kenshujo Senshishitsu, 1979), Ch.1, Table VII.
52. Correspondence with Prof. Saburo Toyama, 10 Jan 1980; see also Kaneyoshi Sakamoto.
53. SPR-222, chronology in Nakagawa's prison file; also Jentschura, 170 & Carpenter, 93 — *I-60* launched 24th April 1929, completed 29th Dec, sunk 17th Jan 1942 by HMS *Jupiter* — *I-63* launched 28th Sept 1927, completed 20th Dec 28, sunk 2nd Feb 39 off Kyushu, raised and scrapped 22nd Jan 1940; Jenkins, 277.
54. Correspondence with Prof. Saburo Toyama, 10 Dec 1979; Sakamoto, Ch.1, Table VIII, 229.

Chapter Three — *FROM PASSENGER LINER TO HOSPITAL SHIP*
1. AAB-361.
2. AAB-858, ref SC2026/13/1755 par.4a-c. (on 18 Aug 1944 Lt-Cmdr George was identified to the Secretary of the War Crimes Commission as a witness who could depose to the Centaur bearing the distinctive markings of a hospital ship).
3. AAB-259, Navy Minute Paper 9 Feb 1943
4. Ibid., War Cabinet Minute, 30 April 1943, Serial No.1451. 20,000 approved 3 Feb 1943, 10,000 approved 12 March 1943; War Cabinet Minute, 13 July 1943 Serial No.A 1689 approved final £25,000 for final cost of £55,000; AAD-157; ADD-270
5. AAB-259, Navy Minute Paper 25 March 1943 by Director of Engineering (Naval) p.1 par 2.;
6. Ibid., pp.1-3, par.(A) 'Army Requirements' (Aa) — par.(Ah).
7. Ibid., p.3 par. (B) 'Crew's Accommodation'.
8. Ibid., p.4 'required by Union Delegates'.
9. AAB-361; AAD-270
10. AAB-410, Letter 11 Feb 1943
11. AAB-362, see Exhibit A9 — distinguishing hospital ship features of Centaur from Assistant Superintendent Engineering, Alfred Holt & Company; *Revue Internationale*, 1944, May — Emploi du signe de la Croix-Rouge Sur Des Navires; *Revue internationale de la Croix-Rouge*, May 1944, 355-360; Refer to Appendix B The Hague Convention of 1907 'The Adaption To Maritime Warfare Of The Principles Of The Geneva Convention'— Article 5.
12. AAB-410, letter 20 March 1943 from Nankervis to Dalgety, par.1 'Services personnel to be borne'; AAB-259, Letter SM 4932 10 March 1943.

13. For example David Milligan AB (Discharge Book No.R104327 — previous WWII vessels *Period, Nairana, Matthew Flinders* and *Kooliga*). Left *Kooliga* in Sydney 17 Dec 1942 signed on Centaur 10 March 1943 (It is highly likely his mate Alfred Ramage was engaged at the same time.) — correspondence with Dept. of Transport 24 April 1980.
14. AAB-410, Navy Minute Paper 19 Feb 1943 ". . . The rates of pay of Master and officers of "CENTAUR" are agreed with Owners and the officers concerned have asked to remain on Holts (Blue Funnel) rates of pay and conditions. The officers are permanent employees of Holts."
15. Ibid, Letter 20 Feb 1943 from Mr.A.N.Nankervis to Dalgety's Manager; AAD-197, After the loss of Centaur — 1 Sept 1944 covers admission of expenditure without supporting receipts.
16. AAB-259, Navy Minute Paper 25 March 1943. p.4. "The total cost of conversion . . . £55,000 . . ."
17. Ibid, Cable 11 Jan 1943 14h42Z/11.
18. PRO-479, Postgram: 21 Jan 1943 DST to ACNB; *Note* — DST letter 23 Jan 1943 notifies FO that both (Canadian vessel) *Lady Nelson* and *Centaur* are being fitted out as military hospital ships. On the same day DST notifies Canadian Military HQ, London, that the *Lady Nelson* ". . . will be included in the British series of military hospital ships and will be given the serial number 46 . . ."
19. Ibid, Cable: No.24 from Australia (Govt) to DO, 25 Jan 1943 8.20 a.m.; AAB-410, message (D241) to PM's Dept. from Navy 25 Jan 1943
20. Ibid, Cable: No. 27 from Australia (Govt) to DO, 27 Jan 1943 11.10 p.m.; AAB-410, Message: (D264) 27 Jan 1943 7.55pm.
21. PRO-723, Telegram: 31 Jan 1943 5.25 p.m. FO to Wash. D.C. (No. 720) to Berne (No. 424).
22. PRO-478, Telegram: (No. 1310) 18 March 1943 Berne to FO.
23. PRO-567, Telegram: (No.1701) 7 April 1943 Berne to FO.
24. PRO-759, Message: (No.1781) 8 May 1943 FO to Berne.
25. PRO-462, Telegram: (No.2450) 17 May 1943 7.50 p.m. from Berne to FO.
26. PRO-812, Nota Verbale: (No.30/14832) Roma, Li-1 LUG. 1943 XXI (21 July).
27. PRO-949, Verbalnote (No. R11714 Ang.III) Berlin, den 9 Juni 1943 (9 July).
28. *Herald.* 18 May 1943 (located in AAD-684), Clipping: 'Equipped For Tropics — Quick Job' (reports that 150 men working 68 hours a week for not quite eight weeks).
29. G.H.Gill, *Royal Australian Navy 1942-1945 (Vol.II)* (Canberra: Australian War Memorial, 1968), 252-253; Jurgen Rohwer, *Die-U-Boot Erfolge Der Achsenmachte 1939-1945* (Munchen: J.F. Lehmanna Verlag, 1968), 282.

30. F.A.Gaf, "Knowing the Law", *Proceedings*, June 1988, 58; refer also to Grider, G & Sims, L. *War Fish* (Little, Brown, 1958); and C.Blair Jr., "Wahoo's January Patrol", *Silent Victory — The U.S. Submarine War against Japan* (Vol.1); it is also instructive to read about the rescue operation of Allied prisoners of war after the USS *Pampanito* sank the *Rakuyo Maru* — A sanitised version is found in J.Blair and C.Blair Jr., *Return from the River Kwai*.
31. Graf, 58-59; J.W.Dower, *War Without Mercy — Race and Power in the Pacific War*
32. Z. Orita, *I-Boat Captain* describes this encounter as a slaughter (p.143). S.E.Morison ("Breaking the Bismark's Barrier, 22 July 1942 — May 1944 (Vol.VI) *History of the United States Naval Operations in World War II*. Boston. Little, Brown and Co 1950) notes that it was the "sickening business of killing survivors in boats, rafts or wreckage" (p.62). M.Caidin, *The Ragged Rugged Warriors* is more graphic — "The water was whipped and churned into a bloody froth, the blood mixing with chunks of flesh and oil from sunken ships" (p.41). Dower refers to this Allied action as 'grim butchery' (p.67); The skip-bombing technique is photographically illustrated in "Skip-Bombing — technique proves deadly in combat" *LIFE* (Vol 15 No.30, 15th Nov 1943, 93-99)

Chapter Four — AHS 47
1. Correspondence with Capt. Mike Carolyn, Port Phillip Pilot, 1991
2. AAB-729, 18 April 1943 Report No.1. to D.G.M.S. L.H.Q. Melbourne, from Lt-Col Manson, OCT. p.1 par.1-2. (hereafter Manson Report)
3. Correspondence with Fred Chidgey and Tom Hobden, 1981.
4. AAB-729, Manson Report, p.1 par.1-2.
5. Ibid., p.1 par.4.
6. Correspondence with Mrs B.Hindmarsh, 1991
7. Walker, 463
8. Goodman, 102; Correspondence with Capt. Rippon, 10 April 1980.
9. Correspondence with Ellen Savage, 27 May 1979.
10. Howlett, *The Oranje Story*, 63-64.
11. AAB-729, Manson Report p.1 par.5-6.
12. Ibid., pp.1-2 par.7.
13. Ibid., Lectures and Routine 26/3/43 to 1/4/43. p.4.
14. Correspondence with Rosemary Brown (nee Clark), 2 Feb 1979.
15. Ibid., p.4.
16. Foley (1982).
17. Correspondence with Fred Chidgey, 1979-1982.
18. Correspondence with Mr D.C.Allard, Naval Historical Center, Washington, 14 Feb.1980 — Of the 17 USS Submarines based at

Brisbane, Australia, in March and April 1943, all of them could
have been expected to render honours in friendly waters to Allied
Ships. *AMBERJACK* (SS-219), *GRAMPUS* (SS-207) and *TRITON*
(SS-201) were lost during this time period. A check of the logs of
the remaining 14 submarines by Brenda A.Beasley (Navy and Old
Army Branch, Military Archives Division) in April 1980 revealed
that only *GREENLING* recorded sighting a hospital ship.
19. Log, USS *Greenling*, Saturday, 3 April 1943.
20. AAB-729, Manson Report p.1 par.9.
21. Ibid., par.10-11
22. Ibid., par.12; AAD-409, Instructions No.004721 Personnel em-
    barkation and stores loaded at Brisbane carried out under the direc-
    tion of Lt A.A.Hinsch, Embarkation Staff Officer (note: this order
    is dated 6th April 1943)
23. AAB-729, Manson Report, par.13
24. Recollections by Chidgey, Cairnie and Rippon.
25. AAB-729, Manson Report, par.14.
26. Ibid., par.16 to par.24.
27. Ibid., letter SM 11817 8 April 1943; MP-259, Fielden's Report: 1
    Feb 1943 pp.9-10 'LIFEBOATS'.
28. Sakamoto, *Military History Series*, Vol.3. Ch.1. p.229
29. SCAP-1781, JICPOA item 5738 Serial ADM 141449 of 14 March
    1944; PRO-037 translation of captured Japanese document; En-
    tire four page order obtained by authors from Lt-Cmdr D.Stevens,
    RAN.
30. JAG-459 Trial Record: Exhibit No.31, Motohide Yanaba, pp 3-4
    outlines how the order passed through various channels.
31. Ibid., Ichioka recounted that Nakagawa maintained he saw the
    order, 208-9. However, the exact date of Nakagawa's first obser-
    vation of the order is not known.
32. *War Diary; Sixth Submarine Fleet, April 1 — April 30th, 1943*
    (10th April 1943, p1605 photocopy obtained from Lt-Cmdr
    Stevens, RAN); Sakamoto, *Military History Series*, Vol.3. Ch.1
    p.229 — Sub Activities March-June 1943.
33. Recollections of Capt. Doug McCormack, 1992.
34. Gill, *Royal Australian Navy 1942-1945*, 257-260; Rohwer, *Die-
    U-Boot Erfolge Der Achsenmachte 1939-1945,* 282; Jurgen Rohwer
    & G. Huemmeichen, *Chronology of War at Sea 1939-1945* (Ad-
    dlestone, Surrey: Ian Allan Ltd, 1974), 311.
35. Sakamoto, 171: Rohwer, 1968, 283

Chapter Five — SYDNEY SWANSONG
1. Gavin Long, "The Six Years War" *AWM*, 1973, 292-292.
2. Correspondence with Rita Dunstan (background material), 11 Feb.
   1980.

3. Ibid., p.2.
4. *Sydney Morning Herald*, 20 May 1943
5. Commander, South West Pacific Strike Force 700 100826
6. SCAP-783, Evidence: A.S.MacKinnon. 8 Aug 1944 p.46 — ref. QM 1487 13 May 1943 — "We instructed Sydney to embark this unit as per our signal QM.30690 on the 8th May 1943." p.46.
7. O'Sullivan, G.J. *Unit War History, Fifth Birthday* — celebration booklet (2/12 Field Ambulance Association: Kuching, 22 Nov 1945).
8. Correspondence with Gordon Rippon, 31 Jan 1980; SCAP-783, Evidence 31 Aug 1944 p.119: Allan Robert Dickson, a driver attached to the 2/12 Field Ambulance, provides detailed description.
9. SCAP-97, Summary of evidence given by Sir William Webb pages 52-77: L.M.Outridge (pp.74-75) "... he was instructed to carry his full war equipment table, being approximately 2,000 rounds of ammunition and 52 rifles; there were no other warlike stores on the ship ..." (p.74); SCAP-783, Evidence: R.G.Carter 14 Aug 1944 p.24
10. SCAP-783, Evidence: A.R.Dickson 31 Aug 1944 pp.119-122 — "THE COMMISSIONER: Did you see any other arms or ammunition on board? No. They had no ammunition? They (Despatch riders) had no ammunition issued to them, and we had none." (p.120).
11. AAB-299, Letter: SM.176 5 Jan 1943, USE OF HOSPITAL SHIPS (cancelled SM.18938 20 Oct 1942 relating to use of hospital ships) signed Col. L.E.Vail; see also, Letter: SM.2023 28 Jan 1943 signed Col. L.E.Vail.
12. AAB-299, Letter: 9484 (M53/4/473) 21 June 1943 from Col. Hector Clayton, H.Q. 1st.Aust Movement Control Group.
13. Ibid., Letters: SM.176 5 Jan 1943 and SM.2023 28 Jan 1943.
14. SCAP-783, Evidence: Albert Edward Blair 14 Aug 1944 p.18, relates "... what I was told by members of the crew ..."
15. SCAP-783, Evidence: W.McIntosh 30 Aug 1944, 103-104; Alexander F.Davidson, 112-115; SCAP-97 Summary of evidence, A.F.Davidson, 59; W.McIntosh, 70-71.
16. Ibid.,
17. SCAP-783, Evidence: W.McIntosh 30 Aug 1944, 104.
18. Foley, 1982, 103
19. Correspondence with Dept. of Transport, Melbourne (M358/27/23/1), 24 Apr 1980 — D.Milligan travelled to Australia as an AB on *Suevic*. Was discharged 30 Oct 1925; Roll of Honour: David Milligan (most likely local Oakleigh, Victoria newspaper)
20. Correspondence with Mrs Outridge
21. Alan E.Smith shared with the authors his correspondence from numerous Centaur relatives. Additional information culled from various newspaper articles.

22. SCAP-783 Evidence: A.E.Blair 14 Aug 1944 pp.18-19 — observed how the A.S.C. and Field Ambulance members were dressed.
23. Correspondence with Vince McCosker (background material), 26 Feb 1979.
24. Correspondence with Maurice Cairnie, 23 April 1979.
25. Gill, Lt G.H. *Royal Australian Navy 1942-1945 (Vol.II)*, 257

Chapter Six — *NORTHWARDS FROM SYDNEY*
1. SCAP-97, Richard M.Salt: Evidence 30 Aug 1944, p.86.
2. G.L.Williams, NCSO Sydney, to Captain Murray, 11 May 1943.
3. AAB-362, Exhibit A6: (Sgd) G.Rawson for RAN Naval Control Service, Sydney, Centaur routeing 11 May 1943.
4. Ibid.,
5. Ibid.,
6. AAB-858, Minute Paper: Additional report from Staff Officer (Intelligence) Brisbane re interrogation of Rippon concerning 'Green Route' telephoned through 1300X/ 16 May (1943); SCAP-97, Richard M.Salt: Evidence 30 Aug 1944, 86; Correspondence with Gordon Rippon.
7. O'Sullivan, 3; Correspondence with George McGrath (1992)
8. AAB-362, Ex. A6: RAN Naval Control Service, Sydney, Centaur routeing 11 May 1943.
9. SCAP-97, Summary of evidence: Leslie MacDonald Outridge, Oct 1944, 74.
10. *People Magazine,* 11 October 1950, 3-6.
11. Correspondence with Matthew D.Morris, 1 Feb 1980.
12. Darwin Clark, letter home — 6 April 1943; Correspondence with Rosemary Brown (nee Clark), 30 May 1979 — "They have some very funny records on this ship. Several Stanley Holloways ..."
13. Ibid., They could have accompanied the other Holloway records on Centaur listed by Darwin Clark ". . . One about Celia the Centipede who had 102 legs instead of the usual 100 . . . another about Anne Bullen's ghost in the Bloody Tower"; Correspondence with Rosemary Brown (nee Clark) 30 May 1979," . . . he was always 'good fun' . . . on his leaves . . . he knew all the words of the current popular songs!"
14. Darwin Clark, letter home — 26 April 1943.
15. Walker, *Medical Services of the RAN and RAAF, Series V,* 462 — Sister Savage describing her experiences.
16. SCAP-97, Summary of evidence: Leslie MacDonald Outridge, Oct 1944, 74.
17. Correspondence with Captain G.Rippon, 1991.
18. SCAP-783 Evidence: Richard M.Salt, 30 Aug 1944, 86-87.
19. Rippon, correspondence with the authors
20. *Argus*, Melbourne, 19 May 1943; SCAP-783, Evidence: Albert John

Taylor, 28 Aug 1944, "the whole ship was " ... brilliantly floodlit", 50; E.Smith described it as lit up like Luna Park.

21. SCAP-97, Summary of evidence: Ronald Charles Isherwood, 71; Kenneth George Murray, 77; Jack Howard Argent, 73; and John Lawrence Bayley, 67.
22. SCAP-783, Evidence: Albert Edward Blair, 14 Aug 1944.
23. Correspondence with Thomas Hobden, 9 May 1979.
24. Correspondence with Vincent McCosker, 10 Aug 1979.
25. SCAP-97, Summary of evidence: Richard Mumford Salt, 69.
26. SCAP-97, Summary of evidence: Ellen Savage, 68.
27. SCAP-97, Summary of evidence: James Carmichael Johnston, 72; SCAP-783, Evidence: James Carmichael Johnston, 14 Aug 1944, 139.
28. SCAP-783, Evidence: Maurice Albert Cairnie, 9 Aug 1944, 124.
29. Correspondence with Mabel Bromley (nee Hess), 10 May 1980.
30. SCAP-783, Evidence: George Richard Carter, 14 Aug 1944, 25.
31. Percy Kelly: Letter to sister quoted in Howlett, *The Oranje Story*, 64.
32. Roll of Honour: David Milligan, May 1943 — quotes by Alfred Ramage.
33. SCAP-783, Albert John Taylor: Evidence 28 Aug 1944, pp.51-52.
34. AAB-121, Sworn evidence: Richard Gordon Rippon, 27 May 1943, Q.5 & A.5; PRA, 24 May 1943, 128A, par.3; Correspondence with Gordon Rippon, 1979.

Chapter Seven — THREE MINUTES OF HORROR
1. Brigadier R.K.Fullford, *The Rous Battery on Moreton Island*, (17 page mimeo, 1985). Copy of paper obtained from Rupert Goodman.
2. Survivor comments have been obtained from the following 'summaries of the evidence' in **SCAP-97**, — Albert John Taylor, 57; Francis Thomas Reid, 58; Alexander Francis Davidson, 59; Allan Robert Dickson, 59-60; Maurice Albert Cairnie, 60-61; Sidney Charles Sandwell, 61; Leo Bidmead, 61-62; Cpl. Thomas Charles Malcolm, 62-63; Albert Edward Blair, 63; Staff-Sgt George Richard Carter, 64; Robert Kneale Westwood, 64-65; Samuel John Cullum, 65; Matthew Morris, 65; Sgt Leonard Richard Hooper, 65-66; Thomas Clark Hegarty, 66; Ronald Jones, 67; Dick Medcalf, 67; John Lawrence Bayley, 67-68; Ellen Savage, 68; Richard Mumford Salt, 68-69; William Cornell, 69; Marcus Jonassen, 70; William McIntosh, 70-71; James Alexander Rawlings, 71; Ronald Charles Isherwood, 71; Jesse Douglas Stutter, 72; Eric George Wallace Taylor, 72; James Carmichael Johnston, 72-73; Jack Howard Argent, 73; Leslie MacDonald Outridge, 74-75; George Sidney Murphy, 75; Clifford George Jones, 76; George Wilfred McGrath, 76;

and, Kenneth George Murray, 77. **SCAP-783,** Cpl Thomas Charles Malcolm, 10-17; Cpl Albert Edward Blair, 17-24; Staff-Sgt George Richard Carter, 24-26; Kevin Francis Reilly, 44-45; Alister Scobie Mackinnon, 46-47; Lt-Cmdr Anthony Victor Hesketh Dalzell, 48-49; Cpl Albert John Taylor, 49a-57; Capt. Richard Mumford Salt, 85-90; William McIntosh, 103-107; Albert Robert Dickson, 119-122; Maurice Albert Cairnie, 123-127; and, W.O.II James Carmichael Johnston, 139-141. Reports from newspaper articles of the time, additional descriptions appearing in journals and books.

Correspondence with survivors and/or family members including Milligan's original 1979-1981 correspondence with survivors, Jack Argent, Ron Bull, Maurice Cairnie, Fred Chidgey, Thomas Hobden, Ron Jones, Vincent McCosker, Matthew Morris, Rupert Paton, Richard Gordon Rippon, Ellen Savage, Ernest Smith, Albert Taylor; and more recent correspondence with George McGrath, Allan Pettiford and Len Hooper.

3. Percy Kelly: Letter to sister quoted in Howlett, *The Oranje Story*, 64.
4. Walker, *Medical Services on the RAN and RAAF, Series V,* 462-463.
5. Gordon Rippon: Letter to his father dated May 1943. A tape recording of Rippon reading his letter was made by Milligan at Sleights, Whitby, Yorkshire 5 Oct 1979. A copy is on deposit at The War Memorial, Audio-visual Section (hereafter Rippon tape).
6. Howlett, 65.
7. Walker, *Medical Services on the RAN and RAAF, Series V,* 462
8. William McIntosh: interview with Jean Devaney, "Bird of Paradise", 1945 (ML ref 940. 950901/D), 163-167.
9. Rippon Tape; Gordon Rippon: Letter to his father, May 1943.

Chapter Eight — A STRUGGLE FOR SURVIVAL
1. *Melbourne Age,* 20 May 1943.
2. *Daily Telegraph,* 19 May 1943, 3 — "Dr. Livingstone"
3. Devaney, 163-167
4. Recollections of Allan Pettiford, 1991.

Chapter Nine — A PITIFUL MUSTER
1. See Chapter Seven, footnote 2, reference to survivor information
2. Fred Chidgey: Two cassette tapes 'recollections of the sinking of the Centaur' Jan. 1980 (hereafter Chidgey tapes); and, Correspondence with Fred Chidgey, 6 Feb 1979–13 Dec 1982.
3. Rippon tape; Correspondence with Rippon 31 July 1979 and Oct 1979.
4. *People Magazine,* 11 October 1950, 3-6.

5. Francis Martin: The following text appears on the sketch Martin drew for the authorities — "Bow slightly raked, height 12ft, higher bow than stern. Large gun — barrel pointing slightly upwards — closer to tower than bow. 2 periscopes, height 3-4 feet. 3 men in conning tower. Noticed black peaked cap on one. Men seemed to be looking forward. Head and shoulders seen. Torpedo tube or aft gun much larger than fore gun & wide raised platform hexagon-shaped. Diameter of barrel probably 24". 10-12ft past gun (or tube), visibility ended. Length — good 300ft. (Appeared as long as CENTAUR, much larger than U.S. submarines in Brisbane River). Painted light grey." Under the sketch appears the following text "Martin stated — while on raft sighted object approx. ¾ mile away paddled with plank for 1 hour sighted above & heard faint thumping of engines. Submarine stationary but half hour later slowly moved off in Northerly Direction and on surface engine revving slowly." Sighting granted C2.
6. SCAP-783, Albert John Taylor, 55-56: Evidence 28 Aug 1944 ". . . but they called out 'Coo-ee', they coo-eed to us in the water, and I said to my mate 'Don't answer them, they are not our sailors.' *Why did you say that?* . . . 'I have always been led to believe that a sailor never uses that word "Coo-ee", that is a digger term; for a sailor's term they always say 'Ahoy'. From that time I gathered myself that they were not our sailors."
7. *The Sun*, Wednesday, 19 May 1943, 3 — 'Tributes To Courage of Woman Survivor'.
8. *Sydney Daily Telegraph*, Wednesday, 19 May 1943, 3 — 'Buried at Sea'; *The Telegraph*, Brisbane, Tuesday 18 May 1943, see Stan Morgan: "We could do nothing for him, and death came as a release from his suffering . . . we held a short burial ceremony at dawn."
9. Chidgey tapes
10. G.Odgers, 'Air War Against Japan 1943-1945' (AWM, Canberra, 19––) 147.
11. *The Sun*, Wednesday 19 May 1943, 3 — 'Tributes To Courage of Woman Survivor'.

Chapter Ten — *STARS AND STRIPES TO THE RESCUE*
1. National Archives Navy Biographies Branch, 0I-450. *Howard G.Corey*, b.22 May 1907, Chattanooga, Tennessee. Graduated Naval Academy (1930). Post Graduate School (1938). Executive Officer and Navigator USS *Henley* at Pearl Harbor 7 Dec 1941. Assumed command of USS *Mugford* 5 Dec 1942. From May 1944 to March 1945 was Captain on USS *Killen* where he received the Navy Cross for extraordinary heroism as Commanding Officer in action against the Japanese Fleet during the night Battle of Surigao

Strait, and the Silver Star Medal for conspicuous gallantry and intrepidity as Commanding Officer in Leyte Gulf, Phillippine Islands. He was awarded the Bronze Star Medal for meritorious achievement as Commanding Officer of the *Mugford.*

2. Log, USS *Mugford* (DD-389), Saturday, 3 April 1943, 04h00–08h00 (OOW. A.F. Johnson).
3. U.S. Naval History Division. *Dictionary of American Naval Fighting Ships. Vol IV.* (Washington: Government Printing Office, 1969),450. — *Mugford* (DD-389) was laid down 28 Oct 1935; launched 31 Oct 1936; Commissioned 16 Aug 1937: dp.1,500: l. 341'8"; b. 34'8"; dr. 9'10"; s. 36.5k.; cpl. 200; a. 4x5", 1 twin 40mm., 4x21" tt; el. Craven).
4. Ibid.; War Record, USS *Mugford* 10 Oct 1945, p.1 — 'moored port side to *Sacramento* with *Jarvis* moored port side to *Mugford.* *Mugford* went to general quarters at 0800. By 0810 she had downed 2 torpedo planes. At 0928 she shot down one Val dive bomber. At 1235 *Mugford* passed through the channel entrance and put to sea.
5. Log, War Record, USS *Mugford* 2-3.
6. Log USS *Mugford* (DD-389) — Saturday, 3 April 1943, 08h00–12h00 (OOW J.R.Shanahan).
7. Correspondence with James R.Cofer (Fire Control Striker Seaman 1/c), 17 Dec 1991. Cofer was a lookout on the bridge who helped identify survivors in the water.
8. Log, USS *Mugford* (DD-389) — Saturday, 3 April 1943, 12h00–16h00: 13h47 (OOW R.L.Clodins)
9. Ibid., 13h57 (OOW R.L.Clodins); and, attached to Log — H.G.Corey, *RESCUE OF SURVIVORS*, (mimeo: 18 May 1943) 1, par.2 (hereafter Corey)
10. Corey, 1 par.4.
11. Correspondence with William Walters Jr. (Seaman 2/c), 28 Nov 1991.
12. Corey, 1 par.3.
13. Correspondence with William Walters Jr. (Seaman 2/c), 28 Nov 1991 — Twenty-year-old Walters could hear screams and spotted survivors "here, there, and everywhere". He had only been onboard *Mugford* for one month and noted that for the young and inexperienced *Mugford* sailors (like himself) the *Centaur* survivors drove home the reality of the war — "We were simply scared . . . for the very first time we actually saw the horrible effects of war."
14. Correspondence with B.W.Middleton, Devon, England, 12 May 1979.
15. Correspondence with Finch Stowell (Fire controlman 2/c), 9 Dec 1991. Stowell retained a vivid recollection of the small number

317

of survivors and the presence of sharks swimming around the area so close to people.

16. Ibid.; AAB-858, Message: (EFD/MV 371) 15 May 1943 T.O.O. 1560607Z; AAD-684, Memos: Ref.031811, Ref.031812 (15 May 1943), Ref.031814 (16 May 1943); AAD-989, Messages: 16 May1943 to PM's Office from Dept. of Defence No.1 (ref.031811) & No. 2 (ref.031812).

17. Correspondence with Bill Records (Radioman), *The Timely Rescue* (mimeo: Nov 1991), 2;Correspondence with James R.Cofer (Fire Control Striker Seaman 1/c), 17 Dec 1991.

18. Correspondence with Frederick Chabot (Watertender 2/c), 27 Jan 1992. Chabot hesitated long enough "to take one last look at this magnificent woman before starting down the airlock to enter the fireroom".

19. Correspondence with Oree Weller (Radioman Third Class), 28 Nov 1991.

20. Correspondence with Joseph Dodson (Executive Officer), 27 Nov 1991

21. Correspondence with James R.Cofer, 17 Dec 1991. Cofer retained the memory of Sister Savage being so cold and her statement that "it was horrible".

22. Correspondence with Phillip Murray (Lt USN), 23 Oct 1991

23. Correspondence with Alfred Alexander (Machinist Mate 1/c), 12 Jan 1992.

24. Correspondence with Joseph Dodson (Executive Officer), 27 Nov 1991

25. Correspondence with Howard G.Corey (Captain), 29 Dec 1980.

26. Log, USS *Mugford* ". . . 15h23 Picked up last group of survivors. Total number of survivors on board 64 . . ." (OOW R.L.Clodins)

27. Ibid., "1532 Underway at 10 kts . . . Commenced search of area for remaining survivors . . . 1758 Completed searching wreckage area . . ."

28. Correspondence with George Johnston (Metalsmith 2/c), 28 Nov 1991.

29. Corey, *RESCUE OF SURVIVORS*, 2 (par.11)

30. Correspondence with Phillip Murray, 23 Oct. 1991

31. *Courier Mail*, (--) May 1943 — 'Ordeal in Darkness'

32. Log, USS *Mugford* — Sat. 3 April 1943, 20h00–24h00 (OOW J.R.Shanahan).

Chapter Eleven — THE SURVIVORS IN BRISBANE

1. D.Lockwood, "Australia's Pearl Harbour" (Rigby, Adelaide, 1966), p.25.

2. Cdr J.C.B.McManus, OBE, RAN. Supervising Intelligence Officer, NE Area 1943-45; b. Echuca, Vic, 11 March 1892.

3. Log, War Diary, USS *Helm* (388), Sunday, 16 May 1943. W.B.Braun, Lt-Cmdr USN Commanding; V.A.Dybdal, Lt USN, Executive Officer;

4. AAB-121, Memo: NQ.43/830 IJB/W, 18 May 1943 — Burch to Dir. of Nav. Melbourne, par.3.

5. Ibid., par.3-4.

6. AAD-684, Message D 1402 15h42 16 May 1943.

7. Recollections of Bill Bentson, member of MacArthur's staff in Brisbane in 1943.

8. Recollections of Sister Joffretta Case, AGH Greenslopes, 1943.

9. AAB-121, Memo: NQ.43/830 IJB/W, 18 May 1943 — Burch to Dir. of Nav. Melbourne, par.4.

10. Log, USS *Mugford* — Sunday, 16 May 1943, 00h45 'Commenced transferring survivors to authorities on dock.' — (OOW R.L.Clodins).

11. Correspondence with Vincent McCosker, 26 Feb 1979.

12. Log, USS *Mugford* — Sunday, 16 May 1943, 01h35 'Completed transferring survivors', (OOW R.L.Clodins); Corey, *RESCUE OF SURVIVORS*, 2 par.9-12.

13. Recollections of George McGrath.

14. Recollections of Sister Joffretta Case.

15. AAB-121, Memo: NQ.43/830 IJB/W, 18 May 1943 — Burch to Dir. of Nav. Melbourne, par.5-7.

16. AAD-989, Copy of message: D.1402. 15h24 (refs. 031811 & 031812) for PM's Office.

17. Log, War Diary, USS *Helm* (388) Sunday, 16 May 1943. p.159 — '00h26 sighted wreckage of life rafts . . . 07h46 Investigated two small objects which appeared to be buoyancy tanks from a lifeboat . . . 12h00 Discontinued search.'

18. Ibid., *Helm* identified *Lithgow* at 03h40 and 06h07. At 12h29 she also sighted five Australian corvettes, passing them to starboard.

19. Correspondence with Capt. Graham Haultain (son of Lt-Cmdr Theo Haultain), 1991

20. Goodman, 1992, 105

21. Written comment by Lt-Cmdr G.H.Gill, Naval Archivist and Historian, 21 May 1943 (source: Lt-Cmdr David Stevens, RAN)

22. Goodman, 'Sinking of Hospital Ship CENTAUR' (mimeo) 1985.

23. Fullford, 1991

24. AAD-989, Message: D.1402 (2nd. Memo 15 May 1943 for Dept. of Defence); AAD-684, Memo D.31814 16 May 1943.

25. AAD-684, Message CS.1958 15h55 16 May 1943 — Copies BXC.384 to PM from MacArthur.

26. Recollections of Allan Pettiford.

27. Correspondence from Mrs E.Thompson (formerly Fortier) 1991.

28. Copy of telegram in the possession of Chris Milligan.
29. Memo, No. SOI185/43 18 May 1943 — 'CENSORSHIP — SHIPPING LOSSES.' signed by Capt.J.Armstrong for Rear-Admiral-in-Charge, HMA Naval Establishments, Sydney, to Secretary, Naval Board, Melbourne. (Source unknown).
30. AAD-684, Message BXM 363 18 May 1943 refers to Q.3877 17 May to PM from MacArthur; also, CRS.A989 BXM363 9h25 18 May 1943.
31. AAD-989, Cable No.120 17 May 1943; also, PRO-432 Cable No.120.
32. AAD-989, Message M.2010 13h40
33. AAD-684, Message BXM363 9h21 18 May 1943 refers to MacArthur's Q.3877 to PM.
34. PRO-432, Message No.171808B, Admiralty to ACNB, and Message No.171811Z original message from B.A.D. Washington; also AAD-989 Message — (ref MAB.250) 10h52 18 May 1943 from Sect. Dept. Defence to Defence Secretariat, Brisbane.
35. AAD-684, Message BXM367 11h40 18 May 1943; Also, AAD-989, Message — BXM367.
36. Ibid., Message BXM368 12h07.
37. AAD-989, 'Draft Statement By The Prime Minister' 18 May 1943; also, message MAB.251 18 May 1943 18h45 text of PM's statement transmitted to MacArthur.

Chapter Twelve — SHOCK WAVES

1. *The Telegraph,* Brisbane, 18 May 1943 — 'Glad He Was Not Aboard'
2. Correspondence with Rita Dunstan, 11 Feb 1980.
3. *Daily Telegraph,* 19 May 1943, 3 — 'Went Down With Ship'.
4. London *Daily Telegraph,* 19 May 1943
5. AAD-684, Message BMX368 12h07 18 May 1943 — G.H.Q. Southwest Pacific Area, Communique No.401, May 18 1943.
6. Ibid., Message No.967 3.00 p.m. 18 May 1943 to Shedden from Hodgson.
7. Ibid., Message BXM.374 12h00 19 May 1943. MacArthur to PM.
8. Ibid., Message 967 3:00 p.m. 18 May 1943
9. Ibid., refer to Message No.962 10h10 18 May 1943.
10. Ibid., Message M2027 11h07 Shedden replies with Army totals.
11. AAD-989, Message: D.1430 17h59 18 May 1943 — To Shedden from Col. Hodgson reply to 967; AAD-684 — Letter (032303) 19 May 1943 from Navy — Explains how mix up in figure count evolved; Memorandum (S.M.12353) 20 May 1943 number of Army survivors.
12. AAD-989, Message BXM.374 12h00 19 May 1943. MacArthur to PM's MAB.251.

13. AAD-684, Letter (032303) 19 May 1943 par.3.
14. *The Telegraph* Brisbane, Tuesday 18 May 1943, p.1.
15. *Herald*, "Shows Country's Real Danger" 19 May 1943, p.8
16. AAD-989, Cable No.110; PRO-731, Cable No.124 "Your kind message of sympathy . . . greatly appreciated by Government and Australian people. John Curtin"
17. AAD-684, Message: No. 988/I.20817
18. PRO-731 Letter: 1 June 1943 to Foreign Office, London. Cable to International Red Cross at Geneva . . . "AUSTRALIAN RED-CROSS INFORM US THEY HAVE COMMUNICATED WITH YOU PROTESTING AGAINST SINKING HOSPITAL SHIP CENTAUR STOP BRITISH REDCROSS IN SYMPATHY WITH THIS ACTION REQUEST YOU MAKE A FORMAL PROTEST TO JAPANESE RED-CROSS. BRITISH REDCROSS HEADQUARTERS 1630."
19. *Age*, 'Replacement of Centaur' 21 May 1943; *Argus*, 'Workers' Gift for Replacement', 20 May 1943.
20. AAS-243, Telegram: FC 1915 3 March 1943 from FEDCENSOR to PRESCENSOR SYDNEY — K.20 Action Sheet issued 7.50 p.m. (e.g. Mrs Still *Smith's Weekly* notified 13 March at 11h27).
21. Ibid., Letter 27 May 1943 (Telephoned from Brisbane 4.10 p.m.)
22. Spector (1985, 451-2) recounts an American example of an unauthorised disclosure or security leak reported in the *Chicago Tribune*. Just after the Battle of Midway the paper reported the US Navy had advance knowledge of the whereabouts of the Japanese fleet. This was picked up and broadcast on radio, and then repeated in public by a politician condemning the newspaper for making it public! The US Navy and its codebreakers were beside themselves. They tried to prosecute the reporter. It was unsuccessful when the Navy refused to explain why the enemy could benefit from the newspaper report.
23. AAS-37, letter: SPC/9914 28 May 1943.
24. Ibid., letter: 31 May 1943.
25. Ibid., letter: SPC/9937 1 June 1943.
26. Ibid., letter: 3 June 1943.
27. Ibid., letter: SPC/9977 8 June 1943.
28. Howlett, 55

Chapter Thirteen — THE WAR OF WORDS: PROTEST AND COUNTER PROTEST

1. AAD-989, Message M.2021 17 May 1943 Hodgson to Shedden.
2. Ibid., Draft Telegram to High Commissioner, London 18 May 1943 (draft with edits).
3. Ibid., Message No. M.2019 17 May 1943 Shedden to Prime Minister (par.2)
4. AAD-684, Cable No.120 0. 13256 17 May 1943 to Dominion Office, London from PM.

5. Ibid., Cable No.109 No.961/I.20556 17 May 1943 (received 18 May 1943) from Dominion Office, London to PM. — refers to No.120 from Berne .. Japanese informed 5 Feb 1943.
6. Ibid., Message No.967 3.00 p.m. 18 May 1943 to Shedden from Hodgson.
7. Ibid., Extracts from Short Wave Broadcasts. Tokio, 15 May 1943.
8. *Daily Telgraph*, Thursday, 20 May 1943 'Japs Claim U.S. Attacks'.
9. *The New York Times*, Wednesday,19 May 1943, 4 — 'Japan Accuses US'.
10. AAD-684, Extracts from Short Wave Broadcasts — 9 April 1943 (alleged attack *URARU MARU* 3 April 1943); 14 April (Japanese Hospital Ship attacked by American plane); 28 April (25 April *BUENOS AIRES MARU* . . . attacked by American sub); 29 April (repeat of 28 April); 30 April (*URARU MARU* arrives back in port . . .'our enemies are not human beings but wild beasts')
11. SRNS-0406, Summary: as of 24th May 1943, par. "IV Japanese Hospital Ships . . .", pp.2-3; AAD-989, Cable No.302 I.21148 from Dominion Affairs, London. 22h20 21 May 1943 concerning attacks on six Japanese hospital ships — *ARABIA MARU; AMERICA MARU; MANILA MARU; URAL MARU; HUSO MARU; BUENOS AIRES MARU*, Gill, 260.
12. Ibid., Cable No.73 0. 13401/18429 18 May 1943 — PM to Bruce, London.
13. PRO-731, Letter 19 May 1943 to Eden from Bruce.
14. Ibid., Background paper 20 May 1943 by Mr D.L.Stewart
15. Ibid., Letter 19 May 1943 to Eden from Bruce.
16. Ibid., Background paper 20 May 1943 by Mr D.L.Stewart
17. Ibid.,
18. Ibid.,
19. Ibid., Cable S.103 21 May 1943 "FOR PRIME MINISTER. MOST SECRET." from Bruce; outward cable filed in AAD-989 Cable: No.S.103.
20. AAD-989, External Affairs Memorandum for Prime Minister: 22 May 1943 — suggests concurrence with Bruce
21. Ibid., Cable No.77 22 May 1943 from Curtin to Bruce
22. PRO-731, Cable No.2014 5h45 22 May 1943 notification to Swiss from FO. Cable No.2015 7h20 — text of protest forwarded.
23. Ibid., Cable No.2804 5 June 1943 4h32 p.m.
24. Ibid., Background paper 20 May 1943 by Mr D.L.Stewart
25. AAD-396, Cables (D. No.301 No.1017/I.21038) and (D.No.302 No.1019/I.21142) 20 May 1943.
26. Ibid., message: (M.2120) 13h38 22 May 1943 — Mr. Quealy suggests to The Secretary that MacArthur be referred to; Letter 24 May 1943 from John Curtin to Gen. MacArthur seeks observations of the General as early as possible.

27. AAD-989 — EXTRACT FROM DEPT. OF INFORMATION BACKGROUND dated 17th May. (General source G.H.Q. Brisbane).
28. AAD-396, Teleprinter 11h41 1 June 1943, text of MacArthur's (6871) forwarded; Letter (6871) dated 30 May 1943.
29. Ibid., Letter (6871) dated 30 May 1943 MacArthur's reply to Curtin.
30. Ibid., Cablegram (No. 142) 0. 16001/4/5/9/12/13 repeated to PM of NZ as No.106.
31. AAD-399, Message (CS.1995) par.1(A) 14h28 20 May 1943 — to Chief of General Staff from Secretary, Dept. of Defence.
32. Ibid., Message (CS.1995) par.2. 14h28 20 May 1943
33. Ibid., Message (D.1499) 12h08 23 May 1943 agreed to by "C-in-C SWPA and our C-in-C ..."
34. Ibid., Message: CS 2080 29th May 1943 — PM's views to Chief of Naval Staff; Message: M.2211 31st May 1943 Chief of Naval Staff views and concerns to PM
35. Ibid., Letter: 035108 30th May 1943 to Defence from Navy — Admiralty views requested.
36. Ibid., Message BXM.479 1st June 1943 to Col. Wilson from Secretary. C-in-C takes exceptions ... PM to be informed; Letter: 5th June 1943 to Minister of the Navy Makin from Prime Minister Curtin "The Chief of the Naval Staff infringed the directive by submitting the matter to the Prime Minister, but the Naval Board had committed the further impropriety, after being informed that it was an operational decision, of recommeding that the ... Government ... confer with the United Kingdom and Washington ... before reaching a final decision. The Naval Board has further violated the directive by referring the matter directly to the Admiralty (which, according to Curtin was a) ... contravention of the instructions that communications between Governments must proceed through the channel laid down, and the attention of the Navy Department has previously been drawn to the non-observance of these directions". Five days later MacArthur received a copy of Makin's dressing down.
37. Walker, *Medical Services of the RAN and RAAF,* 502.
38. AAD-399, Cable from Admiralty T.O.O. 281134B (repetition of JSM 972 dated 9 June)
39. Ibid., (Part 1–Part 9).
40. Ibid., (Part 10); also paraphrase of message.
41. AAD-399, Letter 17 July 1943 from John Curtin to Gen. MacArthur (Attachment 'PARAPHRASE OF MESSAGE RECEIVED FROM ADMIRALTY BY AUSTRALIAN COMMONWEALTH NAVAL BOARD ON 30TH JUNE 1943').
42. Ibid., Letter No.8254 19 July 1943 from MacArthur to Prime

Minister; Message BXM.685 09h42 20 July 1943 copy of Letter
8254 from Brisbane Secretariat to Secretary.

43. Ibid., Cable No.191 26 July 1943. (Note: message D.2427 13h00
23 July 1943 from Shedden to Secretary, External Affairs "In view
of General MacArthur's position in relation to the United States
Chiefs of Staff, it is suggested that no reference should be made
to General MacArthur's views in the reply which is sent to Domi-
nions Office No.165").
44. Ibid., Letter No.049479 30 July 1943.
45. Ibid., Letter No.052086 10 Aug 1943. Navy to Secretary, Dept.
of Defence; also, Message: MAB 479 18h15 16 Aug 1943 — MacArthur advised by Shedden about repainting "Manunda"
46. Ibid.,
47. *Argus*, 2 Dec 1943 — 'Japs Deny They Sank Centaur'
48. *Herald*, 2 Dec 1943 — 'Centaur Sinking "Too Silly" — Mr Forde'
49. PRO-455, Cable No.6035 15 Dec 1943.
50. Ibid., FO note to High Commission for Australia, 20 Dec 1943.
51. AAD-989, Cable No.244 I.51612 SC. 900. received 15h08 26 Dec
1943.
52. AAD-396, Cable D.1192 I.51836 SC216, 28 Dec 1943 rec'd 9.25
p.m. 29 Dec. '43
53. Ibid., Cable No.86 I.2191 SC293 rec'd 19 Jan 1944.
54. Ibid., Cable Copy (W. 356/12/49) Registry No.W.7242/379/49. FO
10 Jan 1944 par.3-6.
55. Ibid., Letter 14207 21 Jan 1944 from MacArthur to Curtin — attachment letter 30 Aug 1943 AG560 (28 Aug 1943) B to Chief of
Staff, Wash. D.C. from Maj. Gen. R.K.Sutherland, Chief of Staff.
56. Ibid., (J. 3. A.6/226) Jap. Dip. Note with reference to W.356/12/49
(10 Jan 1944) a further telegraphic communication — Swiss Legation, Special Division, 10 May 1944.
57. Ibid., FO Diplomatic Note with reference to Swiss No.J 3. A.6/226
(10 May 1944) the FO "would be glad if the following reply could
be returned to the Japanese Government's protest" — 15 July
1944.
58. Ibid., (W.14157/12/49) J.3. A.6./460. Jap. Diplomatic Note with
reference to W.10997/12/49 (15 July 1944) a further telegraphic
communication — Swiss Legation, Special Division, 29 Sept 1944.
59. Ibid., Circular despatch D. No.156 to The Prime Minister, 14 Nov
1944.
60. Ibid., Circular despatch D. No.168 to The Prime Minister, 12 Dec
1944.
61. Ibid., Circular despatch D. No.32 to The Prime Minister, 5 March
1945.
62. Ibid., Draft FO Diplomatic Note with ref. to Swiss No.J 3. A.6/460
(29 Sept 1944). P.M's file No.D.61/2/5.

Chapter Fourteen — UNDER THE LEGAL MICROSCOPE

1. Webb, Hon. Sir William Flood, KBE 1954; Kt 1942; LLD (Hon) Queensland; Justice of the High Court of Australia, 1946-58, retired; b. 1887 d. 11 Aug 1972; Japanese Atrocities Commissioner, 1943; Chm War Crimes Comm, 1944-46, visited England as such in 1944-45 to appear before United Nations War Crimes Commission presided over by Lord Wright; Communicator Censorship Commissioner, 1944 (under National Security Regulations); Member, Senate of the University of Queensland, 1944-46; President of the International Military Tribunal for the Far East for the trial of major Japanese War Criminals (including four former Prime Ministers of Japan: Tojo, Hirota, Hiranuma and Koiso, 1946-48; ... (additional bio info in General Editors, *Who Was Who 1971-1980 (Vol. VII).* (Adam and Charles Black: London, 1980), 840.
2. Appointed to Commission 23 June 1943
3. Appointed to Commission 8 June 1944.
4. SCAP-97, First Schedule. National Security (Inquiries) Regulations. National Security (General) Regulations. 96-97.
5. Ibid., Time and Places of Hearings. 104.
6. Ibid., Second Schedule — Names and Descriptions of Witnesses (in alpha order). 98-103. (Authors Note: These are summaries of evidence).
7. SCAP-783, contains authenticated true copies (by Lt-Col Thomas F.Mornane — VX 102782) of the official transcripts of evidence taken before His Honour, Sir William Webb of: Malcolm, Blair, Carter, Reilly, Mackinnon, Dalzell, Taylor (A.J), Salt, McIntosh, Dickson, Cairnie, and Johnston (J.C.).
8. Ibid., evidence of Cpl Thomas Charles Malcolm p.17 — *THE COMMISSIONER:* This evidence is classified by the Defence Authorities as most secret. You will not mention that you gave evidence? (Cpl. Malcolm) Very well, Sir. *COMMISSIONER:* We want you to come back at half past two and read your evidence, which will be written out by that time, and make any corrections you think fit. Also, if you think of anything you have forgotten tell us then what it is. I want to make sure we get the whole of your evidence? (Cpl. Malcolm) Thank you, Sir.
9. Ibid., evidence of Major A.S.MacKinnon. 46-47.
10. Ibid., evidence of Lt-Cmdr Anthony Victor Hesketh Dalzell, RNVR. 48-49.
11. SCAP-97, 52-57.
12. Ibid., 54-56.
13. SCAP-783
14. AWM54, Written records, 1939-45 war item: No. 505/4/16 — Letter No. 2841, 2892 SDM No.20 3 Dec 1945 from K.Nakamura,

representing the Imperial Japanese Second Demobilization Minister. (Letter obtained from Lt-Cmdr D.Stevens, RAN).

15. SCAP-783.
16. Getty, George Franklin II; b. Los Angeles, 9 July, 1924 d. 6 June 1973; son of J.Paul and Jeannette (DeMont) G; Student Princeton, 1942; Served as 1st Lt. AUS, 1942-47; He spent 16 months in Philippines, Malaya and Japan as a war-crimes investigator in the legal section of the Supreme Commander for Allied Powers. (for additional bio. info refer to *The New York Times Biographical Edition* — June 1973, "George F.Getty 2d, Oldest Son Of Oil Billionaire, Dies on Coast", 965); *Time,* 'Milestones', 18 June 1973; Who's Who In Finance and Industry (18th. Ed) 1974-75, 301; and, Lenzner, R. (1985). *The Great Getty.* NY: Crown Publishers, 145-169.
17. SCAP-783, Memo 14 June 1946
18. Ibid., Letter No.3081(PM) 24 June 1946 from Mr Katsube, Chief of Liaison Section, Central Liaison Office (C.L.O) (Imperial Japanese Government) to GHQ, SCAP.
19. Ibid., Request for Interrogation, 27 June 1946,
20. Ibid., Report of Shichiji Interrogation, 8 July 1946.
21. Ibid., Report of Komazawa Interrogation, 8 July 1946.
22. Ibid., Report of Nakagawa Interrogation, 8 July 1946.
23. Ibid., Report of Kusaka Interrogation,(pp.1-2),19 July 1946
24. Ibid.,
25. Ibid., Report of Nakagawa Interrogation, 9 Oct 1946.
26. Ibid.,
27. Ibid., Report of Investigation Division by 1st Lt., Getty (Infantry), 14 Oct 1946.
28. Ibid., Correspondence (56) WC 231 Australian Div. SCAP to Inv. Div. SCAP 29 Aug 1946
29. Ibid., Correspondence of Investigation Div. SCAP to Australian Div. SCAP, 1 Nov 1946.
30. Ibid., Report of Investigation by 1st Lt Getty (Infantry)., 7 Nov 1946.
31. Ibid., Correspondence by Getty to CLO, 8 Nov 1946.
32. Ibid., Correspondence of CLO No.6264 (PM) 27 Nov 1946.
33. Ibid., Correspondence by Getty to CLO, 2-3 Dec 1946.
34. Ibid., Correspondence by CLO No.6569(PM) 10 Dec 1946.
35. PRO-106, Telegram B89 27 June 1946 from Br. Minor War Crimes (BMWC), Tokyo to ALFSEA — Lt William Salter RNVR — belonged to Naval Intelligence Office UKLIM Tokyo where he was appointed by Admiralty to investigate shipping cases connected with sinkings by submarines. His naval experience and ability to speak and read Japanese made him very valuable as an investigator/interrogator of Japanese submarine crews. He was investigating British, and certain Dutch and American cases at the same time.

The BMWC unit worked closely with Salter on these cases.

36. SCAP-783, Report of Investigation by 1st Lt Getty (Infantry), 17 Dec 1946; Alden, Japanese Submarine Losses in World War II, *Warship International* (1985) details how published articles differ concerning lossess. See pp.17-18 for *I-178*.
37. PRO-041, Letter (M.02750/46) 18 Nov.1946 — Adm. to War Crimes Section, the FO (par. 2).
38. Ibid., (par.4).
39. Ibid., (par.3).
40. SCAP-783, Three Reports of Investigation (i) 21 Jan 1947; (ii) 27 Jan 1947; and, (iii) 18 Feb 1947 all by Lt William Salter, RNVR.
41. Ibid., Report of Inv. by Maj. B.B.Rogers J.A.G.D. (Interrogation of Komazawa), 14 Jan 1948
42. SCAP-783, Report of Investigation by Mr Joseph F.Sartiano 30 Aug 1947
43. Ibid., Report of Investigation by Maj. B.B.Rogers J.A.G.D.(p.3), 14 Jan 1948
44. Ibid., Document No.34895 26 Sept 1947 ATIS translation (Japanese to English) of Masayuki Ikezawa's statement (4 pgs.)
45. Ibid., Report of Komazawa Interrogation, 14 Nov 1947.
46. Ibid., Report of Nakagawa Interrogation, 18 Dec 1947.
47. Ibid., Report of Investigation by Maj. B.B.Rogers, (p.5) 14 Jan 1948.
48. Ibid., 5 pages.
49. AAB-858, Memo (Ref.4087) 16 Feb 1948 for Dept. of the Navy from Army.
50. Ibid., Letter (Ref.01095) 20 Feb 1948 for Dept. of the Army from Navy.
51. SCAP-783, Report of Investigation by Maj. B.B.Rogers (p.3, 1.24) 14 Jan 1948.
52. Ibid., Report of Investigation by Capt. Robert E.Miller QMC., 30 Apr 1948.
53. Ibid.,
54. Yokahama war crimes trial titled *Ichioka vs. The United States of America* culminated in the sentencing of four former admirals (and others) of the Imperial Japanese Navy being collectively found responsible for more than 800 deaths.
55. Shinsho Hanayama, *The Way of Deliverance.* (New York: Charles Scribner's Sons, 1950). Hanayama was the Buddhist Chaplain at Sugamo Prison for three years. His account of the last few hours of the condemned is detailed in his Ch.7 — 'One Minute After Midnight, Dec 23, 1948'.
56. SCAP-783, Handwritten note by Capt. Miller on Report of Investigation 20 Dec 1948 indicating that the file was returned by Salter 23 Dec 1943.

Centaur

CONCLUSION

1. Lt-Cmdr Stevens (mimeo) — *War Diary: Sixth Submarine Fleet, April 1–April 30, 1943* p.1605.
2. SRN 7080.
3. SRN 7125.
4. Orita, 195 — "And 6th Fleet headquarters required reports from us too often, again making for easy discovery through radio detection."; (for example) Lt-Cmdr Stevens has plotted 13 DF Fixes and 2 DF Indications (at various radii); 2 sightings by aircraft, and one contact by aircraft along the Australian Eastern Coastline for the period 3 May–31 May 1943.
5. SRNS 0406 (24 May 1943) — 3 May 1943 Foreign Minister Shigemitsu advised Berne, Switzerland of alleged Allied attacks on 5 Japanese Hospital ships.
6. SRN 7080.
7. SCAP-783, 11 Dec 1947 Maj. Rogers requests a demand be placed on the Japanese Government to produce for interrogation Hajime Obori — best address they had was Hiroshima City. No indication in the Investigation File that Obori was located or interrogated.
8. SRN 6963 (17 May 1943) — "Tomorrow, the 18th at 0500 the I-178 (course 0o) enters via South Channel"; SRN 7707 (31 May 1943) — "Submarine I-178 will carry out firing practice . . . from 0930-1530, 2 June, outside the South Channel. Exercise caution!"; Lt-Cmdr Stevens located in Canberra microfilm copies of National Archives SRH 'Ultra History' series — SRH 104 ('Enemy Combat Ship Losses' 1 Aug 1945) and SRH 263 ('Japanese Submarine Sinkings' 29 Nov 1945). Both indicate that, at that time, the loss of I-178 was established in part by ULTRA information (i.e. SRN 7707).
9. Log, *SC669*: 11.00–11.58am 29 May 1943 made a number of runs on a submarine. Fired mousetraps, dropped depth charges. At 12.05pm two air bubbles observed. At 4.43pm. DD449 USS *Nicholas* heard bubbles at sound buoy No.4 — 5.40pm nothing unusual sighted, results negative. At 2.30am 30 May *Nicholas* ordered *SC669* to investigate sound buoys Nos.4, 5, 6. At 3.10am results negative. At 8.01am *SC669* ordered to resume regular patrol.
10. Roscoe, 'Patterson Kills I-178', 237-238.
11. Orita, 165.
12. *Canberra Times*, 19 Sept 1988, 'Centaur: atrocity or incidental tragedy?' — I.D.Marshall; 'Hospital ship spared' — C.Kennedy; and 'Another volley in the Centaur debate' — A.Garland.
13. Report of Proceedings: 1 April 1943, War Diary Brisbane Command, 'H.M.A.S. "GYMPIE'S" ACOUSTIC MINE'. Report located

in a Naval Historical File (Canberra) by Lt-Cmdr Stevens.
14. SCAP-783, evidence of Lt-Cmdr Dalzell, 48-49.
15. Letter, No. SOI186/53, 18 May 1943, CENSORSHIP — SHIPPING LOSSES, Armstrong to Dir. of Naval Intelligence. Probable source AAB .
16. AAD-883, letter 20 May 1943 & 28 May 1943, No.GS/328/Int, Col. Merle-Smith to Col. Diller.
17. Ibid.,
18. Ibid., 19 May 1943 ("U" FS Sec) — "Investigation of Rumour Concerning Hospital Ship Centaur".
19. AAB-299, Letter 26 May 1943, Gerrand to Curtin.
20. Ibid., Letter No. M53/4/473, 21 June 1943, Col. Clayton to Movement Section, LHQ, Melbourne.
21. AAD-684, Letter 30 June 1943, Spender to Curtin.
22. AAD-684, Advisory War Council Minute No.1199, 3 June 1943.
23. *Western Advocate*, 19 Aug 1988, 'World War II outrage: ammunition on Centaur'.
24. It was reported in the Australian press that Minister of the Navy Makin believed an enemy spy ring was watching ships in Australian ports. He saw sinister implications in the type of ships chosen by enemy submarines for attack which indicated previous information being obtained.
25. SCAP-783, evidence of Bill McIntosh, 104.
26. IMT, Exhibit No.2106 'Interrogation of General Hiroshi Oshima, 1 Feb 1946', 15,187–15,199; JAG-455, Trial Review, Spurlock's summary of events, 36-38.
27. SCAP-78, Lt Salter's reports on Mito and the Japanese Submarine Secret Operational Order.
28. Ibid., also refer to extract of order in PRO-037, 15 Nov 1945. mimeo copy of entire order obtained from Lt-Cmdr Stevens.
29. JAG-459, Trial Record, *US vs Hisashi Ichioka et al.,* 208-209.
30. Ibid., Exhibit No. 31: translation of statement by Motohide Yanaba; JAG-455, Ichioka reported that when he took over command of the 8th. Sqd. in August 1943 Ariizumi ". . . told him that the order of the 6th Fleet had been complied with up to that time" (p.39).
31. Orita, 262.
32. Orita, 143; refer to Chapter 3, note 32.
33. Refer to Roscoe, *Pigboats*, 404-405, — the sinking of *Awa Maru* by USS *Queensfish* 1 April 1945; refer to Ch.13, notes 8-11; see also Graf (1988) for the sinking of the Japanese Hospital Ship *America Maru* that Brittin (1986) notes was not painted white, or marked, or illuminated.
34. Orita, 143. Events in the Indian Ocean were the machine-gunning of Allied merchant crew survivors by Japanese submarines.

EPILOGUE
1. Walker, Use of Hospital Ships (Army Instruction July 1944), 508-509.
2. D.Foxwell & R.Jolley, "The RFA Argus: a gas-tight floating field hospital", *International Defense Review*, 2/1991.
3. Carpenter & Polmar, 105; Jentschura, 172; Sakamoto, Vol.3 Table VII, 484.
4. Roscoe, *Destroyer Operations in World War II*, 442.
5. War Record — USS *Mugford* (DD-389), 10 Oct 1945, Commanding Officer to Secretary of Navy. (mimeo copy forwarded to authors by former Mugford crew member John R.Doyle, Iowa); United States Navy Department, *Dictionary of American Naval Ships*, (Vol. IV), 450-451.
6. IMT, 15,153-15,154.
7. SPR-222, Nakagawa's prison file.
8. Toshio Kusaka, while commanding I-26, was accused of machine-gunning merchant crew survivors in early 1944.
9. JAG-459, Trial record, 172,175.
10. JAG-455, Trial Review, 56-57.
11. SCAP-782, File 520, Report by Capt. W.Hill of *British Chivalry*. On 22 Feb 1944 Hill was captured by Japanese Submarine I-37. While standing on the submarine deck, waiting to be executed, he was approached by the submarine commander (Nakagawa) who asked if he were married and had children. Hill replied yes, and indicated five children. "A smile illuminated his (Nakagawa's) face; and it is this I consider I owe my deliverence . . ." (p.13); Hill also reported that later on ". . . when speaking to the commander . . . he told me that it was the order of the Imperial Nippon Navy, that no survivors must be taken from British and American ships" (p.14).

INDEX

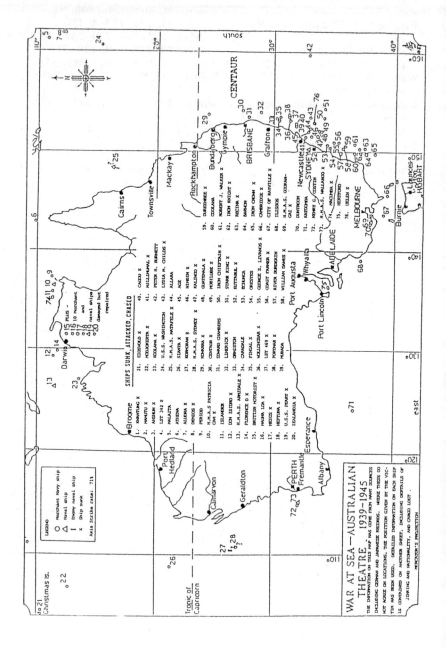

WAR AT SEA — AUSTRALIAN
THEATRE . 1939 – 1945

THE INFORMATION ON THIS MAP HAS CODE FROM MANY SOURCES
INCLUDING GERMAN AND JAPANESE RECORDS. WHERE THESE DO
NOT AGREE ON LOCATIONS, THE POSITION GIVEN BY THE VIC-
TIM HAS BEEN USED. DETAILED INFORMATION ON EACH SHIP
IS CONTAINED ON ANOTHER SHEET, INCLUDING DETAILS OF
JOINING AND NATIONALITY, AND CARGO LOST .
MERCATOR'S PROJECTION

SHIPS SUNK, ATTACKED, CHASED

1. RANATLAG X
2. MAMITU X
3. ANSKAN X
4. LST 342 X
5. MALATA
6. ATHINA
7. ALLERA X
8. DENGOS X
9. PERIOD
10. H.M.A.S PATRICIA CAN X
11. ISLANDER
12. DON ISIDRO X
13. H.M.A.S. ARMIDALE X
14. FLORENCE D X
15. BRITISH MOTORIST X
16. MAWA LOA X
17. MEIGS X
18. NEPTUNA X
19. U.S.S. PEARY X
20. ZEALANDIA X
21. EDSVOLD X
22. MOLDOORTA X
23. KOOLAMA X
24. U.S.S. WASHINGTON
25. H.M.A.S. MATAFELE X
26. SIANTA X
27. KORORAN X
28. H.M.A.S. SYDNEY X
29. KOARPA X
30. CENTAUR X
31. EDARD CHAMBERS
32. LIMERICK X
33. ORMISTON
34. CARADALE
35. FINGAL X
36. HOLLGREDAR X
37. LST 469 X
38. PORTMAR X
39. MAMANA
40. CAZOU X
41. MULLIMIMAL X
42. PETER H. BURNETT
43. LYDIA M. CHILDS X
44. ALLARA
45. AGE
46. NIMBIN X
47. KALINO X
48. GUATAWALA X
49. MORELLBE X
50. IRON CHIEFTAIN X
51. STARR KING X
52. KATTABUL X
53. ECHUNCA
54. ORESTES
55. IRON CROWN X
56. CAMBRIDGE X
57. GEORGE S. LIVANES X
58. COAST FARMER X
59. DUREENBEE X
60. COOLANA
61. ROBERT J. WALKER X
62. IRON KNIGHT X
63. RECINA X
64. BAROON
65. IRON CROWN X
66. CAMBRIDGE X
67. CITY OF RAYVILLE X
68. RIVER BURDEKIN
69. WILLIAM DAWES X
70. H.M.A.S. GOORAN-GAI X
71. ILLISOS
72. DUNTROON
73. KATOOMBA
74. HENRY G. COSTIN
75. H.M.A.S. MILLIARD X
76. MOCIMBA X
77. BEXFORD
78. UHLEN X

LEGEND
O MERCHANT NAVY SHIP
△ NAVAL SHIP
I ENEMY NAVAL SHIP
X SHIP SUNK
Axis Strike rate: 711

Christmas Is.

Tropic of Capricorn

CENTAUR